Heroes All

HEROES ALL

Airmen of Different Nationalities
Tell their Stories of Service in the
Second World War

Dr Steve Bond

GRUB STREET • LONDON

Published by
Grub Street
4 Rainham Close
London
SW11 6SS

British Library Cataloguing in Publication Data

Bond, Steve.
Heroes all : airmen of different nationalities tell their stories of service in
the Second World War.
1. World War, 1939-1945--Aerial operations. 2. World War,
1939-1945--Personal narratives.
I. Title
940.5'44'0922-dc22

ISBN-13: 9781906502713

Cover design and typesetting by Sarah Driver

Edited by Sophie Campbell

Printed and bound by MPG Ltd, Bodmin, Cornwall

Grub Street Publishing only uses
FSC (Forest Stewardship Council) paper for its books.

CONTENTS

Foreword   vii

Introduction & Acknowledgements   viii

Chapter One   Enlistment   1

Chapter Two   Training Days   22

Chapter Three   Defence – the Fighters   58

Chapter Four   Offence – Bomber Boys   90

Chapter Five   The Lonely Sea   133

Chapter Six   The Eastern Front   149

Chapter Seven   Mediterranean & Far East Theatres   189

Chapter Eight   Night Fighters!   220

Chapter Nine   Transports   235

Chapter Ten   They Also Served   248

Chapter Eleven   D-Day to VJ-Day   268

References   291

Abbreviations   292

Select Bibliography   295

Index   297

FOREWORD

AIR MARSHAL SIR ROGER AUSTIN
KCB AFC FRAES RAF (RET'D)

History with its flickering lamp stumbles along the trail of the past, trying to reconstruct its scenes, to revive its echoes, and kindle with pale gleams the passion of former days.

Winston Churchill

The history of air warfare is well documented because every take-off, every landing and every engagement of the enemy was logged and recorded. That record of action is generally accurate and comprehensive but statistics alone do not tell the full story. To complete the picture, eye-witness accounts are invaluable as they bring the story to life by illustrating the tension, the emotions and the atmosphere surrounding the events.

Steve Bond has done a remarkable job in gathering the tales of over 100 people from the armies, navies and air forces of six nations, both aircrew and ground crew, plus civilians such as Alex Henshaw. He has sensibly avoided the temptation to edit their contributions, thus preserving the very personal nature of their accounts which reveal their characters and the differing approaches of the various nations.

The result is a compelling and fascinating compilation of stories from every area of air warfare which add so much to the bare statistics. This is a first class book which will be a most useful reference for anyone with an interest in the history of air warfare.

INTRODUCTION & ACKNOWLEDGEMENTS

HEROES

Hero: "A man distinguished by extraordinary valour and martial achievements; one who does brave or noble deeds; an illustrious warrior."

Oxford English Dictionary

In the world of the 21st century it has become commonplace to refer to high achievers in almost every walk of modern life as heroes. One only has to turn to the sports pages of our daily newspapers to find the term applied to, for example, footballers who have saved their national team from disgracing itself against the opposition. Worthy though such endeavours may well be, turn back the clock sixty years or more, and the common meaning of the term was very different. and indeed little used.

Then, young men – and women – of a similar tender age to today's sporting stars were fighting a very different kind of campaign, with far more serious, almost unimaginable, potential consequences for both themselves and their losing side. A 2007 study of the United Kingdom premier football league revealed that the average age of the team players at that time was a little over twenty-six years[1]. The average age of crewmen in Royal Air Force (RAF) Bomber Command during the Second World War was just twenty-two. An airman in his mid to late twenties was often referred to by his comrades as 'the old man', while at the other extreme, the youngest airman to lose his life during the Battle of Britain, air gunner AC2 Norman Jacobson, was just eighteen when he died during the late evening of his very first day of operations on Blenheim-equipped 29 Squadron. His body was recovered a day later and buried at sea, and he is commemorated on the Runnymede Memorial. Today such fresh-faced youngsters, hardly out of school, are again making the supreme sacrifice in conflicts in far-flung places like Afghanistan.

The toll in human lives throughout the Second World War was enormous. In Bomber Command alone, 55,573 airmen lost their lives in action, out of a total of 70,253 casualties for the entire RAF. Similarly, Luftwaffe losses, which will probably never be known for certain, amounted to 96,917 up to the end of 1944, after which no reliable records remain, even if they were completed. United States Air Force (USAF) records indicate 79,265 killed in action in just the European theatre of operations (ETO).

Looking back, the first wartime heroes I came across were during my school days in the 1960s. At that time, only a decade and a half after the end of the war, there was not the intense interest in that conflict that is so prevalent today, so those who had been there perhaps tended not to be paid much attention. At my school, the master who was the officer in charge of the RAF section of our combined cadet force, one N H 'Blanco' (inevitably) White had been, so I later found out, a pilot during the war, while my English master, John Perfect, a very quiet and unassuming man, had been one of those incredibly brave souls in the Glider Pilot Regiment who had flown Horsas into Arnhem. Again, this fact was not widely known, I recall being told about it by another boy one day, and was only able to confirm it recently. Sadly, in the intervening years, John Perfect had died; how I would have loved to have talked to him about his role in that momentous event.

In recent years there have been many books published that have included the thoughts and memories of those who were there. Hearing the airmen bring to life such well-known events as the Battle of Britain, the bomber war, the air war on the Eastern Front, as well as lesser-known aspects, is a privilege not granted to many today. This is not just because the veterans are reluctant to talk about their experiences; often I have found that they need to be persuaded that the listener is genuinely interested – they worry about boring us! Today, the survivors of the armed forces that took part in that great conflict are all elderly and they are rapidly fading away. Yet still they retain almost to a man, a remarkable degree of self-effacement, and during my many visits to interview them, the conversation frequently starts with something along the lines of: "Oh, I didn't do very much." As former Warrant Officer Jack Bromfield of 158 Squadron put it:

> "The memories are still there; they're there all the time. You can go maybe two weeks and think nothing; there's a little snippet in the paper or on the television and suddenly it all starts to wind up again. Or somebody mentions a name, you've forgotten about him for years, and suddenly you remember about him."

Occasionally too, a subliminal feeling of guilt can be detected; not, by any means, guilt at what they were called upon to do, but guilt that they had survived when their comrades did not. There is rarely any political aside to their stories and for me, this attitude is best summed up by something written by the renowned Luftwaffe night-fighter ace Major Heinrich Prinz zu Sayn-Wittgenstein, who scored eighty-three victories against allied bombers, but failed to survive the war. The following passage appears in his biography *Laurels for Prinz Wittgenstein* written by fellow officer Werner Roell[2]:

> "We soldiers are not born to politicise. That is not consistent with our duty...We go into battle trusting in the justice of our action. Let someone tell me that, in the middle of a battle, he can evaluate what the polit-

ical leadership has ordered. We are too close to events to have the same insight as our superiors into the sense or nonsense, and therefore into the right, and wrong, of things…Discipline is the most pious virtue.

"We soldiers entered an order, whose vow is obedience. One cannot fight the battle half-heartedly. How clear and self evident it is for us in the front line. The orders are clear. It runs: To prevent enemy attacks by night on our towns. No more and no less."

Having decided that I wanted to meet as many of the veterans as possible, and as my sound archive started to build-up, I became increasingly aware that many more of these stories were crying out for a wider audience. The other remarkable discovery was just how coincidental and closely-related many experiences turned out to be. I have spoken to British and German, German and Russian, and British and Italian veterans, who it transpired, all shared the same piece of sky at the same time; still with us despite the passing of so many years. I had somehow managed in a sense, to bring them back together – in one or two cases actually culminating in face-to-face meetings.

This is not a book about the rights and wrongs of war; neither does it discuss the strategies of the various military commanders in order to explain why airmen were doing what they were. The intent is simply to explore the experiences and feelings of those people in the front line charged with the delivery of whatever the strategy was. I have also tried to look at all aspects of their service careers, from enlistment, through training and operations right through to de-mobilisation.

This then, I decided, was to be the main thrust of the work, to take key campaigns of the air war in the various theatres, or even single remarkable events, and examine them from both sides as far as possible. I also felt it was important that the less 'glamorous' sides of service life should not be ignored, so I have included such aspects as selection, training, aircraft ferrying and so on; not of course forgetting those vital unsung heroes (that word again), the ground crew, without whom the air war could simply not have taken place. It must be remembered that most of these men and women were not long out of school, so trying to keep some sort of normality in their lives resulted in some fairly lively interludes away from their operational roles, and these too are included to illustrate further the human side behind the uniform.

I also took the deliberate decision not to edit their words, since to do so would be a breach of faith and would also carry the risk of imposing my hindsight beliefs on theirs. So I simply put each set of stories in context with an overview of where the reader will find his or herself in time through the pages that follow. I have however, added a few explanatory notes here and there where perhaps something has slipped the airman's memory, or where I am able to add to information that he simply did not have at his disposal.

The result is a series of snapshots in time. Over the last twenty years or more, I have accumulated many, many hours of recordings and a great deal of correspondence, far too much to make use of it all in this book, but I have done my very best to ensure that I have done justice to each contributor, and presented their contribution appropriately. Sadly of course, many of them have passed on since I started this project, and I thank each and every one of them. They all gave freely of their time, often with gusto, always with enthusiasm.

Those listed below are all the veterans with whom I have had contact, mostly directly, or in a few cases, such as the Russian pilots, through intermediary family members or fellow-enthusiasts who have been tremendously helpful in solving issues of distance and language. Other airmen quoted in the text have been sourced elsewhere and are appropriately referenced.

Ladies and gentlemen, we owe you a debt that can never be repaid; I salute you all.

AIR TRANSPORT AUXILIARY
Third Officer Joe Dorrington

BELGIAN AIR FORCE
Flight Lieutenant Gabriel Seydel DFC

BRITISH ARMY
Sergeant John Perfect, Sergeant Raymond 'Tich' Rayner

BRITISH CIVILIANS
Bob Clarke, Alex Henshaw MBE

FLEET AIR ARM
Sub Lieutenant Idwal James 'Glan' Evans, Sub Lieutenant Jim Langford, Commander Jack Routley, Lieutenant Peter Twiss OBE DSC and bar

GERMAN CIVILIANS
Gisele Hannig

ITALIAN AIR FORCE
General B A Giacomo Metellini MAVM 2 MBVMs MVBA

LUFTWAFFE
Leutnant Hugo Broch KC, Unteroffizer Gustav Drees, Leutnant Norbert Hannig, Oberleutnant Hans-Joachim 'Hajo' Hermann KC with Oakleaves and Swords, Oberfeldwebel Herbert Koller, Generalleutnant Günther Rall KC with Swords, Oakleaves and Diamonds, Oberfeldwebel Willi Reschke KC, Hauptmann Heinz Rökker KC with Oakleaves, Oberleutnant Ernst Scheufele, Oberleutnant Walter Schuck KC with Oakleaves, Hauptmann Peter Spoden DK

ROYAL AIR FORCE
Warrant Officer Eric Barfoot DFC, Flying Officer Andrew Barron, Squadron Leader Dennis Barry, Reg Baynham, Flight Lieutenant Jack Biggs, Flying Officer Jack Booth, Harry Brent, Warrant Officer Jack Bromfield, Air Commodore Pete

Brothers DFC and bar DSO CBE, Sergeant Charlie Browning, Wing Commander Branse Burbridge DFC and bar DSO and bar, Flight Lieutenant Dennis Busbridge, Flight Sergeant Eric Burke, Flight Lieutenant John Caird, Flight Lieutenant Terry Clark DFM, Flight Lieutenant Eric Clarke, Flying Officer George Cook, W Coombes, Air Commodore James Coward AFC, Group Captain Tom Dalton-Morgan DSO OBE DFC, Flight Sergeant H Dennis, Corporal Norman Didwell, Sergeant Ken Down, Group Captain Billy Drake DSO DFC and bar DFC(US), Squadron Leader Neville Duke DSO OBE DFC, Flying Officer John Eaton DFC and bar, Wing Commander Tim Elkington, Air Commodore John Ellacombe CB DFC and bar, Flying Officer John 'Jock' Elliott, Wing Commander Lucian Brett Ercolani DSO and bar DFC, Squadron Leader Peter Fahy AFC DFC, Flight Sergeant Roy Fensome, Warrant Officer Les Giddings, Squadron Leader Ray Glass DFC, Flight Lieutenant Ray Grayston, Warrant Officer Peter Green, Flight Sergeant Alan William, Sergeant Stephen Hall DFM, Flight Lieutenant Eddie Hancock, Sergeant G E Harris, Flight Lieutenant Fred Harrison, Sergeant Harry Hogben, Flight Lieutenant Cyril Jackson, Pete Jackson, Flying Officer David Johnson, Flight Lieutenant Ernest Jones DFC, AC R M Jones, Flight Sergeant John King, Squadron Leader Pete Langdon DFM, Sergeant Ronald Liversuch, Flight Lieutenant Jim Lord DFC, Wing Commander W H McGiffin OBE AE, George McLannahan, Flight Sergeant Frank Mattinson, Flight Lieutenant Ted Mercer DFC, Flight Lieutenant Ted Milligan, Flying Officer Bill Musgrave, Flight Lieutenant Norman Nava, Pilot Officer Michael Nicholson, Flight Sergeant Bob O'Dell, Squadron Leader Jack Parry, Flying Officer Henry Payne, Flight Lieutenant Joe Petrie-Andrews DFC DFM, Squadron Leader Tony Pickering AE, Squadron Leader J P Rae AFC, Bob Rees, Flight Lieutenant Cecil 'Rick' Rickard, C J Robbins, Wing Commander Jack Rose CMG MBE DFC, Flight Sergeant Peter Skinner, Flight Lieutenant Philip Smith, Squadron Leader Gerald 'Stapme' Stapleton DFC Dutch Flying Cross, Warrant Officer Norman Tayler DFC, Flight Sergeant David Taylor, Squadron Leader Jimmy Taylor, Flying Officer Alan 'Tommy' Thomsett, Warrant Officer John Torrans, Sergeant Tommy Turnbull, Flight Lieutenant Doug Turner DFC, Flying Officer C T 'Reg' Viney, Sergeant Jack Wade, Squadron Leader Michel Wainwright AFC, Flight Lieutenant Russell 'Rusty' Waughman DFC AFC, Warrant Officer Les Weeks, Wing Commander Oliver Wells OBE, Squadron Leader Geoffrey Wellum DFC, Warrant Officer Frank White, Master Navigator Bill Whiter, Flight Sergeant John Whitaker, Flight Sergeant Ron Williams, Flight Lieutenant Norman Wilson, Flight Lieutenant George Wood, Warrant Officer Sid Woodacre, E J Youngman

ROYAL CANADIAN AIR FORCE
Flight Sergeant Grant MacDonald, Flying Officer Bob Sebaski, Flight Lieutenant Rod Smith DFC and bar

ROYAL CANADIAN NAVY
Lieutenant Jimmy Greening

INTRODUCTION & ACKNOWLEDGEMENTS

SOVIET AIR FORCE

Colonel Grigory Avenesov, General Major Nikolay Gerasimovich Golodnikov, Guards Lieutenant Benedikt Kardopoltsev ORS OMRB OPW, Yuri Khukhrikov, Major Vasili Kubarev HSU OL ORB OPW ORS, Alexei Kukin, Colonel Leonid Sergeevich Kulakov ORS OPW OL, Guards Senior Lieutenant Olga Mikhaylovna Lisikova, Vladimir Markov, Mikhail Pomorov, Lieutenant Colonel Vladimir Tikhomirov, Senior Lieutenant Alexei Valyaev, Senior Lieutenant Ivan Zvyagin

UNITED STATES ARMY AIR FORCE

Lieutenant Bob 'Punchy' Powell, Captain Sam Halpert 5 AMs, Captain Norm Rosholt 6 AMs PH

UNITED STATES NAVY

Storekeeper Chief Alfred Rodrigues

I must also thank the many other non-wartime veteran people who have been such a great help to me in putting this work together. If I have inadvertently missed anyone out I apologise, but you know who you are.

Wing Commander Jez Attridge MBE, Simon Attridge, Air Marshal Sir Roger Austin KCB AFC FRAeS, Giancarno Buono, A Dikov, Artem Drabkin, Brian Fair, Colin Fair, Jim Fitzgibbon, Squadron Leader Dick Forder, Flight Lieutenant Peter Hearmon, Colin Heaton, Oleg Korytov, Alessandro Metellini, Dave Paterson, Diane Rickard, Andrey Suhorukov, Judy Tomlin, Tim Whitaker, Dave Underwood, and special thanks for tremendous support over a lengthy period must go to Colin and Rose Smith at Vector Fine Arts, my daughters Elizabeth and Rebecca, son-in-law Stuart Williams, and of course my darling wife Christine for putting up with all the time I have spent on the road or locked in the study beavering away at this project.

Steve Bond
Milton Keynes
2010

Chapter One

ENLISTMENT

C Flight – Ah-ten-shun, the corporal roared,
Four weeks of lectures and bullshit on the 'square':
Your country needs you – What! For this O Lord?
It's wings we want, and combat in the air.
Rifle-drill, fatigues, PT and 'Who goes there?',
Airframes, Engines, King's Regs and ACI
A grounding this – to help you they declare –
Yours not to learn nor ask the reason why.
Learn Air Force Law – full-pack and extra drill,
We yearn for Spitfires screaming overhead
The war will end before we make a kill
Then came Dunkirk – invasion next they said.
And after ITW we learned to fly –
Now disciplined to fight – to live or die.

Squadron Leader Peter Fahy AFC DFC

As the Second World War approached, and re-armament gathered pace in many parts of the world, so the recruiting, induction and training systems of the armed forces began to react and reform to cope with the many thousands of new airmen and women who would be needed. The numbers required for rapid expansion would have completely overwhelmed a peacetime system, and of course as operational losses mounted, so did the need for yet more replacements. In fact the numbers of volunteers coming forward resulted in many people having the start of their service deferred, often by several months, as the training schools struggled to cope.

ROYAL AIR FORCE (RAF)

In the years prior to the outbreak of war, most civilians entered the RAF via one of three recruit depots at Cardington, Padgate and Uxbridge. With the coming of general mobilisation, many more recruit centres had to be opened up to cope with the huge influx of conscripts and volunteers, with Uxbridge alone receiving an average 600 recruits per month by 1937. In that same year a sub-depot was opened at RAF Henlow in Bedfordshire due to lack of space at Uxbridge (officially recruits were required to be accommodated on a scale of 60 square feet per man!).

Flight Sergeant John Whitaker enlisted as a wireless operator/air gunner (WOp/AG) that same year, and after training at Uxbridge and Cranwell, was posted on his first tour with 38 Squadron at Marham, which was the only unit to fly the Fairey Hendon bomber.

> "After a medical board examination at the Aviation Candidates Selection Board, which declared me fit for flying duties, I enlisted as an aircraftman second class (AC2). At Uxbridge I found myself in the same room as David Lord, later to be awarded a posthumous Victoria Cross for extreme gallantry piloting a crippled Dakota over Arnhem. *(David Lord's 271 Squadron Dakota was hit by flak in the starboard engine while running in for a supplies drop, and caught fire. Despite this, Lord continued with two supply runs and then instructed his crew to bail out. Immediately they had done so, the starboard wing parted from the aircraft and Lord fell to his death.)*
>
> "We went on to Cranwell and were put in a hut: twenty of us, and it was pretty primitive, there was no central heating and with doors that didn't fit very closely. There was no hot running water and the central coal-burning stove had to be cleaned out every morning and not re-lit until the afternoon. The chaps in the hut were a jolly good bunch."

In the rush to expand the RAF rapidly during the immediate pre-war period, airmen might find themselves arriving at stations that were not really ready to receive them.

> "On 1 September 1938, the first party of twenty-five airmen arrived at St. Athan, and for the next two weeks, these flight riggers were the only airmen on the station. They arrived by train carrying their own rations, since they could not eat in the dining hall until they had unpacked the tables and benches the next day. Although the station was largely complete, some building work was still in progress and it was extremely muddy under-foot. The first task of the advance party was to clean out the newly built barrack huts and make them ready for occupation. 1,000 trainees moved in by 18 October." [3]

A few young men had already become exposed to what was happening in Germany well before the outbreak of war. Among them was Air Commodore Pete Brothers, who was to have a long and illustrious career, mainly as a fighter pilot. He initially flew Gauntlets and Hurricanes with 32 Squadron at Biggin Hill, Hurricanes with 257 Squadron during the Battle of Britain, then several Spitfire units including 457 and 602 Squadrons, and commanded the Tangmere and Culmhead Wings. In total he scored sixteen air-to-air victories, and finally retired from the RAF in 1973.

> "At the end of '34 or early '35 I was sent to Germany to learn German. I lived with a family for three months, outside Nuremberg. Three boys, Otto, Walter and Harold was the eldest, he was about six foot three, he was older than me and he was Waffen SS. He used to wake me up at six o'clock in the morning, I'd look out of the bedroom window and there was Harold leading a bunch of black-uniformed chaps with spades on

their shoulders, down the street, with a band playing. Otto was learning to fly at a local 'aero club'. He was shot down on the Russian front as a bomber pilot. Walter, the youngest, was six foot eight, and was in the Guard of Honour for Hitler at Nuremberg, and he was the smallest!

"I was standing in the street when a parade came down the road, everybody Sieg Heil'd as the Nazi flag went past, except me. I suddenly had that feeling that somebody was looking at me; I looked to the right, and on the corner were two bloody great chaps, blackish uniforms, with daggers, pistols, and truncheons, and rocking on their toes looking at me. I thought discretion is the better part of honour; the thought of being shot out of hand or something."

Already by this time, Pete had taken flying lessons.

"In '33 my father said, 'This silly idea of yours, which you've had since childhood. You'll learn to fly, and you'll get bored with it. Settle down and come into the family business.' My mother didn't object to my trying to join the air force, because she reckoned I was a weakling boy who'd never pass the medical. I learned to fly at the Lancashire Aero Club at Woodford on the Avro Avian and Avro Cadet. Learning was great, and I had a civil instructor, First World War Sopwith Camel pilot, who I adored. After I'd gone solo, I used to take my father flying.

"I put my application in to join the air force, on 27 January 1936. I reported to Uxbridge to march up and down, have a uniform fitted, mess drill. There was a super little squadron leader who was in charge of us. First World War fighter chap, covered in decorations, stuttered terribly, Welshman – Taffy Jones. He gave us a lecture, and said, 'There's g-g-g-going to be a f-f-f-f***ing war. And you chaps are g-g-g-going to be in it. And when you get into your first c-c-c-combat, you'll be f-f-f***ing frightened. And n-n-n-never f-f-f-forget that the ch-ch-chap in the other c-c-c-cockpit is t-t-twice as f-f-f***ing frightened as you are.' It was wonderful advice. My first combat, I thought 'This poor bugger in a '109 must be having hysterics. I must put him out of his misery! So I shot him down."

A lot of men had already started out on civilian careers prior to volunteering, and in fact some of those that survived the war found their previous employers were happy to take them back again so that they could pick up where they had left off. One such was Flight Lieutenant Norman Wilson, who became a pilot with 209 Squadron on Catalinas at Mombasa, before moving on to fly Sunderlands.

"I left school in July 1939 at the age of sixteen and commenced an aircraft engineering apprenticeship at Sir W.G Armstrong Whitworth Aircraft Ltd in Coventry. (They were building Whitley bombers at the time.) On my eighteenth birthday in 1941 I volunteered to join the RAF as a trainee pilot, was successful in selection, but had to wait until 10 August 1942 to be called."

Flight Lieutenant Eric Clarke was a WOp/AG on 49 Squadron, Hampdens, Manchesters and Lancasters flying mainly from Scampton before moving to Fiskerton. He completed a full tour, which included the first two thousand-bomber raids.

"In the 1930s as I worked in a Doncaster office, I got used to seeing various aircraft flying around and in 1936 RAF Finningley opened and I also became accustomed to seeing the boys in blue in the town mostly wearing an aircrew brevet, pilot, observer etc., and the aircraft were Handley Page Hampdens. I did not fancy myself with a Lee Enfield .303 plus bayonet and I had some ideas about becoming one of those boys so at the first opportunity I visited the recruiting office at Sheffield and applied for aircrew navigation but was refused on the spot as I did not have grammar school education, but I was offered wireless operator/air gunner which I accepted. I was called up on 13 August 1940."

Many such budding recruits had seen something of the unfolding air war even deep in the English countryside. Warrant Officer Jack Bromfield was brought up in Bletchley in Buckinghamshire, and went to work on the railway before he too became a WOp/AG with 158 (Halifax) Squadron at Lissett in Yorkshire.

"As a sixteen-year-old I rode from Bletchley to the top of Little Brickhill hill, and I could see the London docks burning. The first German aeroplane I ever saw was a Dornier 17. Where I worked they asked me if I'd be a messenger boy in the air raid precaution section...and when the air raid siren went, it was my job to go to the council offices. This particular day it was overcast, very low cloud. I was standing on the balcony of the offices, and this thing came down Bletchley Road. I was petrified, I couldn't move. There used to be a painting in the Great Hall at Euston of an aircraft machine-gunning a train. It was that aircraft...we were on the main railway line into London. He aimed for the train and missed. His stick of about four ruined a perfectly good mushroom field!"

The peacetime RAF was largely comprised of career airmen, but wartime recruitment and initial military training needs demanded a very large and complex organisation. A system of initial training wings (ITW) was established with the first such dedicated unit 1 ITW being set up at Jesus College, Cambridge in September 1939. The primary purpose of these units was to transform a civilian into a military man or woman, and on successful completion of the ITW course, recruits moved on to training schools appropriate to their trade, which was not always the one they would have chosen.

Recruits spent several weeks at ITWs, many of which were established in seaside hotels requisitioned specifically for the purpose, examples being 3 ITW Marine Court Hotel, Hastings, 7 ITW Bellavista Hotel, Newquay and 13 ITW

ENLISTMENT

Grand Hotel, Torquay. Here they were issued with a uniform and other personal kit and learned such things as Air Force Law, basic first aid, drill, physical training, route marches, and handling small arms. They were also subjected to a lot of medical attention, including the inevitable plethora of 'jabs', often in both arms at the same time.

At first, the ITWs were fed from two receiving wings (RW), at Babbacombe and Stratford-on-Avon, but in 1941 these too became ITWs and were replaced by a system of aircrew reception centres (ACRC, colloquially known as 'darcy arcy'). The first and perhaps best known of these was No.1 set up in requisitioned properties at St. John's Wood in North London, in and around Lord's Cricket Ground and close to Regent's Park and London Zoo. At its peak, this ACRC had over 5,000 men in attendance at any one time for their three-week stay.

Flight Lieutenant Ted Mercer enlisted in August 1941, and reported to ACRC. He subsequently became a pilot on 83 (Lancaster) Squadron at Wyton, then 44 (Lancaster) Squadron at Dunholme Lodge.

"I reported to Lord's Cricket Ground, and there the catering arrangements were rather abysmal. Breakfast time, the tea was terrible, the story being that it was laced heavily with bromide to keep us quiet, if you know what I mean."

Similar memories of ACRC came from Flying Officer Mike Nicholson. His flying career as a pilot was mainly with 358 (Liberator) Squadron in the Far East right at the end of the war.

"I went to the aircrew reception centre at St. John's Wood, where we lived in new commandeered flats which had never been occupied. I can't imagine what state they were in when they were handed back. We had our meals in the London Zoo, which says something."

At first, an airman would be earmarked for a particular aircrew category at either the RW or ACRC stage, but this was changed in 1942 with the introduction of the pilot / navigator / air bomber system (PNB), where the final category was not decided until the airmen reached the end of the ITW phase. Flight Lieutenant Eric Barfoot recalls his own induction; he went on to complete a distinguished wartime career as a Wellington pilot with 37 and 70 Squadrons in the Middle East, then switched to Dakotas with 216 and 267 Squadrons in Burma.

"I had been turned down by the Fleet Air Arm as too young to be trained as a pilot. They had graciously suggested that I might fulfil the role of marine or stoker. I had therefore offered my services as a pilot to the RAF... and in October 1940 I reported as requested to Uxbridge, hair well Brylcreemed, and I was interviewed by three senior officers. They asked if I had studied trigonometry for school certificate. Did I know what a tangent was? Did I know where the Great Bear was? I did? Good. Did I know where the pole star was? Good. 'You'll do nicely.'

"I was posted to 13 ITW in Torquay. My pay was two shillings and sixpence a day, less barrack damages. We lived in a room at the unfurnished Regina Hotel, drilled on the quayside outside the old Spa Ballroom, and marched all over the place. We did our square-bashing on the jetty. I thought I was an example of a good square-basher, but they called me a ruptured crab. I never quite lived that down." [4]

Flight Lieutenant John Caird had been working for an insurance company in Leeds before joining up. He trained as a pilot and went on to fly Liberators with 159 Squadron in the Far East:

"The first step was to go to a recruiting centre…I was there for three days. The first time away from home and I was very nervous about the whole thing. Did I take pyjamas? Would there be sheets on the bed? How would I like sleeping in a barrack room with a lot of other recruits?"

Flying Officer George Cook, WOp/AG with 49 (Hampden) Squadron at Scampton, completed a full tour, including the first two thousand-bomber raids, before transferring to 205 (Catalina) Squadron at Koggala in Ceylon.

"I joined up in 1939, before the war, a VR wireless operator, and I was called up on the Friday night; that was on 1 September and the war started on Sunday. Then I was posted to Kenley on the Saturday, square-bashing and learning the intricacies of the Lewis gun."

Flight Lieutenant Joe Petrie-Andrews had tours as a pilot on 102 and 158 (Halifax) Squadrons, and 35 Squadron of the Pathfinder Force, which flew the Halifax and later the Lancaster from Graveley. He completed a total of seventy operations.

"In 1940 I was at school, and I decided I would leave the Home Guard and join the air force, so I went along and stuck my age up and they wanted me to be a wireless operator/air gunner, while I'd set my mind on being a pilot. But they said, 'no thanks', and I came away. I went back a few months later and at another recruiting office everything went well. He asked, 'how old are you?' I said: 'I'm eighteen sir.' 'You don't start pilot training until you're nineteen, but you look older than you really are, perhaps you will go through straight away.' I got in and they sent me to America to do my training."

By the time Sergeant Harry Hogben enlisted, the tide of the war had begun to turn in the allies' favour, and the massive training system was beginning to produce more aircrew in some categories than were being lost on operations. Consequently, many men found their service deferred until such time as they could be accommodated.

Flying Officer George Cook (far right) joined 49 Squadron at Scampton, Lincolnshire in 1941 as a Hampden wireless operator and completed thirty-two operations including the first two thousand-bomber raids. Next to George is his pilot Sgt Latty *Cook*

"We lived in Whitley Bay near Northumberland. I was in the ATC there, and I went up in a Blackburn Botha, it was terrible. I was in the mid-upper gun turret, looking backwards, so I could only see where we'd been.

"I went up to Edinburgh for my aircrew medical in '43. I was on deferred service for a year virtually, and they said, 'Try and get yourself into something to do with flying'. I went into a shadow factory in Reading, building Spitfires...and we were doing the fuselages, fitting the engines, tailplanes, and that sort of thing. They all said, 'You won't get into the RAF now'; I said, 'I think I will'. I did, I went up to ACRC at Scarborough."

Jack Bromfield took up the story of his own enlistment.

"I always wanted to be a locomotive man...my Dad wouldn't let me. He said if you go into the traffic department as a train-reporting boy, you can go signalman, right up to signalman's inspector. I wasn't happy. So without telling him, I went to Northampton and volunteered for aircrew duties. I'd only been back about two weeks and a letter arrived telling me to go to Bedford, for a medical. I presented myself to a major, 'Bromfield?', 'Yes sir'. 'Any preferences for regiment, young man?' I said, 'Yes sir, Royal Air Force'. Then he looked up, and there I am, a sergeant in the air training corps; he thought I'd been wasting his time. Anyhow, they passed me A1. Not long after that, I had to go to Cardington...my Dad knew about it now, and he wasn't talking. It was a bit fraught, but the job was done...I'd been accepted and that was it. The station master wasn't pleased, because he explained that I'd chucked in a reserved occupation.

"Eventually, that buff envelope came through the door from King George, and away I went to the ACRC at St. John's Wood. I lived in a block of flats in Grove Court, in Hall Road for about two-and-a-half weeks. Abbey Lodge, which is a big block of flats; that was the medical centre. You went in one end, with your hands on your hips, and all your other clothes draped over your arm, and every time you went through a doorway, somebody had you with a syringe. There were blokes passing out; the bigger they were, the more they seemed to keel over. Regent's Park, which it backed on to, looked like a battlefield, all these bodies lying all over.

"Then we were posted to Bridgnorth, 19 ITW; the discipline was tight. We did a couple of hours of square-bashing a day, some morse and learned how to dig a latrine. Everything was done the way the Royal Air Force wanted. What made me laugh, was my clothing card. I had 'boots, ankle, leather, black, left, one; boots, ankle, leather, black, right, one'. We had two dress uniforms, but didn't have a battledress. And a big kit bag; and the one that made us laugh was 'coats, over'. I thought well, is this the Royal Air Force that we were cheering when they were winning the Battle of Britain?"

Joe Dorrington was working on his father's farm in Lincolnshire and wanted to play his part, but was found to be medically unfit for active service. Undeterred, he became a 3rd officer in the air transport auxiliary (ATA), ferrying a wide variety of aircraft around the country.

"I decided I wanted to do something else; I was in a reserved occupation, farming. There were two things I could have a go at; flying, or bomb disposal, and I applied to go into the air force and went to Padgate. They took one look at my eyes, and they sent me straight back home again. That left me to have a go at bomb disposal. When I had a medical inspection, they graded me down to Grade 2, which meant I couldn't go out of England. The bomb disposal people weren't really bothered about my eyes, but they didn't want to go to all the trouble of training me to have me stuck in England; so that was that out.

"I was still interested in flying, and eventually the ATA started training pilots. I went for an interview, I must admit more in hope than expectation. Anyway, they were perfectly happy as long as you were prepared to have a go, so I was joined up. Then after just over a year, my father died and I applied for compassionate leave to go and look after the farm. After D-Day, we were tearing across France, and it was all going to be over by Christmas, so they said, 'Don't bother to come back, you'll be more useful on the farm than you will be here'."

Warrant Officer Peter Green enlisted as a flight engineer, and completed thirty-three operations with 102 (Halifax) Squadron at Pocklington.

"We had a lot of older people with us at ITW in Torquay, because the average age then of flight engineers was thirty-nine, so there were a few older ones that had been policemen. If the instructor wasn't about, they used to appoint them as sort of instructors, to march us; they had no authority really. Six weeks we were there and we did a bit of everything, dinghy drill, clay-pigeon shooting. For dinghy drill, we had to jump in from the harbour. I didn't like that; I couldn't swim at the time but we had Mae Wests on of course."

After something like eighteen months training in the UK and Canada, Flight Lieutenant 'Rick' Rickard from Aylesbury in Buckinghamshire became a Coastal Command navigator. He started his operational career with 53 Squadron flying Hudsons from St. Eval, followed by 172 and 179 (Wellington) Squadrons at Chivenor and Gibraltar.

"It was the custom for pubs to maintain a wall map with pins indicating the progress of the German advances in Europe, but after a few beers and a bit of larking about, the pins and strings appeared in all sorts of odd places. A great feeling of patriotism had developed throughout the whole of Britain and despite all the setbacks and the bombing, spirits rose to a high level. Although inwardly scared, we couldn't wait until it was our turn to be called up, but the waiting seemed endless. However in May 1940 an official letter ordered me to appear at High Wycombe for an interview. I hadn't a clue what to expect, but I took the precaution of 'genning up' from my school books on the Pythagoras theory and the sine formula and such like and writing them on the back of a cigarette packet. Having left school at near on seventeen and reached the ripe old age of twenty-five, I was amazed at what I had forgotten.

"The board contained plenty of 'scrambled eggs' and they asked me almost identical questions on the subjects which I had mugged up. I left for the return journey feeling somewhat smug. So back to work and back to waiting, week after week. It was difficult to make any plans and life settled down once more to a routine of work. On 3 September 1940 my call-up papers arrived, instructing me to appear at RAF Cardington. After so much waiting this came as a relief and at the same time a feeling of some trepidation. I was given a service number and styled as an AC2. Otherwise known as AC plonk and the lowest form of life! We stayed at Cardington for two weeks, never once going out of camp, although some enterprising regulars were charging for readmission at certain gaps in the station fences for those brave enough to ignore the confined to barracks conditions.

"We were housed at forty a time in large huts and even in those early days, a bond began to form. Occasionally we could get to the NAAFI for a pork pie and a pint of beer, but usually interrupted by air raid sirens. London was taking a hammering and although thirty miles away, we could see the blaze of fires.

"We transferred to Blackpool for ten days in private digs pending drilling instruction…doing practically nothing but enjoying ourselves as far as our little pay would allow. Dancing in the ballroom, organ music in the Tower Ballroom and variety shows, but then we found ourselves posted to Wilmslow near Manchester, where we stayed for six weeks, and were given a stringent spell of square bashing and arms drill. We were taught how to bayonet charge at straw dummies uttering fierce war-whoops!"

The eagerness displayed by many young men anxious to enlist was typified by Air Commodore James Coward, who went on to have a long and distinguished career starting on 19 Squadron at Duxford flying the Gauntlet, then the first RAF Spitfires. Moving to 266 (Spitfire) Squadron at Sutton Bridge he was shot down during the Battle of Britain, losing a leg, and spent an extended period on Winston Churchill's staff at Chequers whilst recuperating from his injuries. He retired in 1969 with the rank of air commodore.

"I couldn't get into the air force before because I left school when I was fifteen. My father went broke in the depression and so I had no hope of getting to Cranwell. They didn't introduce any short service commissions until the expansion began and then they started advertising. My father had told me I had to be twenty-one to get into the air force without his permission, which was completely untrue; he wanted me to go into his business. So when I was twenty-one I joined up."

Because of the huge demand for aircrew and the ever-present threat of disruption to training by the Luftwaffe, the British Government established aircrew training schemes in a number of countries, largely in the commonwealth. In addition, the scale of training required soon outstripped the ability of Britain to provide it all, so the Dominion Air Training Scheme (DATS) was established in Canada. Later renamed the Empire Air Training Scheme (EATS), this resulted in many recruits being shipped out to South Africa and Southern Rhodesia for training, with smaller numbers also going to India. One airman caught up in this process was navigator Flight Sergeant Eric Burke, who flew twenty-seven operations with 13 Squadron in Italy, briefly on Baltimores before converting to Bostons.

"I went up for the attestation and interviews to the Air Ministry, the backlog of aircrew was closing down a bit, that was 1942. I was on so many months deferred service, but I was called up, and reported to St. John's Wood, it was 1 February 1943. I hadn't been there many days when they asked for volunteers for overseas training, and the buzz was that Canada was getting chock-a-block a bit, and that we were going to South Africa or Southern Rhodesia. I thought that was probably a good idea, but I wasn't on the first parade they asked, because I'd lost my hat. I got on the next parade and they did want a few more volunteers, and probably within three weeks we were posted up to Blackpool. It wasn't long before we marched down to Woolworth's and we went into tropical kit. Within a week or so after that, up to Liverpool onto the boat, HM troopship *Otranto*. We were in F3 port, which is pretty low down, and we went out from Liverpool in convoy, and being realistic most of us realised that if anything happened, with the U-boats waiting, we wouldn't stand much chance.

"This was the long way round to Durban, it took us a month. We were in transit in Durban for about three weeks, then we got the train up to Bulawayo, a three-day journey; we reached what used to be the old agricultural showground, and our billets were where the animals used to live. We had pig pens, and it was all very comfortable because it's a wonderful climate in Southern Rhodesia; it was open type billets, just rows of beds."

Rhodesian pilot Flying Officer Bill Musgrave trained in his home country, converted onto Hurricanes in Egypt, then flew a lengthy tour with 237 Squadron on the Spitfire IX in Corsica and Italy, which included the invasion of southern France.

"I joined up at the end of '42, when I left school. I trained in Rhodesia, which was a very big part of the Empire Air Training Scheme. I think the first flying started in '41. When it was added up I think there were ten or eleven airfields and 800 aircraft, so it was quite a thing."

In 1940 the UK started to look into the possibility of having aircrew trained in the United States of America. The Americans agreed to participate even before they entered the war, under the Arnold Scheme, devised by General 'Hap' Arnold. Among the conditions imposed were requirements for trainees to be civilians so as to avoid overt breaching of United States' neutrality. Flight Lieutenant Jack Biggs enlisted in October 1940 and commenced training on the first Arnold Scheme course No.42A. Returning to convert to the Hurricane, he flew with 17 Squadron in the defence of Calcutta, later converting to the Spitfire with the same unit.

"I volunteered in June 1940. As I was in an engineering drawing office, there was some doubt as to whether or not I was reserved occupation. So they put me off, and eventually called me to go to Cardington in October '40. I had the usual aircrew tests, eyesight, medicals and what have you, and we had three days and two nights there. All sorts of intelligence tests, aptitude tests and I got through, and they said, 'We'll send for you'. I went to Babbacombe in Devon, 4 January 1941.

"We didn't have aircrew reception centres then, Babbacombe was the place you went for that area. We were kitted out and had all our usual inoculations, and then I was posted to 4 ITW Paignton. We then did the usual ITW stuff; Vickers gas-operated gun, strip it blindfold and all that jazz, morse code, Aldis lamp, camp hygiene, navigation, mathematics, in fact it was just like a ground school.

"We got to the end of our course and we were going to go on leave, and they said, 'Call out eight names'. The buzz was that they were going to America. It transpired they went to Canada, those eight, but the rest of us went to America! They told us to go home, and that we could take some civilian clothes with us, when we came back to Paignton. They took us up to West Kirby and kitted us out with fifty-bob suits. We didn't know it at the time, we were going to a country that wasn't at war, and we had to wear civilian clothes, we couldn't wear uniform. We had to put 'Arnold Spud' on our kitbags and on all our kit. It was because General Hap Arnold was the instigator of this scheme; 'Spud' was just another moniker they decided to call him. They took us to Gourock, and we then got on the *Britannic*.

"We sailed for our unknown destination, and were then told quietly that we might be going to the United States. When we got out to sea there was this one solitary ship, the *Britannic*, and the *Rodney* battleship and four destroyers, and that was our escort. I like to think it was because we were on board, but it wasn't. The *Rodney* was going to Norfolk for a refit, and being a battleship it needed four destroyers. We got to the point that we were halfway across the Atlantic when it was reported that the *Bismarck* had our course and speed and would be prepared to do something about sinking us; and the *Rodney* and three destroyers left us. We were left with one destroyer, and the *Rodney* helped sink the *Bismarck*. Anyway, the *Britannic* got us to Halifax.

"We went to the manning depot in Toronto, and that was the reception centre for the Royal Canadian Air Force, eastern. We were very well treated, they took us out in motorcades, and the people brought their cars and took us around and showed us the sights. We were there for about a week, then we were all ushered in to what was the sheep-judging pen, because it used to be a big cattle place where they had all their exhibitions. They said, 'You, you and you, you're going to Arcadia Florida; you're going to so and so'. They put us on a train on a

Saturday, and we travelled all the way down from Toronto, through Detroit and all the other states and we got to Arcadia Florida – dropped people off at Lakeland, which is another flying school – at about six o'clock on the Monday morning."

FLEET AIR ARM

The Royal Navy had a similar, but largely separate system for recruit training. All potential Fleet Air Arm aircrew started their service careers with two months of basic training at HMS St. Vincent, Gosport before progressing to dedicated flying training establishments. Commander Jack Routley joined as a pilot in September 1939, and flew operationally with 805 Squadron in the Western Desert, flying Martlets 1941-43. Subsequently he became officer commanding 885 (Hellcat) Squadron aboard HMS *Ruler* and HMS *Indefatigable* in 1944-45. He retired in 1970.

"I was a clerk in a Co-operative Society bank in Gillingham in Kent. I saw a picture in the paper, it was about mid 1939, of some naval aviators standing nonchalantly alongside some aeroplane or other, holding their wings prominently into the foreground. I thought to myself, 'That looks pretty good'. I reckoned rather than wait to be conscripted, I would pre-

Lieutenant Jimmy Greening RCN(R) first flew the Fairey Barracuda with 713 Squadron in the summer of 1944, including deck landing practice on HMS *Rajah*. *Greening*

fer to volunteer for naval aviation. So I got in touch with the recruitment people and had all the paperwork ready for my father to sign when they got back from holiday. He was very pleased, though my mother wasn't."

Canadian born Jimmy Greening came to England in the late 1930s and subsequently enlisted for service as a pilot in the Fleet Air Arm during the latter stages of the war, flying Barracudas with 822 Squadron from Thorney Island in Hampshire.

> "My interest in aviation stemmed from early days in Prince Albert, Saskatchewan. My cousin George was a bush pilot and Prince Albert, being at the end of the railway line, was the base for aircraft serving the northern half of Saskatchewan, including Fairchild 71s, Norsemen, Wacos, etc. My interest continued when I arrived in England in 1938 to work for de Havilland at Stag Lane and I managed to get the occasional flight with the Civil Air Guard. I joined the navy on 28 December 1942."

Sub Lieutenant Jim Langford also trained to fly Barracudas, but converted to the Avenger to fly operationally with 820 Squadron aboard HMS *Indefatigable* including bombing operations against the Japanese mainland in 1945.

> "I was called up in February '42, but didn't actually join the navy until the following December, which seemed an awful long time to have to wait before going down to the south of England to two naval establishments to learn all about how to do a bend and a hitch and to learn all about naval history. So then came the ground school, square bashing, how to fire a rifle, and do guard duty on the camp at night."

LUFTWAFFE

In Germany, recruits entering the Luftwaffe, including officer cadets, were similarly sent to a recruit depot, *Flieger Ausbildungs Regiment*, which was roughly equivalent to the RAF's ITW system. They would spend between six and twelve months here, almost exclusively devoted to military and physical training, with limited instruction in map reading and wireless principles. As the war progressed, this period was progressively reduced down to about two months.

Recruits then moved on to a pool called the *Fluganwaerterkompanie*, where they spent another two months studying aeronautical subjects before commencing training at an elementary flying school. However, by 1942 the system was beginning to break down under the pressure of ever-mounting losses as the tide of war turned against Germany.

Leutnant Norbert Hannig flew the Bf 109 and Fw 190 with Jagdgeschwader 54 'Grünherz' (Green Hearts) on the Eastern Front, scoring forty-two victories. He then flew the Me 262 with Jagdverband 44 and Jagdgeschwader 7 'Nowotny'

Leutnant Norbert Hannig volunteered to join JG54 'Green Hearts' on the Eastern Front, where he flew the Bf 109 for a short while before converting to the FW 190. *Hannig*

and returned to the Luftwaffe after the war, ending his flying career on the F-104 Starfighter.

> "In the Hitler Youth you got meals, you got the uniform, you had nothing to pay but could do what you wanted at that time. You had more or less anything, youth sport and paid from the state. I had seen Hitler only once, as he went from Berlin to Beelitz *(training airfield south of Werder)* on the train and drove his Mercedes down the road to Sudetenland. As a boy I sat in a tree beside the road, and that was the only way I really could see one of the politicians very close to me. My class were in a gymnasium, thirty-five boys all Hitler Jung. If we had a state day, 12 May or something like that, everybody in the class had to be in uniform. The teacher was a very simple SA man *(Sturmabteilung [Storm Trooper] 'Brownshirt')* but that never made any difference to us."

Generalleutnant Günther Rall transferred from the army to the Luftwaffe in 1939 and flew Me 109s in the Battle of Britain leading 8./Jagdgeschwader 52. He went to the Eastern Front and finished the war as the third highest scoring fighter pilot in history with 275 victories. He had a distinguished career in the post-war Luftwaffe.

> "I was already in the army, an army of soldiers. Then Hitler came. I wanted to go into the air force, because I wanted to fly. And when I was in the air force, then I wanted to be a fighter pilot. I think this is my temperament to be a fighter pilot; it was by choice."

Hauptmann Peter Spoden was a night fighter pilot with Nachtjagdgeschwaders 5 and 6, flying sorties against allied bombers in the Me 110G and Ju 88G, scoring twenty-four victories. He too served in the post-war Luftwaffe and retired in 1981 as a Boeing 747 captain with Lufthansa.

> "Only two or three in our class became Hitler Youth leaders, like for example my good friend Hans Adelhütte. He was one of the few who frequently turned up at school in uniform, for which he was made much fun of by some of us who went to the Thielemann Dance School in the town centre of Essen wearing baggy trousers. Hans was a nice, sporty type, not a fanatic, good at school and full of enthusiasm for national socialist ideals. Despite that, he never denounced any of our teachers. He volunteered for the Luftwaffe at the outbreak of war, and became a night fighter before I did, and was shot down over the North Sea after twenty successful combats with RAF bombers. He is buried in my home town, Essen."

Oberleutnant Adelhütte, who possessed the German Cross in Gold, had between fifteen and twenty confirmed victories, but the unit on which he served, and the date of his loss, are not known.

Hauptmann Peter Spoden during training at C-Schule 17 at Pütnitz, Pomerania in 1942. *Spoden*

SOVIET AIR FORCE (VVS)

The normal route for those hopeful of becoming a pilot in the VVS was to gain entry to a local aero club, which were essentially quasi-military establishments set up on the direct orders of Joseph Stalin. Here recruits were assessed for both their aptitude and medical status before commencing flying training ahead of formally entering the VVS. Colonel Leonid Kulakov was a pilot with the 103rd GuIAP (*Istrebitel'nyi Aviatsionnyi Polk* – Guards Fighter Air Regiment) stationed in Kovalevo flying the P-40 Kittyhawk.

> "I always wanted to be in military service. About 100 men enlisted from our school, but only about twenty passed the commission. Father was against my choice of profession; two pilots crashed and were killed in the aero club. He came to me and kept asking: 'Are you training to become a pilot?' I replied, 'No, no, dad, I'm going to be a mechanic, and later I'll study to become an engineer'. 'Then why do you need these flight goggles?' 'Oh, those. When I work under the aircraft, motor oil drips straight to my face and I have to protect my eyes.' When I received an acceptance letter, I finally told my dad that I'll become a pilot, 'I'm going to continue my training!' He thought for a while and replied, 'If it's your choice, go on. I won't object.'"

Lieutenant Colonel Vladimir Tikhomirov was a pilot who flew with 12 IAP KBF (12th Red Bannered Fighter Aviation Regiment of Red Bannered Baltic Sea Fleet) using the Yak 7 and Yak 9. He scored thirteen victories, and stayed on in the air force after the war.

> "I worked as an electrician, and at the same time I studied in a local aero club. In 1939 I was appointed to Lugansk Military Aviation School (*In the Ukraine, 200 miles west of Stalingrad*), but after theoretical education, which lasted for three months, I failed the medical test due to a punctured drum in my right ear. I was denied the chance to fly, but the school suggested a place for me as a driver. I was very upset, and went home, where I took a post as a mechanic at the same aero club I had left earlier. In March 1940, due to the lack of crews, the chief of the aero club asked me to return to flying. This time the medical commission allowed me to fly if I had good character references from the commanding officers."

Guards Lieutenant Benedikt Kardopoltsev flew in combat from October 1943 to May 1945, flying the La-5 and La-7 with 2 GuIAP, which was stationed in Belorussia. He ended the war with six victories plus one shared.

"I always wanted to get to the aero club, but when I first applied I was rejected by the medical commission, they thought I was too short. I used to be a yachtsman, and since I had no chance to become a pilot, I decided to participate in yacht races. We were racing for two-and-a-half months, and during this time I built myself up quite a lot, so in the autumn I had no problems with applying to the Second Leningrad Aero Club."

Senior Lieutenant Ivan Zvyagin flew the Yak 7 with 43 IAP, shooting down four German aircraft (one Me 109, two Fw 190s and one Ju 88) before being shot down and injured on his forty-second mission.

"It was decided that I should move to the city for further education. I went to my sister's house, but when I came to the school, which we were supposed to live in, I simply ran away – it was too cold and there was nothing to eat there. So, I went back home. While I was in 9th class, Stalin had issued an order to create aero clubs. The medical commission decided that I was suited for flying and I ended up at the aero club in Leninsk-Kuznetskii."

The Soviet air forces were recruiting female pilots from an early stage. Guards Senior Lieutenant Olga Lisikova initially flew medical evacuation flights in U-2 (Po 2) aircraft, then converted to fly both the C-47 Dakota and the locally-built Li 2 variant.

"In 1934 I travelled to Tambov civilian flight school. There were already four young girls there. In 1936, all of the girls from Balashov and Tambov schools transferred to Bataysk flight school, where a female squadron was being formed. It consisted of three detachments, and I completed training in 1937. In that year a film came out: Bogatyri nashey Rodiny! [*Warriors of our Motherland*] If you are able to see it, you would see only me, although the film was an artistic work. After that our young men could not pass by without calling out to me, 'star of the screen!'"

ITALIAN AIR FORCE

Italian air force pilot recruits initially spent two months basic training at the military school in Capua, near Naples before proceeding to flight training. General Giacomo Metellini joined in 1929 and flew CR 42s during the Spanish Civil War. He went on to fly the G 50 in North Africa, and then joined 2 Stormo flying the Re 2001 during the Malta campaign, claiming two victories. He rejoined the Italian air force in 1949 and finally retired in 1961.

"Girls were the motivating force in the beginning; they pushed me to make a career in aviation. One day I was walking along the seafront in

Trieste when I saw two young airmen in their beautiful uniforms, grey-blue and with a shining golden Aquila pinned on the chest. I was seventeen years old; they looked so good and attracted admiring glances from passers-by, I thought, why can I not be like one of them?

"These young people convinced me that to get into aviation could be the best solution to get to know beautiful girls, and to let me escape from the grind of daily life and to lead an adventurous life. The Italian air force had an advertisement, looking to recruit 400 new pilots. Therefore, I decided to enlist as a student petty officer first class pilot. It was 1929."

UNITED STATES ARMY AIR FORCE (USAAF)

As with the other major powers, the rapid expansion of manpower in the USAAF and a large influx of volunteers from 1942 onwards, meant major problems for the training organisation, with the result that a lot of the basic training in soldiering

Captain Norm Rosholt was shot down on his thirty-first mission and taken prisoner. *Rosholt*

skills was cut from the syllabus. Lieutenant Robert 'Punchy' Powell was a P-47 Thunderbolt and P-51 Mustang pilot with the 328th Fighter Squadron, 352nd Fighter Group 8th USAAF at Bodney in Norfolk. He claimed two combat victories.

"I enlisted right after Pearl Harbor when I was at West Virginia University. My friend and I skipped school for a couple of days and hitch-hiked to Pikeville, Kentucky to take the aviation cadet exam. We were sworn in as privates after passing all the tests and told to standby at home. They called me in during April '42 as a cadet to take basic training and then start flight training."

Captain Norm Rosholt, six Air Medals, Purple Heart, flew the B-17 Flying Fortress in combat missions over Europe with the 452nd Bomber Group based at Deopham Green in Norfolk.

"I was born in Montana, went to high school in North Dakota and college in Iowa. I enlisted in the reserves in 1942. I then went to the south-west US to do my flying training."

Chapter Two

TRAINING DAYS

Today we have naming of parts. Yesterday,
We had daily cleaning. And tomorrow morning,
We shall have what to do after firing. But today,
Today we have naming of parts. Japonica
Glistens like coral in all of the neighbouring gardens,
And today we have naming of parts.

This is the lower sling swivel. And this
Is the upper sling swivel, whose use you will see
When you are given your slings. And this is the piling swivel,
Which in your case you have not got. The branches
Hold in the gardens their silent, eloquent gestures,
Which in our case we have not got.

This is the safety-catch, which is always released
With an easy flick of the thumb. And please do not let me
See anyone using his finger. You can do it quite easily
If you have any strength in your thumb. The blossoms
Are fragile and motionless, never letting anyone see
Any of them using their finger.

And this you can see is the bolt. The purpose of this
Is to open the breech, as you see. We can slide it
Rapidly backwards and forwards: we call this
Easing the spring. And rapidly backwards and forwards
The early bees are assaulting and fumbling the flowers:
They call it easing the spring.

They call it easing the spring: it is perfectly easy
If you have any strength in your thumb: like the bolt,
And the breech, and the cocking-piece, and the point of balance,
Which in our case we have not got; and the almond-blossom
Silent in all of the gardens and the bees going backwards and
forwards,
For today we have naming of parts.

Henry Reed

Having successfully passed through their basic military training, recruits were streamed onto their various specialist trade training courses. In the case of air-crew, this typically consisted of basic and advanced flying training of some sort, followed by a shorter course to convert to the particular aircraft type they were destined to fly on operations. Similarly, engineers would usually follow their basic skills courses with some specific type training.

PILOT

Regardless of their country, pilot recruits started with some form of elementary flying training. In the UK and its dominions, the usual aeroplane was either the ubiquitous Tiger Moth or the Magister; in the United States it was the Stearman PT-17, in Germany the Fw 44 Stieglitz, in Russia the Petlyakov U-2 (later known as the Po 2), and in Italy the Breda Ba 25.

On completion of the basic course, and following the award of their wings, pilots then proceeded to advanced training, with separate streams for those destined to fly singles, and those chosen to fly multi-engined aircraft. This was usually followed by operational training to learn the necessary combat skills. In RAF Bomber Command for example, this was the point at which aircrew of various disciplines would come together and be 'crewed up'. This simple process took the form of herding all the aircrew newly arrived at an operational training unit (OTU) into a hangar and telling them to form themselves into crews by natural selection. The final link in this particular chain prior to arriving at an operational squadron was a spell at a heavy conversion unit (HCU).

GAINING THEIR WINGS
Despite having already learned to fly in the civilian world, Pete Brothers still found himself going through the RAF basic training system.

"I went to Brough, (4 ERFTS). Arthur Loton, the chief instructor was a nice chap. (*Wg Cdr A G Loton AFC was CFI at Brough for twenty years.*) I then went off to do advanced training at Thornaby, 9 FTS. Harts and Gauntlets, Harts was the advanced side. It was a dreadful step up to a Hart; the power from the engine taking off was battering your head. I thought I'd never get used to this, but we were by the second flight.

"One of my instructors was Flying Officer Grandy, and during our course, a notice went up in the mess to say that he had been promoted to flight lieutenant and awarded a permanent commission; so he threw a party. Most at this young age had never drunk alcohol, only a drop of Vimto, things like that. So I drank beer, and I got thoroughly pissed. In ensuing years, I was able to say to my chief of air staff: 'You're the chap who introduced me to alcohol, don't you ever accuse me of drinking too much.'"

Norman Wilson found himself shipped off to Canada on his way to qualifying as a Sunderland navigator.

"Training in Canada at 33 EFTS at Caron, Saskatchewan and 33 SFTS at Carberry, Manitoba. I was gratified to achieve 'honour student' awards, 'above average' assessments as a pilot, and receive a commission as a pilot officer. At that time, flying boat pilots had not only to be assessed as 'above average' but had also to be qualified navigators so I was very encouraged to believe that I was on course to achieve my ambition when I was sent to 31 GRS at Charlottetown, Prince Edward Island and obtained my air navigators certificate on 10 February 1944."

Flight Lieutenant Philip Smith mainly served as an instructor on advanced flying units with Oxfords. He also completed his pilot training in the United States on the Arnold Scheme and described his return back to England.

"I crossed the Atlantic in '42 in an old French tramp steamer, it was awful. We were escorted by two First World War American destroyers, with three funnels. It was at the height of the U-Boat war, but we had prisoners on board so I suppose the Germans were under orders not to sink us. The *Queen Elizabeth* and *Queen Mary* were too fast for them, 25 knots, but we were only doing 10 knots. I came back with my wings in '43."

Jack Biggs continued the story of his training under the Arnold Scheme.

"On the Arnold Scheme, the rules were very different for us because we had Americans as our upper classmen. We were going to a flying training school in peacetime, and those blokes who had graduated before us never had any idea that they would be at war, because they'd joined in peacetime.
    "When you were a lower classman, which was the first five weeks of your course, you wore green overalls and hat, and you were allowed five demerits, which meant you could have five black marks during the week. Anything above that meant you had to walk for half an hour on the ramp, outside the orderly room. The only Fourth of July I was out there, I happened to be room orderly that week, and I accrued more than the five demerits, because if you were room orderly, no matter what your mates did, and there were four of you to a room, you got the blame for it. I accrued another three demerits over my five allowed, and on 4 July 1941 I was walking up and down the ramp for an hour-and-a-half. That was Independence Day, and I thought: 'My God, this is not much independence.'
    "Everything was done by a system of bells. You had a bell that woke you in the morning, then you were allowed twenty minutes for your ablutions. Another after that which meant you had to be out on parade; and we had to salute the stars and stripes every morning at about five o'clock. Your clothing had to be folded in an exact way; they used to

bring a protractor round – the duty officer used to come round and check you had a 45 degree angle on your blanket. You weren't allowed rat-tails under the bedding, or anything showing out under the spring mattress. If you did, when you came back you would find it all on the floor, and you had to make it up again, and got demerits. Tedious little things, but I rather enjoyed it.

"We had ten weeks of primary on the Stearman PT-17, you went solo and had civilian instructors. The senior check pilot was an Embry-Riddle man, and then you had as a last resort, a lieutenant in the Army Air Corps who had the final say, if you got to the wash-out point. I think there were fifty-odd of us out of that ninety-nine who went on to basic, the others all got washed-out, because they were up to their standard of peacetime. They weren't looking for cannon-fodder, they hadn't changed when we were there, being the first course.

"From there we went up to Montgomery, Alabama – Gunter Field. We went on to Vultee BT-13s – I liked the BT-13 – and that's where we did our first bit of formation flying, our first bit of night cross-country, and various other things. Then we got Army Air Corps instructors for ten weeks. The student flew from the back seat, and they allowed you ten hours to go solo before checking you out. I went solo in about seven-and-a-half hours. We stopped in the middle of the field and my instructor said: 'Time you had a go on your own.' There's nothing to compare with your first solo, up there all by yourself.

"We finished basic, and we singles went to Craig Field, Selma, Alabama. They were nice; I think they found us strange, because we didn't talk their language, I mean we didn't drawl the way they did. But it was very worthwhile, and we went on to AT-6s. The beauty of night cross-countries in America was that you had the weather, you didn't get clamped down with fog or anything like that, and you had the beacon system, whereby you used to fly along and got signals to differentiate, and when you got the cone of silence you were over the beacon. It really made life very easy.

"There were occasions when you thought: 'Will I ever get through?' Once you'd got over basic training you were fairly confident that you were going to get through, although people were still washed-out at advanced; some people just couldn't land a Harvard. It's a unique little aircraft, in as much as you're skimming the ground if you're not too careful, and you can do the wrong thing if you handle it badly.

"We were out on the Saturday night that Pearl Harbor happened. The Yanks came up and said: 'You Limeys, we'll soon get this war over.' But the sad thing was when we went back to get into camp they wouldn't let us in because we were civilians. So they had to get the RAF officer to come and vouch for us, and they then let us wear our uniforms.

"It was Christmas of '41, and we were the senior cadets, we were due to pass-out in January. So we were put on readiness, they fitted a gun to the AT-6, and they gave us this little bull-talk about, 'The AT-6 is a match for any Jap aircraft that might come'; they had visions of them coming up the Gulf of Mexico. Apparently, one of the generals said that if the Japs do come up through the Gulf of Mexico, Florida will be given to them, they wouldn't defend Florida. So they obviously had thought about it. We got called out when we were in the cinema. Whether or not it was just a practice I didn't know, but I got down there, and mine was up on bloody stands, they were doing undercarriage tests on the aircraft that I was allocated. They did panic a bit, but nothing came of it, and then we graduated on 4 January. They called our names out, we marched up smartly to the front, and saluted the colonel or general, whatever his name was, and we were given diplomas.

"I think thirty-five to forty of the original ninety-nine were left and they were ruthless. One chap had a passion for orange juice, because we'd gone to Florida, and he drank it as if there was no tomorrow. He became so sick with it, that he got washed-out. Another chap took a camera up in the 'plane, and was told, 'no cameras', so he got washed-out. It wasn't always flying ability, sometimes it was just sheer disciplinary things."

Bill Musgrave started his flying training in Rhodesia.

"I trained at Guinea Fowl *(26 EFTS Rhodesian Air Training Group)*, which is near my home town *(Gwelo)*. Then at Thornhill *(22 SFTS)*, which had become the main base. I started on Tigers then going on to Harvard Is, which was a bit of a dicey aircraft. It had a terrible habit of dropping a wing about five miles per hour above stalling speed. You had to be very careful. Then we went on to Harvard IIs, those were beautiful aircraft."

Master Navigator Bill Whiter also commenced pilot training in Rhodesia, but was remustered as a navigator. Having enlisted in April 1942, he first served with 18 (Boston) Squadron in the Mediterranean. Returning to the UK, his war ended while he was on 203 Squadron Lancasters at Stradishall. Bill had a lengthy post-war career, finally retiring from the Hercules fleet.

"I went to Rhodesia to train on Tiger Moths at Induna *(27 EFTS)*. I got through that all right, and then I went onto Oxfords, at Kumalo, just outside Bulawayo *(21 SFTS)*. I went right through the course to train as a pilot, got to within a couple of days of the wings. We'd sat our ground exams and everything, so I thought it's all over. But then the chief instructor said, 'Mr Whiter, sergeant, come with me'. He took me up for a flight, he said it was just a final CFI's test, and when we landed he said: 'Sorry, no more flying for you, not as a pilot. You were too tight on the control column.' Air Ministry at that time sent out an order to all training schools to increase their failures as pilots, they had a surplus; that was June '44. They said: 'Right, if you want to, you can go and train as a navigator.' I enjoyed flying, so I thought I might as well. I think with hindsight, it was a better thing."

By contrast, Mike Nicholson was undergoing his training in the cold of Canada.

"At grading school, we were to fly twelve hours in Tiger Moths and if we were OK, fly solo then on to pilot training. If you failed, it was on to other aircrew training. I was OK, but I made a terrible landing on my first solo. Then we went to Heaton Park in Manchester, crowds of chaps milling around waiting for posting overseas. I went off to Canada in the *Queen Elizabeth*. There were 17,000 troops on board and the trip took four days before we landed at Halifax on 24 March 1943. We then had a 2,200 mile journey by train to Neepawa, Manitoba (*35 EFTS*) arriving on 5 April 1943. This was an elementary flying training school with Tiger Moths.

"It was freezing cold, and one day four choughs came round the corner of the hangar and dropped dead through the wind chill! If an aircraft wouldn't start, it was pushed to one side in the snow and we got on with flying the rest. Then at the end of the day it was pushed into the hangar to thaw out. We lost a lot of people off our course, and the original sixty was down to forty by the time we left. We then went on to service flying training school to fly the Oxford. I liked the Oxford. Again, when we finished, our forty had come down to twenty-five."

ADVANCED TRAINING

Having mastered basic airmanship, pilots continued with advanced flying and conversion onto operational aircraft types. Flying Officer Henry Payne converted to fly the Hampden, before finally arriving at a Stirling Squadron in 1944.

"I went on to Hampden torpedo-bombers. That was an OTU where we flew at 70 feet to drop our torpedo and we simulated targets, and we were on anti-submarine patrol over the Pacific. We went 500 miles out. If you look at the Pacific, 500 miles is just a blip, so we never saw a thing.

"That was in Victoria, at Pat Bay, (*32 OTU Patricia Bay*). It was in the middle of a forest, and we lost more 'planes in the Rockies than we did on anything else. Because Victoria and Vancouver in particular are very fog prone and we used to come back after we'd been out for seven or eight hours, in dense fog they just used to miss the aerodrome and go straight into the Rockies.

"I got back to England in '43. I was first put on a Mosquito squadron at Swanton Morley. (*Probably 2 Group Support Unit, a holding unit for aircrew.*) I was only there a few months, because they shipped me off to a Whitley conversion squadron to do airborne dropping (*possibly 81 OTU Ashbourne*). We did parachute dropping and glider towing in preparation for conversion to Stirlings."

Having been passed over as a pilot, Bill Whiter continued with his type conversion prior to joining his first squadron as a navigator.

"I was off to the Middle East, to 70 OTU at Shandur, on Baltimores. It was a nice aeroplane, lovely position for the navigator, because you were sat right in the nose of the aircraft, with a great big glass dome in front of you. You couldn't get out apart from the door and you couldn't get back to the rest of the crew. It wasn't a bad aircraft, it was quite fast, but I think it had problems with stalling. They lost quite a few when pilots got a bit careless and went in.

"Then we went to Italy to convert to Bostons before the war finished. We went on about 10 May, to a conversion unit at Paestum on the Salerno beach-head. My conversion was at 5 RFU on B Flight. 5 RFU had several landing strips on the Salerno plain. Our strip was situated on the coast at the southern end of the Salerno beach and we were there between 10 and 27 May 1945. We then went back to the transit camp, where we were told: 'Oh, they don't want any more aircrew.'"

For the single-engine fighter boys, there was a parallel process of learning how to use aeroplanes in anger and converting to fly their chosen type prior to joining an operational unit. Squadron Leader Geoffrey Wellum joined in 1939 and started his operational career with 92 (Spitfire) Squadron at Pembrey in South Wales, and then Biggin Hill. He later served with 65 (Spitfire) Squadron at Debden, in Malta in 1942, and then became a test pilot for the Gloster Aircraft Company. He enjoyed a successful post-war RAF career until retirement in June 1961. During his wartime service he was credited with two confirmed victories, one probable, two damaged, and one shared damaged. He recounted just how rapid a baptism of fire life could be for new fighter pilots during the testing times of 1940.

"Just before the completion of my training, I was at armament practice camp at Warmwell, firing a gun for the first time, and at a moment's notice I was posted to 92 Squadron flying Spitfires. 'There's a Spitfire, laddy, fly it, and if you break it, there'll be hell to pay!' It certainly gave one food for thought as I came to realise that I now found myself in a front-line fighter squadron within ten-and-a-half months of leaving the cloistered existence of boarding school. With only 146 hours total flying, and never having seen a Spitfire let alone fly it. I was of little use to them because the day after I joined, they were in combat for the first time over Dunkirk."

An uncertainty of what was to come next was true in many cases, a typical feature of life for newly qualified aircrew. Mike Nicholson was typical of those towards the end of the war who found themselves held in instructing posts due to a diminishing requirement for replacements in the operational squadrons.

"After we graduated and got our wings, what next? Back to Bomber

Command in the UK, where we might survive on ops for three weeks, or go on to instructor school in Alberta, which is what I did. I flew 1,084 hours instruction on SFTS in Oxfords, and I specialised in beam-approach training. A friend of mine was instructing on standard beam approach (SBA) in Norfolk. It was very foggy and he told his pupil to trust the beam and land, even though they couldn't see a thing. They landed safely and then switched off because there was no way you could taxi because you couldn't see anything.

"Stations started to close in the autumn of 1944 as the need for crews started to tail off, so I was transferred to fly the Liberator, but first the Mitchell as an introduction to tricycle undercarriages. I liked the Mitchell very much, it had lots of power. I went to Abbotsford for my first introduction to the Liberator."

This anticipation of where pilots would end up often resulted in disappointment. Joe Petrie-Andrews found himself in one such situation.

"By the time I got back from training in America the Battle of Britain was over; they didn't want me in Fighter Command. I was going to be a night fighter or a day bomber pilot, and ended up in a Whitley (24 OTU Honeybourne), which I thought was the pits. I volunteered for Pathfinders, because they said that if I did a couple of tours on Pathfinders that I could do whatever I wanted, but it didn't work out that way."

Others however, were more fortunate, and managed to end up on their chosen aircraft. Squadron Leader Peter Fahy enlisted in May 1941 and after training joined C Flight 543 Squadron at Benson flying photo-reconnaissance Spitfires. He later moved to 16 Squadron at Northolt in the same role, and after serving post-war, was invalided out in May 1958.

"I went to EFTS at Desford, near Leicester, flying Tiger Moths. (7 EFTS.) That was fun, but they didn't let me stay there. I dive-bombed the cathedral in a Tiger Moth and I was sent to Canada, and eventually got my wings. I always wanted to fly Spitfires, and my wish was granted. I think I must have said I wanted to fly Lancasters so I was actually posted to Spitfires."

Even though advanced training was over, there was often a long road still to travel, with many changes along the way before crews arrived at their first postings. Bill Musgrave's experience at this time was typical; to him it seemed the air force was in no hurry to decide what to do with him.

"We finished training in Rhodesia in November '42, and we went overland to Egypt, it took three weeks. By road, rail, steamer across the lakes, and Sunderland flying boat from Kisumu, Lake Victoria, to

Khartoum, then Khartoum to Egypt. Christmas in Jerusalem, was the coldest Christmas I'd ever experienced, and there was no hot water. Then we were posted to a Hurricane OTU at Ismailia *(71 OTU)* on the canal. Going onto Hurricanes, not a waste of time, but eventually we went to a rest station before going on a squadron.

"A group of us fresh from 71 OTU, including two other Rhodesians, were posted to a place which was a bus ride from Tunis, where we sat for six weeks doing absolutely nothing. What a dump this was – virtually a staging post boarding house. The name was RAF BPD *(personnel depot)* Tunis. It was within walking distance of El Aouina air base. They were trying to decide what to do with us. To get on, some of us volunteered to go onto air sea rescue, the Walrus. But eventually, about six of us Rhodesians were posted to a Rhodesian squadron."

There was another surprise in store for Jack Biggs and his fellow graduates from the Arnold Scheme; the RAF wanted to submit them to further training, in essence going over much of the ground they had already covered in America.

"We came back from Canada and then were posted to Bournemouth, which was an aircrew centre. Then they said, 'Well you're going to have your postings now'. Typical air force, they didn't trust the Americans, they didn't think the Americans had taught us to fly properly, so they opened up a series of advanced flying training schools. They hadn't existed before, so I went up to Watton in Norfolk. We were on Masters, Master I wasn't half bad, that had the in-line engine, Master II had a bloody great radial engine, and it was so nose heavy, that if you just touched your brakes you'd be up on your nose."

OPERATIONAL TRAINING
A problem for trainees at OTUs was the fact that the units usually relied on either obsolete aircraft types, or early examples of current types which had been handed down from the squadrons in a war-weary state. Flight Lieutenant Dennis Busbridge completed one tour on Coastal Command with 224/233 Squadrons (Hudsons) from Leuchars, Aldergrove, Limavady and Tiree, from September 1940 to July 1942. However, later he was confronted with the dreaded Blackburn Botha, which had earned itself an unenviable reputation as a generally bad aeroplane, unfit for service.

"The Blackburn Botha and I crossed paths momentarily only, for which I am truly grateful. On posting from 12 Flying Training School at Grantham (Spittlegate) on Ansons, several of us arrived at Silloth towards the end of August 1940 where, having reported to station headquarters we were immediately detailed for duty the very next morning as pallbearers to the crew of a Botha which had crashed during training a day or so previously. *(Probably L6203 which suffered a loss of engine power on take-off, lost height and crashed one mile south east of the airfield on 24 August.)* Completing this not very pleasant function, we reported to flights to learn of our future activities – I was suitably unimpressed to find myself allocated to the Botha Flight.

"By this time, of course, we all knew of the Botha's reputation. Designed for the Hercules engine but having to make do with the much less powerful Perseus, with a subsequent non-existent single-engine performance, it was said to be a kite much-loved by the grim-reaper. Shortly afterwards I was even less enthusiastic about the type during my first cockpit familiarisation lesson, when having settled into the pilot's seat, it was pointed out that the nose and pistol of the torpedo it was designed to carry would appear to be not more than a few inches from my right cheek (not the facial one!) My future seemed extremely brief.

"However it was proved to me the very next day that there is a providence when the whole course was switched to Hudson aircraft and the Bothas were withdrawn from flying training for Coastal Command pilot courses. Thankfully, I never flew in one and I do not recollect ever seeing one again and happily played with the Lockheeds (complete with efficient heating systems, ashtrays, toilets et al) from then on. My instructor during the Hudson course was Squadron Leader Jan Johannes Moll, the Dutchman of Parmentier and Moll fame, who raced the KLM DC-2 into second place in the 1934 England-Australia Air Race. I was really chuffed."

Having completed his post-Arnold Scheme training at 17 (Pilot) Advanced Flying Unit (AFU) at Watton in Norfolk, Jack Biggs also experienced less than ideal machines as he started his operational type conversion.

"After AFU I got posted to 55 OTU at Annan for eight weeks. We were flying clapped-out Hurricane Is. If a new Mk II came in, the wing commander flying got it, and his name was Dennis Davey. When I was out in Ceylon subsequently, Wing Commander Davey came out. He came in the mess one day and he said, 'I know you don't I?' and I said, 'Well sir, I was at 55 OTU'. Whether or not he remembered me I don't know, but he said, 'I enjoyed those days at 55' and I agreed that it was a good OTU.

"We had the usual lectures and the wing commander engineering officer was an ex. pilot. He said: 'I want you to look at your partner, because it's odds on that one of you won't be here at the end of the course, you'll be killed.' We did have one of our course members killed, but he had been sick and he got put on two courses later. He went into the Solway Firth in a Hurricane and ploughed in."

Sergeant Charlie Browning was another Hurricane pilot, who served on 42 Squadron in South East Asia. Similar to Geoffrey Wellum, Charlie had to find out very quickly how to cope with a high-performance aircraft.

"I trained out in Rhodesia – Bulawayo. *(21 Service Flying Training School.)* From there I went to Egypt and they taught me how to fly a Hurricane, which was great. *(71 Operational Training Unit at Ismailia in the Canal Zone.)* On the course they decided to have a Spitfire crew and a Hurricane crew; we were in training on the Harvard. The top group got the Spitfire, and the lower group got the Hurricane. But the one thing about it was, if you banged it down on the ground, it would stay there, and there was no question of it wobbling about like a Messerschmitt 109; once down they stayed down.

"We had a Hurricane up on jacks that we could sit in, which we used to do in the evening in our own time, and get to know where everything was; for example how to get your hand down to where the undercart was. After some time an officer of the flight would come and check you out, and he put a cover over your eyes so you couldn't see, and he would say, 'Air speed indicator, put your left hand on it', and do the same for all the instruments, so that he saw you knew where they were. 'Get down, get the undercart – up, and drop your hand down', and this kind of thing. So in the end when you had done all that, we would pack up and have our Hurricane first flights.

"I was detailed to fly, but they had trouble with the parachute section, trying to get me fitted when I got down there; everyone had gone, 'It's national Hurricane day', they said, 'They've all gone! Where have you been? Get in that one over there.' So I leaped in the thing, went through the cockpit, said I'd done all my calls – 'The cockerel is crowing, the cockerel is crowing', that was switch on the IFF (Identification Friend or Foe) so that you didn't get hit by friendly fire.

"And away you go. I went down the runway, and after flying the Harvard this was a really, really good aeroplane to fly. You hammered off down the runway with this beast that you'd never had before. Get the thing airborne and then get down to get the undercart up. It splattered about, but you'd done this a dozen times, if not more, put your hand down. Could I find it? No! I looked down and finally I got the undercart up. I don't know what made me do it, but I looked over the side. Fortunately, one thing they always told us in training, if you've got a problem, and doubt, bang the throttle open. So I grabbed for the throttle; instead of it being right forward, just giving it petrol, it was halfway back. I hadn't tightened right up after all the panic of getting off – you had to keep one hand on the throttle when taking off, especially when it's your first time. It gradually lifted back, so I'd gone off. Everybody told me afterwards that when I disappeared from view, they'd put their hands over their ears."

Experienced aircrew were frequently rested from operations to fly as instructors at OTUs. Pete Brothers spent some time at two different OTUs in between his operational tours and experienced some of the difficulties of putting senior officers into this kind of position.

"Taffy Jones became station commander at Hawarden; a Spitfire OTU. (57 OTU.) 'Station commander, you ought to fly a Spitfire.' He put the wheels up too soon, finished up at the end of the runway on his belly. He got out, all the chaps rallied round, and he said 'Bring me another f-f-f***ing Spitfire, this one's b-b-bloody broken.'"

OTUs were frequently called upon to support Bomber Command Main Force by participating in raids, although this was normally done using staff crews rather than those under training. However, Flight Sergeant Ron Williams, wireless operator/air gunner, was a member of a crew under training called upon to join main force for an operation. Ron subsequently served a full tour with 150 (Wellington) Squadron in Tunisia and Italy.

"On 15 September 1943, while I was training at Moreton-in-Marsh (*21 OTU*), I took part in my first operational sortie when I flew as W/Op to Pilot Officer Ken Hammond and crew on a six-and-a-half-hour Nickel *(leaflet dropping)* raid to the city of Rennes in Brittany. I had told my parents beforehand, and my mother sent me a telegram wishing me: 'God bless and a safe return.'"

Pilot Flight Lieutenant Jim Lord served with 550 (Lancaster) Squadron at North Killingholme. He described the crewing-up process at OTU.

"We crewed up together at 83 OTU Peplow, Shropshire (*Wellington*). We got into a huge hangar, everybody was milling around, 'get your-selves sorted out gentlemen'. This tall lanky fellow came up to me, he said, 'are you looking for a wireless operator?' I said, 'yes, I suppose I am', and we took to each other. We thought, well we could tell that we were much the same sort of breed, grammar school boys. I said, 'all right then, let's go and find some more crew'. We wandered around and got a crew."

The 'tall lanky fellow' Jim speaks of, was Wireless Operator Flying Officer John 'Jock' Elliott, who takes up the story.

"Then we looked around and found a navigator, Bob Sebaski, a Canadian, and then the bomb aimer, another Canadian, Gus Vass. The rear gunner at that time was an Irishman from the Irish Free State, and when we finished OTU, he went back to Ireland and never came back. So we got another rear gunner, at OTU, and that was Jack Schomberg, an Australian. The mid-upper gunner was a chappie from London (*Sgt P J Scully*), so we were a very mixed crew really.

"Having finished OTU, we had to hang about waiting for another rear gunner, and then we went to Sandtoft Heavy Conversion Unit, Halifaxes. (*1667 HCU.*) Those who worked on Lancasters loved Lancasters, and those who operated on Halifaxes were very happy with

Halifaxes, and they were a different beast from the ones we used in Training Command. You've got to appreciate that the training ones were clapped out, and they were Merlin-engine Halifaxes, rather than Hercules. We very rarely came back on four engines."

Jim Lord continued:

"That was a hairy time, they weren't very good aircraft to be honest. They were a bit teased out, and they were superannuated. We had a bit of trouble in them now and again. I never told the rest, but we came nearer to killing ourselves on HCU then we ever did on the squadron. We were doing a cross-country and were down to two engines, so I said to the flight engineer, 'we're on two, I'd better find somewhere to land'. So we called up, got permission to land at a place called Halfpenny Green. We did all the necessary things, got onto the approach, and we were just coming into land when we got a red from the caravan. How do you overshoot a Halifax, on two engines?

"So very quickly, we un-feathered the two that we'd closed off and we went round. It took us twenty minutes to get some altitude. We came round again and got another red, so I ignored it and landed by the side of the runway. That was the hairiest landing I ever did. When we got up the next morning and went to look at the aeroplane, there were bits of twigs on the underside of the mainplane; and that is a line that nobody else would believe.

"After we'd finished at HCU we went on to Hemswell, 1 Lancaster Finishing School. We just did two weeks there, then we were posted to 550 Squadron at North Killingholme. That's where the real stuff started; where you suddenly realised that you hadn't joined the air force to fly, you'd joined the air force to die!"

WIRELESS OPERATOR / AIR GUNNER

Up to the outbreak of war, wireless operator training still mainly followed the pre-war pattern of a six-month course at the electrical and wireless school at Cranwell in Lincolnshire, which was followed by a one-month course at a gunnery school. A second wireless school had been opened at Yatesbury in Wiltshire in 1938, but additional training capacity was still needed, and supplementary schools of wireless telegraphy were opened at Hamble in Hampshire and Prestwick in Scotland. The wartime training pattern went through a number of changes before settling on an increased number of radio schools plus bombing and gunnery schools (B&GS).

George Cook followed the early wartime system, before moving on to an OTU to crew up with the rest of his Hampden crew.

"I did my initial wireless operator training at Prestwick, and I was at Cranwell for the second part of the wireless operator course. Then it was a gunnery course on Fairey Battles at West Freugh in Scotland, (*4 B&GS*) where I got my sergeant's stripes and aircrew brevet as a WOp/AG. Then I went to Upper Heyford (*16 OTU Hampden and Hereford*), and all that training took about fifteen months and I was ready for an operational squadron."

Jack Bromfield did not enlist until much later, so he went through the fully-developed radio school / B&GS system.

"We were posted to 2 Radio School at Yatesbury, for twenty-six weeks. The first half was sometimes four hours morse a day. It was beginning to get to some; you could see them at breakfast with a pint mug in this hand, knife, fork and spoon in the other hand, rattling morse on the mug. At the end of the first half of the course, I came home on a week's leave, and Dad took me out for a pint. First thing we did when we got back – flying kit! Suits, Kapok, Sidcot, masks, oxygen; all the kit, and these beautiful boots. The next thing we know, we're booked to fly, in Dominies.

"Dominies had a wooden propeller on one of the inboard struts, which made the power, so until you were tail up and hammering down the grass, you were powerless! It worked once you were airborne, and supposing there were maybe five students and an instructor, and the driver of course, you had about twenty minutes on the set, which was on a card and you just contacted those VF stations. Just for practice, that's all it was.

"At the end of twenty-six weeks we'd lost four of the original thirty. At the end of every month, there was an exam, and an intake came in every two weeks. At the end of the first month you had an exam; if you didn't pass, you were FT – further training. You could manage two FTs before you were scrubbed, and then of course you had the choice – ground crew or straight air gunner.

"Then I had indefinite leave, and when the telegram came I was posted to 8 Bombing and Gunnery School, Evanton, Inverness. We did eight weeks there, and three of you would go up with an instructor, in an Avro Anson, with a Blenheim turret. The turret only has 45 degrees of traverse from dead astern. You had two foot pedals, and you'd press the pedal and the gun went round and your head went round with it. I suppose it gave you another 5 degrees of traverse. You had something like a motorbike seat you sat on, with two handles. You only had one gun, and what we would do is each have our own belt of ammunition, the three of us; and one would have blue dye on the tip, red dye or green dye. So you loaded your belt in your ammunition, some were about 250 / 300 rounds. They fired about twenty a second, so you didn't have much firing time, which was good really, because the guns were clapped

35

out. When your hits went through the drogue, it would leave this coloured dye, so they could tell which of you had hit, and how many.

"We had one trip with two lads who were air gunners, and we went through the whole drill before we got in the aircraft, with the instructor. No. 1 stoppage; the cocking stud right at the front of the slot, take your cocking toggle out of your flying boot, cock, and fire again. No. 2 stoppage; stud would stop half way back; same process, cocking toggle, cock and fire again. No. 3 stoppage, where the breech block is right at the back, you can't cock it. So what you do, is to get your cocking toggle and jam it under the rear seat, which is like a freewheel pawl, and it will go forward and you start all over again. The young lad that went in last had a No.3 stoppage. So, instead of jamming his cocking toggle under the rear seat, he lifted the breech cover. So the gun went forward and fired and he had a black face. Frightened the life out of the poor lad. When we got on the ground, of course the pilot was a bit miffed with this explosion in the turret.

"Then we were posted to Madley, down near Hereford. (4 *Signals School.*) We did a quick refresher course on the 1196 radio, and then we were posted to Bishop's Court in Northern Ireland. (7 *[Observers] Advanced Flying Unit.*) All they sold in the sergeant's mess, was Guinness, Irish whisky, or milk, they didn't sell any beer. So we found out there was a guy down the road who had his front parlour as a bar; he sold beer. If you went down to see Shaun in this pub it was hilarious.

"If the pilot was a bit browned off, and you were coming down the east coast of Northern Ireland in the old Annie, instead of a gentle turn, suddenly you'd do a very steep turn, and he said, 'We were nearly over the Free State border then'.

"The next telegram said: 'Report to 21 Operational Training Unit, Moreton-in-Marsh.' I thought that can't be bad, summer time, and Bromfield's going to the Cotswolds, where all the pubs are thatched, and you can drink your beer in the sun. This is going to be good this is! We had a fortnight's ground school, refreshing everything you had learned. The pilots had carte blanche to go and listen to any lecture. Then at the end of the two weeks it was a sort of tea and sticky-buns day, and the pilots just went around and selected their crew. I got crewed up with Arthur Robertson, a Canadian regular; his trade was armourer, so the gunners couldn't pull the wool over his eyes.

"I was the only Brit in a Canadian crew. We did a fair bit of flying; first you had an instructor, then you went solo. They were mostly Wimpey IIIs and Xs, and you just started flying, but we lost our navigator. Apparently, he couldn't cope too much with night flying. He was a very quiet man, and the others were very boisterous, typical Canadians.

"We were supposed to go and simulate bombing at Rhyl, then up to Ramsey to do it again, and then go up over the Mull of Galloway and across the North Sea, down to the Wash, and then back to Moreton. I knew when we'd turned into Ramsey, but after Ramsey we didn't turn.

Warrant Officer Jack Bromfield (fourth from left) and his crew during training on Wellingtons at 21 OTU Moreton-in-Marsh, Gloucestershire. Jack was the wireless operator and was shot down on his twelfth operation in January 1945 while serving with 158 Squadron on Halifaxes. *Bromfield*

I thought, I wonder what's gone wrong. I looked over his shoulder, and the plot finished at Rhyl. So I did lift up the pilot's helmet, I didn't want to yell over the intercom, and said: 'The plot finishes at Rhyl.' Of course it was dark, so I couldn't see what the expression on his face was, but he called the bomb aimer. The bomb aimer went and looked and said, 'Yes, it does'. We need some means of getting home, because apparently he'd just lost it.

"Well I found a beacon at Limavaddy, and I checked with the pilot, 'There are your needles, now turn around', and they all shouted: 'What?' 'Turn around, fly towards it until the needles come up again, and then when the needles come together we're at Limavaddy in Northern Ireland.' Then the bomb aimer looked on the map and gave you a rough course to steer. So suddenly, there was the River Severn. I then called Moreton-in-Marsh and up went the searchlight. He was finished, that nav.

"On a cross country from Moreton we had two gunners in a Wimpey, but only one turret. Halfway round they would change over. On that last long straight leg, they would tell the pilot, 'Ready for the exercise', and he would do gentle S-turns. One of the gunners reeled out

37

the drogue, which was sort of fishtailing behind you, and the other gunner shot at it – he couldn't hit the side of a barn if he was in it! On this particular night, Robby had told the rear gunner to stream the drogue, because Doc was in the turret.

"The skipper called me up, he said: 'Have you got communication with Doc?' I said, 'Yes'. He replied, 'I can't get anybody'. I said I'd give him a shout and I called Doc in the rear turret and said: 'Has he streamed the drogue yet?' 'I can't see any drogue, he should have streamed it fifteen minutes ago.' The skipper said to me, 'Disconnect, walk down the back and have a look.' I saw this little short man, he'd stepped back to admire his work and gone through the canvas; his legs were hanging outside. We missed the best bit didn't we, Robby should have told me to go down and tell him when to start running!

"From there we were posted to 6 Group Battle School at Dalton, up near Thirsk. There we had talks by people who had evaded capture, we also had a dear old lady, she must have been in her seventies, who was trying to teach us a smattering of French. By the time we had her out for a lunch in the sergeants' mess and back again, she only spoke Dutch – of the double variety! She said, if you could learn to count in German, you can progress from there quite easily if you took note; and she taught us all to count in German. French, well you know it might well have been Japanese, to all these idiots, I think half of them were asleep. Then we were posted just a couple of miles down the road, to 1659 HCU at Topcliffe, Halifax IIs and Vs. We flew long night cross-countries, circuits and crash landings, you know, circuits and bumps!"

Flight Sergeant Roy Fensome was a WOp on 216 Squadron in the Middle East in 1945-46, mainly in Dakotas, but including the occasional trip in a Halifax or Lancaster.

"I was at 4 Radio School, RAF Madley, Dominies; that was when I found I loved flying. But the problem was there were seven students, an instructor and a pilot, and a lot of people who were airsick. It was terrible – we had an old biscuit tin. Fortunately, I wasn't sick, but I can understand it, with the aviation fuel and first-time flying, some people were really bad. In the end, the brats, they used to have to clean it out, but they got so disgusted with it, the person who was sick had to do it themselves.

"From there we went on to Proctor IVs, with just the pilot and operator, although there was one other seat at the back. It was good, and I knew I was going to make it when we went up one day, and of course the weather was really tremendous. But they said fly, so we flew. The pilot, a young pilot officer, after we'd been up for three-quarters of an hour, said he was lost. I immediately looked at the altimeter, because the Welsh Black Mountains were close, about 5,000 feet I think, but he was at 6,000 feet so we were all right.

"He wanted me to get him a QDM – a fix. I contacted the headquarters, and they told me to change frequency, and fortunately they informed the DF station that I was going to contact them. So when I tuned in the receiver I could hear their call sign. I tuned in the transmitter and I got him his fix, and was quite happy with that, and I got him another one. They were both first class fixes, so when he come down below cloud, we were almost over the top of the airfield. So he was happy, and I was happy, because I thought I'd done well, and that was that.

"After posting, we landed at Port Said after a terrible journey by sea. We then went to 13 Air Gunnery School at El Ballah, where we used Ansons and, I think it was Martinets that did the towing. They always said, 'Sergeant, you shoot at the drogue, not at the aeroplane!' 'We don't want all the paperwork', you know what I mean? I scored 69%, so not bad. There were about three or four of us in the Anson, and I thought to myself: 'How do they know who hits the target and who doesn't?' But each student had a different coloured tip bullet, so mine was 300 red, or 300 blue. So when the drogue comes down they could see the coloured holes in the drogue. Then with the 25 feet of film, we used to watch that, and see whether you had done well, or whether you had done badly, or you wanted some improvement and so forth."

Having completed tours of operations on Whitleys and Halifaxes, Flight Sergeant Harry Kent found himself employed as a staff pilot on 12 Radio School at St. Athan, flying pupil WOps.

"I was a staff pilot from January 1944 to July 1944 and the flying field only had one 1,000 yard runway. In the event of a crosswind, there was a Sommerfeld track strip, but unfortunately, there was a large dip in the middle of the airfield, which meant that if one did not touchdown reasonably quickly, one found that the runway suddenly dropped several feet, which did not make for smooth landings.

"I flew Oxfords and Ansons, which at least gave us the choice that if we had been out the night before and were not feeling quite on the ball, we chose to fly an Anson, which was almost impossible to prang, as about 10 feet off the ground one closed the throttles, pulled back on the control column and she landed herself, whereas the Oxford had a nasty habit of dropping one wing if one did not land it correctly. There was also a Tiger Moth which we used to take up for aerobatics if so inclined, but of course this was more for a break from flying around with trainee wireless operators.

"I wonder if there are any local householders still living on the approaches to the runway, who remember the trailing aerials that we used to wrap around their clothes lines, when the wireless operator forgot to reel them in before landing? I believe it used to cost him 7/6d to have it replaced."

AIR BOMBER

The trainee bomb aimer, more correctly referred to as an air bomber, underwent a six-week course at a B&GS, followed by six weeks basic navigation training at either an air observer's school or at an air navigation school. Flying Officer Ted Milligan had wanted to be a pilot, but in common with so many others, found himself being streamed off in a different direction, completing his air bomber training in Canada.

> "I trained as a pilot in Canada, initially on Tiger Moths. I failed the course after a crash-landing in the States, and getting lost at the end of advanced flying, so I was re-mustered as observer (navigator/bomb aimer). I completed about 350 hours as a pilot and 100 or so as nav/bomb aimer, plus some gunnery and radar training. I came back to the UK and did my Wellington conversion at 30 OTU, Hixon, then on to 21 OTU at Moreton-in-Marsh where I spent some time and we crewed up. Then it was 1668 HCU at Bottesford for Lancaster conversion, before we were finally posted to 460 Squadron at Binbrook, an Australian outfit, where I completed thirty-three ops."

FLIGHT ENGINEER

The training of flight engineers was concentrated at 4 School of Technical Training St. Athan in June 1942. The first trainees were recruited from airframe and engine fitters since they would need a shorter course. Direct entry training lasted twenty weeks, after which the trainee was promoted to sergeant and sent out on operations. At its peak in late 1943/early 1944, the school had more than 5,000 flight engineers under training. One notable feature of flight engineer training was that the course was based almost exclusively on the use of grounded airframes for instruction, so that it was quite usual for a newly-qualified flight engineer to be awarded his badge without ever having flown in an aeroplane.

Flight Sergeant Bob O'Dell however, started off as a trainee pilot but the declining need for replacement crews in 1944 led to his being re-mustered. After passing out of St. Athan he was posted to 408 'Goose' Squadron at Linton-on-Ouse in Yorkshire, completing thirteen operations on the Halifax before the end of the war intervened.

> "I went up to Yorkshire to fly the Tiger. I did twelve hours on Tigers; soloed at twelve hours. I went to Heaton Park, Manchester, ready to go to Canada to complete the training. But when we got there it was all scrubbed because all the schools were full in Canada. Then I was no longer wanted as pilot, they wanted other crew members. I had to go to London then for a series of aptitude tests, and I had a natural aptitude for engineering, say no more. Then I went to Locking (5 SofTT) to do

the first of the engineering training. Then I went to St. Athan in Wales (*4 SofTT*) for type training, and I was typed on radials, Hercules, so I knew very well I was going on Halifaxes.

"After that I went to Dalton (*6 Group Aircrew School*) to meet the crew. I did a bit of hanging about at Boscombe Down, just gaining some flying experience. I had quite a few trips in Airspeed Oxfords, bloody awful they were, ever so noisy, and of course I didn't have a flying helmet! Then at Dalton, that was where we met the rest of the crew. Got crewed up and then we went to Dishforth for con unit (*1664 Heavy Conversion Unit*); and then Linton-on-Ouse on squadron."

Flight Lieutenant D C Tritton had previously served with the rescue launches of the marine branch of the RAF before being selected for flight engineer training.

"Selection for training for different types of aircraft was achieved in the simplest manner. A parade of the complete entry (usually of 100 men), was separated into parties of the required sizes for Lancasters, Stirlings and Halifaxes, with a small number for Sunderlands and Catalinas. I requested that I be allowed to change to flying boats, as I had previously been a fitter, marine and was thus familiar with waterborne life in Coastal Command. The request was refused, and I carried on as a Lancaster man as selected. At this stage, all were given the opportunity to withdraw from their voluntary commitment; I am not aware that any did, but certainly there was no obvious reduction in numbers.

"Obviously there was an aircraft of each type available for ground instruction of the trainee flight engineers, and it is interesting to note that the Sunderland was flown into St. Athan, alighting on the grass on its hull. Subsequently, it was jacked up and mounted on its normal beaching gear. I examined the underside of the hull, and found that it bore minor scratch marks but was probably still watertight! In fact, this was a method used on several occasions by operational Sunderlands with hull damage as a result of action. *(One incident involved a Pembroke Dock-based Sunderland, which was successfully landed on the grass at the nearby airfield at Angle.)*

"The instructor's technique course I considered to be excellent, and it was followed by a refresher on advanced Lancaster airframes. Primed with this lore, I reported for duty as an instructor, to find there was a class actually seated and waiting for a lesson on aircraft instruments. Fortunately, I knew enough about the subject to get through the first lecture or two, this gave me a breathing space sufficient to launch into a high-speed teach-yourself situation. My first pupils were Free French air force cadets, and they all passed the course – fortunately they spoke English. I was most impressed when one of these lads brought back a pound note that I had overpaid him on pay parade, even before I had missed it!

"During my operational tour, the rear gunner of another crew on the squadron had died of anoxia in his turret, unbeknown to the rest of his crew for some time. On discovering that there was a decompression chamber at St. Athan, I requested a run in it. The chamber held six men, three on each side of a table.

"When air evacuation commenced under the supervision of a medical sergeant, one man of each pair would be connected to the oxygen supply, while his partner opposite remained disconnected. Starting disconnected, I sat and waited for something to happen while watching the altimeter needle rise to 30,000 feet. I became aware of the NCO suggesting that I might like to loosen my collar and tie; on reaching up I found that I was wearing neither and that my oxygen was plugged in! Clearly I had been unconscious, and my partner produced my collar and tie. Altogether a very disturbing experience and we all became very conscious of this danger on operations."

Another strange aspect of flight engineer training was that they did not routinely go on to OTUs, only meeting up with the rest of their crews at the later heavy conversion unit (HCU) stage, shortly before reaching their operational squadrons, as Peter Green described.

"I did my flight engineer training at St. Athan like everybody else. I didn't go to OTU, as flight engineer, we went straight to the conversion unit. This was at Riccall, in Yorkshire (1658 HCU). And then we went to Pocklington (102 Squadron). The mid-upper gunner as well, he missed OTU."

Flight Sergeant John King served as a Halifax flight engineer with 296 Squadron at Earls Colne, 644 Squadron at Tarrant Rushton and 47 Squadron at Fairford.

"I came in during 1943, but I got right through my course, flight engineer, and my appendix burst. I was rushed into hospital and I was out of action for six to eight weeks. Of course, when I got back, I had to start again. My course had gone on. So I did two courses more or less.

"Eventually I passed the course, and was posted to HCU at Saltby (*1665 HCU, Halifax and Stirling*). I got put with a crew, flight sergeant pilot, and the rest were sergeants, but they were all from the north country, right on the borders. I mean they talk about the north / south divide; I was poison to them more or less. I had a hard time with them, because they would never drink with me or anything. If they went in a pub, they went on their own.

"I started getting airsick, so I had to go to the MO, and he put me on cheese. Every time I flew, I had to go to the cookhouse and get two lumps of cheese; it worked. I used to eat one and take the other one with me and nibble on the flight. But he complained about the psychological effect of being with the crew, and I was transferred to another crew. The pilot was an Australian flying officer, the wireless op was Australian, and the bomb aimer was Irish, from Donnegal. They were great, fantastic after the last lot."

Harry Hogben, who had already had his service deferred for many months, subsequently found that right at the end of the war he was no longer required as a flight engineer, and was retained in a ground trade.

"I went to St. Athan for flight engineer training. Actually, the entry that I was on at ACRC was 2,000; there were seventy-three flight engineers. Got through that, prop-swinging and all things like that; and I was at St. Athan on VE-Day in fact. So what happened was I did Merlins and then I did Hercules, and then I did Pratt and Whitney Twin Wasps, I was going to go on Liberators. That was at the tail-end virtually, so it was a longer course. I went home on leave, and came back and was told: 'Sorry, you're all redundant.'"

Sergeant Ronald Liversuch also found himself taken off the flight engineer programme, but for rather different reasons in his case.

"Having finished my flight engineer's course I was ceased training and not posted. This was because both my younger brothers had been killed in action; Raymond was shot down in a Wellington and Albert died when the Dakota he was in was hit by ground fire and exploded on the way in to Pegasus Bridge on D-Day. I was the last of the Liversuches and it was said I would be unsuitable for aircrew material."

Sergeant Raymond Liversuch was a WOp/air gunner with 109 Squadron at Stradishall, whose Wellington was shot down on 3 July 1942 by a night fighter flown by Oberleutnant Egmont Prinz zur Lippe Weissenfeld of II./NJG2. The remains of Liversuch and second pilot Warrant Officer William Allison were not found until 1982.

OBSERVER / NAVIGATOR

Sergeant G E Harris was trained as an observer in the pre-war scheme which persisted for some time after the outbreak of hostilities, and due to the urgent demand often resulted in some very abbreviated courses.

"I was a direct entry observer mustered in June 1939. After doing well at 9 Air Observer's School RAF Penrhos, I was rewarded with an astro navigation course at St. Athan in November '39. I was there exactly four days, the object of the course was speed and as soon as qualified, candidates were shunted on. I was sent to OTU at Upper Heyford. I thought the shortness of the course was noteworthy, six hours ten minutes flying time. Less than a year later I was shot down over Holland

and spent the rest of the war as a POW."

Sergeant Harris was shot down by anti-aircraft fire in his 44 Squadron Hampden on 13 August 1940 during a raid on Bernburg. All four crew members were taken prisoner.

As the war progressed and technology advanced, it became clear that extensions to the basic skills of the observer were needed, and the aircrew category of navigator was phased in with various specialisations. Air bomber training was also intended to take over and develop some of the tasks previously in the remit of the observer. These changes were brought in during 1942. Having joined up during the transition period, Flying Officer Jack Booth completed observer training and had a lengthy operational career with 88 (Boston) Squadron at Hartford Bridge (now Blackbushe) and Vitry-en-Artois, flying forty-two sorties in 1944-45.

"Joined up in September '41. I did my OTU at Bicester. (*13 OTU, equipped with Blenheim IV and V.*) We used to travel from Bicester to Finmere, 'cause Finmere had the runways; Bicester was grass. On completion of my OTU, my pilot and gunner, (that's all we had) a crew of three in those days in the Boston IIIAs. My pilot was Flight Sergeant Creighton Cowley, my gunner was Syd Milne, who came from Cambridge."

Rick Rickard took up his story again, with lengthy training in Canada, followed by Coastal Command operational training back in England.

"Myself and Butch Smith were drafted to go to ground defence to Shawbury in Shropshire for three months to the end of January 1941. As U/T Aircrew we sported white flashes in our hats, which looked quite smart and made us feel very important and we reported to the guard room. Incidentally our CO was Henry Cotton, the famous golfer. We were directed to Oxford Block, an old wooden hut housing about fifty airmen and left to get on with our new surroundings. Our room mates were a motley crowd – a large number of which appeared to be 'Brummies' – and as we sat round one of the iron stoves in the evening, we listened to boastings of what prison sentences had been served and for what crimes. We suspected this was all put on for our benefit.

"Apart from square bashing and arms drill, part of our duty was to man posts in the airfield at dawn and dusk against possible surprise, German fighter attacks etc. Needless to say the weather was bitterly cold, particularly at dawn and these watches usually took about two hours of foot stamping and hand blowing and an occasional drag. On one evening 'stand to' with snow beginning to fall, there was a four-engined bomber approached the 'drome with one engine u/s looking for an emergency landing. It turned out to be a Stirling being ferried by Jim Mollison and he successfully managed to lob in to the grass 'drome.

"Eventually we ended up in Canada, at Mount Hope, 33 ANS, which was to be our base for the next twelve weeks. We were the first contingent of RAF trainees under the Empire Training Scheme and as usual the billets were only partially completed. The war was almost eighteen months old and we sometimes felt guilty that so far we had hardly taken any part and in fact we were more secure from bombing and 'Y' rockets than civilians at home. However we took pride in our specialist training and the knowledge that we could put this training to effective use.

"Since flying in the Canadian summer was often uncomfortably warm, we took bottles of Coca Cola with us as a quencher and disposed of empties by throwing them out of the aircraft. We didn't really appreciate that on the way down these bottles whistled like a banshee and alarmed local residents in villages and towns – as a result a notice appeared on DROS that this practice 'must cease forthwith'. We were becoming rather blasé about our importance as trainee airmen, with our special Irvine flying suits, expensive Longine Swiss watches, bubble sextants and rapidly acquired knowledge of astral matters to the point of almost being blinded by science. We were constantly reminded of the importance of occasionally looking out of the window to check position visually against DR theory (always assuming the ground was visible beneath cloud).

"By this time my stomach had become used to flying, but I was constantly apprehensive of take-offs – two engines spitting flames as the antiquated Ansons trundled down the runway in an effort to become airborne. Once airborne and my composure regained, I settled down peacefully to carry out navigation duties. The flight and the landings never worried me, but my fear of take-offs stayed with me for the whole of my flying period, whatever the type of aircraft.

"Next it was 31 Bombing and Gunnery School on the northern shore of Lake Ontario on a four to five week course to learn about the obvious. Imagine our dismay to find that we were to fly in Fairey Battles, with a crew of three in a line, i.e. pilot and a pair of trainees. The pilot naturally sat up front and communication was by means of a length of hose-pipe. We were required to blow down this pipe before speaking and sometimes nearly blew the pilot's helmet off! The small bomb bay was a well in the middle of the aircraft where we were required to lay down over a bombsight and issue instructions to the pilot before pressing the 'tit' and releasing a practice bomb on to the lakeland target. The gun placement was naturally in the tail of the craft and here we were required to stand up in the slipstream to operate a Vickers gas operated machine gun. This was somewhat hairy as we were not harnessed in any way and the top half of our bodies was exposed to the elements. Also the fumes from the glycol cooling system tended to induce sickness with dire results. To place a pan of ammo on the spigot was a tricky business, particularly with the turbulence and the yawing aircraft and it was not unknown to drop a complete pan of ammo overboard into the lake below.

"Our bombing runs were over a target staked out on the lake and we had to carry out a run-in on a marker to release bombs on target and hits were recorded from the spumes of water shown by the small bombs. The gunnery practice was quite fun and we were required to shoot at a white drogue being towed by a Tiger Moth or a Lysander over the lake. Several risks were involved, first you might hit the towing aircraft (worst still, the pilot), or you might pierce the cord thus releasing the drogue beyond recovery or you may miss altogether (most likely).

"After practice and returning to base with a few rounds 'up the spout' it was often the sport to let a few rounds off over land, the favourite target being the stacks of pumpkins put out after harvesting. Bullets on impact would cause the pumpkins to burst and spew out pips and flesh. On one occasion one of the lads thought it fun to chase some horses in the fields, but after a claim that one had been hit and killed this practice had to cease forthwith! We got to know some of the 'erks' whose job it was to recover the drogues on release and record the number of hits and colours. After a few jars of ale and supply of different coloured crayons, we were able to increase our score of direct hits quite appreciably!

"After eighteen months all we had to show were sergeant's tapes and observer brevets, so guess what, on our return to England, we were sent on another course, this time to Thornaby near Stockton-on-Tees, to 6 Coastal Command OTU. I stayed with my pilot Sgt Dai John and flew Hudsons, for a period of eight weeks. We picked up two WOp/AGs as our permanent crew, Sgt Thomas (Taffy) an ex-master baker from Torquay and Sgt Waldron (Shag) a lad from Wiltshire. Our stay at Thornaby was very expensive in aircraft and crews and I suppose during the period our numbers were reduced to just over 50%. Unserviceable aircraft, reckless behaviour, enemy action or angry seas, whatever the cause, we were constantly moving beds closer to each other to avoid the ominous gaps in between. Two of my close contemporaries both 'bought it' and naturally we took it on ourselves to volunteer for funeral duties. This meant shouldering the coffins at slow march to Stockton-on-Tees cemetery; the real side of war had belatedly begun to dawn on us.

"Our training consisted of lots of circuits and bumps (day and night), and various DR navigation over the North Sea and plenty of low flying over the Pennines. Shoot-ups became a pastime and it also became normal practice to get down low enough to fly under electric pylon cables. It was around this time that the RAF was about to launch its first thousand-bomber raid on targets in Germany, which would stretch its resources to the limit. The general idea was, 'as long as it flies get it up into the air' and under close secrecy we were ordered to 'stand to' for twenty-four hours, confined to camp, ready for immediate action and banned from the bar. We hung around expectantly for the whole period, smoking, yarning and playing snooker and cards, but luckily for us the 'stand to' was eventually called off and we all cleared off to our pits for much needed sleep."

Eric Burke successfully completed his navigator training in Rhodesia and the Mediterranean theatre.

"I went up to Salisbury, Belvedere, on Tiger Moths (25 *Elementary Flying Training School*). I suppose I did about sixteen hours on Tiger Moths, until the CFI tapped me on the shoulder. He took me up and said, 'really, I don't think you've got the hang of this'. So, we came off the pilot's course, a few of us, and I went up to Moffatt, near Gwelo (24 *Bombing Gunnery and Navigation School*), and joined the nav course. We did about six weeks, which was ENT – elementary nav training. We stayed with Ansons through our training. Beyond that we did the main navigation course, and we actually did a bit of air firing and bomb dropping, bombing practice. We then had quite a journey, as we'd been posted to the Middle East.

"When we reached Cairo the wireless operator got a message through that they'd landed in Europe, it was D-Day. Having been down in Rhodesia, we didn't really know what was going on. I then went on to Giancalis, 75 OTU. That was on Baltimores, and we teamed up. I'd met my pilot, as it happened, in hospital. We were posted to Palestine, in error as it were, someone said we shouldn't be here, and they sent us back to Cairo. I somehow developed sand-fly fever, so I went in dock for a few days, where I met my pilot. So we crewed up, and we found a gunner."

Flight Sergeant Frank Mattinson initially trained as a pilot, but remustered to navigator and trained in South Africa before returning to the UK and becoming an airfield controller.

"I went to training school at Brough near Hull (4 *EFTS*), flew solo, though not many of us did. But at the end of that they told us that they weren't particularly short of pilots, but they were a bit short of flight engineers, wireless operators, air gunners. They couldn't make us volunteer because we had only volunteered for the PNB, failing which they'd discharge us and we would get called up for the army. Most of us signed up.

"From there we went to Heaton Park, back down to ACRC, and we were doing psychological tests in Lord's Cricket Ground, June '44 when the V-1s were coming over. Although I thought being one of the few to go solo I should be on a pilot's course, they discovered that I was top of maths at school, so I did rather better and was sent on a navigator's course."

FLIGHT MECHANIC

As well as the various aircrew categories, an equally essential part of the RAF structure was the ground crew. Various training schools were established throughout the UK during the war to supplement those such as Halton in Buckinghamshire, and St. Athan which were already in place; John Dodd trained as a flight mechanic at the latter.

> "Part of our training involved starting a Tiger Moth by swinging the propeller; switches off – throttle closed – suck in – switches on – contact! There was someone's little Jack Russell terrier, who used to bark excitedly every time the engine started until one day it jumped up and down and tried to bite the prop, which removed its lower jaw! The camp was in turmoil that night, with SPs crawling under the huts with guns looking for it. No-one dared to go out in case they got shot in the legs! Eventually they found it, but not until after several panics."

ITALIAN AIR FORCE

The Italian pilot training system proved to be woefully inadequate as the war progressed, having seriously under-estimated the scale of losses that needed to be replaced. The quality of the training was also considered to be inadequate, with insufficient flying time being allowed to ease the transition to operational flying, at first without any kind of operational training mid-way stage. Giacomo Metellini described the pre-war training scheme, which was still essentially unchanged under wartime conditions.

> "After two months of training at the military school in Capua, near Naples, I was sent to the 6th Breda Flight School 'Saint Giovanni', close to Milan, on 16 March 1930. At that time the training of military pilots happened at several civil flight schools, some managed by the companies that built the aeroplanes, like Breda, others managed at airfields with the first flying clubs. The aircraft on hand at the school for the first flights were the Breda and the Aviatik A.3 biplanes. They were large aircraft that we approached with a little apprehension. We not only asked if and when we could carry out our first flight but, above all, if we were capable of flying those types!
> "Learning to fly was relatively easy, but like anything it required a certain amount of time. Before taking flight lessons, it was necessary to learn how to guide an aircraft with a motor that produced enough power to taxi fast on the field, but not enough power to take off. We called it the 'Checca', that is the hen, because like the hens, we were not capable of flight.
> "In this way we were familiarising ourselves with the cockpit.

General Giacomo Metellini joined the Italian air force in 1929. He is seen here in an Ansaldo SVA 5 during flying training at the 6th Breda Flight School 'Saint Giovanni' in 1930. *Metellini*

Learning the controls and the art of taxiing, was taught to the student pilots in an aircraft that was quite quick. Those aircraft had poor forward visibility, because the nose was raised in front of the pilot, and therefore for taxiing it was necessary to zigzag on the track, watching to right and left.

"On 4 June 1930 I carried out my first solo flight (*after nine hours*); I remember it still as if it was yesterday. After the first flight there followed others, more and more difficult, learning different procedures. I became very interested, and it increased my enthusiasm. As training proceeded, we also changed the aeroplane. I continued with the Breda 4, and the SVA.9 two-seater, the same type of aircraft on which Gabriel D'Annunzio performed his famous flight over Vienna. Then, the SVA.5 single-seater, the SVA.3, also called 'Ridottino' because of its small dimensions, and finally the SC.4, an aeroplane that we called 'da naso' (the nose) because, wherever you aimed the nose, there you put the wheels.

"These aeroplanes were more and more manageable and as such

49

allowed the pilot to acquire mastery with practice, and to carry out more and more complex manoeuvres and aerobatics. After having obtained my civil pilot's licence, we were assigned to training for the military pilot's licence. I was transferred to Ghedi, close to Brescia and, then to Aviano, close to Pordenone, to the 2nd Fighter Training Squadron. Here, after some hours flying on the CR.20 aeroplane, on 14 December 1930 I became a military pilot of Regia Aeronautica as a petty officer first class. I was selected, it wasn't my choice, but I was obviously very happy."

LUFTWAFFE

When the war started the Luftwaffe transferred most of its well-proven flying training activity to the safer skies in eastern Germany, Austria and Czechoslovakia, and was also rapidly grown to an eventual total of twenty-one schools. A key difference from the RAF system was that operational units had to take on the burden of operational training, receiving new crews from *Erganzungseinheiten* (formation replacement units). In the later stages of the war however, flying training was seriously shortened, training units were frequently robbed of their instructors who were needed on the front-line units, and students were being sent on operations with pitifully few hours under their belts.

Hauptmann Heinz Rökker became the seventh highest scoring Luftwaffe night-fighter ace, with a total of sixty-four victories scored while flying the Ju 88 (primarily) with NJG2.

"I did my night fighter training in Berlin, nine months I was at Gatow. There I trained as an officer and as a pilot. It was the best time during the war to fly. Most of our aircrew were officers; maybe about half and half."

Norbert Hannig expanded the story to describe a little of the basic training system.

"Our pilot training started in different schools. First of all I attended officer's school in Berlin *(Fahnenjunkerkompanie LKS III at Werder/Havel, from 25 February 1942 to 29 November 1942)*. That was for flying and ground school experience. From there I was assigned to the fighter school in Werneuchen *(1 Staffel Jagdfliegerschule, 30 November 1942 to 17 January 1943)*. At Havel I was in the south of Berlin and at Werneuchen was in the north east of the city. There I learned to fly the Me 109. I started out with the B series, C series, D, E and F."

SOVIET AIR FORCE

The Soviet aircrew training system centred on aero clubs, which took people from school and gave them further education, basic military training and selected them for various aircrew categories. Benedikt Kardopoltsev went through this system.

"We were pilots! We finished at the aero club, and although they tried to scare us, we were too young to be afraid. Flat spins were more common to the UT-1, it required exceptional training. But we never flew it, we ended the programme with the UT-2 and moved on to the UTI-4. By this time the Germans had captured Taganrog, almost captured Rostov, and we were moved from Bataisk to Azov."

After completing training General Major Nikolay Gerasimovich served with 2 GuIAP, and flew the I-16 and Hurricane.

"I was in the Yeysk military-naval pilot school; the course lasted two years. We were the first in our school to graduate as sergeants, before us the graduates were junior lieutenants. We were already measured up for the uniform of command, but at that point Marshal Timoshenko's order went out that everybody who completed the air school in 1941, regardless of the duration of training, graduated as sergeants. Our graduation was three days before the start of the war.

"The students had around thirty to thirty-five hours flying time on a combat aircraft and on the UTI-4. I, in contrast with the others, flew around forty-five hours only on the I-16, and this is why; in our flight, there was a type 'ten' I-16 with a slight peculiarity. After repairs and replacement of the wings it did not react well in high altitude. Just before landing it dropped the right wing. I knew this peculiarity well, literally, I had picked it up from the first flight and the instructor planned a full schedule of flights for me on this aircraft. Of the students, I alone flew this aircraft, in as far as the commanding officer forbade the other students to fly this aircraft after an incident when a student did not hold course on the landing run. After the aircraft were transferred to the front, this I-16 remained in our flight and they did not risk giving it to the active unit.

"In the school, apart from the I-16, we studied the LaGG-3. There were a few of them and they came a month before the war. The students were not trained on them, only the instructors. Naturally, I became familiar with it. I went to the front line with my own last group. I passed ten people in March and I went to the front with five of them as their senior officer. Initially in a Douglas to Moscow, then in a Douglas to Arkhangelsk, and from there, in the bomb bay of a strategic bomber, to Severomorsk."

The initial training was often found to be very basic, and pilots were leaving to go to operational units with little or no instruction in combat techniques, as Ivan Zvyagin explained.

"The most noticeable drawback of our training was too few flights and flying hours. We were well trained, but still not enough; tactics were given mainly by word of mouth. We were not really expecting war."

By contrast, although she had proved herself to be very competent at the aero club, Olga Lisikova found herself being subjected to repeated and detailed examination of her flying skills before she was finally assigned to operations.

"I completed training with distinction, and was able to choose where to go; I selected Leningrad. In Leningrad I was immediately assigned to a training detachment. At that time it was comprised only of men. Our instructor, Lebedev, checked me out on the R-5. He was a top pilot, who later became Zhukov's personal pilot, but then he was an instructor. He gave me a test ride and then assigned me another task, and he ran off like a crazy man, it turned out, to the chief of the training detachment. I looked up, and here came the chief of the training detachment, Gosha (Grigoriy) Semenov. Now *he* gave me a task, I did it, and did everything that he ordered: zooms, various turns, stall, etc. I then landed but he said nothing. Later they told me that he called Volodya (Vladimir) Drozdov, the commander of the 31st Detachment, which serviced the Leningrad-Moscow route, and they had the following conversation: 'I would like to recommend a pilot to you.' 'I don't need any pilots right now.' 'Don't you understand? I am recommending a special pilot to you. Lebedev and I checked her out and this is the first time we have encountered such a pilot. Whatever you tell her to do, she does it. Go ahead, try it. Give her an assignment.' 'This is a woman?' 'Exactly – a woman. Give her an assignment.' I received an assignment to execute a flight from Leningrad to Moscow and return. Then I understood why they gave me this particular assignment, in order to get me out of their hair."

After initially serving as a mechanic, Mikhail Pomorov flew operationally with 12 KBF Naval Aviation in the Yak 7 and Yak 9.

"I applied for a place at Molotov Naval Aviation Technical School. In 1941 I finished the school early with a degree as a 'plane mechanic. We trained for around two years. We were supposed to become officers, but we got the rank of senior sergeants.

"After the Finnish campaign, we were stationed on the eastern shore of Kama. There were aircraft of all types, even flying boats. They were disassembled, and we studied how to repair them. The 'planes were damaged by our teachers, and we were shown the ways to repair the damage. We fixed the 'planes independently in all weather conditions and temperatures; of course we had frostbite. But we got all the knowledge we needed. I finished the school with 'good' and 'exceptional' marks.

"I finished school as a mechanic of the MiG 1. It was a very respectable aircraft, but it did not participate in the war in large numbers. Its development was the MiG 3, but it was good at heights, but the majority of air combats were at low altitudes, where it was not good enough against Messerschmitts. I was on leave with my friend, when we heard Molotov's speech about the start of the war."

Colonel Grigory Avanesov trained as a navigator and served on MBR-2 flying boats.

"The instruction was great. I studied at the Yeysk aviation school, in the navigation department. We had to know about navigation, camouflage and countermeasures, bomb aiming and MG use as well as piloting skills. I finished school in 1939, and was sent to Baltic fleet aviation at Khanko peninsula. My first 'plane was an MBR-2."

Senior Lieutenant Alexei Valyaev had some lucky escapes during his flying training. He went on to fly the La 5 with 180 GuIAP, ending the war with two victories and two probables.

"There was an aero club in Obuhovo, where I, along with my two brothers and two cousins finished primary flight education with a Po-2. Once I was about to fly with instructor Leonov in a UTI-4. My friend and squadron commander Pavel Artemyevich came to me and told me to get out. I tried to object, but he insisted – his relatives had sent him some vobla (a dried fish), and he wanted me to join him. So I got out of the 'plane and went to the canteen. As we started some pilots ran to us and shouted, 'Leonov crashed!' It was the 'plane that I was supposed to fly in. Both pilots were instantly killed.

"The second time I flew with an instructor in a U-2, our engine failed, so we had to make a forced landing. We had broken the propeller. So, the instructor went to the air base, and mechanics brought us a new propeller and spares for the engine. We fixed the engine, and I brought it back to base by myself. It was quite easy, about two hours to change the cylinder. We had to learn everything at the front, life is different there, even our attitude towards death, and life changes. Everything changes. School is school, and war is war."

FLEET AIR ARM

Jack Routley continued his story as he started his basic flying training and Fleet Air Arm operational training, a system which in many respects closely mirrored that in the RAF, and at the *ab initio* stage, shared facilities. For example, over 5,000 Fleet Air Arm pilots received their flight training under the British

Commonwealth Air Training Plan.

"I started my flying training in December '39. My elementary flying training was at Elmdon, near Birmingham, on Tiger Moths. I did six hours before solo, and we had a couple of months or so at Elmdon doing typical elementary flying training. Went on then to RAF Netheravon on Salisbury Plain, and we did intermediate and advanced flying training on Hawker Harts, Hinds and Audaxes. It was very powerful stuff I must say; still biplanes nevertheless. But it was a very good, several months' worth of advanced flying training in the Salisbury Plain area.

"Then I went for operational training to Abbotsinch, which is near Glasgow. I flew Swordfish there, and was trained as a torpedo bomber pilot; it was just what happened. We dropped torpedoes in an area around the North Sea, and did all the operational training, including deck landings on a little training carrier called HMS *Argus*; when fully qualified, we went to war.

"I didn't find it particularly difficult to learn to fly. I had the worthy Sergeant Hymans who was my elementary flying instructor, who reckoned that I was heavy-footed in my Tiger Moth. He made me fly without flying-boots, in the winter of 1939 / 1940, to teach me to be lighter-footed. That worked OK.

"After I'd finished my flying training, I did a bit of flying at Arbroath on the Scottish coast, and they had Rocs and Skuas. (*758 Squadron*) I had an engine failure in a Skua from Arbroath, and managed to get that down in more or less one piece. The Roc and the Skua were really bad aeroplanes, but I suppose we ended up having them because the aircraft companies were churning out whatever they could, in the thought from their lordships that whatever you put out will be useable by us at that critical time. Until the flow of Spitfires and Hurricanes improved to the extent that the navy could have some and the lease-lend aircraft began to arrive, we were flying pretty sub-standard aircraft, to say the least.

"There was a long period of waiting while I flew Blackburn Sharks at Worthy Down (*755 Squadron*), a small grass field near Winchester where we trained telegraphist/air gunners in the back seat of Sharks – poor fellows. They practiced their telegraphy and they did some firing at drogues. We had an interesting variety of mess-mates including Laurence Olivier and Ralph Richardson, and a steeplechase jockey called Bissell; they were flying these monstrosities too. The Shark and the Swordfish were both slow and lumbering, though I think the Swordfish might be a slightly better aircraft, in fact I'm confident that it was a better aircraft than the Shark.

"Then I was troop-shipped off to the Middle East in the *New Amsterdam*, which was one of the Dutch passenger liners pre-war and was transformed to become a troopship, via Cape Town and Durban and through the Suez Canal."

A similar programme of operational training was also experienced by Jimmy Greening.

"It was intended that I went on onto Hurricanes, but the very high air-crew loss rate in the Barracuda squadrons forced a change and I found myself on 53A Barracuda conversion course at HMS Jackdaw, Crail, flying with both 785 and 786 squadrons between mid June and mid July. At this point pilots and observers were free to choose with whom they wished to team up, and the pairings were then kept together right through to operational postings. The next move came three days later to join 44 Course at the Deck Landing Training School at HMS Peewit, East Haven and a further month's flying on yet more Barracuda IIs, this time belonging to 713 Squadron. The course flew up to Arbroath, from where I carried out a total of eight deck landings aboard the M class carrier HMS *Rajah* in the Moray Firth.

"The final part of the Barracuda conversion took place between August and November 1944, still with 713 Squadron, but now at HMS *Urley*, Ronaldsway. Here the operational skills were taught, including the all-important dive-bombing techniques which had proved so disastrous for the earlier crews. The correct technique for the Barracuda was to commence a torpedo attack at 10,000 feet and at an angle of 60 degrees to the bow of the target, before putting the aircraft into a 60-degree dive. Dive brakes were selected out at 5,000 feet, the aircraft was pushed over to the vertical and dive brakes put in again at 500 feet immediately followed by a pull out into level flight at an altitude of 50 feet before releasing the torpedo at a speed of 180 knots. The many fatalities had largely been the result of simply failing to pull out of the dive in time. The Barracuda had stalling and landing speeds very similar to those of the Swordfish and since most pilots had been biplane trained, their experience had not prepared them for the high sink rate of a monoplane."

Jim Langford was another Barracuda pilot, who after lengthy training, eventually found himself joining an operational squadron on a completely different type.

"We did our advanced flying unit on Masters up in Scotland (9 [P]AFU *at Errol*) then went on to our operational aircraft, the Fairey Barracuda. A beauty, she was wonderful to fly. I spent eight months on that, including a month doing nothing but AADLs, which are assisted dummy deck landings, in preparation for landing on a carrier. The only thing that was different was that the runway didn't move, but we still had a batsman standing on the end of the runway waving us down. Talk about circuits and bumps; there used to be five of you going round, and round, and round for about forty-five minutes – you got dizzy.

"Having passed, you then flew out to a little escort carrier. If you land on a small one, then they always said you could land on a big one no problem; we duly did two landings on HMS *Khedive*. One of the best pilots, who was with me right from the very start on Tiger Moths failed to make the grade to land on a carrier, which meant he was shipped out to the West Indies to fly heaven-knows-what at a school where observers were trained. A bit of a comedian, and he was one of the most disappointed people I have ever met.

"The instructor would get in his aircraft and three of us trainee pilots would follow, and we'd take off and climb to 7,000 or 8,000 feet – talk about 'Chase Me Charlie' around these clouds, we just had to keep up, and heaven help you if you lost the tail of the feller in front. Then we came to do our practice torpedo dropping. Climb up to 8,000 or 9,000 feet, stick her down in a 45 degree dive, 300-315 knots, and pull out at about 150 feet above the sea and aim towards one of those American four-funnel destroyers, which the Yanks had lent us. And they were our target ship, so you had to get down to 150 feet, drop your torpedo and pull away.

"Doing that was absolutely wonderful. To go from that to a Grumman Avenger was like going from a sports car to a double-decker bus."

Jim's Barracuda courses were in Scotland on 785 Squadron at Crail in Fife, 769 Squadron at East Haven in Angus, and 786 Squadron back at Crail.

UNITED STATES ARMY AIR FORCE

The usual system of basic flying training, followed by advanced training and then operational conversion, was very much the same in the United States Army Air Force (USAAF). 'Punchy' Powell entered the training system in 1942 before coming to England to join the 8th Air Force.

"I went to Santa Ana, California for boot camp, then to Oxnard, California for primary flight training flying PT-13s; then to Gardner Field at Bakersfield for basic flight training flying BT-13 Vultee 'Vibrators' (*Vultee Valiant*); then to Luke Field, Arizona flying AT-6 Harvards. After getting my wings and commission as a 2nd lieutenant at Luke Field, I was sent to Dale Mabry Field, in Tallahassee, Florida and then to a satellite base at Cross City, Florida to transition onto P-47 Thunderbolts."

Norm Rosholt followed the same basic process, but as was so typical in many air forces, found himself being sent off to fly operational types that he would not have preferred, as the need demanded.

TRAINING DAYS

"I did my flying training in the single-engine open cockpit PT-17, single-engine closed cockpit PT 13, twin engine and then four engine B 17. I found it easy to learn to fly, I'm well co-ordinated. We had no choice about whether we would fly fighters or bombers; everyone on our course went into four-engine bombers."

Chapter Three

DEFENCE –
THE FIGHTERS

The tardy dawn has burst in sullen fire,
Grey mists along the level acres lift,
The pilot looks upon his heart's desire,
A clean sky with the westering cloud adrift.
There in the height of his 'plane
Will mount, and climb again,
And there his spirit, breathing power, will rise
Swift as a swallow's, free, in English skies.

So clear the air; he drinks it as he smiles.
This is his element, his realm of dreams,
In measureless immensity of miles,
Swirling beneath a vault of stellar beams.
For this he grew and planned,
To claim with eye and hand
Unhindered passage where no feet may tread,
Where men, like migrant birds, use wings instead.

His helmet fixed, he gives the word and then,
Waving his squadron as their engines start,
He soars and sings above the world of men,
The beat of battle racing in his heart.
In mortal combat there,
Far in the upper air,
He fights for freedom, one of freedom's sons,
Lone in his airy sphere of blue and bronze.

What destiny is his he does not know;
He does not ask, for asking names a fate;
He goes where duty summons him to go,
He'd sweep undaunted up to heaven's gate.
He holds one purpose well,
In flying to excel,
To roll and loop and bank and dive and spin,
To meet the foe in battle, and to win.

This is the Happy Warrior, this is he.

DEFENCE – THE FIGHTERS

On his gay courage all we love depends;
His is the valiant heart that keeps us free;
By him a commonwealth its life defends.
We praise his hands and eyes,
Knight of our war-torn skies,
True son of Britain, fearless in his faith,
Ready to serve her, even unto death.

William Kean Seymour

The fighter forces of what were to become the allies went through a very rapid build-up in strength as the war became increasingly inevitable. Pete Brothers was serving on 32 Squadron at Biggin Hill, which was still equipped with Gauntlets less than twelve months before the outbreak of hostilities.

"In October 1938, 32 Squadron re-equipped with Hurricanes, and that was great fun; a very nice aeroplane. Because we had them so far in advance of the declaration of war, we really got to know them, and that was a great survival fact. The fact you knew what it could do and what it couldn't do, and that was very necessary knowledge.

"They still had the fixed-pitch two-blade prop to start with. Then we got some de Havilland variable-pitch metal things which were terrible. They hadn't got a great pitch range, they chucked oil all over the windscreen, and then we got Rotol wooden-bladed jobs, and they had a greater pitch range, and were dead dry, and were splendid. And had the advantage that if somebody nosed up in soft ground you didn't have to change the engine because the propeller suddenly stopping in the mud usually stripped the reduction gear on the engine. The wood just broke up, you did a check of the reduction gear, and put a new propeller on."

James Coward meanwhile, was serving with 19 Squadron at Duxford, also flying Gauntlets, when the RAF's first Spitfires arrived.

"The Spitfires arrived in 1938, and that was a wonderful change. It really was a great aeroplane, really fun to fly. I was the first chap to spin a Spitfire. I was trained in one for about three hours, and I went up one day and thought let's see how many vertical rolls I can do. I got up to very high speed and pulled up and started rolling and I fell out at the top into a spin. Spitfires hadn't been spun at that time, and they had a little knob in the cockpit just above the throttle, and you were told if you get into a spin, pull that knob and a parachute would shoot out, and that was supposed to pull you out of the spin. I didn't think of that, I just did the normal spin recovery and it came out perfectly. I went up and tried to spin it the other way and that worked just as well, so I tried an inverted spin and that too worked just as well. They took them all out after that.

"I think the Spitfire was the best, it had wonderful control, and so easy to handle. I've never flown an aeroplane quite like it, it was just part of you; you felt so much in control. A bit tricky when landing in a gusty wind, and that sort of thing; a Hurricane was easier to land.

"When the war started, nearly all of us were posted to new flights and new squadrons forming. I was supposed to join a flight on 266 Squadron. (*266 Squadron was formed at Sutton Bridge on 30 October 1939.*) I was flight commander on the squadron, as the other flight commander had flown Hurricanes, and I was the only one who had flown Spitfires. To start with we had a little Magister to fly as a way of getting practice in formation flying and that sort of thing. Then we were given Fairey Battles which were modern to us, and then we finally got our first Spitfires. (*266 Squadron received Battles in December '39 and they left in May '40. Spitfires started to arrive in January '40.*)

"There weren't people with fighting experience to take over these squadrons, because you had to have had quite some experience to be promoted to squadron leader. When I became flight commander I went to meet up with the new squadron commander. He said, 'I expect a great deal of help from the two of you. I've only been a flight lieutenant for eight years, and they've promoted me to squadron leader.' We didn't like to say well, we've only been a flight commander for three months, and they've promoted us to flight lieutenant.

"He never flew with us. We got Spitfires and when we went to Dunkirk, it was the first time we'd ever seen him fly with anybody. I knew he did fly the Spitfire before I came along, because I was in charge of night flying, and when we started I said to him, 'I'd really like the pilots to do night flying tonight, would you like to come along?' He did, and I was at the Chance Light, I gave him a green, and he went off, and when he turned into wind he was so far away I could hide his navigation lights with my thumb. He was right on the deck, came motoring in on the deck, hit a lone tree on the side of the airfield and knocked the wing off the Spitfire, flipped the aircraft, and hit the ground about twenty yards from me. I rushed across and I looked down and said, 'Are you all right sir?' Luckily he was."

The allies however, had no opportunity to hone their combat skills, unlike the German and Italian air forces, both of which were involved in the Spanish Civil War. Giacomo Metellini flew Fiat CR.32s during that campaign.

"At the start of 1939 I asked to be sent to Spain, and in March, I was sent to 'Legionaria Aviation', the 102nd Squadron of 10 Group ('*Baleari*'), on CR.32s, to defend the Balearic Islands. We were on two types of missions, surveillance missions and also intercepting incoming enemy 'planes. On a descent you would get an indescribable headache, because of a lack of oxygen. We were flying above 5,000 metres, with no oxygen.

"The principal battles had already been fought around that area, so by the time we arrived it was more as a reinforcement, and we were to continue defending if any enemy fighter pilots were still alive. The enemy aircraft were Russian types, Polikarpov – Rata."

OUTBREAK OF WAR TO THE FALL OF FRANCE

Very quickly after the outbreak of war, the RAF found itself having to change many aspects of the way it operated in transitioning from a peacetime role, as James Coward remembered.

"We thought we were going to war, but we didn't take it terribly seriously until it actually happened. We were under tremendous strain to start with because of the stupidity of Command. The first night of the war, 19 Squadron was airborne three times, and we slept out on our camp beds under the wings of the Spitfires in our full flying gear, for the whole night. We shot off before dawn to a coastal airfield up in Norfolk. We spent the whole day doing convoy patrols up and down the coast; every time you approached them they shot at you, and we came back in the evening to Duxford after dark. We spent the whole week doing that. It was absolutely madness, they were wearing us out and we were achieving absolutely nothing.

"It was amazing we had no accidents. The first night we went off, just two sections of two, and I jolly well nearly shot down a Blenheim. You know what it's like first time – 'one bandit three miles ahead, closing rapidly, two miles' – and I got all ready to let go and suddenly recognised that it was a Blenheim; just in time, as I was just about to press the trigger.

"The same night we went off about an hour later, the whole squadron in formation; at night, no navigation lights, close formation, you could see the exhausts. We went off over the coast, we came back terribly short of fuel and we had to land in two flights, in tight formation landing together just on little glim lamps. For navigation we just had the chart and the red light flashing away, and you were told what distance it was, how far from the airfield, and what bearing. It wasn't very funny, it was so unnecessary to keep the whole squadron on readiness all night and all day like that.

"We were always individually under control when the war started. There was a minimum height that you could go down to – we didn't do any low flying exercises – and you weren't allowed to do dogfighting training anyway, it was too dangerous.

"Each day when you went flying, you did quite a lot of navigation exercises so that you could find your way around all right. Quite a lot of formation flying, and formation attacks on other aircraft. We were very limited in the number of hours we were allowed to do, we were lucky to get twelve hours a month. When the war started you did what you wanted to do. Of course they were very keen to keep the accident rate down, but we didn't have many accidents."

The so-called 'Phoney War', a period of relatively low levels of activity, came to a sudden halt when Germany invaded the Low Countries in the spring of 1940. Bill Coombes was a fitter on a fighter squadron that had already been sent to France.

"It was very soon after the declaration of war that we set sail for France to become part of the British Expeditionary Force. It was more than nine months later that we, along with many others, were obliged to return to England. My date of departure was 17 June 1940."

Pete Brothers had his first encounter with the enemy during this time.

"The first time in combat for me was over France. We used to go to France daily from Biggin Hill. Take off at first light, or preferably half an hour before first light, go to France, and land at some airfield, refuel, which we had to do ourselves, for we had no ground crew. We refuelled from tins, and then we had no contact with anybody, the headquarters was on the move somewhere, retreating fast, communications were bloody awful.

"No food. Well, the chap who was the best man at my wedding spoke fluent French, so he managed to get us some bread from a local, but otherwise you didn't eat. Then we'd put the starting handles in the Hurricanes, I'd get in the cockpit, and chums would wind the starter and I'd leave it ticking over, I'd do the next one and so on, until we'd got 'em all going. Then we'd go looking, to see what was going on.

"There was absolute silence, we couldn't get any instructions. I have to say we could see a lot of refugees clogging up the roads. Our first combat, I thought, 'Oh, those bloody de Havilland propeller oil specks all over the windscreen', but they grew bigger very rapidly, because they were coming in the opposite direction, '109s! And a chap came and swept just over my head. Fascinating sight, I can picture it now; you could see the rivets, the oil streaks from the engine, and mud on the undercarriage, as he went over the top. I thought, 'Christ, where's he gone?' Looked round, he's not up there, he's turning round, and he's coming down. He dived on me, and I had a shot and missed, he went straight past me and I got on his tail. Shot him down. I thought, 'Oh my God', when I saw him go down. 'Oh my, his chums will have seen that, I'm in deep trouble. They're going to beat the hell out of me, where the hell are they?' Searching the sky, by which time it was all empty.

"Then we came back from France. We used to arrive back at Biggin just on dark, half-past ten or so, have a meal, and go to bed. You were woken by the batman at about half past two, so that you were up, washed and shaved, breakfasted, out to the airfield by three o'clock and airborne by quarter past four say. And then land in France.

"Trouble was, being flight commander, I thought I ought to do the right thing, and I'd get a case of beer to go out to the chaps at the squadron, to my flight. They were anxious to know what had gone on, where we were, and so on. So you told them as best you could, which meant another half an hour. But, you had to look after these chaps, they were the salt of the earth."

The date of Pete's victory was 18 May 1940, when 32 Squadron was operating from Moorsele. It is possible that the Me 109E was an aircraft flown by Fw Heinz Pohland of 1.(J)/LG2, who baled out and was taken prisoner, uninjured.

Wing Commander Jack Rose had enlisted in 1938 and during the French campaign was flying Hurricanes with 32 Squadron at Biggin Hill. He went on to have a very distinguished career on a number of Hurricane and Typhoon squadrons, scoring three combat victories, before retiring in 1946.

"We started flying down to Manston for the day and the Germans, they started off on 10 May, and two days after that, we were ordered off to The Hague at the airfield which we were told had been taken by the Germans, and to shoot up any German aircraft that we came across. We flew across there from Manston and Pete Carter saw one chap he thought might have been a German in uniform struggling somewhere and he let off a burst in that direction but that was about all. But a lot of paratroopers were dotted around and after we returned to Manston, we were told that on the BBC news while we were on our way over there, they said the Dutch had re-taken The Hague that day! (*Flying Officer Peter Carter was lost in a flying accident returning to England in bad weather on 18 October 1940.*)

"About 14 May, we were suddenly asked to produce four pilots and aircraft to fly to France. I thought at the time that things were going to be easier, much the same as in the first war, and so I volunteered. We were told that we didn't have any maps of France or anything and we were going to Merville where we would link up with 3 Squadron. A Fairey Battle would come and fly over Manston and we were to be ready to take off and link up with it and it would lead us to Merville. Well the whole flight from Manston to Merville, which should have taken about forty minutes, took two-hours-and-a-quarter. The Battle didn't know where the hell Merville was, and we couldn't help. Eventually we appeared over the top of somewhere which turned out to be Merville, which was very surprising. We landed there, but we had very little fuel left.

"We had no armour plate but all the chaps there did have. Our radios didn't have the right frequencies so we couldn't communicate with anybody and then we had to wait for calibration and I don't think

I heard anything from anywhere else the whole time I was there. Jones and I went off on patrol and we saw something going on, people whirling around and it was always the way; lots of stuff happening and then after a very short time, we'd look around and there was nothing there. There were '109s milling around and one of them went suddenly vertical, straight up, and I thought somebody else had hit this chap and he'd gone up vertically to get out of the way. Anyway, I followed up behind this chap and then I couldn't believe it was so easy! I shot this chap, and he baled out and I was still shooting. (*This was possibly a Bf 109E-3 of Stab I./JG52 flown by Hauptmann S von Eschwege [gruppenkommander], between Namur and Dinant.*) I got a '110 a few days later, that was very quick. A sudden appearance and – just there – he popped up ahead of me.

"Another time, I shot at this thing and finished up rather too close to it. The port side exploded and I was covered in oil. I pulled away and everybody passed on so I looked all around and couldn't see anything, so very stupidly, I pulled back, dropped the speed right down, pulled the hood back and I couldn't get round to wipe the windscreen. I managed to get a hanky out of my trouser pocket and I couldn't get it round there, so I undid my Sutton harness, waffling along at about 150, leaning right out of the aircraft, wiping the windscreen with my handkerchief! All the stuff I didn't want to see was whistling past me and I could feel the shudder as I was being hit. So I instinctively whipped it down and disappeared from sight.

"I ended up in a spin going straight down and I could see all the oil, coolant, fuel and everything spewing out. I switched off everything and just carried on and I was about 12-14,000 feet, a reasonable height so I had a bit to play with, and I luckily saw when I got down to about 5-6,000 feet, an aerodrome which was Lille/Ronchin, just south of Lille. I pumped the wheels down and they came down and locked, and then at the last minute pumped my flaps, and landed. I was very pleased with myself, landing in those circumstances with no further damage to the aircraft. The first chap I saw was a flight sergeant as I was walking towards these parked Lysanders; it was 4 Squadron and everyone was wearing tin hats. None of the shots fired had gone straight down the middle because they would have gone through me as I had no armour plate on my aircraft. But both wing tanks had bullets in, the starboard flap was gone, there was a cannon shell through the radiator that was underneath, and all sorts of damage, and I started to rattle this off to the flight sergeant and he very quickly told me that there wouldn't be any repairs to mine; it would be blown up with all the other unserviceable aircraft.

"We were told that arrangements had been made for a French aircraft to pick us up and fly us back to England. While we were waiting, someone began frying some bacon on a small field cooker to make a few sandwiches. Before the bacon was cooked, a French civilian aircraft landed and taxied across to us. It was a DC-2 whose pilot jumped out, leaving his engines running, and told us that we had just thirty seconds to climb on board before he taxied out for take-off. The bacon was still cooking when we left, and none of the small rear party had the opportunity to collect any of their clothes or other possessions. *(Air France had leased a single DC-2 from the government for trials in 1939.)*

"The pilot flew very low until we reached the coast and were over the Channel. While still over France we had close-up views of miles of roads packed with French civilians fleeing to the west, most on foot, some pushing loaded handcarts, a few in cars and other vehicles forced by the mass of people to move at a walking pace. Among them were the owner of a restaurant, the Seraphin, with his wife and five daughters, where we had eaten a number of evening meals during our short time at Merville. Just before their departure, the restaurant's patron had given one of the 3 Squadron pilots a key to his establishment with the request that we drink as much of his cellar as we could manage before the Germans arrived. Sadly, there was no chance for us to take advantage of this opportunity of a lifetime."

Jack had probably been brought down by Oberleutnant Karl-Gottfried Nordmann of I./JG77.

Flying Officer Reg Viney was one of the transport pilots flying hazardous missions into France to keep the British Expeditionary Force flying units supplied.

"I was told to report to Doncaster (*271 Squadron*). Here was assembled Bombays, (ex Middle East), Ensigns, HP42s, (ex Imperial Airways) and one Ford Trimotor. The nucleus here was two Bombay units from the Middle East. We flew the length and breadth of the UK, carrying various bits and pieces, mostly for fighter squadrons. Completely unarmed and without parachutes we backed up many a fighter squadron when on the move, carrying their essential ground equipment. In the middle of '40, Eastchurch received a pasting. Two of us spent all day ferrying from here to Hornchurch in an attempt to evacuate this airfield. I seem to remember a few unexploded bombs around at the time, which rather hastened our efforts.

"I was sent down to the Med, on a bit of a hush-hush do, no maps, no radio, and no parachutes. I hung about until our friends capitulated, and couldn't make our contact, so decided to head for home. There were quite a few stranded RAF ground bods hanging about, so I told them to give us a shout up front when no more could climb aboard and we'd try and take off. We made it OK and after an anxious flight, (you should have seen those Peggy cylinder head temps), including refuelling problems at Bordeaux, hit the English Channel. Here we were challenged by various 'planes and warships. I hadn't got a clue what the colour of the day was, so fired off a few hoping for the best, and came through without being shot at. Into the first 'drome available to a doubtful reception, you might even call it hostile, until producing proof of identity. At long last we were able to make the sergeants' mess and grab a pint. I put my hand in my pocket to pay, but had French money only. Fortunately, the sergeant who had arrested me in the first place was in attendance and did the honours.

"We got back to Doncaster the next day, and were cussed by the CO as we had been reported missing, so we had to undo a hell of a lot of paperwork. We also got cussed by the flight sergeant fitter for modifying/repairing a broken tail-wheel without AMOs (*aircraft maintenance orders*). Fortunately, we had the old bits with us so we were able to fit them, make the aircraft serviceable, and peace was with us. I nearly gave the 'old man' a heart attack when applying for a few days leave to see my wife and daughter in Gloucestershire. But in the end I suppose he decided it was worth it to get me out of the way!"

As the ground situation became hopeless, Operation Dynamo – the evacuation from Dunkirk – was set in motion on 26 May. France finally capitulated on 17 June and all RAF operations in France ceased the next day. Squadron Leader Michael Wainwright was flying Spitfires with 64 Squadron from Kenley in Surrey during the evacuation.

"On our first trip over Dunkirk (*29 May*), we lost seven aircraft out of 12. We were in lovely formation; four lots of three sections stepped down, and our leader made a land-fall by Cap Griz Nez in the afternoon with the sun over on the right, turned to go towards Dunkirk, and we were bounced by Me 110s...we had seven aircraft shot down. I don't know whether it was accidental or coincidental, but Keith Park came to see us after we'd got back and asked me about the incident, I said, 'Well Sir, we were all in this formation, we were busy trying to keep in formation instead of doing what we ought to have been doing. We can't do that any-more. What we must do is go up in pairs, and one would be looking out to see what's coming, while the other's looking for somebody to bash.'

"Over Dunkirk I realised there was somebody after me so I went into a defensive right hand turn and slowed right down so I could tighten up my turn, and this '109 was plocking away, bullets passing me and suddenly, I saw this bugger spun into the sea. He must have been in a hell of a panic because we weren't all that high. We were about 10,000 feet...he must have got himself in a bit of a tight spin and couldn't get out of it.

"If we were on early morning things when the Germans were still sleeping in bed, we would go and shoot the aerodrome up where they were, when they started to use aerodromes in northern France. What we didn't really appreciate at the time, was that they had never come up against any serious opposition, so their morale was very good at the time and they just thought it was going to be over quick hence the Blitzkrieg term, so they were a bit more surprised."

James Coward flew Spitfires over the evacuation beaches with 266 Squadron.

"When we went to Dunkirk, we were told one night we had to take-off at dawn the next morning. We flew down to Martlesham Heath and refuelled, off we went, no briefing of any kind, we didn't know where the hell we were going or what it was all about. We flew up over the North Sea to Dunkirk, flew straight up and down the coast, straight up into the sun and back again, at 25,000 feet. As we turned to go up the second time, I suddenly saw a flash of light, and I saw a little stick of Messerschmitts diving down. Obviously they hadn't seen us, so I looked over the side, and there was a Spitfire squadron going the other way in tight formation in the other direction.

"I thought, they're about to be bounced, so I rolled over and went down after them, they saw me coming and they broke inland. I got a bead on one and I opened fire, but I was out of range. The Messerschmitt was a bit faster than the Spitfire in a dive, and he had a head start anyway, so I couldn't get any nearer than that. When I climbed back, he'd gone. I landed back at Manston to refuel, and flew up to Wittering. When I landed the CO was there, absolutely red with rage; he turned on me and he tore me off a strip in front of the whole squadron. How dare I desert him in battle! On and on and on; and about a fortnight later I was told to go to the group for an interview with the AOC Leigh-Mallory. Leigh-Mallory said: 'I've got a report from your squadron commander; you're quite unsuitable to be a flight commander, and he's sending you back to your old squadron.' So that's why I was back in 19 Squadron when things started."

FREE EUROPEAN AIR FORCES

Large numbers of military personnel escaped from Europe to England and many were quickly organised into training schemes to absorb them into the RAF. As an example, a Czechoslovak depot was established at Cosford, later moving to Wilmslow and St. Athan, tasked with training pilots for OTU and teaching them English. As France and the Low Countries fell, many aircrews fled to England in their own aircraft. Ronald Liversuch and Eric How were AC2 mechanics at St. Athan who witnessed the arrival of some of these escapees.

"A runner came out of the hangar office with a message that we were to expect visitors in aircraft with French markings that morning. There was a siren of the station ambulance, followed by the fire trucks as they drew up near the duty flight Hurricanes. The sound of approaching aircraft drew nearer, until circling overhead, they got a green from control, went into a landing pattern and taxied in. We watched amazed at the strange aircraft from Europe, giant string-bags that we had never heard of. (*The types included Caudron C445 Goeland, Caudron C620*

Simoun, Dewoitine D520, Farman 222 and Potez 63-11.) From these machines came as motley a mixture of uniforms as we had ever seen; they all looked like admirals, or characters from a grand opera, with long flowing capes, pillbox hats and much gold braid. I heard a sergeant say: 'Must be bloody Romanians or something!'

"One morning there was a long line of airmen on the parade square. I was told that they had escaped from French airfields. They had all got away just before the German army arrived. They had brought their best uniforms, their flying skills, a determination to fight on, and little else."

Flight Lieutenant Gabriel Seydel was just one of many Belgian air force personnel who made it to England to continue the fight.

"I joined the Belgian air force at the outbreak of war and was accepted for aircrew training. I completed twenty-five hours dual and thirty hours solo before my unit was forced to withdraw through France and eventually we ended up in Morocco. About twenty-eight Belgian air force officers and men arrived at Cardiff by sea on 5 August 1940. We were temporarily housed in a requisitioned house in Tenby, before the aircrew went on to St. Athan, arriving on 14 August; there was a Dutch party at St. Athan at the same time, and we were held there pending organisation of our flying training. We were not given anything to do while we waited and generally kept a low profile.

"On 2 November 1940 we started our flying training at Odiham on Magisters (*Franco-Belgian Air Training School*), and on the 20th we went to Uxbridge to sign an oath of allegiance to the king. After Odiham I went to 5 SFTS at Ternhill in April 1941 and then to 58 OTU at Grangemouth to learn to fly the Spitfire. I finally reached a squadron in November 1941 when I was posted to 350 Squadron at Valley, which was one of the newly formed Belgian squadrons. I was moved to 349 Squadron in July '43, and had periods in both squadrons at various times until the end of the war."

THE BATTLE OF BRITAIN

His place was laid,
The messroom clock struck eight,
The sun shone through the window
On his chair.
No-one commented on his fate,
Save for a headshake here and there;
Only old George, who'd seen him die
Spinning against the autumn sky,
Leaned forward and turned down his plate.

DEFENCE – THE FIGHTERS

And, as he did, the sunlight fled,
As though the sky he'd loved so
Mourned her dead.

Hannah M Hunt, 1940 [5]

As the Luftwaffe commenced bombing operations against RAF airfields in preparation for the planned invasion, code-named Operation Sea Lion, so the squadrons so recently returned from France found themselves in desperate circumstances. Geoffrey Wellum flew throughout what Churchill dubbed the Battle of Britain, and described what it felt like to be in the thick of it.

"The transports taking those on dawn readiness round to dispersal, the tranquillity and peace of the pre-dawn and the beginning of a new day. The ground crews quietly readying their charges for the testing hours to come. The little things: dew on your flying boots as you carry your parachute across the grass to your waiting Spitfire, looking at the sky thinking at the time it's going to be a lovely day again. Resignation. Total resignation. 'Oh God, another dawn.' More often than not one offered up a little prayer: 'It's going to be a very busy day...if I ever forget you, please don't you forget me. Just give me this day, please give me this day.' An early scramble and at 20,000 feet you would see the sunrise, and for those of us who returned to an earth still slumbering in the pre-dawn twilight, you would see the sunrise again all the time suppressing thoughts of those missing and unaccounted for...A time literally packed with life or death and the day had just begun.

"One recalls quite clearly sights and feelings of unbelievable horror. Aircraft on fire, parachutes, sometimes as many as half a dozen at a time floating down, parachutes that did not open, and Roman candled... streaming with the shroud lines twisted and therefore not opening...followed by the plunge of its unfortunate pilot to the earth 20,000 feet below. A German aircrew man who had baled out of a Heinkel 111 had opened his parachute too early and he got caught up round the tail unit of his aeroplane and there he was, banging around like a rag doll plummeting down waiting until the ground got in the way. I remember thinking: 'Great God. Is this really 20th century civilisation? What are you up to allowing this sort of thing to happen?' And all this with the twisting and whirling of aeroplanes, tracers and smoke trails in the vast panorama of blue sky and the contrasting green fields of England below. Total war. No quarter asked or given."

Pete Brothers outlined the way in which typical encounters developed.

"During '40 you were very often scrambled so late you couldn't get the height you wanted. People used to complain like hell, saying, 'God, the bloody controllers...' The poor old controller had to make sure the raid was not a spoof. It was one thing to launch us off because a raid was coming across the Channel, and then as soon as we were well and truly airborne, the raid would turn round and go home, and we would land. Then the real raid would arrive whilst we were refuelling. So, he was inevitably cautious, which gave us problems.

"The reason I got mixed up with fighters so often; A Flight of course led the squadron, B Flight followed. A Flight went in for attack, we followed, by which time the '109s were coming down. So we got mixed up with the '109s to try and divert them from A Flight, it was hard. That really is the way it worked out.

"But of course a head-on attack was a good one, they didn't like head-on, particularly the Heinkel chaps, sitting in their great conservatories. The same with the fighter chaps actually, and I suppose I survived because I thought the instinct head-on when you're about to collide, is to pull up. Don't do that, go underneath. By going underneath, you also build up more speed, so you can turn round and do another attack.

"It was on 18 August 1940 when I shot down Wilhelm Robb in his Dornier 17. I think the Wilhelm lot was the first, because he was leading the formation, and I thought, 'You've got to take the leader out'. It was a bit stupid, because I was trapped in the crossfire. But I got his port engine nicely burning.

"On another occasion, after one of these crazy, mixed-up things where nobody hits you, and you don't hit anything, and suddenly the skies empty, everybody's vanished, I saw a lovely sight, five '109s in vic, steaming way above me, heading for home. I thought: 'What a super thing, I should creep up behind these buggers and pick 'em off.' So full power, chase after them, draw near, and as I was getting nearer, the right hand chap started pulling away, and I thought: 'Oh yes, you're looking over your shoulder; you've seen me coming.'

"Right, I won't be ambitious, you'll do, just you; I won't worry about the rest. I got into position, and I was about to open fire, and he banged the throttle open. There was a cloud of steam because they had a water-injection on the '109, and he shot up, and I pulled up, and thought, 'I'm going to lose out on this, he's going to pull out of range'. I was just about to open fire when all hell broke loose! God, a chap appearing in my mirror, tracer flashing past. Of course the first of the other four '109s went whizzing past, followed by the next, followed by the next, all having a go. I was terrified. More than terrified, I was furious! 'What the hell are you doing, you're an experienced fighter pilot, flight commander? What are you doing taking your eyes off the main threat to go looking after some solo chap? You've gone mad, it's the sort of thing you tell all your chaps not to do.' I was staggered at my own fortune that they hadn't hit me. There were holes in the Rotol propeller – the wings were riddled. I didn't have a wingman with me.

I was just on my own, that was it, everybody had vanished. Stupid things people do.

"I suppose it was my closest call, because usually you were more alert. One other; I had a new boy we were training up, so of course he was flying number two to me, in line astern. I'm sure everyone has had occasions when you feel somebody's looking at you. I had this, and I looked in the mirror, and there was the biggest, fattest '109 I'd ever seen in my life; he filled my mirror. As I saw him, his whole front end lit up into a blaze of red. I pulled and pushed everything in sight, got out of his way by shooting upwards, and I was going round in a circle, looking to see where he'd gone. My number two was miles behind. I thought, 'Christ, you never told me, you were supposed to tell me.' There he was, cutting the corner off beautifully, and I thought, 'Well now you're going to catch up quickly.' The next minute, his wings lit up, my number two was shooting at me! I suggested he desisted; that it wasn't a good idea.

"When we got back on the ground I thought, 'Well, I don't want to destroy him, but it's about time he learned a lesson.' So I said, 'You're grounded operationally for a week, and you're going to do a course in intensive gunnery. Of course you should have shot me straight out of the sky, and you were nowhere near.'"

Pete Brothers was to meet Wilhelm Robb after the war. Michael Wainwright also had a post-war meeting with one of his wartime victims.

"We were on a sweep patrol, and suddenly diverted because of some '109s pissing around. Just near the Isle of Wight we encountered a whole lot of them all milling around. My section, between the three of us, we managed to account for a '109. If I got the chance to shoot at something I did, but my main aim was to keep my section intact, not to get shot because we couldn't afford to lose pilots, so we were always being asked whether you were being a bit timid instead of up guards and at 'em, but we were more concerned with not being killed. We couldn't afford to be killed; we didn't have enough pilots."

Air Commodore John Ellacombe flew Hurricanes with 151 Squadron during the fall of France and the Battle of Britain. He later flew both Hurricanes and Defiants on night-fighter operations, followed by Mosquito fighter-bombers during the Normandy invasion, scored three combat victories, and served on until 1973. He was shot down twice in two days during the Battle of Britain.

"I arrived at my squadron and went to see Victor Beamish and he said, 'I don't have any information about you coming, but I'm delighted to see you. I can very quickly get you converted, we need all the pilots we can get.' On about my third sortie, we were given instructions to attack a formation and we couldn't see them as we closed. Then suddenly, I saw these tiny little flies and then big bees, and he kept on just saying 'Roger' and 'Roger'. When we landed, John Willy Blair said 'Did you see those?' and I said 'Yes. Why did we break off?' He said: 'Because you and I are the only two – we both have exceptional eyesight.' Pete Gordon, the CO heard this and said: 'You will fly as my number two from now on if you've got eyesight like that.' And I did. I flew again till sadly, he was hit by return fire, burst into flames and he baled out. He landed in a river in Essex, and as he walked out, I thought he was taking his gloves off, but as he was doing that all the skin was coming off his hands. From then on, we all flew with our big leather gauntlets which came right up and fortunately, when I was shot down, my hands were not burnt so I didn't get what was known as 'the Hurricane hand'. You had a lot of chaps with a clutching hand when it was recovered.

"We were scrambled and we went through cloud, and as we came through cloud at about 18,000 feet, we were bounced by '109s and everybody broke. When you break, you just pull and heave and when you come to again and look around, nobody is in sight. I was about ten miles from North Weald and then I suddenly heard, 'This is Bengal calling'. That was our call sign from North Weald and they said, 'We have a large formation heading for our base' and I was not very pleased because we'd already been bombed. Then I suddenly saw in the distance these tiny little things coming so I flew towards them and I did a head-on attack from about 2,000 feet; I opened fire underneath the Heinkel, blew all his perspex off and both engines, and as I went underneath, my engine stopped. The man put one bullet through my spinner; the Heinkel had a large calibre gun in the nose. I nearly baled out but then decided that I shouldn't chance it; we had instructions not to bale out; force-land if you can because the German fighters will shoot you in your parachute. So I saw this huge field and I circled round and landed, and when I got out of the aeroplane, a man rushed at me with a pitchfork: 'I'm gonna kill you, you bloody German!' I was running round the Hurricane shouting out 'I'm British!'

"I did about three circuits, when thank heavens the army arrived and they just grabbed this lad and an army sergeant from the nearby gun battery said, 'There's the Heinkel you hit; he's circling round and he's going to crash on the other side of this big field', and he went across, had a look, and came back and said, 'Don't go and have a look. They're all either dead or dying so your head-on attack must have been very efficient.' I got back to North Weald having had to wait for some transport; it was while they were getting the harvest in and they had some barrels of cider there and I had about three pints, so when I got back to North Weald, I went into the bar and there was the station commander and he said, 'John, get another Hurricane, you'll fly as my number two, there's another raid coming in,' and I said to Victor Beamish, 'Sir, I'm half pissed, I've had some cider'. 'How could you?' So I told him the story and he said, 'Oh well, I'm not going on my own', which I reckoned saved his life, and probably mine as well. But it was a pretty hectic day!

"When I was shot down the second time, it was a most extraordinary experience because we attacked some aircraft, and I could see return fire coming. We were up at about 16,000 feet and as I burst into flames, I got out quickly; we had practised this; you pulled the hood back, you undid your belt, and went. I came out, looked up and I was watching to see all the aircraft which were were tiny and then I felt my face getting uncomfortable and I took my helmet off and saw that it was badly burnt, so I foolishly threw it away, and I couldn't reach it again (I thought it would be a nice souvenir to keep) and I looked down and saw I hardly had any trousers on. They had been burned off and my legs were burnt. As I was coming down, I suddenly saw a chap pointing a rifle at me. The old LDV (Local Defence Volunteers) who became the Home Guard and I was screaming at this bloke, 'Don't shoot! I'm British!' But he fired two shots and I reckon I heard the second one pass me. I dropped into the ploughed field and was dragged along until I undid my parachute straps and he was very apologetic, and took me to a farmhouse, where the lady said: 'Oh your legs! I'll go and get my bottle of vinegar and pour it on your burns.' I said, 'Please! I don't want that – just get me an old sheet.' So I had this sheet put on my legs and the farmer was very kind and he got a pint of water 'cause I was very thirsty and he said, 'I'll put a little bit of brandy in that'. Foolishly, I drank it. Now I realise when you've been shot, you shouldn't drink.

"The door burst open and two policemen came in and the first one took a swipe at me and hit me on the shoulder and the Home Guard, the LDV bloke said, 'Look, he's got his RAF wings up' and they were very apologetic and took me to Southend General Hospital, where a very nice nurse took one look at my face and said, 'We must take you in and treat you' and then the doctor came, smelt my breath and said, 'Are you young buggers always flying pissed?!'"

Corporal Norman Didwell was serving as flight rigger with 99 (Wellington) Squadron at Rowley Mile, Newmarket, when an unexpected visitor arrived.

"We were duty crew one Wednesday morning during the Battle of Britain, and they said report to the pilot flight op tent, 'cause we had no watch office in those days at Newmarket. It was a caravan, with a duty pilot, junior sergeant pilot, wireless operator and an electrician. We nipped down to where this Hurricane came in and this fellow was wearing blokes' overalls, with his helmet on and that, and he got out of the cockpit very awkwardly. So we looked at one another and thought 'he must have been wounded', but couldn't see any bullet holes in the aircraft. What the hell's wrong with him? Anyway, Bob thought he must be a flight sergeant. 'Have you been wounded

Chiefy?' 'I'm not a Chiefy,' he said: 'I'm a bloody squadron leader!' He stomped off, 'Where's your operations room, have you got one here?' We said, 'Well you've got to go through that little gate there, and you come to the big building, and that is the operations room which is the old jockey's weighing room.' 'Um, bloody long way to walk!' Well, the next morning, Bob went up to get the papers, the *Daily Mirror, Daily Sketch*, and I think it was in the *Daily Mail*, and they detailed people who'd won the DFC, who had gone missing in action, and all the rest of it, well, there was one photograph: 'Legless pilot awarded the DFC.' Bader! He was commanding 242 Squadron at Coltishall."

James Coward lost a leg during the Battle, an injury that resulted in his being attached to Winston Churchill's staff while he recuperated. He subsequently returned to flying.

"On the morning I was shot down, we took off and flew to the east of Duxford, and at 20,000 feet we were still climbing, and we saw a formation coming towards us of 15 Dornier bombers and about, they said, eighty fighters. We were led by a flight commander – our CO had been killed about three days before – and he did one attack, each section of three went into line astern and each section went across to the bombers. *(James's memory is playing tricks with him slightly here. The CO he refers to was Flt Lt Philip Pinkham AFC, who was shot down and killed over the Thames estuary in Spitfire P9422 during combat with Bf 109s, on 5 September, a few days after James's event described here.)*

"It was absolutely marvellous, suddenly they all went, each went after three bombers, and gave the fighters no chance of getting at us, and I was taking on the one on the far side. I didn't know it at the time, but my number two pulled out, he saw a Messerschmitt coming down on his tail and he pulled out. Anyway I had no-one, number three was on the other side. When we opened fire, none of my guns were working. We were the first squadron to have cannons fitted, we had four cannons. So when I pressed the trigger, I had a jolly good sight of the thing and I expected to see the whole thing explode in front of me, but nothing happened at all, none of my guns worked; we never discovered why, whether they froze up or not.

"I could try the single shot, but by that time I was getting jolly close so I decided it was time to break away. I had a hard kick on the shin; I looked down and thought something heavy must have fallen from one of the dashboards or something. I looked down and suddenly saw my bare foot sitting on the rudder bar, the shoe and sock had just disappeared; my foot was just hanging on by some ligaments and such. I didn't have time to think about it because I was still going down and the elevator controls had gone so I couldn't pull it out, and I baled out. *(The*

74

Spitfire Mk I James abandoned was X4231, and the date was 31 August 1940.)

"I was sucked out of the cockpit – the hood was open – and my parachute became caught on the back of the cockpit. I was thrown back along the side, and my arms were blown back and my goggles were blown off, and my foot was thrashing around my knee. I started to fall head over heels, and it was so painful with my foot I decided to give up this idea of a delayed drop and I opened my parachute. I started swinging in a huge figure of eight and I had a wonderful view of Cambridge, I could see a hundred miles in all directions, and there wasn't a sound or a sight of an aeroplane anywhere. I suppose I was about 1,000 feet lower or something, but then they'd all gone.

"I suddenly looked down, and I saw my blood pumping slowly below me, quite a long way down, it looked brilliantly red up there in the sky. I had to do something quickly, I had my helmet on still with the radio cord hanging down, so I pulled the radio cord up and started tightening up to stop the bleeding. My foot was then up by my bottom, which stopped it twisting about, and was much more comfortable.

"I sailed across Duxford at about 12,000 feet. I saw one or two pilots at refuel, and one or two of them circled around me on the way back, they gave me a wave, I waved to them. When I got almost to the airfield I started to drift backwards again. I spent some time turning myself round so I was facing the way I was drifting, and I landed with a great thump in a stubble field. There was a young lad about sixteen, who was helping to stook corn. I was putting the pressure on my leg and keeping it off the dirt, and I suddenly saw this chap dashing over with a pitchfork thinking I was a German. He made me absolutely livid; I gave a great bellow: 'Piss off and get me an ambulance!'

"The first car he stopped was an army medical officer from the anti-aircraft guns, and he was on his way to the mess for breakfast, so I got very quick attention. I wasn't in any pain, it was all numb; the petrol had taken all the skin off, but the pain wasn't worth worrying about. After about twenty minutes the station ambulance with the medical officer arrived and I was carted off to Cambridge.

"When I came out from the anaesthetic, lying in the casualty ward there, my wife was sitting beside me. There was a wonderful show of flowers on the bedside table, which I assumed she'd brought. Fifty years later, we stayed for a week with a sister of mine, who lives near Cambridge. Her husband asked me if I'd speak at a dinner in Cambridge about my experiences during the Battle, and after the dinner, a little white-haired woman came up to me and said: 'Did you ever get my flowers?' It turned out, on the morning I was shot down, she was waiting outside the church in a little village called Foxton, about ten miles out of Cambridge, waiting for her bridegroom to turn up for her wedding. He was in the army, and all the trains were delayed because of the air raids. So she was there looking forlornly towards the railway station, wondering if he was ever going to turn up, whether the vicar was still waiting to marry them (which he did), when my Spitfire crashed on the other side of the road and made a great hole in the field.

"She saw my parachute about 20,000 feet in the air, a little white dot in the sky. She watched it going very, very slowly across the sky until I disappeared behind some tall trees. Then she saw people looking up again, and I was getting quite low, she could see me quite clearly, and because I was holding my knee up under my shoulder, it looked as though I only had one leg left. So after the wedding, she sent her wedding bouquet to the hospital for me; that was where these wonderful flowers had come from."

Jack Rose also found himself on the wrong end of a combat encounter.

"I was flying number two to Michael Crossley, flight lieutenant *(left the air force in 1946 as wing commander DFC OBE)*, and the aircraft were Dornier 215s on the way back to France and I was just pressing the button to shoot one. Earlier we had seen '109s but they were way up and away, we just thought they looked like gnats. The trouble was, we didn't have quite enough height and instead of being able to come down on something and clearing off, to attack something while you're still climbing is obviously not the best place to do it. I suppose it allowed enough time for this chap to come and knock me down. We were above cloud; it was about 6-8,000 feet, so I was quite surprised when I jumped out, pleased that the parachute worked, happy about that but not so happy when I came through the clouds and I wasn't over the vicar's garden in Kent! I was over the Channel.

"I came down in the Channel, and there was a bit of a sea running, and I hung on to my parachute. I had the initial, old-fashioned Mae West with Kapok, stuffed, to blow it up a bit and that was it. There was a whistle I think. It so happened that they'd come around that morning while we were waiting in readiness, with little packs of fluorescein and they dished out one for each chap and the others were going to wait and get their batman, or their girlfriend or whoever to sew them on their Mae West later on. I don't know why, I decided to try it on my parachute. I got a tacking needle and just tacked it onto my Mae West. So there was this long trail of fluorescein in the water. I found I could only swim on my back (with the buoyancy all on the front) and I could see the balloons over Dover, they were there by my feet but the next minute they weren't there, because the tide was taking you round. Fortunately one of our chaps spotted this slick in the late afternoon and got a boat out from Dover."

Pete Brothers summed up just how difficult and confusing a time much of the Battle was.

"I changed squadrons to 257 as 92 were taking a bit of a beating. It was the new boys we lost like crazy, and we were moved up to Acklington for a rest on 28 August. I thought 'I could do with a rest, thank you very much'. A few days went by and I was posted to 257 Squadron Martlesham Heath. 'Oh, what's with this?'

"Both the flight commanders had been killed on the same sortie; and the squadron was in dire need of morale. I got a lift in a Blenheim down to Martlesham Heath, walked in, to see all these glum looking chaps. Two experienced flight commanders shot down, what bloody chance have I got of some support? You could see it sinking away. Bob Tuck arrived, and he took over A Flight, I took over B Flight, and we decided, 'Right, get stuck into this'. The CO, he was rather an old fellow. First flight we did, he led, and we were told to patrol the Maidstone line at 18,000 feet, which we did. Then we saw this great phalanx approaching. 'There they are!' CO said, 'We've been told to patrol the Maidstone line. That we will do until we do otherwise.'

"So we pissed off and left him, Bob and I. I discussed it with Bob when we landed, and I said 'I don't know whether we were right on this. The controller could have been holding us for a second raid or something.' This happened three more times in succession. So Bob and I rang up 11 Group, and insisted on speaking to the AOC, nobody else. We got onto him, we told him the problem. The next day Bob was promoted to squadron leader, CO of the squadron, he was six months senior to me, and the CO vanished. Then we got on very well, Bob and I, and we took the chaps out boozing like crazy, and told them how to behave. And they did well, bless 'em."

James Coward described some of the key personalities he encountered during this period, including Air Marshal 'Stuffy' Dowding, who was AOC-in-C Fighter Command throughout the Battle.

"Douglas Bader was not a popular fellow, because he was very abrupt. He was a very senior chap, although he was only a squadron leader, his contemporaries were AOCs and people like that; heads of the air force. So he thought nothing of picking up the phone and asking for somebody in the Air Ministry. He was a very good pilot, a very good leader; he had plenty of guts. When he went into attack he went straight in. He had a Canadian squadron to start with, *(242 [Hurricane] Squadron Coltishall, an RAF squadron comprised almost entirely of Canadian pilots)* and they were terribly impressed with him.

"Dowding was a very doddery old man when I met him. After my CO had crashed his Spitfire he was in hospital, so I was acting CO, and he came down to look at the squadron, and said: 'Have you got any problems?' I said, 'Yes sir, we've got no gun-sights. We can't be operational until we get gun-sights.' He replied: 'What the bloody hell do you think I can do about it, produce some out of my hat?' I thought, 'you silly old man, if you didn't want to know, why did you ask?' But I think it was getting a bit too much for him then. He was an excellent staff officer, an excellent planner and organiser, but he wasn't a leader of men.

"Leigh-Mallory *(Air Vice-Marshal Sir Trafford Leigh-Mallory, AOC 12 Group Fighter Command during the Battle of Britain)* was a pompous old bastard. I knew him quite well. He never flew a Spitfire, or any other aircraft on his own; I don't think he'd flown an aeroplane since the First World War much."

> You see them in the 'local' anywhere
> In town or country near a fighter station
> In flying boots and scarves – their ruffled hair
> Like schoolboys out for a jolly celebration.
> Eight in a car for four had raced along
> And miracles were wrought to bring them here.
> To pass an hour with banter, darts and song
> And drink a pint or two of English beer,
> And talk of 'binds' and 'dims' with lots of natter
> Of 'ropey jobs' and 'wizard types' and 'gen'
> Amid much laughter glasses chink and clatter.
> Deep underneath was hid the real men,
> Who saw their comrades fall out of the skies,
> And knew too well the look in dead men's eyes.

W A G Kemp [6]

AFTER THE BATTLE

With Operation Sea Lion abandoned, the RAF took the opportunity to start rebuilding its fighter force. Pete Brothers was involved in setting up a new squadron.

"I was sent to set-up 457 Squadron at Baginton and there were eighteen Spitfires, scattered round the airfield, pointing in all sorts of directions, as left by the ATA or whoever. I had a flight sergeant and a couple of English airmen. Then a chap arrived, and said 'Flight Lieutenant North reporting for duty', grey moustache, and grey hair. What the hell are they sending me? 'How old are you?' 'Twenty-one sir.' 'Who the hell frightened you?' He said: 'My father.' He was a Battle of Britain chap, New Zealander. *(Flt Lt Harold 'Knockers' North was lost on a bomber escort sortie in 1 May 1942 and awarded a posthumous DFC.)*

"The other flight commander arrived, a Canadian Battle of Britain chap. He was shot down in a Spitfire at 19,000 feet, on fire. He couldn't open the hood to get out, it was jammed. He said, 'Down we went, controls had almost gone, nothing happening when you played with the stick. Of course you built up speed, and as it built up speed you pulled it up until it stalled. I did this several times, and I could see the field and the trees I was going to land in. At the bottom of a swoop, we went into this wood, and the engine went on ahead, the wings came off.' He crawled out from under the instrument panel, of course he couldn't open the hood. He bent his nose a bit on the gun-sight, but was otherwise unhurt. He said, 'I think my flying boots got a bit warm, but there was no draft, so the flames didn't come through. If I'd opened the hood, well it would have been an inferno.' I thought: 'You're a very brave chap to continue doing this.' Oh boy.

"We were on the Isle of Man, just about operational. I was leading the squadron in formation when one of the chaps on the right, his wings folded up suddenly and he vanished down into the sea. Course he could-n't get out, the waves closed over the top anyway. So that afternoon, everyone was worrying about the Spitfire falling apart like that. I thought they needed a demonstration of confidence, so I did an aerobat-ic display over the airfield. We raised the wreck and discovered mild steel bolts instead of high-tensile steel in the wing root. Aircraft so fit-ted with mild steel bolts were to be grounded and changed; all my squadron, including my aeroplane, were struck off. Funny if they'd all come apart! So the bolts were replaced. C'est la vie.

"457 went home to Aussie and I took over 602 (in June 1942) because they needed a bloody good lesson. They had been in the Kenley Wing with my 457 Squadron, and they were led by a wild Irishman, Paddy Finucane. The first sortie we did with the Kenley Wing, being the new boys we were sandwiched in the middle, doing a bomber escort. I forget which squadron was bottom, we were in the middle, and Paddy with 602 was on top cover. On the way back, halfway across the Channel, there was no sign of Paddy and his chaps above us. All hell broke out on the radio – 'Look out Paddy, there's one behind you...blah...blah...blah'. I thought, 'What's going on?' So I pulled away from the wing, as the bombers were all right, they'd got their low support squadron, they were halfway across the Channel. I called up and said: 'Where are you Paddy?' '20 miles in from Calais', was his response.

"Right, we swept round up sun, saw a great melee of wings flashing; dived into this, and they were all bloody Spitfires. Went home, landed, and got a bollocking from the wing leader. 'I will tell you when you can leave the wing. What the hell did you think you were doing?' 'Well we were going to help Paddy in 602.' He said: '602 are always in trouble, shouting "look out" and so on. They come back having amassed an enormous score and nobody's been lost; it is quite remarkable. You do as your f***ing told and stay with the wing.'

"A little while later we were all split up again, and we were dispersed to Redhill, and the wing was returning to Kenley. We saw aircraft over-hauling us, and someone said: 'Aircraft following behind.' I said: 'OK, keep an eye on them.' Steaming home, and suddenly they attacked us.

A chap dived on me, I said: 'Christ, they're Spitfires, don't fire!' One of my Aussies said, 'Any bastard who shoots at me, I shoot back.' We tangled round, and they were all Spits; they were 602. We all landed back, I rang up the intelligence reports from Kenley, and said, 'How did the show go?' 'Oh, Paddy Finucane got a Spitfire just south of Beachy Head.'

"Poor old Paddy. When I took over from him I rang up group, and said: 'Would you make 602 Squadron non-operational whilst I teach them aircraft recognition and tactics?' I pulled them out of the line. They were all horrified, this was a great loss of presence and morale, however it taught them a bit of a lesson. I had them for a very short time *(June to October '42)*, and was then promoted wing leader Tangmere."

FROM DEFENCE TO OFFENCE
With increasing strength came a gradual change of fighter tactics to take the war to the Germans while still acting primarily as defence against continuing Luftwaffe attacks on Britain. Squadron Leader Dennis Barry was a Hurricane pilot during this early period.

"I volunteered for the RAF in October 1940, at the age of nineteen and commenced my aircrew course on the first day of January 1941. In October, I was posted to 504 Squadron, stationed at Ballyhalbert in Northern Ireland. Our job was the defence of Belfast, flying Hurricanes, but after a month these were replaced by Spitfires. During the period in Northern Ireland, the squadron was used on convoy patrols and scrambles in the Irish Sea area, when on one occasion I claimed a Ju 88 damaged. On 20 October the squadron moved to 10 Group at Middle Wallop, then on 30 November to Ibsley. During this period I was able to claim three Fw 190s damaged. At this time we were escorting bombers and flying fighter sweeps over France.

"I was posted to 616 Squadron, still at Ibsley as a flight commander. We flew Spitfire VIs, a high-flying model with extended wing tips and a pressurised cockpit, plus a modified engine. These were originally used to intercept high-flying aircraft, but with the change in the pattern of the air war, the wings were clipped for use at lower altitudes, escorting bombers and fighter sweeps over France. On September 14 the Spitfire VIs were replaced by VIIs; another high-flying model, with fuselage modifications and more powerful engines. These enabled us once more to fly high cover on sorties where top cover was required."

Wing Commander Tim Elkington enlisted in September 1939 and on 1 July 1940 joined 1 Squadron, Tangmere, flying Hurricanes. On 15 August he shot down an Me 109 over the Channel, but the following day was himself shot down over Thorney Island. Subsequently he took Hurricanes to Russia on HMS *Argus* in 1941 and later flew with 67 Squadron, retiring in 1975. He described the varying qualities of the aircraft he both flew and encountered in the air.

"With our German opponents there were really two considerations. Firstly, there were good and less good enemies, like with us. In a dog-fight, the better man/aircraft could win. But anyone with height and sun – as they so often had – could be a killer. Secondly, my engagements were all of a following nature, where all the chap could do was open the throttle wider. No great skill there.

"As for their aircraft; no wonder they had successes with the Me 109 with its dive speed. No wonder they had fun with the Fw 190 (which I flew in 1945) with its incredible roll speed. Its ailerons went right out to the wing-tips. I didn't have time to be critical with the Fw 190 as I did only one trip, but was fascinated with the handling. I also flew the Me 110, but I only had a few minutes before some auto feature brought the flaps fully down and I had to put my feet on the control column to hold the nose down while I tried to get it in to land."

Former Me 110 pilot Peter Spoden commented on this.

"We had a lever for the flaps in the '110 and no automatic feature. Of course if you are out of trim you get a heavy control load on the stick, but that's what we had a trim wheel for. I used my feet for the rudder and not for the stick on landing; the story sounds like many shortly after the war."

Tim Elkington continued:

"Flaps, yes – finger trouble, obviously!

"The split stick in the Hurricane was great, a flick of the wrist rather than shoulder and arm. And, of course, your knees didn't get in the way. The straps were so tight you could barely breathe; this was good for prolonged inverted flying. I could sink a Hurricane in to land actually on the stall, without any viciousness as it was generally a bit sluggish. Trim was really only important on full power take-offs and when settling down to a period of almost hands-off flying. As for maximum engine power, ''through the gate' was the term. You got hell if you used it, as a major service followed. I used it once chasing a Ju 88, but it didn't seem to make a lot of odds. There was no heat in the Hurricane, so we were never warm; I had my fuel selector freeze at 35,000 feet. I even tested heated gloves at that time.

"Skill certainly showed, but so much depended upon the situation. The Hurricane could always defend itself by turning. Except with the Zero! The '109 could always run for it. We dropped the 'Vic threes' pattern soon after the Battle. In Russia we often went up as a pair. Some folk had a knack of spotting the enemy aircraft but, for most, it boiled down to a disciplined search pattern – the same as if looking for a dinghy in the sea. With night vision, you often saw things when you were not looking directly at them. Sometimes it was just a yellow nose cone that caught your eye.

"One thing that we did on Typhoons was cut down the paintwork with meths to give us another 5 knots. Frowned on because you shone like a mirror! And another thing; the covert Lysanders were working from our base, the black painted ones, but the ones we were escorting carried life rafts for downed crews.

"Mud: the P-47 and P-51 had a floor to the cockpit, we didn't. So, when you went inverted, you were often showered with debris. Even by something as large as a spanner. Yes – you got the lot – there was no boot-scraper. Many of us wore white sea-boot stockings inside the boots. With my aim of being airborne, I could not spare ten seconds to change my footwear. Despite the toughness of the flying boots, my lower legs were peppered with shrapnel.

"I believe that I was the only person who kept his 'chute in the cockpit; all the others were struggling into their harnesses and then clambering up the wing like apes. They risked damage to the 'chute as they swung into the cockpit. Rather, I could be inside in three leaps, harness would be offered by a crew member either side, 'click, clunk', as they say, and I was off! I reckon that if you could walk in your harness, it was dangerously loose."

A very difficult time for the RAF came with the abortive Dieppe raid on 19 August 1942, which proved to be extremely costly. John Ellacombe flew three times that day.

"The Dieppe raid was the most ghastly experience; we flew down to Tangmere for the briefing. I was then a flight commander at 253 Squadron and Leigh-Mallory said: 'We're going to attack Dieppe and the troops will be going in. I have cancelled the orders which were going to bring the bombers in to bomb all the guns there and this is going to be done by *my* Hurricanes. I have ten squadrons and I don't mind if we lose 50% of them.' That was a hell of a thing to say to your chaps. We had to go back and say to our blokes, 'it's going to be pretty sticky'.

"On the first sortie, my number two was shot down, a very nice fellow, he crashed right next to me and I wrote to his mother and said, 'I don't think you're likely to see your son again', but actually, he was thrown out of the cockpit and landed in a haystack and was perfectly all right.

"On the third sortie, we were bounced by Focke-Wulf 190s and the squadron broke up, but my number two stuck with me. I had a four-cannon Hurricane and my number two had a 12-machine-gun Hurricane. He saw this gun in a field, there were about 4/5 88mm guns there. As we attacked, a lot of flak came up from the side and my aircraft was hit. My throttle was shot away and my engine was hit, so I knew I had about thirty seconds before it seized. I turned right immediately and flew through the gunfire of my number two who took a perfect picture of the

Hurricane going through. So he had twelve guns firing. He must have hit my aeroplane but not me. I reached the coast just as my engine stopped, it absolutely seized solid and I managed to ease up to about 600 feet and baled out. All the guns were firing at me. I looked up at my 'chute, which I thought was on fire but it was all the tracer going through, and when I landed in the water, all these machine guns kept firing and I was absolutely petrified. Suddenly, they all stopped and I started to kick my shoes off to start to swim back to Newhaven, there was no point in going towards the coast 'cause you'd just get killed. Thank heavens the navy sent a little landing craft and they lowered the ramp and pulled me up and I said to the skipper, a Sub-Lieutenant Hall RNZNVR, 'Can't we go a little faster?' He said, 'We've only one engine left, we're only making 4 knots', and there were shells exploding in the water and alongside us.

"The navy sent back a fast patrol boat, they threw us a rope and towed us off at great speed and we rejoined the convoy, and for the next eight hours as we went back to Newhaven, we were bombed a lot on the way. We had a marvellous view of all the British fighters attacking these German bombers and shooting them down but it was a pretty hair-raising day. When I got off the boat, an army officer came up and said: 'You haven't got any shoes, would you like some boots? We've got a lot of men who have died here. What size boot would you like?' I said a size eight so he went off and took a pair of boots off a dead body. They were all lined up there these poor chaps who'd died on the way back. We lost fifty Hurricanes that day."

FIGHTER INTRUDERS

Long-range intruder aircraft such as the Beaufighter and especially the outstanding Mosquito enabled the RAF to spend extended periods over enemy-occupied territory seeking out targets such as Luftwaffe aircraft in the landing pattern at their home airfields. Squadron Leader Clive Knowles started his war as a photo-reconnaissance pilot on Spitfires and Blenheims, before moving on to Mosquitoes with 605 Squadron at Castle Camps in Cambridgeshire. He enjoyed some success, as shown by his following combat report.

"After ten minutes patrol we saw aircraft lights on the far side of the aerodrome (*Soesterberg*), we were then on the north side, but we were unable to make contact. Fifteen minutes later two enemy aircraft were seen making their approach from the north, burning red-white recognition lights. The hinder one doused his lights shortly after and we dived on the first, and I gave a three-second burst of cannon and machine guns from 350 yards, closing to 50 yards from astern and above, using 5 degrees deflection, at 1,500 feet. We saw strikes on the port engine and fuselage, which burst into flames, in the light of it we recognised it to be

Squadron Leader Clive Knowles spent much of his war flying photo-reconnaissance missions. He was photographed in late 1940 flying a Blenheim of 140 Squadron from Mount Farm, Oxfordshire. *Knowles via Judy Tomlin*

a Do 217 and we saw the hood jettison. We broke away to port and saw the enemy aircraft crash to the east of the aerodrome at 02:30 hours. During our dive and combat, and until breaking away we were held by a searchlight on the line of the Lorenz (*radar beacon*) at the north end, and by others round this end of the aerodrome, and were engaged by flak from the aerodrome defences."

His log book entry is rather more explicit:

"Soesterberg. Do 217 pranged. One-and-a-half seconds burst, 10% deflection and above. Flamer into deck. Wizo! First shots fired in anger this war."

Knowles's second combat victory (in a Mosquito) was claimed on the night of 23/24 September 1943 in the Mannheim area. During the patrol around the

aerodrome at Ober / Olm, four enemy aircraft were seen to land without navigation lights, and though attacks were attempted on two, they were unable to position in time. However, success was to come, as Clive wrote in his combat report:

"We followed this enemy aircraft round the circuit, closing our range to
200 yards. When at 1,500 feet, with our wheels down and radiator flaps
open, I gave a two to three second burst from dead astern and slightly
below, closing to 150 yards. Strikes were seen on the cockpit and port
engine, which immediately burst into flames, by the light of which the
aircraft was identified as a Do 217 with its wheels down. It went
straight down and crashed, bursting into flames, with many explosions
of ammunition going off being seen on the ground."

A third and final victory came on the night of 22/23 October over Wunsdorf
which was seen to be active, with several colours of the day being fired. Course
was altered to investigate, and on approaching, an enemy aircraft was seen to
overshoot, burning its navigation lights.

"The enemy aircraft slowly climbed away, and as he did so, we positioned ourselves for an attack. As he turned down-wind, I opened fire
with the cannon only at a range of 200 yards at 1,000 feet, giving a five
to six second burst from below and slightly to port. We saw many
strikes on the fuselage and starboard wing, and the starboard engine
burst into flames, by the light of which we identified him as a Do 217.
The aircraft had long-range tanks on, rather like the drop tanks of a
Mosquito. We broke away to port in a steep turn, and saw him discharge a considerable number of small brilliant white lights, like the
flares which the night fighters drop to illuminate our bombers over and
around the target. The Do 217 crashed on the east end of the flarepath,
exploded and burnt for a couple of minutes, but the aerodrome lights
remained on."

USAAF FIGHTER MISSIONS

United States Army Air Force flying units began operations from Britain with the
8th Air Force in 1942, and thereafter rapidly built into a formidable force, which
included large numbers of fighter wings to escort the daylight bombing missions and
carry out their own offensive operations. 'Punchy' Powell flew many such missions.

"When I first got to England in April '43, about fifty of us were assigned
to an RTU at Atcham where we were to get a little more P-47 training.
(6th Fighter Wing, a combat crew replacement centre, which flew
Spitfires and Airacobras, these being replaced by P-47s.) They didn't
have enough Jugs for us so they said to just go out and get some flying
time in any of the 'planes, including the Spitfire. So we got someone to

show us how to start the Spits and began flying them. We were sent to an RAF gunnery base and I flew my gunnery missions in the mornings and towed targets with a Lysander in the afternoons. I had to get someone to show me how to start the Lysander, too.

"On 352nd, our primary mission was bomber escort; some were combined bomber escort and ground strafing. Some were strictly planned as ground strafing missions to destroy enemy aircraft on their airfields, transport such as trucks and trains and other targets of opportunity. Our D-Day period missions and for several days thereafter, were ground attack missions. We were assigned sectors of France to stop anything moving toward the invasion beaches.

"Any mission was a good one if we were able to keep the enemy aircraft away from the bombers so they could complete their mission or when we managed to score victories over enemy fighters without loss. Some missions were 'milk runs', meaning that we flew without enemy contact with everybody getting home.

"On an escort mission which had turned out to be a milk run, en route home we went down to strafe an airfield. My wingman, Jamie Laing, and I both took hits as we pulled up off the field. Jamie's was in his radiator and he soon lost his coolant, his engine froze, and he had to bale out about fifteen miles from the airfield we strafed. He was captured and a POW for the rest of the war. I took an explosive shell in my right horizontal stabiliser which tore a hole about the size of a bushel basket. I prepared to bale out as soon as the aircraft zoomed up high enough but as its speed diminished, it became more stable and I managed to get it back to Bodney and land.

"My worst day was when I was taking off, got about 300 feet in the air, wheels up and my 'plane suddenly burst into a ball of flames. I managed to dodge some trees and belly it into a farmer's field adjacent to Bodney. Fortunately, the farmer had just ploughed the field and the loose dirt coming back across the aircraft as it slid to a stop knocked the flames down long enough for me to get out and run about thirty yards from it before it exploded. I do not know what caused the fire on takeoff; most likely a fuel line broke loose and spilled gasoline onto the hot manifold, but I will never know. I suffered no injuries, luckily, but I had difficulty getting the canopy off after landing, but managed to kick it loose after pulling the emergency canopy release. The flight surgeon gave me a physical check up later that day and I flew a mission the next day. As he often did, God was riding with me on that one.

"On one mission, we all wished we were back on the ground. The overcast extended from about 800 feet up to and above 27,000 feet. Flying very tight formation as squadrons, we climbed to 27,000 feet and were over enemy territory hearing close flak around us before the bombers aborted the mission and we were ordered to do so too. The tension that existed when flying close formation for that long was almost unbearable, but we lost no aeroplanes or pilots on that one.

Lieutenant Bob 'Punchy' Powell with his P-51D Mustang 'The West By Gawd Virginian' at Bodney, Suffolk in 1944. Punchy served with the 328th Fighter Squadron, 352nd Fighter Group and also flew the P-47 Thunderbolt. *Powell*

"I shot down an Me 110 on my seventh or eighth mission. Later, I shared credit for the destruction of an He 177, we were flying a mission in the area of Nancy at about 25,000 feet when we spotted this lone bomber several thousand feet down. Our leader figured it might be a decoy, so he held most of the 'planes up for top cover when we, the lead flight, went down after it. Colonel Ev Stewart and Captain John Coleman were White 1 and 2 and I was flying as second element leader (White 3).

Colonel Everett Wilson Stewart was the CO of the 328th FS, before taking over command of the 355th FG at Steeple Morden, then the 4th FG at Debden. He ended the war with 180 missions and 510 combat hours, being awarded the Silver Star, four Distinguished Flying Crosses and eleven Air Medals. He retired from the USAF in 1966. The action Punchy describes took place on 1 May 1944.

"Just as we got into range, the Jerry evidently saw us coming, chopped his starboard engines and pulled into a tight turn to starboard. Since the colonel and his wingman were coming down so fast, they could not really turn enough to take a good lead on the bomber, but fired as they scooted past him. Since I was in the number three position and slightly behind them in combat formation, I saw him turning and I had more time to turn with him and when he started rolling out of his turn I was right up his giggy shooting like crazy and getting shot at by their tail gunner. As he was still in a slight turn as I was firing, my fire cut through the centre section of the aircraft and it started breaking up. We pulled up and watched it go down in two big pieces.

"Both the colonel and the captain claimed they got hits on the bomber and I, being only a lieutenant at that time, was not about to argue with them, so when we returned and made our claims we were each credited with a one-third victory. However, I will go to my grave convinced that they did not get hits on that '177.

"The Me 110 I got was a day fighter-bomber. I was flying Colonel Stewart's wing on one of our early missions and I was patting myself on the back for having maintained good wingman position throughout the mission. Looking back over my left shoulder to check for enemy aircraft I was shocked when I looked forward again and Colonel Stewart had disappeared. Looking frantically for him I looked down and saw him inverted doing a split-S, so I quickly followed. As we came out of the split-S I was fish-tailing to keep from overtaking him when I noticed that he was firing his guns. Looking forward to see what he was shooting at I saw him getting strikes on a two-engine aircraft.

"Since I was in combat formation some few hundred feet to his right, I also saw movement in front of me and when I looked I saw another enemy aircraft, the same type, and I was right behind him. I just started shooting and couldn't miss. There were two others we chased but they escaped us by going into the clouds. When we got back on the ground, he said, 'Punchy, what were they?' and I said, 'Damned if I know, colonel, but they had big black crosses on them and they sure as hell were not ours.' Then, when we saw our combat film we recognised them as '110s. It was the first time either of us had fired our guns at an enemy aircraft in the air.

"It was difficult or impossible accurately to claim either air or ground victories. Sometimes your gun camera worked properly, sometimes not. Sometimes other pilots observed your victory; others not. I daresay that the British in the Battle of Britain, the Germans, and the Americans all made claims which were inaccurate and usually on the high side and that enemy aircraft were sometimes destroyed that could not be claimed officially for lack of proof, i.e. gun camera film or observed. Ground claims were easier to confirm since many of those flamed up or exploded. Hence, I look at claims with a jaundiced eye.

"The German pilots were outstanding, and particularly during the fall of '43 and most of '44. And why not? Most of them had been flying combat during the Spanish Civil War, the Blitzkrieg of Poland, the

Low Countries battles and the Battle of Britain. Most of them had thousands of hours and multiple victories before they ever encountered us in the air. I only had fifty hours in a P-47 when I flew my first combat mission. We had tremendous respect for the German pilots and learned combat tactics while flying against them.

"I probably respected the Me 109 most, but the Fw 190 was also a very formidable fighter. I didn't have combat with any jets. I saw some but never got close enough to engage them. I also saw a German 163 attack our bombers but none of us could get close to him.

"As regards the P-47 versus the P-51, no doubt, the Jug (P-47) was the greater aircraft for ground-strafing and dive bombing although we didn't do much of the latter, mostly, of course, because of the ruggedness of the 'plane. It could take a lot more than the '51 and still bring you home. One .30 cal in the radiator of the '51, if you lost your coolant, you went down. However, the Jug's range lessened its effectiveness. But the Jug was equal to or better than the German fighters above 20,000 feet, and it could out-dive anything. No doubt, again, the Mustang was the overall superior aircraft and particularly for air to air combat, for its range, its visibility, rate of turn, climbing rate, etc.

"I completed eighty-seven missions (two combat tours) in September '44 and was sent to headquarters, 8th Fighter Command at Bushey Hall as an advisor to the public relations section there for a few months. Finally got orders to return Stateside in December and arrived back home on Christmas Eve, 1944. Betty and I were married on 4 January 4, 1945."

Chapter Four

OFFENCE – BOMBER BOYS

Lie in the dark and listen,
It's clear tonight so they're flying high,
Hundreds of them, thousands perhaps,
Riding the icy, moonlit sky,
Men, machinery, bombs and maps,
Altimeters and guns and charts,
Coffee, sandwiches, fleece-lined boots,
Bones and muscles and minds and hearts,
English saplings with English roots
Deep in the earth they've left below.
Lie in the dark and let them go;
Lie in the dark and listen.

Lie in the dark and listen
They're going over in waves and waves
High above villages, hills and streams,
Country churches and little graves
And little citizen's worried dreams;
Very soon they'll have reached the sea
And far below them will lie the bays
And cliffs and sands where they used to be
Taken for summer holidays.
Lie in the dark and let them go;
Theirs is a world we'll never know.
Lie in the dark and listen...

Noel Coward 1944

TARGET FOR TONIGHT

Without question one of the most debated air campaigns of the Second World War was the joint RAF/USAAF bomber offensive against Germany and her allies, not least because of the huge numbers of airmen lost, with more than 55,000 killed or missing from Bomber Command alone. The well-known and oft-quoted statement by Prime Minister Winston Churchill to the House of Commons on

20 August 1940 about 'The Few', is generally considered to be entirely about the fighter pilots who fought in the Battle of Britain. However, the full text also includes substantial reference to the RAF's bomber crews:

"The gratitude of every home in our island, in our empire, and indeed throughout the world, except in the abodes of the guilty, goes out to the British airmen who, undaunted by odds, unwearied in their constant challenge and mortal danger, are turning the tide of world war by their prowess and by their devotion. Never in the field of human conflict has so much been owed by so many to so few. All hearts go out to the fighter pilots whose brilliant actions we see with our own eyes day after day, but we must never forget that all the time, night after night, month after month, our bomber squadrons travel far into Germany, find their targets, often under the heaviest fire, often with serious loss, with deliberate, careful discrimination, and inflict shattering blows upon the whole of the technical and war-making structure of the Nazi power. On no part of the Royal Air Force does the weight of the war fall more heavily than on the daylight bombers who will play an invaluable part in the case of invasion and whose unflinching zeal it has been necessary in the meantime on numerous occasions to restrain." [7]

Against this background, memories of those days remain very vivid amongst the survivors. Jack Bromfield is typical, thinking of his experiences every day, even though sixty-five years have passed.

"You'd got up at five o'clock in the morning, gone to briefing, gone out for five-and-a-half hours over Germany, got back, had your meal and gone to bed. Being woken up in the middle of the night with blokes coming into the billet was common. Always the padre with a couple of military policemen, who'd come to collect the effects of blokes who hadn't come back. That was tough, you couldn't get back to sleep after that.

"Leave was a waste of time, we were wasting getting the war finished. At home they knew nothing about war, they were carrying on with their lives, and good luck to them. It was what everybody would have liked to have done, but their lives were not mine, and my life wasn't theirs. I think with families in the east end of London or Liverpool, where the whole family had been bombed, it may have been different. But these little country towns like those where I lived, war to them was remote, it was just something they read about in the papers."

The campaign was equally hard for the Luftwaffe defenders. The fighter crews fought extremely fiercely in defence of their homeland, however the survivors have frequently stated that their aim was not to kill the bomber crews, their target was the aeroplane; night fighter pilots especially have said they tried to aim for the inner wings to disable engines and start a fuel leak and fire to force the crews to abandon their machine. This is typical of the respect airmen held for their opposite numbers; an appreciation that both were simply doing their job. Heinz Rökker outlined his views.

"We couldn't win the war; we had too many enemies; the world was against us. But we couldn't see it, we had our duty and we tried to save our country from bombing. Today people see the bombing of Germany with other eyes I think; they say it was not gentleman-like.

"I had a meeting with Hermann Göring. I got my Oakleaves there, I had to go to Karinhall, near Berlin. It was at the end of the war, March 1945, he gave me the award and shaking hands, said: 'Carry on as you are and be a good fighter.' At the beginning of the war you could get the Knight's Cross if you have ten victories, but when the war was longer we got it for twenty-five victories and Oakleaves was for fifty, seventy-five earned you the Swords. After that was the Diamonds, that was for 100; we had only one (*night fighter*), Schnaufer."

Nonetheless, the scale of losses amongst bomber crew was such that the chances of a crew surviving a full tour of thirty operations was extremely slim, even after the balance of air superiority started to move in the allies' favour. Jack Bromfield:

"What used to get me was seven empty beer glasses on the shelf. We would learn if someone was missing next morning, at breakfast. You'd expect to see seven blokes sitting at that table and they weren't there. You sat around for a while, wondering whether they had landed away from home, but by dinner time you knew."

George Cook arrived at his first squadron in 1941 and was shocked by the speed with which friends were lost.

"When we were training, there were twenty of us who stayed together and we got to know each other very well. We were told that when the time came for posting, we could ask to stay together with our friends. There were four of us who wanted to do that and we took the form to the office. When the postings came through, we were split up. I went to 49 Squadron at Scampton, and the others went to 106 Squadron at Coningsby. When I got to Scampton I went to the sergeants' mess to have a beer, and one of the regulars asked me what squadron I was posted to. When I told him 49, he said, 'You poor bugger'.

"About a month later I was crewing a Hampden that was doing some target towing, and we had to stop at Coningsby to pick up the target. I asked the skipper if I could go over to the squadron office and see if any of my mates were about. I found the office and asked if Butler was around. 'He's gone.' 'What about Burrell?' 'He's gone.' 'What about Clifford?' 'He's gone too.' All three of them had been lost in their first month on ops."

Sgt Eric Butler of Blackheath, London, was lost during an operation to Düsseldorf on the night of 10/11 April 1941, when 106 Squadron Hampden X3148/ZN-E was shot down by Hptm Werner Streib of NJG.1 and crashed at Limburg in Holland. Sgt William Burrell of Eltham, London, was lost during an operation on Köln in the early hours of 21 April 1941, when Hampden X2986/ZN-F crashed near the target. Nothing is known about the third airman, Clifford. George was fortunate to survive his first tour, but not without some nervous moments.

"I went to eighteen different cities, some of them two or three times; in the end I did thirty-three trips. My worst moment was when I had a trip to Duisburg, and this was going to be my last one to complete my tour. It was known somehow that everybody on their last trip went for a Burton.

"When we got to Duisburg, we had a horrendous reception. That was the alternative target, and I think we were the only aircraft that arrived there. We had heavy flak for about half an hour, and on the Hampden the part you sat in was the cupola. The flak was so bad that it actually sucked that part away and just blew it off, so you were left with all you were sitting on and that was only half your seat. The shrapnel was hitting the aircraft, you could smell the cordite and feel the heavy flak bursts.

"We had twenty-nine holes in us and we eventually crept back. I got wounded in my hand, a bit of shrapnel caught my fingers. Through all the evasive actions we had to do, the poor old navigator didn't know where we were. So the skipper said, 'Go in SOS conditions, and get a fix'. I said to the wireless operator, 'Will you be able to cope?' He said, 'Yeah'. I couldn't do anything because it was the hand I used on the morse key. After about half an hour, the fix hadn't come through, and the skipper said to me, 'You get back on the set George', so I had to use my left hand. We swapped over, and when I looked at the receiver, he'd got the receiver on HF and the transmitter on MF. So when I switched it over, the station was coming through with the fix, and within about five minutes we were all right. The navigator got his position, and we finished up OK, but that was a horrendous night; I was on the sick list for four months.

"After that I went to Cottesmore (*14 OTU*) in 1942 as a screened instructor and safety wireless operator, still on Hampdens. While I was there, the thousand-bomber raids came on, they got hold of us staff people as well, and I went on the thousand-bomber raid to Cologne and to Essen. On the Essen trip, we were attacked by an Fw 190 but fortunately, he was a poor shot."

The raid on Duisburg resulted in good bombing accuracy, but 49 Squadron lost two Hampdens to night fighters. Wing Commander Lucian Ercolani also flew on the second thousand-bomber raid, while a pilot on 214 (Wellington) Squadron at Stradishall in Suffolk where he completed twenty ops. He later took command of 99 and 159 Squadrons in the Far East.

> "Bomber Command was trying to prove to the powers that be that if they'd only help them, let them have enough aircraft, they couldn't half do a hell of a lot of damage. So they used every aircraft that they had any control over at all (quite a lot of which were on training) and concentrated them. We took off with as many bombs as we could, and got as many aircraft into the air as we could and we were all rather excited about it. We knew that something rather special was happening and knew you had more company. You get more spread out actually, you don't see all that many, unless you get one that comes a bit too close!"

Lancaster pilot Ted Mercer also experienced the shock of losing friends, in his case, the rest of his regular crew.

> "Initially I went to a PFF (*Pathfinder Force*) Squadron – 83 – not as Pathfinder crew, because I had only just finished training. It was just an idea to see how we fitted in. I never operated with that crew because I went down with appendicitis. When I came back...they had all gone missing. I went to Dunholme Lodge and joined 44 Squadron, where I met a great crew; we got on very well, and finished our tour together."

Flight Lieutenant Russell 'Rusty' Waughman joined the RAF in 1941 and trained as a pilot. He flew Lancasters on operations with 101 Squadron from Ludford Magna in Lincolnshire.

> "I feel very lucky to be alive considering Bomber Command's losses. Figures published about aircrew losses in Bomber Command state that out of every 100 aircrew fifty-one were killed on operations, nine were killed crashing, three were seriously injured and were unable to fly again, twelve were taken as POWs, one evaded capture, the remaining survived but many suffered health and mental problems. I was indeed lucky to survive."

Jack Bromfield started his tour much later in the war during the second half of 1944.

> "We were posted to 158 Squadron at Lissett, 4 Bomber Group. Crew were a bit upset because they thought they were going to 6 Group, the Canadian group. We were a night bomber squadron, and for our first raid where did we go, to Julik (*16 November '44, troop concentrations*) in daylight! That frightened the bloody life out of me. I've never seen so much flak in all my life. It really was a baptism of fire. From what I could gather from the briefings, there were two big crossroads, and if

we could shut those crossroads out it would stop the armour from going whichever way they wanted to go.

"New crews would not get their own aeroplane for a while. Z-Zombie was quite well known on 158; she'd done quite a few. So as a new crew, you generally got an aeroplane with a lot of bombs painted on the side, but Sugar hadn't got many. We flew Queenie once I think, but Sugar was the one we normally had. We did about four before we got 'our' aeroplane.

"We were on our way back from a daylight on Mulheim. (*Christmas Eve 1944.*) We were nearly home; and all of a sudden Pop! Pop! Pop! Flak bursts all around us, one of our convoys was shooting at us! My call light came on – the skipper – so I got on the intercom, 'WOp, get onto those bastards and find out what the hell they're doing!' 'I don't know what frequency they're on.' 'You've got a lamp haven't you?' So I leaned over his shoulder and flashed down to them, 'Piss off'. Pop! Pop! Pop! They took no notice.

"You could do no more than do your best. If you haven't done your best, it's your fault, but if you've done the best that you as a person can possibly do, then you tried and you deserve the honour of the people of your country, to be looked up to because you tried."

Amongst the targets that crews feared the most, 'Big B' – Berlin – stood out for them as somewhere they would really rather not have to visit. A long flight over Germany, running the gauntlet of night fighters, was followed by a very hot reception from the flak batteries defending the German capital. Philip Smith was serving as a flying instructor on Oxfords when he experienced Berlin first hand during a short attachment to 100 Squadron at Waltham, near Grimsby, and flew an operation as a second pilot in a Lancaster.

"We went to Berlin, it was a hell of a trip; eight hours there and back. We got shot up by a night fighter attacking from underneath; it injured three of the crew. The pilot – he was only twenty-one – had to make the decision. Do we bale out and leave the three of them to it (they couldn't bale out), or do we carry on and try to make it back? No choice really, so we got back and landed at one of the big emergency runways, at Carnaby. The wheels came down OK, but we were on two engines. That was in April '44. The three injured crewmen all recovered."

WHAT WAS IT LIKE TO BE ON BOMBER OPS?

Surviving veterans have frequently been asked how flying operations felt. Flight Sergeant David Taylor was a Lancaster flight engineer with 49 Squadron, and put his feelings very simply. "We were always scared."

Wireless Operator/Air Gunner Flight Lieutenant Eric Clarke crewed Hampdens, Manchesters and Lancasters during his tour with 49 Squadron, and he described vividly what bomber operations were like for him.

"On Sunday 21 September 1941 I arrived at RAF Scampton having completed a twelve-week course of operational training at 16 OTU at Upper Heyford on Hampdens. I was to learn later that our course suffered the most losses in training.

"The following morning we found our way to the wireless operator's crew room in No. 2 Hangar; Guy Gibson's dog Nigger's memorial is now there. There were about twenty WOp/AGs; about six or seven would be in their late twenties, the rest seemed to be quite young. Two of us were both twenty-eight – old boys! The Hampden had a crew of four – pilot, navigator (who also combined bomb aimer) wireless operator and rear gunner. There were no 'straight' air gunners, so the crew comprised pilot, navigator and two wireless ops. One WOp would be 'on the set' in the upper position and the other in the lower gun position, known as 'the Tin'.

"What was it like being on ops? Normally, we got word in the crew room by 9 a.m. that aircraft, say nine, were serviceable and Flt Sgt Jack Gadsby would detail us to carry out a DI (daily inspection) on a specific aircraft and usually it would be the aircraft that you later flew in on an NFT (night flying test) to certify its fitness for an operation. This involved a ten to fifteen minute flight, usually the pilot with whom you would fly that night, but this did not always happen. Later in the morning, we could see from our crew room window a tractor towing a string of bomb trolleys and we might just get an inkling of the type of operation that night. Ruhr, happy valley. Or mining, known as 'gardening', but we just speculated. Sometimes Flt Sgt Gadsby would be able to say that you were flying with such a pilot in, say, K-King. The rest of us would not know until we saw the ops board at briefing but if your pilot was an NCO, he would know and he would contact you; if your pilot was an officer you would not see him until briefing."

"There were a few occasions in the early days where a crew stayed together in the Hampdens, but not many. The merits of the pilots were certainly discussed in the WOps crew room, comments like 'spot on', 'super', 'wizard' and so on, but also not so others who might merit 'dopey', 'crazy' and other unspeakable sorts. Obviously, affinities were formed but of a tenuous nature. When we got the Manchesters, we had seven crew and the majority stayed together, but we might not see much of the officer members until we assembled for boarding. They had their own crew rooms.

"The daytime was a mixture of DIs, NFTs, a lecture, parachute repacking, and some local flying, otherwise it was cards and dominoes for some. I did not get airborne until 12 October, actually 00:10 hrs on the 13th and it was an op. I had not been informed that I was flying that night until Flt Sgt Gadsby told me at tea time to be at briefing 18:00 hrs. Arriving at briefing I found I was crewed with a Sgt Pilot Robinson, navigator Sgt Black, and Sgt Mossop wireless operator; I was in the Tin. The target was Halse (also called Huls) and it was my first flight with 49 Squadron. I did not know the pilot or navigator but of course I knew the WOp Sgt Mossop, who was a buddy of Flt Sgt Gadsby and a 'veteran'.

"The briefing was short, the squadron commander pointing out the target, the reason for the operation, and the route out and back, followed by specialist officers, meteorologist, navigator signals and intelligence, and take-off times were also announced, then the individual crews got into a huddle over the navigator's chart after which we returned to our messes for a night flying supper. There was no excitement, just quiet conversation and discussion.

"We all met at 23:00 hours in front of the hangar, fully kitted up, extra jerseys and the like as it was very cold in the Hampdens and along came the wagon. No more smoking, cigarettes stubbed out. An officer would sit in front with the WAAF driver and we piled in, two or three crews at a time and we were off to dispersal. No sign of nerves, but quite a lot of banter. I think to some of the younger ones, it was an adventure of a sort with little thought of the possible horrors. You would hear: 'I have done ten now, how many have you done?' Or, 'Get some in' or similar. I did not announce it was my first.

"The pilot, who was addressed as 'skipper' was in conversation with the ground crew flight sergeant, after which he just said, 'Let's get going'. All this was in black-out conditions and then the sound of engines starting up. The pilot and navigator entered through the front hatch, the WOp and myself through the rear lower gun position. I was the last, we were all in and individually commenced connecting up routines, I stowed my 'chute, checked the safety catches on my guns – twin Vickers gas operated, plugged in the oxygen tube, and then listened in to the crew checking intercom contact with each other but firstly with the pilot. 'Hello skipper, navigator here', from the WOp and myself. Good intercom was so vital, as just one defective headset could cause the whole intercom to fail and possibly the whole operation. For take-off and landing, the Tin gunner had to squeeze in with the wireless op. The engines were started up, with some vibration as they were warmed up and we checked the intercom again, and then we commenced taxiing to take off.

"Waiting for take-off, I found myself musing. I went back to the time when I hitch-hiked home on a '48' and found myself on the London North Circular road, making my way to a lorry park at Finchley where I could get a lift up the A1 to Yorkshire through the night. The 'all clear' had just sounded and I had to wind my way through bomb damage, with fire engines and others doing their job, water mains burst, shop windows out, glass and goods all over the place, maybe because we were in uniform the wardens took no notice of us. As I sat in my bomber I began to ask myself what damage were we going to do? I also remembered, when on leave, the red sky over Sheffield some eighteen miles away. I thought of the reports by radio and newspapers of the damage, and countless civilian deaths in London and our big cities. Why was I here, listening to the engines of my bomber about to take off to do untold damage and death to another people? I consoled myself that my country was fighting for its very existence, and that I was a very small cog in a massive war machine. Germany had over-run Europe and England could be the next victim. So horrible to think and yet possible.

"With these and other thoughts I began to ask myself, 'What happens now? Are we going to be successful and carry out our mission with a safe return, to do more? Or are we going to be shot down, shall I have to bale out?' I had no qualms about baling out, but would I be able to? I certainly feared coming down in the sea.

"My musings were interrupted, 'OK boys we are off', and with a surge of the engines we rumble down the runway, gathering speed and then the rumbling ceases and we sense a slight lift – we are airborne and I am sweating. I hear the navigator telling the pilot, 'Wheels up OK', and then remind him of the compass course to the coast. I clambered down to my lower gun position, and then re-checked my intercom. During the steady climb I swung my guns from side to side checking my view. I did not want this, I wanted to be on the set, however, my turn would come. We were now flying level and the engines droned, what is to be will be. My thoughts flew home, to my wife. Past midnight she would be in bed. I suddenly felt very much alone, isolated, and apprehensive. We had decided not to have children because of the war, but when I commenced flying training she changed her mind.

"I heard the navigator give the pilot a new course, we were crossing the Norfolk coast, goodbye England! Hopefully just for the time being. We were at about 10 to 12,000 feet, and the navigator sounded crisp and confident and the WOp reported, 'nothing from group'. Throughout the trip the WOp must listen out to group HQ every fifteen minutes from the hour in case of recall or diversion, W/T silence was observed except in case of emergency and only with the pilot's permission. As we approached the enemy coast the pilot warned us that we were in a night fighter zone but there was now a lot of cloud and I could see nothing. My first operation; in the next fourteen months I was to survive twenty-six of these with nine different pilots, in three different bombers: Hampdens, Manchesters and Lancasters.

"The Air Ministry report reads: 'AD979 Sgt Robinson,10/10th cloud at Wesel on ETA, set course for target, dropped flare without success for twenty-five minutes at 2000-4000 feet looking for target spending fifty minutes in area, Essen and Ruhr under 10/10th cloud, bombed 'drome and flarepath in Holland on return.'

"We landed at base at 07:50hrs, we had been airborne six hours and twenty minutes. We piled into the waiting wagon, to de-briefing and then to breakfast, somebody said, 'everybody back'. With a strange sense of elation I went to bed. The next day I was able to have a talk with Bill Mossop, the WOp, and discussed the flight. He laconically summed it up as, 'a fat lot of good'. He said he was about finished and I don't remember seeing him again; I think he had completed his tour. There was constant movement in the WOps crew room – on leave, on a course, failing to return, new arrivals. One sergeant arrived (Sgt Way) who made it known that he was expecting his commission to come through. He was on the 'Channel Dash' detail the same week and did not return. He was posted missing as Pilot Officer S W A Way; in total we lost fifteen NCO aircrew, including seven WOps."

The Channel Dash operations, code named Fuller, against the German capital ships *Scharnhorst*, *Gneisenau*, and *Prinz Eugen* resulted in the loss of sixteen bombers, including four 49 Squadron Hampdens. Flg Off Way's aircraft, AE240/EA-P skippered by Sgt M H Holt RAAF, was, like the other three, lost without trace. The crew is commemorated on the Runnymede memorial.

"On Hampdens, I went on to do nine more ops, one in the Tin and eight on the wireless, with six different pilots, including two with Squadron Leader P D S Bennett DFC our B Flight commander. I was happy to be on the set and felt that I was really doing the job I was trained to do.

"My second op was with Sgt Bow as pilot and a different crew. The target was Mannheim and the Air Ministry report reads: 'Flak and searchlight opposition over Belgian coast, cloud necessitated flying at 18,000 feet. Target bombed at 14,000 feet and pin point at river junction seen. Electrical storms prevailed over target area.' We diverted on the return to Horsham St. Faith in Norfolk in pouring rain. We slept in the sergeants' mess lounge and flew back to Scampton next morning.

"In late 1941 news began filtering through that Coningsby had been given Manchesters and we began wondering how long it would be before we got them, we certainly felt that the Hampden had reached the end of its service. In early 1942, 83 Squadron got the Manchesters; and we always seemed to play second fiddle to 83, but on 2 May I did my first Manchester op, a leaflet raid on Rennes. The next few days we did local day and night flying and on 8 May we did our second op laying mines off Heligoland Bight. I was beginning to feel comfortable in this big bomber...a major contrast in every respect as far as the Hampden was concerned, like converting from a Ford 10 to a Rolls-Royce.

"On 30 May we were briefed for the thousand-bomber raid on Cologne, but I do not remember any particular emphasis on the number except that some OTU crews would be taking part. When we arrived at the target there were a great many fires and palls of smoke. Our bombing run seemed strangely devoid of flak although there were many searchlights. Of 1,047 aircraft taking part forty-one failed to return; 49 Squadron lost two, its first Manchester casualties. The second thousand-raid took place on 2 June, and to me the raid seemed quite uneventful – 49 Squadron lost one. It turned out to be my last operation in Manchesters.

"I did eight ops with Flt Lt Cooke DFC – 'Cookie', and he became my 'Icon'. I had a warm feeling for him, he had a sort of laid back attitude, and a very dry, laconic humour. His style was: 'You clueless clots, pull your finger out!' Somehow I felt safe with him. On three occasions we returned to base on three engines, even two-and-a-half engines. And I was instructed to break W/T silence and obtain emergency fixes for the navigator. When we disembarked, he just said, 'Good show Sergeant', I felt great!

"On 24 October we bombed Milan, an operation I remember vividly; an early briefing, take-off midday in our regular Lanc. After night bombing since October 1941, this was a low level daylight. Eighty-eight Lancasters from 5 Group, independently due south from Scampton over the Channel and to the river Loire where we turned to port for the Alps and we rendezvoused at Lake Annecy from where we flew through the top of the Alps to Milan. As we did so I had my head in the astrodome and an unforgettable experience. Looking forward, easterly, I saw at eye level a big white full moon and looking aft, westerly, I could see, at eye level, an equally large orange sun; it was quite unique. Down in the now dark valleys we saw quite a lot of twinkling lights, no black out there. We bombed at dusk descending through cloud. We had a real scare on our bombing run as a Stirling crossed just below us. We bombed below the cloud base at 4,500 feet. We returned, in the dark over Germany but fortunately without hindrance, steering round two flak concentrations.

"Why was I on ops? Our country was fighting for its very existence. I have had to live with the knowledge that some of the bombs from my aircraft must have killed many innocent civilians, women and children, I think I have read somewhere that our enemy killed 30,000 civilians in Britain. What of the many colleagues, pilots and crews, and some very close friends who were killed or missing – they were denied the life that I have had. Bomber Command lost 55,500 aircrew; my squadron lost 907. I shall continue to mourn them for the rest of my days.

Halifax pilot Flying Officer John Grenville Eaton later flew Mosquitoes with 105 Squadron, and recalled extreme cold and some of the incredible sights he witnessed.

"Freezing conditions at height, sometimes minus 56, the cold could freeze your breath into an ice beard and freeze your eyebrows if your heating failed, and at anytime could immobilise vital instruments. On one occasion when we carried wing-bombs, they froze to the wings and did not release until the shock of landing, exploding and causing several casualties.

"The view from 30,000 feet was very wonderful. The south coast of England, for example, just as it is on the map, or the daytime view of a never-ending stream of 1,000 bombers, dog-legging to the target and away again. At night, the Zuider Zee glinted in the moonlight, or the sight of V-2s rising at the speed of sound and disappearing far above us. Or seeing the sunset, then climbing fast and actually seeing it set again. Or, awe-inspiring and awful, the view of the Ruhr aflame, exploding as far as the eye could see, sheer hell, flak, searchlights with planes and 'scarecrows' flaming down. Our height gave us a grandstand view, but we did not hang around after release of our load and the photoflash. A sight that was unforgettable, but I would hope never to see again."

The reference to scarecrows perpetuates a long-held belief that the Germans had some kind of device that caused violent explosions at altitude. Subsequently it has become clear that these really were bombers exploding as a result of being hit by flak or fighters.

Warrant Officer Les Weeks trained as a navigator and flew ops with 467 (Lancaster) Squadron RAAF at Waddington, and 83 (Lancaster) Squadron Pathfinder Force, at Coningsby.

"My first op was Aunay-sur-Odon, troop positions, on 14 June '44. My watch gained half-an-hour before we got to the target, so according to my plotting we were falling behind. I was saying, 'OK, another 10 knots skipper'. We'd gone ahead and there we were all on our own, some way from the target, somewhere down the South of France. The skipper said, 'How much longer to H-hour nav?' So I told him. 'Oh, what time is H-hour then?' Told him. 'Well,' he said, 'that doesn't correspond.' That was when we found my watch had gained half an hour. We did a dog-leg away to waste time until he said, 'When do we turn back nav?' 'Well, you'd better turn back now.' So, we did, and we were just coming up towards the target all flaming away and flak and everything, and the bomb aimer takes over, 'OK, bomb doors open...left...skipper...left...right...right'. Then the wireless operator came up with a message, 'Message from base skipper, hold bombs and return'. Oh, you ought to have heard the bomb aimer's voice: 'Please skipper, please let me drop 'em!' 'Bomb doors closed.' We came through the target, and had just got out the other side. 'Another message from base, skipper, drop bombs and return.' So round we went again, through and then back home.

"Somewhere well into Germany, we bombed the target OK, and turned to come home. The bomb aimer said, 'skipper, there's a bomb hung up'. 500 pounder, we didn't know if it had a delayed action or not, 'cause we'd been given a mixed assortment. The skipper started jinking the 'plane about, bomb doors opened, but it wouldn't come off, so we carried on with it, and tried several times. Just crossed over the Channel and it dropped into the bomb-bay, and was rolling around! We were diverted, and we put down in the early hours of the morning at a training place with Wellingtons. After an hour or so, they got the skipper and the flight engineer out of bed, to go and shift our kite in case it blew up and damaged any of theirs. After breakfast they had to get in it and bring it back again, still with the bomb in it.

"Another time we were out on our own, way down in Germany and couldn't get a fix. The rest of the crew were looking out trying to spot somewhere for a fix, but couldn't. Eventually got one and identified it on the map. We were miles port of where we should have been, it was a heck of a way. I took a direct course from where we did eventually find ourselves, and looking at it afterwards, we got there OK, marked and everything, we'd gone right over Peenemünde – just one little Lancaster on its own.

"We were asked to go on Pathfinder Force, so we joined 83 Squadron in September. It wasn't different, navigated just the same, perhaps a little bit more accurately, dead to time, more or less working to seconds. Some of the ops were a little bit hazardous. I used to get close to the target, work the course to come back, come out from behind the curtain and I'd stand behind the skipper watching what's going on, seeing the bombing going on and all the flak and everything. Then as soon as we'd got clear of the target, give him a course and we'd start back. I saw some of them go down, some of our 'planes. I think one was hit by a bomb from above; went down, like a falling leaf.

"We diverted to an 8th US Air Force station once, and after landing, the bomb doors are opened. Of course the Americans come round to look, and they saw the size of the bomb-bay and they had open mouths."

Peter Green had a difficult trip resulting in a crash-landing at Woodbridge in Suffolk, one of three very long and wide emergency runways built for just this purpose – a safe haven for badly damaged aircraft returning from the continent. The other two such runways were at Carnaby in Yorkshire, and Manston in Kent.

"We had a daylight one on Munster, 12 September '44. We were hit by flak on our bombing run, but fortunately although the nose and tail were badly damaged, the only injury was the bomb aimer, who got some shrapnel in his shoulder. The bomb doors wouldn't close and the tail got shot up pretty badly. The rear gunner was very fortunate, he didn't get injured, and nobody else was wounded.

"We managed to maintain an airspeed of 135 knots although the bomb doors were open and the undercarriage lowered due to the failure of the hydraulic system. On our final approach at Woodbridge I remember seeing a Lanc on the runway that had approached in the opposite direction. On touching the runway, our port undercarriage leg, which was cracked, collapsed, and the aircraft went ahead on its belly and we finished up in a ploughed field adjacent to the runway. Fortunately the old Halibag didn't catch fire, but we all scrambled out of her very quickly with the roar of the fire engine and blood wagon amongst us.

Everybody was fairly shaken and I well remember an extra tot of rum. We were picked up the next day by another crew from our squadron and flown back to Pocklington, as our kite was a write-off."

Halifax III LL555/DY-W took off from Pocklington at 16:19 and bombed the target at 18:39 from 19,000 feet, but was hit by flak. The aircraft crash-landed at Woodbridge at 20:24. The crew was captained by Flt Sgt Vernon George 'Taffy' Fitt, who was awarded a DFC in July 1945.

Bomb aimer Ted Milligan and his crew also had occasion to be thankful for the availability of these emergency runways.

"I was posted to 460 Squadron in May '44, and completed thirty-three operations, crewed with P/O Lyall J Notley RAAF. On our fifteenth op, a daylight to Trossy St. Maximin, we bombed visually from 13,000 feet and were hit by flak five minutes before the target, which holed the leading edge of the starboard wing. We mistook hydraulic fluid for petrol pouring out, and were unaware that the bomb doors failed to open and as the bombs did not fall I assumed the electric supply had been cut. We eventually belly-landed at Carnaby with a full bomb load.

"Our tail gunner reported seeing V-2s on more than one occasion before their existence was generally known, but not much else exciting happened until we finished our tour, after which I was posted out to 1667 HCU at Sandtoft in October '44."

Bob Clarke was an aero engine fitter at Elstree airfield in Hertfordshire when it was taken over by Fairfield Aviation Company (FAC) from Croydon. Fairfields were bombed out at Croydon in August 1940 and they moved to the private airfield at Elstree with their main plant in a part of the Odhams Press factory a few miles away at Watford. Bob witnessed the aftermath of the sad loss of two damaged bombers struggling to get back to base in April 1943, and recorded them in his diary.

"RAF twenty-five years old today, said to now be the biggest in the world – it needs to be as we are losing about thirty bombers a night. The fire we saw last night was quite close, at Bushey, caused by a crashed Whitley. Bits were strewn all over the surrounding area. Our crash wagon and ambulance went to the scene. I wasn't on duty.

"Sirens tonight for the sixth night in succession. Working until 10 p.m. and saw a Wellington crash in flames quite close at London Colney. Found out later it was a Lancaster."

The Whitley was an Mk V AD679 of 81 OTU Sleap, on a 'Bullseye' exercise, and had taken off at 20:15 with eight others. Two hours later it flew into the ground at Finch Lane, Bushey and burst into flames. It is thought the pilot became so dazzled, when caught in searchlights, that in taking evasive action he exceeded the safe limitations of the mainplane. The crew were all killed and comprised:

Sgt W Hall (pilot), Sgt A L Culley (navigator), Sgt W Harrison (air bomber), Sgt I F W Pead (wireless operator) and Sgt A C Strolin (air gunner).

The Lancaster was an Mk I L7575/UG-Q of 1654 Heavy Conversion Unit (HCU) Wigsley, also on a 'Bullseye' exercise. It had taken off at 18:55 and it is suspected that the crew encountered very severe turbulence and, possibly, icing which led to structural failure of the outer wings and tail. Thus, at 20:12, debris literally rained from the skies over Warren House Farm at Colney Heath. The crew were all killed and comprised: Plt Off E M Taylor RAAF (pilot), Sgt A Rooks, Flg Off E Williams, Sgt J F Thwaite, Sgt H T Green, Flt Sgt G B Davies RAAF and Sgt E P Stock.

Almost exactly one year later, Bob's diary made brief reference to Bomber Command's worst night of the entire war in terms of losses. "We lost ninety-four heavy bombers last night."

This was the disastrous raid on Nuremberg on the night of 30/31 March 1944, when the expected cloud cover failed to materialise and the German night fighters were not drawn away by the planned diversions. The actual number lost was ninety-five.

Bombers who had lost their way making for home could call England for emergency directions using the 'Darkie' system of a dedicated radio frequency with airfields listening out for calls in order to guide the aircraft in trouble. Jack Bromfield recounted one such event he overheard.

> "Coming up the North Sea my pilot called me and said: 'What can you make of this?' And a voice said, 'Hello Darkie, Hello Darkie' and it went on, and the pilot asked me, 'Where is he?' I said, 'Well he's close', 'Why isn't he picking up somewhere in England?' I figured he was too far out, and on the 1196 (*the dedicated Darkie radio*) he wouldn't reach the coast, so he was east of us. He kept repeating, 'Hello Darkie, Hello Darkie', on and on and on, nobody answered. My pilot said, 'Get him on the big radio', and I said: 'You'll get me sacked using that thing on that frequency, it'll just blow everybody else off the air.' But he kept on, 'Hello Darkie, Hello Darkie; where are you, you little black bastard!' The skipper said, 'You heard him didn't you?' 'No, I never heard a word.'"

Some crews were more fortunate than most and either had a comparatively uneventful tour, or started flying very late in the war, so were unable to fly their allotted thirty. Flying Officer Bob O'Dell was one such; a Halifax flight engineer with 408 (Goose) Squadron.

> "I joined 408 (Goose) Squadron at Linton-on-Ouse in the autumn of '44, but I didn't complete my tour, because the war finished, I did thirteen. The first one was Bremen, the last one was Heligoland, that was a daylight. We bombed the airfield, and the Lancs bombed the submarine pens. Nothing much happened really. We were fortunate I suppose, had a very good crew, and an extremely good skipper...he'd got two-

Flight Lieutenant Jim Lord and his 550 Squadron Lancaster crew at North Killingholme, Lincolnshire on completion of their thirty operations. Jim is in the cockpit and wireless operator Flying Officer John Elliott is in the centre of the group. The aircraft is ED562 BQ-G 'We Dood It'. *Elliott*

and-a-half-thousand hours instructing in Canada, so he was a very good pilot; very solid, and very quiet. The rest of the bods were a good bunch as well.

"I was one of the few people who flew Hally 7s. A super aircraft, they really were; the engines were. When they fired up a Merlin it sounded like Heinz 57 beans, bloody awful things. But ours used to waffle, ooh a lovely sound they were. They were reliable, a lot of people had experiences with one or two pots knocked out, and they still kept going."

Jim Lord (JL) and John Elliott (JE), who having already described some of their training days, continued the story of their tour on 550 Squadron at North Killingholme.

JE – "We were very lucky, we had a good tour of operations; we did thirty-one. The one that stands out in our memory is the thirteenth op, on

Wednesday 13 July '44. We were coming back from Revigny, and it had been a particularly nasty one. Coming back across the Channel everything was clamped down with fog.

JL – "We lost an engine over the Channel, obviously it had been hit by flak and I came in, saw Beachy Head, it was a beautifully clear morning. We flew up England and about halfway up we got a call to divert to Norfolk. By the time we got to Norfolk, missing the odd church steeple by a hair's breadth, we decided we couldn't land because it had already clamped down there. We just flew around until we ran out of fuel. We jumped out and came down two miles from Needham Market.

JE – "Jim says he's never seen six greener faces go past him. We all went in a fairly orderly fashion. Our navigator was told never, if possible, bale out on a full bladder. So Bob had a can, he did the necessary and stood the can very carefully on the navigator's table so it shouldn't spill. Five minutes later the aircraft *(Lancaster III ED562)* was in little pieces on the ground; so that was how we became members of the 'Caterpillar Club'.

"We were pretty lucky, we got shot at now and again. We did one or two daylight raids. The bomb aimer used to say to me, 'we don't want daylights, just nights'. We saw one or two night fighters. My job was to watch the 'Monica' screen, on the wireless operator's cathode tubes. Often they would come from behind, and I was on the first course of radio operators, to become wireless operators air, because we had this Monica.

JL – "He saw coming on the radar screen, something that was faster than someone who was keeping pace with us. We knew it might be a fighter. My story is that he used to wake me up and tell me.

JE – "One of the first daylights we did over Paris, I was standing up in the astrodome having a look around. I looked above, there was a Halifax just above us, and their bombs came down, and of course that happened all the time. Scary.

"We flew in the famous Lancaster, *(Phantom of the Ruhr)* twice. Once on a fighter-affiliation exercise against a captured Ju 88. It had landed intact in England (this is the aircraft now in the RAF museum at Hendon). As soon as I switched on my Monica set, the Ju 88 knew where we were, so we had to switch it off again."

Inevitably, for many crewmen, an operation came to an abrupt end when they had to abandon their aircraft. Flight Engineer Warrant Officer Les Giddings:

"They posted me to 102 Squadron Pocklington in September '43; and the first operation was Kassel. When I went on ops first time I had twen-

550 Squadron Lancaster EE139 BQ-B 'Phantom of the Ruhr'. *Elliott*

ty-six flying hours under my belt. I think I did seven ops and was shot down on the eighth; that was February 19/20, and at that time, that was the heaviest loss of the war."

This raid was on Leipzig with 823 aircraft; 561 Lancasters, 255 Halifaxes and seven Mosquitos. A total of seventy-eight aircraft were lost (forty-four Lancasters and thirty-four Halifaxes), 9.5% of the force. The Halifax loss rate was 13.3% of those dispatched and 14.9% of those Halifaxes which reached the enemy coast after early returns had turned back. [8] Les continued:

"We thought it was going to be easy, because we were making a direct approach to Berlin, and ahead of us were Mosquitoes. Then we were starting an attack on Berlin, and when we got near we turned starboard, we were going to attack Leipzig. But it all went wrong. A night fighter took out the port outer engine with Schräge Musik (see page 225), port inner, set the tanks on fire – thank Christ they still had fuel in, 'cause the shots come up from underneath – if they'd been empty... It was an emergency bale-out. I couldn't get the skipper's parachute clipped on him, 'cause he had the stick so hard pulled back. He let go and I tried to clip it on, the aircraft went uncontrollable. He ordered me to bale out, and he knew he wasn't going to be able to get out. So

107

I went out the entrance door.

"The mid-upper gunner was married to a WAAF...she got hold of me one night and said, 'You help him out if anything goes wrong', and I said I would. But as I ran past his turret, he was out of it and I said, 'For Christ's sake come on Taffy'. The whole port wing was a sheet of flame – I didn't see him again. As I opened up the door, the rear gunner was out of his turret and plugged in at the door, on the intercom. I pulled his hat back and said: 'For God's sake you can see the flames!' They were past his turret by that time, and whether he got out or not, I don't know. I know where they're all buried. My skipper was twenty-one on 17 February, but he was dead on the 19th.

"I don't know whether I went unconscious because we must have been at 19,000 feet. I thought I ought to have been able to see the enemy 'plane, but I couldn't. The outlay of the Halifax heating system meant that the pilot, the flight engineer, and the wireless operator (who was sitting beneath the pilot), got all the heat. So we didn't need to wear flying suits. First thing I noticed was how quiet it was without the roar of the engines. As I didn't have a flying suit on, I could get my hand inside my top pocket, so I got my fags out, and had a cigarette on the way down. It must have been minus 25-30 and we didn't go as high as we could either. When it got down to the stub, I thought if I throw it away it'll go up and set fire to the parachute, so I managed to drag one foot out and sort of stub it out on it."

Bomber operations could be every bit as tough on the ground crew, who frequently saw their charges – both aircraft and the crew they had got to know – fly away on an operation and not return. Flight rigger Norman Didwell remembered his time on 99 Squadron. He later served at various Middle East staging posts, and with Transport Command during the Berlin Airlift.

"Old 'Ging', during his rest period at Waterbeach, had the job of collecting aircrews' kit that had been shot down or went missing. He saw a pair of flying boots on a dispersal one day, and picked them up. He took them round to his little store, 'cause sometimes a bloke would lose things and give you a couple of bob, 'Got some spare?'

"Two or three days later, Ginger was cycling round the peri-track, and he saw the CO's car coming towards him, Wing Commander Dixon-Wright (*DFC*) pulled up and said, 'Sergeant Ware, I've lost a pair of flying boots'. 'Oh have you Sir?' He said, 'Have you got any spare ones in that little store of yours?' 'I might be able to find you some sir.' 'Bring them to my office.' Ginger promptly arrives with them, 'Oh yes, they look all right, how much do you want Ginger?' He said: 'Before you pay me sir, you'd better look inside!'

"I worked on one of Percy Pickard's aircraft. He came from 214 Squadron to Newmarket. On 14 December 1939, they had to do a reconnaissance of a German fleet reported steaming off Heligoland

Right. A lovely morning, frosty but beautiful sunshine – they took off at about eleven o'clock, we watched them...all twelve of them. We heard no more until about half past three, it was starting to get dark. One of the wireless ops on duty said, 'We've had some signals from returning aircraft; they haven't half had a bloody pasting.' The first one came then another one, then another one – five – then another one. I watched this one coming round, he'd got his navigation lights on, and all of a sudden he went over on the port side and down.

"Wing Commander 'Square' McKee, who'd served on the squadron before the war, was at group headquarters, but he came and did one or two ops on the squadron, and he was on this, in fact he flew the leading aircraft. He came along with this little Ford van and asked: 'Airman, where did that aircraft go down?' 'Right jump in', he said, 'and point where it is, we'll drive'. It had crashed the other side of Devil's Dyke. By this time, the fire tender and the blood wagon had got there, and he said, 'Go and find out', and I went up over the top and oh, that was a mess. We could hear somebody groaning inside and that was Sergeant Parton, the observer. Fight Lieutenant Hetherington was the crew. (*The Wellington was N2957, and it had been badly damaged by an Me 110. The squadron lost a total of six aircraft that day, and all crews were killed in the other five.*)

"Sergeant L W Parton WOp/AG was very badly injured...there was a bit of geodetic stuck into him, in his shoulder. We got in the aircraft, one or two of us, and got him out. The stern frame had broken in half, and AC2 Lofty Craig was still in his turret, he'd been wounded. We got him out, with a stepladder, and they carted them off in the blood wagon. Lofty came back to the squadron after he'd recuperated from the wound. He was eventually killed on his second tour. We lost thirty-three aircrew that day. I believe Air Vice-Marshal Baldwin in his report, said it was like the 'Charge of the Light Brigade', because it was daylight. There was only one aircraft of the five that actually got back that had no battle damage.

"There were some great officers there. Ian Cross came to the squadron as a flying officer, finished up as a squadron leader; Jack Grisman was ex-Halton apprentice, and came to the squadron after we'd been at Newmarket a while, as a sergeant observer. He got his commission, and there was Kirby-Green, and all these three were taken POWs. Those three were among the fifty officers shot (*after the Great Escape*). Kirby-Green had a son, and he was eight-years-old when he was told by his headmaster that his father had been shot by the Gestapo. Tom Kirby-Green was my flight commander. One day he came into the line tent and said, 'Anything going on Didwell?' 'No Sir'. 'Might as well go and get some tea then.' When we came back we could hear an almighty din; he was a great banjo player.

Squadron Leader T G Kirby-Green was shot down on 16 October 1941 during an operation on Duisburg, in Wellington Z8862 of 40 Squadron. Pilot Officer

W J Grisman was shot down on 5 November during a special duties operation in Wellington T2565 of 109 Squadron. Squadron Leader I K P Cross DFC was shot down on 12 February 1942 during an attack on warships in Wellington Z8714 of 103 Squadron. All three later took part in the Great Escape, and were murdered by the Gestapo.

HALIFAX OR LANCASTER?

Airmen were fiercely loyal to the aircraft type they flew on operations, none more so than those who crewed the Halifax or Lancaster. Joe Petrie-Andrews flew both types to complete his seventy operations.

"I was very fond of the Halifax because it was an extremely well built aeroplane as opposed to the Lanc, which, although it was a good aeroplane, after all was only a twin-engine Manchester; when they put four engines on it did very well, but you always felt so very secure in a Halifax. We hadn't got the great depth of bomb bay needed to carry 22,000 pounders, but our bomb load was quite substantial. The weight of the aircraft unloaded was 30,000 to 40,000 pounds heavier than the Lanc, which made a difference, but I did like the Halifax."

Jack Bromfield was a Halifax man through and through.

"When people look at the bomb bay in the Lanc, this cavernous hole underneath, and then look at the Halifax they say it's shorter. But what they don't realise is that in the wings, inside the two inner engines, you could have four or five 500 pounders.

"I got inside a Lancaster and felt that I wouldn't want to be in it for very long; getting over the main spar was like getting through a cat flap, if you could imagine getting through with all your kit on. In a Hally it was so easy, the forward end was double-decked, and the driver sits up top and the WOp sat underneath him. The escape hatch for the bomb aimer, WOp and nav was underneath the WOp's feet. All you had to do was kick the over-centre spring back and out goes the hatch. The engineer could go out the rear door, which didn't have a step over it, because it was part of the fuselage. Once lifted up you could get out so that you didn't clobber your head. The only bale out problem that I thought of my rear gunner sussed. He said: 'If it goes pear-shaped I've got to get out of the turret, climb over the elevator bar, grab my 'chute and get to the door; I'm not gonna make it.' He got himself a fighter pilot's 'chute and sat on it, and when we were downed, he turned the turret round 90 degrees and fell out backwards. I found the Halifax to be a very well-built aircraft."

USAAF DAY BOMBING

While RAF Bomber Command pounded German targets mostly by night, the B-17s and B-24s of the USAAF's 8th Air Force kept up the attack in daylight. Flying Fortress pilot Norm Rosholt did not quite complete his full tour as he was shot down and taken prisoner on his thirty-first mission out of an expected thirty-five.

"Our missions started with a wake up call at 03:30 with breakfast at 04:00; to briefing at 05:00 and dressing at 06:00. The clothes consisted of long johns, an electric suit, shirt and trousers, sheep skin trousers and jacket, flak jacket, Mae West, parachute harness, helmet, goggles and heavy boots. With an oxygen mask there was no skin exposed as the temperature was 20 to 30 below zero, and one day it was 50 below.

"At the beginning of the bomb run, the bombardier took over the steering of the 'plane and the pilots maintained speed of 150 miles an hour and maintained altitude. The bomb run lasted for thirty minutes and we were at the mercy of anti-aircraft guns. The Germans would build a cube of exploding shells in front of us. So for thirty minutes we would see a black square and we knew that the black was powder and the sky was full of shrapnel.

"We went to Berlin half dozen times to destroy the rail yards. We went to Hamburg to bomb the submarine pens. On one mission to Hamburg the German fighters drew our fighter escorts away from us and then we were hit by fighters from the front and they shot down our lower squadron of thirteen planes – that was 117 guys. We hit Merseburg and Magdeburg a few times; the oil storage tanks. All our gunners claimed fighters, but with thirty-eight 'planes firing, no-one received credit for any of them. We mostly encountered the Me 109, and some jets.

"On my final mission, to bomb a jet fighter base, our 'plane got four direct hits; number one engine, number four engine, the waist and the lower turret. The waist gunner and the lower turret operator were killed. I had the two inside engines to steer the 'plane and they were running at half speed. At 5,000 feet I told the crew to bale out. Six of us were captured and the co-pilot evaded capture. On the first night our guards marched us twenty-two hours straight till we got to a jail on an airfield. Little did I know I wouldn't receive any food until I got to prison camp."

Captain Sam Halpert was a B-17 navigator with the 324th Bomb Squadron, 91st Bomb Group, based at Bassingbourn in Cambridgeshire. He flew a full tour of operations in 1944-45, ending with an especially traumatic final mission.

"I am a life member of the 'Lucky Bastards Club', an exclusive club, no rules, no officers, no meetings. Open only to those who have paid their dues by completing a tour with the 8th. After returning from a particularly rough mission, one of the gunners on our crew muttered, 'You know, you just can't beat a real good war'. That attempt at gallows humour, and his way of dealing with the horror of the situation, remained with me.

"It is still difficult to think of Merseburg without recalling the feelings of alarm and dread it held for crew. Deep in the heart of central Germany, lay the site of Leuna, the world's largest synthetic oil refinery, and by mid 1944, it was the primary producer of oil for the Third Reich. Merseburg became Hitler's most fortified stronghold, encircled with hundreds of flak battery emplacements and numerous Luftwaffe squadrons. In November '44, the 8th sent 421 B-17s to Merseburg led by our group, the 91st. The weather was bad from the start, and by the time we were over Germany we found it close to impossible to maintain formation inside massive clouds reaching higher than our altitude at 25,000 feet. Our squadron commander, Major Immanuel Klette decided to lead the groups in a descent, seeking to find a break in the clouds. When we finally broke through at 17,000 feet, we discovered that more than half of the groups had left to seek secondary targets, targets of opportunity, or returned to their bases. Merseburg at 25,000 feet was perilous enough, 17,000 feet was madness.

"Nevertheless, our group bombed from 17,000 feet and miraculously lost only one ship of our thirty-six aircraft to flak. We discovered at interrogation that the group behind us, the 398th, decided not to follow us, but to climb above the cloud cover. When they broke out at 31,000 feet, over fifty Fw 190s jumped them from out of the sun and destroyed five of them. We lost two aircraft from our twelve-ship squadron. (About 500 Luftwaffe fighters attacked the bomber formations that day, with thirty-four aircraft being lost, three from Bassingbourn.)

"We were amazed to learn about the ship we lost, last seen on the return home with two engines out and the third about to blow any minute. The pilot put the ship on auto-pilot before the crew baled out over enemy territory. The crew was captured and spent the rest of the war in a German prison camp. The empty ship flew on without any of the crew on board and landed on its own in a snow-covered pasture in Belgium where it was discovered by two bewildered British soldiers.

"Our regular B-17 was 'Mah Ideel'; there was a popular song in the US at the time, 'My Ideal'. The southern accent made it come out as Mah Ideel, and we were all trained in the south. The ship had completed forty-five missions and at the time we all stood in front of it for a crew photograph. Aircraft were not allocated to the same crew. Aircraft could fly every day, crews could not; HQ wanted to make the most use of the airplanes. If that 'plane was available, and not in the hangar for

Navigator Captain Sam Halpert (end front row on the right) and his
crew with their B-17 'Mah Ideel' from the 324th Bomb Squadron, 91st
Bomb Group, Bassingbourn, Cambridgeshire in December 1944. His pilot
Welden Brubaker is at the other end of the same row. Sam completed his
thirty-five-mission tour in February 1945. *Halpert*

repairs or on some other maintenance, then if you wanted it, you had it;
they knew the preference of the crews.

"In case somebody was unavailable to go, through sickness or whatever reason, they'd break-up the crew. Crews could be split in half; there
was not much choice in the matter. They'd post an alert list the night
before, to see what crew you were with. I flew maybe twenty missions
with my own crew; Welden Brubaker was the best pilot in the whole
damn 8th Air Force, and we were all aware of the many times that only
his skill and judgment saved our collective ass. Henry Jensen, the bombardier, was my room-mate through the whole thirty-five missions, and
his friendship pulled me through many a dark day.

"On February 3, 1945 we were on our way to Berlin, my thirty-fifth mission. Earl Sheen was the bombardier and I the navigator on the number two ship, alongside the squadron lead ship leading the entire wing that day. All went well until over target at bombs away. A burst of flak demolished the lead ship, breaking it in half at the waist. Then we lost the number three ship. We were the only ship left in the lead element. I didn't know that the hose between my mask and the oxygen regulator had been punctured by flak. When I failed to reply to a call from the pilot, Sheen turned around and saw me slumped on the floor. Thirty seconds without oxygen at our altitude and you are gone. I'll never know how long I was out, but he managed to revive me by hooking me up to one of those walk around oxygen bottles.

"It had been a rough mission. I didn't feel too much like celebrating the completion of my tour that night. We all had been close to the guys who had gone down that day, and the base was as quiet as a church on Tuesday. The next afternoon, I left Bassingbourn. I didn't have to leave the next day; they told me I could take my time. But I was very disturbed by the events on my last mission; good friends went down in those two ships. I couldn't even feel good about finishing my tour, I just wanted to go home.

"I was told to report to Stoke, there was a depot for crews going home and awaiting transportation. I changed trains at Crewe, and I stayed drunk and happy in Crewe for a week. We had to take the ship back home. Not like when we came out, we flew, but they needed the aircraft in Europe, of course the war was still on. I came out of the air force in September '45. They asked me if I wanted to stay, but I'd had enough."

As the scale of the daylight operations continued to build, the Luftwaffe was forced to include night fighters in efforts against the huge American formations, as Heinz Rökker recalled.

"In Parchim we had the order to fly in daylight against the Americans over the North Sea. They had to fly daylight, and they suffered many losses but were overall successful in their daylight bombing offensive. When we were in Kassel we would fly against American bombers because they had no day fighter cover at that time. I once heard the order to fly that day, but the attack was already finished by the time I got there, so I flew back. But others in my group started earlier so they had losses, as it was not possible with our big Ju 88 to attack the Fortress. Later our gruppe kommander stated he couldn't fly at that time because his observer was ill, and he got my regular observer as a replacement. So they flew together but were shot down; of the crew, only my observer survived. The kommander died, not far away from his house. That was Hauptmann Schulz, Arnie we called him. He was a very good man." (*Hauptmann Albert Schulz was lost on 30 January 1944 when his Ju 88 was hit by return fire from a B-17, one of four air-*

craft lost by his unit. The Luftwaffe claimed five aircraft shot down but lost thirty of their own number.)

RAF pilot Michael Wainwright had a brief but memorable experience of the B-26 Marauder, a type used with considerable success by the USAAF for light bombing missions, but one which was not without its handling issues.

> "I was offered a ride in a Marauder by an American pilot. He told me that on take-off it had to adopt a flying-boat attitude to lift off. We headed off down the runway, and it seemed to adopt the flying-boat attitude, but it wouldn't lift off. We were rapidly running out of runway, and at the end was a South Pacific steam locomotive. The pilot was bouncing the aircraft on its nosewheel, and eventually it got off the ground, the 'plane was shuddering like mad, and just about cleared the locomotive. He said to me: 'You know something? I wish we were watching this!'

Warrant Officer Frank White was a Marauder gunner seconded to 25 Squadron South African Air Force. Initially operational on Venturas, the squadron re-equipped with Marauders at Biferno in Italy.

> "The Marauder was quite fast and had a high take-off and landing speed. It had a bomb load of 4,000 pounds and we sometimes returned and landed with them still on board if we were unable to carry out the raid due to cloud cover over the target or engine problems."

LUFTWAFFE OPERATIONS AGAINST ENGLAND

Although large-scale Luftwaffe bombing operations against Britain reached their peak during the winter 1940/41 Blitz, they nevertheless continued to send attacking forces throughout almost the entire war. Heinz Rökker was involved in smaller attacks on a number of occasions.

> "A bomber group had orders to bomb over England (*24 October 1942*), I think it was Lincoln, and we started with two crews. We had to fly to another airfield where the bomber squadron was, Gilze-Rijen, for bombs. The first time I was caught in searchlight, they got me, but there was no flak. It was not good to be in the light, I had never experienced that before. I tried to get out, I dived very fast and two or three times they got me, but they always lost me. Nobody had said what we had to do if we were caught. We were bombing at 1,500 metres, which was not very high; so you could see all the lights on the airfield."

Bob Clarke witnessed and documented many raids while working at Elstree aerodrome.

"Another raid at 04:30, coming over low overhead and getting heavily plastered with ack-ack. Showers of shrapnel falling down on the field, and large lumps banging on the fire station roof. Apparently 178 people suffocated in a London shelter.

"Sirens at 01:00, heavy continuous gunfire, distinctly hear the aircraft milling around overhead. The main railway line is blocked, and several fires still burning. West London all lit up, looks fantastic with blood-red blotches in the sky as flares drift down through the clouds. London had a bad time last night. Found strips of foil all over the field that had been thrown out by raiders to confuse our radar."

Attacks against RAF and USAAF airfields by small groups or lone raiders were frequent. Norman Didwell was on the receiving end of one such attack at Rowley Mile, Newmarket.

"One afternoon, during the Battle of Britain, Fred Caldecotte and I were filling up the bowser, and all of a sudden...'That's funny, that sounds like it ain't one of our kites in the circuit.' There was low cloud, all of a sudden this bloody kite came out of the cloud, and it was an 'einkel. It started bloomin' red flashes from its front gunners. I dived in to where the turnstiles were in the old grandstand. Where do you think Fred went? Under the petrol bowser!

"They came over and we got a stick of bombs that afternoon. He came across and dropped them between the two race courses, but he dropped them a bit too early, or else he'd have bombed a line of kites at A Flight dispersal. There was one kite on which they were doing an engine change, and the last bomb hit the corner of the grandstand, and bounced over this aircraft – with blokes working on it – and it hit some stables and thankfully never went off.

"I was on the flare path one night. We'd got a new crew doing circuits and bumps, and I could see little shoots of red coming down towards the Chance Light, and all of a sudden it went out. A bloke came running down: 'Douse the flares, douse the flares!' He had dropped his bombs in an open field."

SPECIAL OPERATIONS

In addition to the regular bombing operations by Bomber Command's Main Force, there were many specialised operations, both one-offs (such as the dams raid) and longer-term support such as that provided by 100 Group for jamming enemy radar.

THE DAMS RAID
While 617 Squadron's epic attack on the Ruhr dams in May 1943 is well docu-

mented, it followed a period of intense training in low-level flying over England, which on occasion provided practice targets for fighter pilots who happened to come across the Lancasters, as Michael Wainwright recalled.

"I went to do my fighter leader course at Sutton Bridge when 617 were getting ready to do the dams raid so they were flying low round the place, and in our Masters we used them for practising our various attacks. We used to try and get them to fly higher if they could so we could do a C3 attack. A C3 attack was very interesting because you attacked your target aircraft from underneath. You came along fast and then you went up on your back and you were shooting ahead of him and hopefully, you'd knock him out of business."

HIGHBALL

Formed at RAF Skitten on 1 April 1943, 618 Squadron, equipped with the Mosquito, had one primary role – Operation Servant, to sink the battleship *Tirpitz* in its lair in Alten Fjord. To do so, the aircraft was to carry a weapon known as Highball, which was essentially a scaled-down version of the Upkeep weapon to be used by 617 Squadron against the Ruhr dams in planned concurrent raids, which in the end did not take place due to serious doubts about the survivability of the Highball operation.

Flight Lieutenant Doug Turner, who at the time was flying Beaufighters, was one of the airmen suddenly selected to join a newly-forming squadron, all the crews being hand-picked and asked to volunteer, with a choice to opt out if they wished.

"Wing Commander Hutchinson was a fantastic bloke, anybody would follow him. I came out of a Beaufighter at Leuchars with my navigator, we'd been off Norway doing a recco, and the lad came up the ladder outside and said: 'They want to see you right away in the Command quarters.' I thought: 'Oh God, what the hell have we done wrong?' Went in and there was the CO, and all the flying people were there. We were told that nobody would think any the less of you if you didn't want to join, just return to your squadron, and nobody would ever mention anything. 618 was the special squadron. We used to move everywhere and nobody would know us.

"Highball was a bouncing bomb. There were years when we couldn't even mention it, because it was so secret. We had special armour plating, and just the four machine guns. We had to sort of semi prove it; we went off to the lochs in Scotland to practise because getting at the *Tirpitz* you had to get down to a certain height and a certain speed, to drop the bomb. The boss invented some gadget that, as soon as you looked into the lens, you could put it between the points.

"This lake we found in Scotland, (*Loch Striven off the Firth of Clyde*) was north of Glasgow, and they had an old French ship to use as a target. I was one of the ones who did the tests, with a Mossie. She was very snappy, a lovely machine. But we were using Bomber Command ones at first, and we were getting the newer ones in all the time. They were doing the dams at the same time, and wanted to co-ordinate these two things. They didn't know if they would do a fantastic amount of good, but it was more to show Jerry that we'd still got a lot of guts in us.

"It was a case of practice low flying, practice all sorts of things for safe living. We went right the way up the Caledonian Canal, we used to go there and do our exercises. There was one Canadian, he was a hell of a nice bloke; but sometimes he was a swine! He led three of us, I was on the right, and he was doing a low level cross-country flight. He came towards these blinkin' mountains, he put his nose up and kept going. The speed was going down and I could see I wouldn't have enough to get over. I had to break off, and this chap said: 'Ha, ha, ha, got you!' All the controls were sloppy. I had to peel off, but very gently, the controls were absolutely rubbish; we were right on the edge of the stall.

"I thought, 'I'll never get through this'. The sinking of the *Tirpitz*, there was no return; 600 miles was too far to come back, as she was in Norway. If we did it, that was it. The battleship was underneath the overhanging rock, so you had to get in, get the ship, then you had to get out again. The bomber boys did a hell of a job getting in on the Möhne dams. We were waiting for Bomber Command to say they'd done those dams, then we were doing the *Tirpitz*, but it was called off. They were realising that aircraft coming in low at a certain height, were just pea-shooting. Poor old Barnes Wallis, he was absolutely stuck because it was chewing his idea in half, in the sense of putting Bomber Command on the dams, and ours on the *Tirpitz* at the same time."

100 GROUP

Formed in November 1943 for special duties, 100 Group specialised in night fighter intruder operations, electronic warfare and countermeasures, and was mainly based in East Anglia flying a wide variety of aircraft including the Wellington, Mosquito, Liberator and Fortress. One such unit was Wellington-equipped 192 Squadron based at Foulsham, and pilot Flying Officer Alan 'Tommy' Thomsett, who had enlisted in 1942, flew forty-and-a-half operations. He later instructed and carried out trials work, also on Wellingtons, and worked for the British Aircraft Corporation at Filton post-war.

"The main job was to locate the beams coming out of Holland and France in particular, track them and ring up Radlett (*80 Group*) and say: 'There's one.' How much of a use that really worked out to be I don't know but it was quite tricky actually locating them. The other part of the job which I only did once, was to come in with the German bomber stream and check the efficiency of the ground jamming. We tracked them in from our base at Ford, and then just rushed into the skies at an enormous rate of knots in a Wellington to clamber up there and then follow the beam. It was unreadable at Croydon but of course from Croydon you could see London so it would only require one incendiary or one flare and then they had the target illuminated. We were behind the German bomber stream I imagine, 'cause I'd no way of knowing. All you would get was a telephone call saying there's a radar image of a gang approaching from France and you get up there quickly with an approximate location and just drag the thing up into the sky until you hit the beam.

"Our regular ops were all coastal. We covered the coast from half way up Norway, down Denmark, Germany, Holland, Belgium and France right round to about almost seventy miles north of St. Sebastian in Spain. We did quite a bit of western approaches but of course it's almost cloak and dagger to a large extent. The briefing we got was minimal for obvious reasons, and the special operators were given a minimum briefing as well but obviously told more than anybody else. They were told to search a certain frequency band and note everything that happened and they had a wire recorder so they could record the signals. The only time the pilot came into it (apart from having to put the thing in the right place) was using a switch so he could bring a signal through to me at the front and if he was picking up a beam...he might switch me through and then I could follow it.

"The trip we loathed was down...in sight of the St. Sebastian lighthouse because there we were at about 2,000 feet and the understanding was that we were looking for the V-3 (*the long-range gun*) which was under trial there. I don't think it was anything to do with it in point of fact; it seems to have been homing beacons for U-boats coming into St. Nazaire or wherever. Then we got much mixed up with the V-2, because the Air Ministry wanted to prove that the V-2 was or was not radio controlled in any way, and the only way we could do that was to go and sit off the Frisian Islands and when something went up, see if it produced any signal; of course it never did. We did that by sitting out there for six hours at a time going up and down, and we kept that going for twenty-four hours, day and night.

"With the V-1s we were asked to plot them if we saw them coming over but this was really rather absurd because you couldn't plot with any accuracy when you saw a flame going across underneath you. I think it really was nothing to do with the V-1 at all, it was just a general search and if we saw something like a V-1 coming over, to say so. I don't think it was anything of significance, it was so grossly inaccurate.

"The astonishing thing was only once knowingly, did the German air force come and show any interest in us. A lot of the time we were the only aircraft out in Bomber Command, so we were a rather sitting target if anybody could be bothered to put us into the North Sea. I've no idea why they left us alone; everybody knew we were there! Somewhere off the Dutch coast there was a white light flying in formation with us; that was a Ju 88, you could see it silhouetted and we knew it was a German night fighter because we knew what their colours of the day were of course; they knew ours, so it was a game of cat and mouse immediately. He stayed with us and paid no attention whatsoever and after a moment or two, I decided it was about time we went somewhere else but he never followed. Sometime later a signal came round all Bomber Command stations to say: 'Be careful! Keep your eyes open. Don't talk.' They reported an incident when an aircraft was identified and it quoted the registration letters of the aircraft and it was said to be believed to be based at Foulsham, with 192 Squadron; this was a German signal! It was probably that night; funny game.

"In some cases particularly on the V-1 and down the English Channel and that sort of stuff, they were classed as half ops, and we had to do forty to complete a tour. Forty-and-a-half! I'm still waiting to come home from the last one!"

Flying Officer Andrew Barron was a Liberator navigator with 223 Squadron at Oulton. He completed a full tour and subsequently moved onto to 196 (Stirling) Squadron at Shepherd's Grove. His description of the 100 Group operations again shows how vulnerable they were away from the mutual protection of Main Force.

"I was the second navigator and really I was redundant. So they said, 'Well, you can fly as front gunner and spare navigator if you like', so we started off on the 'Big Ben' patrols; flying up and down the Dutch coast looking for V-2s because at that time, they thought they were radio controlled and the idea was that the special operators would jam this equipment, but the only useful service was broadcasting the fact that one had taken off.

"The bulk of our ops were 'Window' diversionary sorties which were designed to confuse the Germans as to which was the main target. The Window force would have been about a couple of dozen aircraft flying parallel tracks and spaced out and they were throwing out bundles of Window and it would simulate a force ten or fifteen times the size of what it actually was. The main force was always on a circuitous route. This was one of the lessons they learnt from the fiascos like Nuremberg. The force would fly perhaps ostensibly towards Cologne then it would dart off either to the north or the south of the Ruhr, perhaps towards Frankfurt and then added to that were perhaps a couple of Window forces.

"When we flew with the bomber stream as the jamming cover en route and over the target, (when we got to the target, we would have to orbit for anything up to about ten or twelve minutes) we were normally 2 or 3,000 feet above the bomber stream, which itself was at various

Navigator Flying Officer Andrew Barron in front of his 223 Squadron Liberator at Oulton, Norfolk in 1944-45. The unit was part of 100 Group which often meant flying operations as single aircraft away from the main bomber stream to confuse enemy defences. *Barron*

staggered heights depending mainly on the performance of the aircraft. The poor old bloody Stirlings were always down the bottom, then the Halifaxes and then the Lancasters.

"We had two special operators, and where their equipment was situated actually varied from aeroplane to aeroplane...I think the whole installation was a bit ad-hoc. The RAF kept on producing different jammers and putting them into the aircraft and I think on occasions, we thought, 'well, where have we got a space to put this?' In our particular aircraft, they were above the bomb bay. Others were actually in the bomb bay itself, and others were up on the flight deck where the wireless operator and his equipment were. I'm sure it was a case of, bunged in wherever they could find room for it.

"I logged a report of an aircraft that seemed to be being attacked, and about twenty minutes later we passed over burning wreckage – it was the wreckage of Ayres' aircraft. (*Flt Sgt N S Ayres and crew were shot down in Liberator VI TS526 6G-T of 223 Squadron, by Oblt Johannes Hager of 6./NJG1*) So obviously, we knew a night fighter was in the vicinity.

"We were homing back to Oulton and a Lancaster with its wheels down went over the top of us – close enough for me to hear its engines. Then on the night of 'Gisela' we got to the circuit just as a Fortress was being shot down. I only learned recently when I was talking to my old co-pilot in Canada that they had seen a night fighter. Presumably, he hadn't seen us or if he had, he was on the tail of the B-17 so he ignored us. As far as I was concerned, I just got the order: 'Course for Brawdy'. I was always rather envious of the fact that the B-17s had H2S radar but of course at the time, I didn't know that the night fighters could home onto it. The Forts had one or two other things; they had ABC (Airborne Cigar) which was the German speaking operators. I think we did as well but I'm not sure; we weren't told, we didn't ask, and that was it. They were special operators and they did their job."

ON THE RECEIVING END

The joint Bomber Command and USAAF raids on Dresden in February 1945 which resulted in the notorious fire-storm remain a controversial subject to this day. Luftwaffe pilot Norbert Hannig's wife Gisele was in the city when the raid occurred and recounted a sobering view of the campaign from the civilians' perspective.

"I was in Dresden that time; it was a wonderful town and a nice evening. I went over the bridge and it was about eight o'clock. I had no shoes. (I came from East Prussia to Silesia and I had to walk two days in the snow and wet. I couldn't walk any more, and I couldn't put on my shoes.) And then: 'woooo'. (*Air raid siren.*)

"I had to hide in a cellar, there were lots of noises…'woomf' (*bomb explosions*). I was there for one hour, and everybody prayed – 'help us'; there were only wives and children and some old soldiers from the barracks. Eventually I went to see what had happened outside. Everything was burning, and there came a storm from the town, it was terrible. There were burning trees in the air. I had only a jacket from Norbert. In all the cellars there were huge puddles of water, so I put the jacket in the water then over myself and ran out. Just outside the tiles fell from the roof, on my head. Then I saw a car, everybody wanted to drive away from this town. I saw my reflection, it was white, I looked like I was wearing a wedding veil, with all this ash in my hair.

"I ran and jumped on a truck and held on with my hands stretched over my head; I held on for ten minutes. Then I saw the wall of the cemetery; the wall was 2 metres high and the town was burning. I lay down with a towel over me. When I woke, I thought it must be morning, but it was dark, about eight o'clock I think. I walked about 5 kilometres when I came across a very nice family. There were more than thirty people lying on her carpet, but she made coffee for everybody."

SHOT DOWN AND EVADING

Many were the bombers brought down over enemy territory, by the efforts of fighters, flak, or sadly, mid-air collisions or being struck by bombs from other aircraft. For those crew members who were able safely to abandon their stricken aircraft, the challenge was then to avoid capture and try to make a 'home run' back to England. Jack Bromfield and his crew fell victim to a night fighter on the run in to the target, but none avoided capture for long.

"We were attacked by a night fighter, which I found out from the rear gunner was a Ju 88, but other than that we didn't know a great deal except that there was a hell of a lot of bangs and thumps and crashes. Then the fire started…and there were bits flying off here, there and everywhere. I didn't know until some days afterwards that I'd been shot. The bullet hit my flying boot, on the outside of the foot, but my feet were so bloody cold I didn't feel it. The aircraft didn't do anything strange, it was just losing height. I looked past my curtain at the pilot, and he looked at me and pulled the control column backwards and forwards and I shouted, 'I've got no control', so he said, 'Right, time to go.' So I opened the hatch between me and the nav, and I gave the pilot his parachute, because it was stowed next to mine, and when we'd gone, he would jump. The mid-upper, the rear gunner and the engineer, would all go out of the rear door. So out we went.

"I went through two lots of cloud, and it was a white-out on the ground. I could see the target burning, and I could see flares going down, so I knew we weren't far, but the bombs were still on when we left her. I looked at two black lines, one was a bit shiny, and the other one was dull. I thought, 'the shiny one is the river, or canal or whatever; the other one is the road. I can't steer this bloody thing, and I'm going straight down into the river.' So I thought I had to turn the buckle and hit it, which I did, and I fell out of the harness, straight on my arse in the middle of the road; the shiny one was actually the road, it was like a sheet of glass. But I was grateful, because only about 20 or 30 yards away was a mucky old canal. If I'd gone in there, I'd have had no chance, especially if the brolly had sat down over the top of me.

"It was a very wooded area, so I buried all the gubbins, and I kept my Sidcot; although I didn't want to walk in it, I thought it would be good to lay on the ground to sleep on. Having seen the direction of the target, I knew which was west, so I just buggered off in a westerly direction, thinking I might bump into somebody, but I didn't see a soul. I didn't see another 'chute as I was coming down. We think one of the blokes didn't get out, however the mid-upper heard from a Yank that he was captured with, that the engineer was shot, trying to escape from a German hospital.

"I had eight days on the run, and I thought I was doing quite well. I walked at night, but I gave that up after two days because I got fed up of tripping over tree roots and falling down ditches in the dark. On about the third or fourth morning, I was walking just off a road in the woods, and I heard voices; I could understand what they were saying. I got towards the edge of the wood and looked down the road, and there were two blokes with shotguns and three blokes standing with their hands up. The latter were Americans, so I went deeper into the woods and just kept on walking.

"On the eighth day, I was following a single-line railway, it was going more or less westerly which suited me down to the ground. I saw something that looked like a potato field. I was getting bloody hungry by then. I was silly, I didn't think first, I was just hungry. I was scratching about, and I felt something in the middle of my back, and a voice said: 'Hande hock!' So I hande hocked, and I turned round, and there was this guy in a railway uniform. Just round the other side of the trees there was a small station, and I hadn't seen it. Then two guys from the Luftwaffe came in a clapped-out Beetle.

"I was taken to a night fighter station. I didn't know where it was, but there was a guy who brought me some porridge; the first real food I'd had, and I tried to make him understand: 'Where am I?' Then I wanted to go to the toilet, so I rattled on the door and the old boy came and took me to the toilet. When I was ready to come out he gave me a little piece of paper. When I got back in my cell I looked, and it said 'Diepholz', and that's where I was.

"I had about two or three days in there. One guy came in and he was obviously a pilot, and he gave me some cigarettes, and they brought me some bread and a sort of sausage sandwich. He did a bit of interro-gating, but he didn't get very far, so he cleared off. Then this little guy came, and I thought he was fighting everybody all by himself. He was about 4 feet 12 tall, and he had a Mauser rifle, a small Walter pistol, and a machine-carbine. He was Luftwaffe, and he'd got a big pack on his back, and he said 'Kommen ze mit'. They gave me a loaf, under one arm 'cause they'd handcuffed me then. I said, 'Geneva Convention', 'Oh we're not bothered about the Geneva Convention', was the worrying reply. I had some margarine under the other arm, and I was given a box of fish cheese. We went to the station, and then we went through Hannover, which was the target! The siren went, and I thought, 'Oh shite, that's all I need!' Here am I, in RAF uniform and Bomber Command comes when Bromfield's on Hannover station.

"This idiot, when the people, the civilians were around, asked who I was, he said 'Englisher flieger', and there was a siren going! So I lost my bread...but I was rescued by a guy. I couldn't speak German, but I got the gist of the message: 'It's your job to get him to Dulag at Frankfurt, sound in wind and limb so we can interrogate him. Not let these idiots have him.' So I was grateful to him. We caught the train to Dulag, and what a forbid-ding place that was! It was just grim huts and barbed wire; lots of Kriegies wandering about inside. They chucked you straight in a cell; there was nothing said. There was a knob inside, which, when you turned it, made a little signal arm come out which meant you wanted to go to the loo, and you would hear them push it back, that'd make you use the bucket.

"They turned the heat up 'til you cooked, then turned it down 'til you were freezing cold. Three o'clock in the morning was their favourite time. They had a sheet of paper that said 'Red Cross Geneva', and 'Red Cross' in German in the other corner, and it had number, rank, name, squadron, aircraft, all lots of other gubbins. I did the usual thing: put my number, rank and name down, and scrubbed out the rest, which made them a bit peevish. This just went on, and on. We weren't getting any sleep, and I thought, well I've got this far, they obviously know a lot more than they let you know, so why just compound it, keep playing them dumb.

"I was there for about eleven or twelve days. Then suddenly the doors opened, and everybody was ushered into a big room, and given a couple of slices of bread and a cup of black ersatz coffee. Then we were marched out and taken down to Betslaw, which was just south into Frankfurt itself, and then we were on the train to Luft 1."

Warrant Officer Gerry Marion was another member of Jack's crew.

"I was the mid-upper gunner and was taken prisoner after parachuting onto a highway. I was wounded with a broken leg caused by gunshot, roughed-up and taken to a guardhouse. The next morning I was taken by car, with two guards, on a two-hour drive to another guardhouse.

Here I spent two weeks in solitary, the only POW there. I left on 19 January with a German officer, and met another guard and a burnt American flyer and guard at Kassel. We spent two days on a train to Frankfurt, with lots of problems. We arrived at Frankfurt then went to the air force interrogation centre (sweat-box). Later that month I went to Hohemark hospital by truck, for medical treatment; my leg was in a bad shape. There were fifteen to twenty other POWs there."

Flight Engineer Warrant Officer John Torrans was posted to 582 Pathfinder Squadron at Little Staughton, Bedfordshire in April 1944, to start his second tour following his first tour with 103 Squadron.

"On the night of 7/8 August '44, on the way home from the target we were attacked by a night fighter as we approached the coast at Le Havre, our gunners had already spotted him and were passing evasive tactics to the captain. We were raked along the underneath of the aircraft by cannon fire, and our aircraft caught fire. The navigator, Squadron Leader Hill, made signs at me to abandon the aircraft as the fires were completely out of control. I descended feet first out of the hatch and on glancing upwards towards the aircraft, which was trailing flames from both wings, the fighter which was clearly illuminated, was still firing at it.

"I landed in a field not a mile away from where the aircraft had crashed and I could see the glow of the flames and hear the ammunition exploding. I discovered that I had a bullet wound in my right thigh, also that my battledress trousers were badly burnt and scorched. I managed to evade capture and met up with the navigator after a few days; he had a badly sprained ankle and severe leg burns. We were accommodated in a farmhouse outside Oudalle near St. Romain. We arrived back in England on 6 September. We were flown out from St. Romain by two Auster aircraft to Bayeux and then by tank landing craft to Newhaven."

The aircraft was Lancaster III N817/6O-S. Of the rest of the crew, pilot Sqn Ldr R Wareing, and plotter Flg Off R V King RAAF were both taken prisoner, while the remainder all perished in the crash. They were: bomb aimer W/O E J Hawker, WOp Flg Off R W Blaydon, mid-upper gunner Flt Sgt R G Campbell and rear gunner W/O W Gaughran.

Wing Commander Oliver Wells was a Lancaster pilot with 7 Squadron at Oakington. He was shot down on his seventh operation, but evaded for five months thanks to help from the Belgian Resistance before finally being caught shortly before crossing into France.

"I was moved to Brussels and was holed up in a flat for a couple of weeks over Christmas in '43/44 and then I was taken down to the station and handed over to a guide. We were taken to the station by a girl who was dressed as a school girl, she looked very young, she and another chap and I. Another bloke appeared from somewhere else, he was a sergeant pilot, and this young guide took us onto the train. The object of the exercise was to take the train to just before the French border, get off and then cross the border, going round the side as it were, and get on the train again to Paris.

"Just before the border, we were rounded up by some thugs in plain clothes who had followed the school girl. Instead of arresting the girl, they let her carry on with her trade, and followed us onto the train. So really we were caught red handed, and there was nothing much we could do. We were taken to a very nasty prison in Lille. I had a horrible month there with the Gestapo, being interrogated but not actually beaten up. You were only supposed to give your name, rank and number, but as this was five months after I'd been shot down I thought I may as well tell them who my crew were, as it couldn't do any harm. They must have checked through the records because shortly after that I was passed onto the Luftwaffe, going into another interrogation centre and then Stalag Luft III."

KRIEGIES

For the huge numbers of aircrew who had survived the loss of their aircraft, statistically it was most likely that their ultimate fate was to spend the remainder of the conflict as a prisoner of war. They called themselves 'Kriegies', from the German word Kriegsgefangener, meaning prisoner of war.

Gerry Marion took up his story again.

"Still in January, I had to endure a forced march and boxcar ride with fifteen POWs and five guards to Nürnberg POW camp, Stalag XIIIC, with approximately 2,000 POWs. Then in February, the camp was evacuated and we were marched to another camp at Moosburg, Stalag VIIA. At both Nürnberg and Moosburg we slept in tents.

"We were released in April by American Army General Patton. (Moosburg was the largest of all the German POW camps, and at the time of its liberation there were approximately 40,000 in a camp designed to hold 10,000.) I was flown back to Reims, France, then to army hospital in England. There was nothing first class on this trip."

Jack Bromfield continued:

"The others in my crew had all been captured the morning after we got shot down, and it was nearly a month by the time I got to the POW camp. It was March when my mum got that telegram, so six weeks probably, before anybody knew. They thought I hadn't made it, they hadn't seen the engineer or me. There they were, but I wasn't put in that compound. The west compound was British, dominion and allied, and then north 1 and 2 were American, and I went in there.

"I made a request to see the senior British officer, Group Captain Weir. (*Group Captain C T Weir was shot down in 49 Squadron Lancaster PB300EA-K from Fulbeck, while attacking the Mitteland Canal on 21 November 1944. He was blown out of the aircraft and was the only member of the crew to survive.*) I said, 'I'm stuck up in the American compound, and I'm not too pleased about that.' After a couple of days, I was marched through the Vorlager (*German accommodation area*), and put into block 11, and there in a room up the corridor were the other three, we didn't know where Doc was, the mid-upper. Apparently, when baling out he was pretty badly wounded.

"In February we suffered some reprisals from the Germans for having a secret radio. We were made to stand in the snow all day and were counted eleven times. Everything from our room was thrown out in to the snow while they looked for the radio; they didn't find it though!

"It got bitterly cold, and on Monday 30 April we were informed that the Germans were evacuating the camp and leaving us to it, this meant that we were no longer prisoners of war, but we were still not allowed outside the barbed wire. Most of the boys had a good feed, but I saved mine until the next big day, liberation by allied forces. I had a bar of chocolate and a packet of sweets, but that was all. The only thing wrong was the water supply, which was kaput.

"We went to kip, and slept on a shelf, six of us, like sardines in a tin. We heard bangs, and thumps, and somebody said, 'That's the Russian guns'. A voice said, 'Don't talk bloody daft. I was at Alamein, and that's not artillery fire.' When we got up next morning, there were indeed Russians in the compound! There was a lot of conversation going on outside between the commissioned types in the camp and the Russians, and then they cleared off, they were an armoured column, and the infantry came through...and just left us to our own devices. The Germans had all gone; it seemed funny not having guards about all day and seeing the searchlights shining outside the barbed wire instead of in. The thumps we'd heard were them blowing up the buildings on the airfield. They hadn't got enough sense to blow up the runway!"

Having finished his cigarette (see page 108), Les Giddings landed and was rapidly captured. This heralded the start of an extended period 'behind the wire'.

"I don't know the name of the village I landed near, but there were a few Luftwaffe people going through there. They took charge of me, 'cause they'd watched me come down, and the only place they could take me was to the local pub. So we sat in the bar – I went to sleep with my arms tied. I woke up and there was a: 'Your country needs you' SS poster; I thought, 'Oh Christ Almighty!' A policeman turned up with a pony and trap, and took me to the railway station. When I got there, my navigator had been carried piggy-back by a POW, and we were the only two survivors.

"They took us to a Luftwaffe airfield, Diepholz. The navigator had broken his leg, broken his left arm and he was taken to the hospital; I was put in the cell. In the evening they took me from my cell into the guardroom, and sat me down, 'cause I only looked about fifteen or sixteen. There were their equivalent of WAAFs coming in and pointing me out, 'Englischer flieger'. I think they were implying – 'Look, they're sending young boys', that sort of thing.

"The next day a siren went off about lunch time, and there were Messerchmitts roaring off into the air, and the Yanks decided to bomb Diepholz. The Germans ran away and I was left in the cells. The bombs were getting bloody close and all the tiles were blown off, and the building was on fire. It blew the frame off the door, and I managed to prize that open and get outside. They grabbed hold of me, and made me be a stretcher-bearer for a Luftwaffe bloke; he had a hole in his back you could put a fist in. Using one of the doors from the guardroom, four of us carried him. Then we heard the whistle of more bombs coming down; the three Germans left him and we jumped into a ditch. Somebody jumped in by the side of me, it was the bloke with a big hole in his back!

"The three Germans decided they'd had enough, and pushed me underneath the barbed wire and off we went, we left the poor thing there. So the next bombs that came down showered us with dirt, and he must have been hit on top of the head, poor devil. Then I was taken back to the cells after the raid was over. Consequently, it was a long time before the nav and I got to interrogation. What I didn't like about the interrogation was the fact that the Luftwaffe bloke who was interrogating me knew more about my squadron than I did. He could name names, and all things like that, and show me the book of what was shot down.

"In the end I had to ask for interrogation, because we'd been told that if you were there for more than seven days, you were giving them information, and I actually had nobody to talk to, apart from the feller with the Red Cross letter, which I refused to sign. They said, 'Your parents will never know. This is the only way you can get through, through the Red Cross, and we don't open it.'

"After interrogation, I was released into the main compound. We actually looked like holiday-makers, because we were issued with a cardboard suitcase, from America, with everything in there: shirts, cigarettes, chocolate, everything. We walked down to the train and they put us in carriages that had painted on the side, 'forty men or eight horses', and it was divided in three parts. Thirty-odd of us – I was the only RAF chap, the rest were Yanks – were in one third and the German guards were in the other two thirds. They were First World War men I should imagine, because they looked it, and they suddenly called me over and said, 'Tommy?' because I had a different colour uniform. 'You Tommy?' and I nodded 'Tipperary', and they finally got it across to me, they wanted me to sing Tipperary. So I sang it, and from then on, when they had some bread, I ate; they wouldn't give anything to the Yanks.

"We were about nine days on it, and we went up to Heydekrug, which was Luft VI. It wasn't a bad camp. Dixie Dean was the British man of competence, he spoke perfect German. He'd been a newspaper correspondent in Germany, and he got us out of a lot of trouble. (*Camp Leader Flight Sergeant Dixie Dean had been a POW since being shot down over Holland in a 77 Squadron Whitley on 10 September 1940.*)

"Bloody cold it was. They called a special parade one day, and they lined us up three sides of the square, which was unusual. They brought in machine guns and they placed them facing each of the three sides, and we thought: 'What the hell's going on?' There was snow on the ground, and the commandant announced that there'd been a big escape from Sagan, Luft III, and he said fifty had been killed. I don't care how good a shot anybody is, there is always bound to be some wounded. So we started shouting out, 'How many wounded?' 'No wounded'. So we knew they'd been executed. We snow-balled the bloody machine guns, and they didn't want to shoot us, the Luftwaffe, so they evacuated, and Dixie was calming us down.

"As the war went on, we could hear the Russian guns, and we thought they'd soon reach us. The Germans moved us out into Poland; it had two names, one was Toruń and the other one was Thorn for the same place. (*Stalag XX-A*) They mixed us up with army then. What surprised us was in Heydekrug, all aircrew had been locked in every night, and shutters put across the windows, and lights out. But in this camp as long as they kept to the footpaths, prisoners could go out and go to the toilet and come back into the billet. They moved us out and we stopped on the borders of Lithuania, and it all blew up in the middle of Poland, so we had to be moved out. They tried to march us up into Denmark. Part the way up there they realised that we were clogging the roads up; so they turned round and started marching us back. Then rocket-firing Typhoons came in and killed any people walking towards the front. They shot our column up, killed thirty-odd prisoners and eight guards, but they didn't know. Then they took us back to Diepholz. I ended up at Fallingbostel, (*Stalag XI-B*) which was about 11 kilometres away from Belsen; I never want to see a sight like that again. We were liberated by the British.

"The Luftwaffe didn't treat us bad, 'cause they were frightened of the SS who, without telling them, would suddenly put on a search of the camp. They would first of all move into the German quarters and kick everybody outside, then kick the Germans out of the guard boxes, and check to see if they'd been trading with us. Then they would check through us, we had some very smart cookies in the camp. They got us in, like a sheep-pen, and you went to where the SS were sitting, and they checked you against your photograph and ID. Then you were sent back to the barrack and locked in. At the end of the day – don't ask me how it was done – 200 of the identity cards disappeared, and the Germans never did know, to the end of the war, how many people were in that camp."

Oliver Wells found himself on the notorious 'Long March' as the Germans attempted to move large numbers of POWs away from the advancing Russian forces.

"Ours wasn't as long as some of them were. But we marched for a week in the snow and ice and took as much as we could, we made some sledges out of the so-called furniture we had in the camp which were mostly RAF and Red Cross packing cases. Piled whatever we could onto these, pulling them along through the snow, and then the snow evaporated and so we had to carry them after that. After a week we were loaded onto a cattle truck on a train and taken up to a place called Lückenwalde about thirty miles south of Berlin.

Norm Rosholt found himself in the same prisoner-of-war camp as Jack Bromfield.

"We were held in a jail on an airfield until they rounded up thirteen prisoners. We began marching to Hamburg, sleeping in barns, in bomb shelters, in ditches and in fields. On walking through Brennan, we were told to look straight ahead and the guards faced the German people. Not a building was standing and smoke was rising out of chimneys as they were living in the basements. The people were vicious and I don't blame them. They threw rocks, sticks and stones at us. I was kept at Hamburg for a week of interrogation as the rest of the crew went on.

"When they got thirty of us we started our march to Stalag Luft I. We had no money as it was taken away from us and the guards had only coffee and black bread and they weren't going to share any. Thus I lost fifty pounds in fifty days. We got rides on the back of flatbed trucks and on trains on our way to Luft I near Barth, on the Baltic Sea.

"This was towards the end of the war and they were not building any more buildings so we ended up sleeping in the sitting position with our knees tucked under our chin. Likewise they hadn't updated giving us Red Cross parcels to our room. If they received one parcel a week for one person, we got one parcel for ten people. Our bathroom was a telephone box lying lengthwise over a ditch. But with very little food we never went there much.

"In the middle of the campground was a map of Germany that was updated daily to show where the front lines were. The guards would come every day to look at the map. Someone in the camp had a secret radio so that they could listen to the BBC. Our guards throughout Germany were older men who had served their time and were now retired."

Chapter Five

THE LONELY SEA

"Bombers or Fighters?" his friends used to say
But when he said "Coastal", they half turned away
Yet Coastal's patrols which traversed the Bay
Forced the U-boats to dive for most of the day

With the U-boats submerged for much of the day
The convoys ploughed on, midst the salt and the spray
While the men on the ships did silently pray
That his 'plane would appear; both to circle and stay

When his plane did appear; to both circle and stay
Then the Wolf Packs held back; wholly robbed of their prey
And the convoys sailed on in their purposeful way
And the seamen reached port where their loved ones did lay

"Fighters or Bombers?" his friends used to ask
"Coastal", he said, his face a tired mask
"Though not in the spotlight where others may bask,
We've a tough job to do and I'm proud of the task."

Squadron Leader Tony Spooner DSO DFC AE

O, slinky, slimy, slithering snake,
You make poor trawlers quiver and quake,
But following your elusive feather
In every kind of dirty weather,
In rain or hail, snow or fine
Come those who'll catch you – 269.

You hide beneath the waters green,
But we will find you, submarine.
Although you in our channels lurk
To try to do your dirty work,
That death-portending screaming whine
Means you've been seen by 269.

Your conning tower, that glorious sight
Comes into view just on the right.
The bombs are live, the eye is keen
Crash-dive you cowardly submarine,

133

This bomb will break your slinky spine –
A job well done by 269.

Now, submarine, take this to heart.
Ere your next raid is due to start,
Your chance is NIL; the odds too great;
So shoot yourself; it's not too late.
If you're not blown up by a mine
You sure will be by 269.

Hudson aircrew of B Flight 269 Squadron [9]

ROYAL AIR FORCE

Throughout the war one of the key roles of RAF Coastal Command was to protect merchant shipping convoys from attack, primarily from U-boats, and keep the vital sea supply lanes open. The long-range aircraft fleet necessary to accomplish this task consisted of both landplanes such as the Fortress, Halifax, Hudson, Liberator, Wellington and Whitley, plus Catalina and Sunderland flying boats.

Having completed a Bomber Command tour and moved to instructing at an OTU, George Cook was presented with an opportunity to retrain and move to coastal work. His subsequent experiences of long, lonely hours patrolling over the ocean were typical.

"They asked for volunteers for WOMs training (*wireless operator mechanic*), so I re-mustered and went on a course at Cranwell. When that course came through, I was going to be sent back on my second operational tour. I was crewed up with a navigator and a pilot on Lancasters, but my WOMs course took preference, and I did another three months wireless course. That made me eligible to fly on long-range aircraft.

"Then it was Carew Cheriton (*10 Radio School*) to get twenty hours flying experience on Oxfords (and Ansons), even though I'd flown 200 operational hours on Bomber Command! I was transferred to South East Asia Command in the Indian Ocean on Catalinas. I went to Alness in Scotland (*4 [Coastal] OTU*), where we did flying training exercises while we waited for an overseas posting.

"On Christmas Eve 1943 we picked up a Catalina and flew it out to Gibraltar. We always had to have 'plane guards whenever we were away from base and usually it was the airmen who took turns. On Christmas Day a terrific storm blew up; we were moored in the harbour and the skipper, flight engineer and two others were on board as gale crew. During the night we could see a dark shape in the distance which gradually got bigger and bigger. It was an American navy ves-ael that had broken its moorings in the storm and was drifting straight for us. There were loads of sailors lining the deck and the skipper called up to them and asked where they were going. 'Wherever the tide takes us', was the reply. The ship hit us and damaged a wing tip. We broke our moorings and started drifting towards another Catalina, which we hit; it swung around and hit us again, damaging the tail. So there was a ship and two Catalinas drifting about in the harbour. We were stuck there for fourteen days waiting for repairs. Then we carried on through Aboukir, Cairo, Habbaniya, Bahrain and Karachi, where we had another long stop because the kite had gone U/S. We finally arrived at Koggala three months after we left home to join 205 Squadron on 23 May 1944.

"Our duties included anti-submarine patrols, convoy escorts, air-sea rescue searching for survivors and homing vessels for pick-up. We operated from other bases including Addu Attol and Kelai in the Maldive Islands, Diego Garcia in the Solomon Islands, and the Cocos Islands. We flew a thirty-hour mail trip from Koggala down to Perth and got 'The Order of the Double Sunrise'. We were down there flying submarine patrols; never found any, but we did find surface ships.

"While we were at Diego Garcia there was a hurricane warning and we were ordered back to base. A couple of months later we went back there and the whole marine section had been torn from its moorings and washed out to sea. There was no refueller, so after a twenty-hour op we had to refuel the Catalina with five-gallon Jerry cans, which had to be rowed out in a dinghy from the shore. With the aircraft needing 2,000 gallons, this used to take between two and three hours and had to be done as soon as we were moored up so that it would be ready for operations. I got my commission in February 1945 and became the squadron's signals leader. I flew 1,000 operational hours on Catalinas, came back to England after VJ-Day and was demobbed in 1946."

Flight Lieutenant Norman Wilson flew Catalinas and Sunderlands in the latter stages of the war, primarily in the Japanese theatre.

"After being on leave in the UK on D-Day and being slightly ashamed of sitting in the garden watching hundreds of allied aircraft overhead on their way to support the invasion of Europe, I eventually found myself in Mombasa, Kenya joining 209 Squadron as a second pilot on Catalinas. My first operational flight was an anti-submarine patrol between Mombssa and the Seychelles on 19 February 1945, returning on the 21st. In the month up to 24 March, a number of similar flights to such places as Madagascar, Pamanzi and Dar-es-Salaam were undertaken during which time we were told that we were to convert to Sunderlands before departing to the Far East to participate in the Japanese conflict.

"I joined the Sunderland crew of Flying Officer Gibson initially as third pilot. During the work up to become operational, many exercises were undertaken. Whilst on a bombing practice, during which a smoke bomb marker was dropped into the sea and then bombed by other smoke bombs, we had our first emergency. The apparatus for dropping the smoke bombs was somewhat primitive, in that the bombs were individually loaded onto a small rack attached to the sill of the drogue hatch in the downstairs galley and then swung out ready for the pilot to operate the electrical release. Unfortunately our navigator dropped one of the primed bombs inside the aircraft, which detonated and filled the 'plane with dense smoke. In the cockpit we could not see the control column let alone the instruments.

"The captain shouted that we must be on fire and he would try to land – we were some fifty miles from land – I could not even see him. In an effort to see outside I attempted to put my head out of the rear, sliding window on my side of the cockpit but to no avail. I then slid the window panels back to see if I could do so out of the front window when the changed airflow over the cockpit window miraculously sucked the smoke out of the 'plane in a second. We were by then straight and level, about five feet above the water, calm waves but a large swell. The captain landed and all seemed well until the starboard wingtip float hit the swell and was knocked rearwards and upwards lifting the starboard aileron, knocking the control wheel from the captain's hands and dipping the starboard wingtip into the water. Looking out of the cockpit I could see the starboard outer prop was thrashing up spray. I instinctively grabbed the wheel and applied full power. Luckily the aircraft responded and took to the air at an incredible nose up, wing down angle. We were able to resume normal flight, less the starboard wing float, return to Mombasa and land. Me and another crew member climbed onto the port wing to keep the starboard wing up, whilst being towed to a mooring. The aircraft was taken out of the water, and a new aileron and wingtip float fitted.

"On the night of 14 May two crews were assigned to fly one aircraft on a night radar training exercise, the crews taking it in turn. We all got onto the aircraft and realising that there were more than enough pilots to carry out the work, I said to our navigator, 'I don't feel like going tonight' to which he replied, 'Nor do I, let's ask the skipper if we can get off'. Both captains agreed and although the crew boat had left the aircraft, we managed to shout to him to return and the two of us went ashore. Later that night when the aircraft was due to land, a thunderstorm covered Mombasa and they were told to remain out at sea until it passed. The aircraft flew into a hill and although some survived, there were many who did not.

"We flew to our advanced base at Rangoon. Over the next few weeks, until the Japanese surrender, the squadron flew many anti-shipping sorties in the South China Sea. The routine was to fly halfway down the west coast of Malaya to where there was a gap in the hills which would allow our limited altitude to cross into the South China Sea. Here we patrolled up and down the coast and attacked coastal shipping with which the Japanese were supplying their troops in Singapore and Malaya.

"During that time we flew five operational missions and sank one Sugar Dog supply ship, one tug and two barges. Also attacked and damaged were, seven Sugar Dogs and one large junk. (Sugar Dog was the code name for small freighter ships used to supply the Japanese troops in Malaya and Singapore.)"

The majority of Coastal Command landplanes were adaptations of existing bomber types, such as the Whitley, which was flown by Wing Commander 'Hunter' McGiffin, who found himself involved in trials of early air to surface vessel (ASV) radar.

"In August 1940, I and two other pilots were sent to 10 OTU Abingdon to convert to Whitleys and my conversion consisted of one hour thirty minutes dual day instruction. It was then decided to equip our 502 Squadron Whitleys with ASV and I was sent with my crew to Telecommunications Research Establishment at Christchurch. We flew co-operation with a submarine off the Firth of Forth, this was the first aircraft to be fitted with ASV, but the trials were not successful. We tried again with new aerials and we had a boffin on board with a long cylinder in the fuselage, which it was hoped would detect a submerged sub. It transpired that the device only worked if the aircraft was within 150 feet of the sub, so the idea was scrapped!"

Having completed his training in Canada, Rick Rickard found himself back in England and starting operations on the Lockheed Hudson. He soon moved on to a Wellington squadron helping to guard the Western approaches, before moving on to the Mediterranean theatre.

"After 6 OTU at Thornaby we were posted to join 53 Squadron Coastal Command at St Eval in Cornwall. We arrived there on 6 June and stayed for three or four weeks, and it was arranged to swap aircraft with a squadron based at North Coates on the Lincoln coast as at that time activity in the North Sea became more important than the Atlantic, so in short we sent good aircraft in exchange for semi-clapped out kites.

"By the end of the month it was decided that 53 Squadron had too few serviceable Hudsons to use up the new crews, so off we went to Chivenor in Devon and Wellington aircraft, and we reported to 172 Squadron to convert to Wellingtons flying with ASV equipment. Apparently we needed two more in the crew, so we picked up a second pilot, J O'Sullivan from Hull and an Australian flight engineer from Perth (Keith). We were a happy crew, all sergeants and no bull, but we had to go through local flying, circuits and bumps and bombing practice all over again.

"On our first hop local flying, we got off the deck OK thanks to lengthy runways and spent a good hour nipping in and out of the Cornish coves and generally admiring the scenery. On return to Chivenor however, we found the Wellington had different habits from the Hudson and we just couldn't get down. We made several uncertain approaches too high, too fast and finally lopped in from about 30 feet having just missed two or three armoury sheds. We did several kangaroo hops before coming to rest on the grass, having got off the concrete runway. The flight commander tore off several strips and thankfully checked that the aircraft was still intact – and so we were well bloodied into 172 Squadron.

"On one night exercise over the Irish Sea we had settled down for a boring stooge trip and had set the automatic control otherwise known as 'George'. Jimmy was up front in the nose, Dai had wandered down to the Elsan for a slash, Keith was having a quiet kip, and Taffy was half asleep at the radio and Shag was in the rear gun turret. I was standing up in the astrodome getting a bearing on a flame float to check wind direction when all hell let loose. George had slipped and we were not much above 1,000 feet over the drink! We nose-dived to a couple of hundred feet but somehow Dai and Jimmy defied gravity and got back to the control column and jointly gave a great heave. The aircraft staggered back to 500 feet, stalled and dropped again, this time almost into the drink, but again lumbered back to a few hundred feet and after a few similar hops and jumps Dai and Jimmy were able to give the engines a few more revs and gradually restore the aircraft to normal habits. We all suffered cuts and bruises from being thrown around so much, so we promptly set course for Chivenor. To restore confidence we went through a few choruses of 'Green Grow the Rushes Oh' over the intercom and other less polite ditties and touched down safely about 04:00.

"By this time we were much overtrained and wondering when we would be able to make any contribution to the war effort. The buzz went round that U-boats were knocking the hell out of Russian and other convoys in and around the Faroe Islands and so off we went to Wick, almost to John O' Groats. Six aircraft were involved and we went with all our kit and equipment including my dismantled bike hidden mid-aircraft. The runways were too short for take-off with extra fuel tanks and depth charges on board, so we had to fly the unladen kites to Skitten, a god-forsaken 'drome fifteen or twenty miles away, where the runways were longer. There we were loaded up with extra fuel and six depth charges each weighing 200 pounds, for night anti-sub patrols around eight or nine hours a time in the far North Atlantic waters.

"Coastal Command seldom flew more than 1,000 feet up, depending purely on DR navigation and at night time on flame floats to check drift and sextants to take bearings on any stars visible. The Wellingtons we flew carried ASV which transmitted a pulse to the sea surface and was returned on a screen as wiggly lines. Any sizeable item such as submarine, fishing boat, or other vessel would show up as a blip on the screen and could be picked up at a range of twenty to thirty miles; the larger the blip the bigger the vessel. Having read a blip, our drill was to home in, reducing height to 100 feet over the top and then switch on our Leigh searchlights and swivel them around to identify the target. If we saw the enemy, we'd drop depth charges and then scarper. One snag, they had guns to pop off and quite often our own surface vessels would shoot first and ask questions afterwards. Other times it could be a harmless fishing vessel, but with a barrage balloon flying from a very dangerous steel hawser.

"Between 20 August and 3 September we did four such night anti-submarine sweeps, each taking around nine hours. On our first trip the weather was grim, the winds were strong and six kites took off for a creeping line-ahead search of the Faroe Islands. After half an hour a recall message was sent and five aircraft returned to base. Somehow we didn't pick up the recall signal and we just soldiered on to the position for starting our search. In a search, each leg south to north was to be twenty miles and each west to east, five miles, so that eventually a large area of ocean could be covered in the exercise. We had been briefed of southerly winds approx 40 knots, but I estimated stronger, say 50 knots. In truth the gales were raging around 70 knots. The only means of verifying this was the occasional sight of wave cap pattern, but not very visible in the dark.

"As a result, on each leg up we went up thirty miles instead of twenty and on the down legs came back only fifteen instead of twenty so after a dozen legs completed, we were much further north than intended (way inside the Arctic Circle). Setting course for base we would have been able to pick up Wick beacon fifty miles out, but at the ETA there was no semblance of a blip and we were some 200 miles out and with a veering wind we emerged at dawn amongst the barrage balloons of Scapa Flow, a hazard in itself, but luckily air fleet could identify our aircraft and therefore held their fire, hoping we could weave away safely from the balloons. We did and finally touched down at Wick, one-and-a-half hours overdue and almost written off. On de-briefing, we were asked why we ignored the recall message. We said we didn't receive it and did our best to complete what we set out to do. The flight commander said, 'Well done lads, especially on your first trip'.

"We returned to Chivenor as it seemed that more activity was required in the Bay of Biscay, there was an operational flight every three nights, where invariably we were flying nine, ten and sometimes eleven hours non-stop. This involved a briefing where all the crew attended, clambering into the aircraft, taking off, setting course for Biscay and then patrolling, returning at dawn. Not only was the observer awake the whole trip, he was required for de-briefing at the end. The rest of the crew could relax at some time during the trip, but I was constantly checking and counter-checking, keeping position, taking astro shots and working fixes with the use of the astro tables and only when we picked up Bishop Rock beacon in the Scillies could I relax, and we would come up the Cornish coast with a sing song.

"We did twenty-two trips round the Bay of Biscay and they were generally negative, but very tiring and somewhat boring. We frequently got shot at but luckily survived. On one occasion we came across what we thought to be the *Bismarck* or the *Scharnhorst* way out in the Atlantic. Being unable to use the radio for fear of being fixed, I was able to use a carrier pigeon, attaching a message indicating position and description to its leg and shoving the bird down the flare chute. Apparently it flew into Cornwall and Devon and our naval forces were diverted to the area. As far as we were concerned we continued to circle the convoy, but out of firing range long enough to leave us just enough fuel to return to base.

"I celebrated my second wedding anniversary with a rather hairy trip off the Lorient coast well known for all the U-boat pens based there. We were the only crew involved and had orders to fly into the estuary with ASV aerials transmitting pulses alternately fore and aft and amidships and to stooge around for three hours or so. We should have attracted flak from shore battery guns or fighter aircraft, but neither occurred. It transpired that our single 'plane gave the impression with signals from all directions, of an approaching heavy bombing raid.

"By this time the squadron had lost several aircraft for reasons unknown and one couldn't help but wonder who would be next. Of our original number in Canada, a good third were missing or dead. So be it, we carried on up to and including a last trip on 3 January. It then appeared that 179 Squadron in Gibraltar badly needed reinforcements and we asked to be included in the six crews required, and so down to Portreath we went. There was great panic as we were due to go that same night. Eventually with very bleary eyes, we took off at 06:15 only becoming airborne by virtue of the runway disappearing out to sea over 100-foot cliffs. We flew in darkness halfway across the Bay of Biscay coming in closer to Cap Finisterre. We had been warned to keep a look out for any Focke-Wulf Condors but luckily we met none. Although we were supposed to respect neutral countries by flying out thirty miles to sea, we more or less flew down the Portuguese and Spanish coastlines shooting up a few towns and fishing boats en route. Reaching Cap St. Vincente, we headed into Gibraltar, landing at 15:10 and immediately saw what kind of place we had come to. A Beaufighter had just belly landed, a Wimpey caught fire and Spitfires were gun testing out to sea incessantly.

"Our first op from Gibraltar was ten-and-a-half hours night flying in the Med between the Tangier and Spanish coats. Take-offs from Gibraltar were always hairy, no choice but up or down and barely 1,000 yards runway crossing the La Linea road full of donkey carts. A Wimpey with full fuel tanks, four depth charges and Leigh light (*anti-submarine weapon*) virtually shrugged off the deck. Our patrol produced nothing more than the odd fishing boat and we got back in the early hours, shattered and ready for kip. We seldom flew at more than 1,000 feet so Mae Wests took preference to parachutes and we tooled around in the dark constantly watching the ASV screen to detect the presence of submarines or other enemy vessels. Use of the radio was strictly forbidden, so fixes were hard to come by, or took ages to work out.

"Off the south east coast of Spain – groaning along at 120 knots – a lovely clear night and the Mediterranean sky was full of stars and the coastline was full of lights. We were turning in towards Algiers, and observed heavy ack-ack fire and what appeared to be exploding bombs. Soon after, we were diverted by code to search for a U-boat sighted off Alboran. This involved a cross-over patrol in the suspected area, but obviously Jerry knew we were around and wouldn't surface. We descended and lit up a terrified Spanish trawler, luckily with no barrage balloon and steel cables.

"We were called to do a convoy patrol off the Canaries going under the code name of Teapot. The convoy was in from the USA carrying supplies and equipment to support the Casablanca landings. We circled the convoy for several hours, receiving and transmitting morse code messages by Aldis lamp. Not only was it difficult to keep up with their transmission speed, but it was tricky to keep them in view from the starboard wing of a constantly circling aircraft. However we managed to cope until it was time to leave. It being broad daylight, we thought we should have a good look at the Sahara Desert before returning to base, so inland we went at 100 feet above the dunes. We came across what looked like a foreign legion fort, but as we got nearer it appeared to be a harem and we could see many heavily garbed female figures dashing for cover (station orders subsequently posted said that the practice of low flying over Moroccan properties must cease forthwith).

"We carried on further to Dar Sibena in the Spanish Moroccan territory of Sidi Ifni and we came across what appeared to be a small flying strip. On closer inspection and still at only 100 feet we saw several three-engined Junkers transport 'planes lined up on the tarmac and next thing we knew was gunfire and the fabric of our 'plane was peppered in several places, one uncomfortably close to my ear. As an all white 'plane against a pure blue sky and at very low level we offered a sitting target and having broken rules by flying over neutral territory (so called) we had still to explain how we had incurred damage. We got out of this by claiming that when we took off in the dark, several loose stones and rocks had hit us (the runway was quite primitive), but we had decided that no serious damage was suffered so we proceeded with the patrol. Luckily this was accepted without question and we buzzed off to catch up on some much needed sleep.

"By March '43, after something like forty operational trips since 20 August 1942, the strain was beginning to take its toll. Not only had we scooted around the upper North Sea, the Bay of Biscay, the North Atlantic and most parts of the Med and always at night, we had played as hard as possible. We hoped all this effort had done something to suppress U-boat activities. So on 11 June I turned up on my own at 105 OTU Bramcote near Nuneaton with the intention of being part of screening crews to fly with some sprog crews coming in for training."

In addition to these long-range patrols, Coastal Command also fielded a substantial force of Beaufighters and Mosquitoes for shorter-range search and attack work against both U-boats and surface vessels, as Doug Turner recalled.

"During my first operational sortie with 235 Squadron, in a Beaufighter, I managed to sink a 6,000-ton merchant vessel off the Norwegian coast, that was in January '43. It was the most heavily armed aeroplane you could get, she had six machine guns in the wing, and four cannons in the nose, it was fantastic. We all carried rockets as well under the wing job, lovely aeroplane, I really enjoyed her.

"On the Mosquito they decided to put this ruddy great six-pounder gun in it. It shook the whole aeroplane right through, but the old Mosquito could take that quite easily. If I'd been a German I'd be scared to shit of it! It had everything. It had the speed and you could knock bits off it and it would still fly. Nobody thought a wooden aeroplane could do it. Commonly enough, it would come back with six feet of the wing off at the end, and half the tail blown off. It was a fantastic aeroplane.

"I actually got a number of U-boats with them; I met their captains afterwards. (*Doug Turner was awarded the DFC, together with his navigator Des Curtis, for their attack and sinking of U-976 off St. Nazaire on 25 March '43, flying Mosquito XVIII MM425/OP-L.*) We had one special one, it was amongst the ones coming back after attacking a convoy. They used to call up, 'Airborne number 3', and 'be there at say, six o'clock in the morning', and you'd find a submarine was just about there. You'd just catch them, they were all asleep; they'd be on the surface there. They were being led in by a couple of destroyer types; of course you could ignore them, they'd start popping away at you, but you could waggle these aeroplanes around and make a dive attack.

"You got a bit scared at times, but that faded away with the mere fact that it was an interesting job you were doing – 'get him!' that sort of thing; 'sorted that bugger'. Life was wonderful. I used to feel so sorry for other squadrons who hadn't got people looking after them as we were looked after. Our chief, the way he had to put up with things that we did. But I was one of those blokes, I couldn't care what happened."

In late 1940 it became apparent that the Luftwaffe was beginning to pose a serious threat to convoys, and the decision was taken to equip merchant ships with Hurricanes, launched by catapult from the foredeck in the event of the approach of an enemy aircraft. The plan was that the aircraft would recover back to a land base if possible, or if not, for the pilot to either put down on the sea or parachute out and be picked up by a convoy escort. The ships were known as Catapult Aircraft Merchantmen (CAM), RAF pilot volunteers were called for, and deployments began in 1941.

Squadron Leader Gerald 'Stapme' Stapleton was a South African pilot who flew Spitfires with 603 Squadron from Turnhouse and Hornchurch during the Battle of Britain. He later commanded 247 Squadron Typhoons during the D-Day period, operating from B6 ALG in France in August 1944. He finished the war with six victories, and says he was shot down twice 'without spilling any blood'. In 1941 he volunteered to fly CAM Hurricanes.

"I flew cat-ship Hurricanes, not in anger though. I was fired off at Speke aerodrome during trials. You needed 25 degrees of flap, fully fine on the prop; the acceleration was really fierce, the run was only about 30 feet or so. My colleague was launched in anger over a convoy. We took it in turns to be launched; I was in cockpit readiness too. Anyway, he went off by which time the Condor had flown away. If the sea was rough you had to bale out; if it was fairly calm you ditched. It was calm, so he ditched and was picked up by a destroyer. We used an Aldis lamp to signal the destroyer and ask how he was. They said he was OK but wet – inside and out!"

SOVIET AIR FORCE

The Soviets too, established coastal patrol units with both their own indigenous aircraft types and lease-lend aircraft such as the Catalina. Colonel Grigory Avenesov started the war in the Baltic and finished it in the Black Sea as a flying boat navigator/bomb aimer.

"War for me started in 1940. We had several reconnaissance missions to fly. We painted over red stars, and flew over the Baltic to see what was carried by the cargo shipping from Germany to Finland.

"At the start of the Great Patriotic War, I was supposed to check the 'chutes of the squadron, so I woke up early. When I reached the airfield I heard a radio message that the war had started. On 25 June we were shot at by large calibre guns from Finnish territory, but with no result. Then we were moved to Tallinn. From there I got my first order. We were told that a submarine had left Helsinki or Kotka with torpedo boats as escort. The mission was to prevent them from getting to Tallinn port. We scrambled two Beriev MBR-2s with four FAB-100 bombs each. We found the submarine, but it was submerged. No surprise, our cruise speed was about 160-180 kilometres an hour. But the boats started to shoot at us. We shot back with ShKAS machine guns, with no result, but we managed to sink one of them with bombs. No damage was inflicted on us, those gunners were really bad!

"From Tallinn we flew to Libava port, and bombed some airbases at night. Then we were moved to Ezel and Kogul. From there we flew recon missions. In July 1941 we were told that new fighters would arrive at the bases to show them to us, so that we would be able to recognise them. We were standing at the beach, when we saw three 'planes coming from the south. We cheered, but they threw bombs at us. Those were Me 109s. We spread out, and tried to hide. At the same time the Messerschmitts strafed our 'planes on the water. Several were lost. Our AAA defence were hiding with us, but we threw them out of the fox-holes to carry on fighting. The AAA fire started when they left. In about ten minutes three 'planes came back. We started firing, but these were the promised Yaks! Someone shouted: 'Yaks!' We answered: 'Huyaks!' (*a very rude swear-word*) and continued firing. Luckily, we killed no one. This led to some problems later as we shot at our fighters. After the evacuation from Ezel we were stationed at Kronstadt. Our main work was anti-submarine warfare. We had a special method of finding U-boats. They left a trail of oil on top of the sea. If it was cone shaped, we dropped a series of bombs a bit ahead of the trail. If it was still, we dropped bombs amidst it. We could not see the damage we did, of course. It was rather boring, really. In 1943 I was moved to the Black Sea.

"We were sent after torpedo boats that attacked ports. They went to Kertch. We found them almost at their port and bombed them, but after the bombs were gone we were intercepted by fighters. The pilots went down to ten metres in height. The Germans did not like low altitudes. We started gaining altitude almost at our shore, I radioed that we were arriving, when they told me that a fighter was behind me. Then everything exploded around me, we fell into the water, and when I came to the surface I saw an Me 110. Its pilot strafed us and set off. I shouted that I was sinking, when I saw my pilot, Komesk shaking his fist at me and shouting something like: 'If you will sink I'll go down after you and I will torture you instead of the devil, and I will do it better!' That helped a lot. I lost consciousness in the boat. It took us to the AAA battery, where soldiers fixed my damaged knee. The last thing I can remember, we were flying at approximately 150 metres, and went down without 'chutes! The tail gunner was killed in the air.

"The Catalina was a marvellous 'plane. Apart from all it was able to carry 600 kg of bombs instead of 400 on the MBR-2. We were patrolling the Black Sea with it. We managed to kill three U-boats with it. Four more boats were damaged by our squadron alone.

"The Germans were great fighter pilots. There were some tricks that helped, but we lost a lot of pilots to their fighters. Our pilots were excellent at the start in 1941 and from 1944 onwards; in between they were rather weak. The AA defences of surface vessels were not really good, sometimes we flew above them until they would shoot off all of their ammo, then get low and shoot passengers and personnel by machine guns. In 1941 we did this to a German troopship, which was crowded with people. When we left more than 100 dead soldiers were afloat in the sea, and those who survived were waving white flags. We managed to make so many holes in that ship that it sunk...when we came back, I had only one bullet left. After the war I found out that this ship was thought to be lost in a storm, since no survivors were ever found.

"We received notification of our fleet positions for the duration of each flight. Enemy ships would reveal themselves very soon, as they would throw everything at you on approach. The ship we sunk by machine-gun fire was depleted of ammo, and that was the only reason we got close enough to shoot. Two or three times a year we would lose one of our 'planes to friendly surface fire. In July 1941 we lost one from a two-plane flight to the patrol boat, but stuff like that happened.

"For defence we could cover above us in both 'planes, but the underside was undefended. One of my colleagues managed to shoot down two Me 109s with ShKAS. Meeting a fighter would often end up in being shot down, no surprise really. But usually we would meet Do 18, Do 24 or Fw 200 patrollers. It was not our business to deal with them, though a neighbouring regiment's pilot flew under such a flying boat and his gunner shot up its belly seriously. Most likely it sank after landing.

"If we had a damaged belly, on landing we would have a fuselage full of water, so the 'plane would gradually sink. If the side floats were damaged, we wouldn't even have time to get out. On take-off the biggest threat were the wild ducks. There were lots of them, and at take-off speed about 150 kilometres an hour, a duck would do the same damage as a 20mm explosive shell. Landing on level 3 sea was considered as dangerous, and 3.5 was impossible. Surprisingly, most 'planes were lost on still water (because the pilots couldn't see where the water level was), so we had speed boats going across our landing approach to create waves. If we landed on a log under water the 'plane would disintegrate, and these were only visible in wavy conditions."

FLEET AIR ARM

The principle anti-shipping aircraft used aboard the Royal Navy carriers were the torpedo-carrying Swordfish, Albacore, Barracuda and later the Grumman Avenger. Sub Lieutenant Idwal 'Glan' Evans was still flying the obsolescent Swordfish on anti-shipping patrols when he and his crew came to grief at the end of 1942 and spent the rest of the war in captivity.

"I had been in the front line with 805 Squadron Fulmars from October 1940 to January 1941, then flying with 815 Squadron from Takoradi to Alexandria from January 1941 to January 1942. There was an exceptional affinity between officers, TAGS and ground staff, probably because we were a mobile squadron put onshore when HMS *Illustrious* returned to the USA for repairs and refit. We lived in tents in the Western Desert and Crete and it was a very close-knit squadron.

"I joined 815 at HMS Daedalus *(Lee-on-Solent)* after the Channel do, moved to 825 Squadron the following month, and stayed with it until 29 December 1942. I came back from leave to Pompey to await transport to Thorney Island. I met Captain Skirts Harris RM with whom I'd flown in Fulmars from Takoradi to Alex with 805 Squadron. He was going to start a night fighter squadron for fleet work and wanted me to join him as we had also been in Crete together. I said I would consider it and let him know in a few weeks. I got back to Thorney and was asked by one of the lads if I'd do his trip so that he could get off on leave earlier. I foolishly agreed, so I flew with Dan Timms and Sid Winder (and I had been brought up never to volunteer!) We were tasked with mine-laying at Le Havre.

"I had not flown from Thorney during daylight, let alone at night so whilst taxiing around the perimeter track, I could have, during 'swinging jinks' just got off track. All I remember about it is keeping an eye on a radio mast illuminated with a red light on top and thinking how I must remember this on return to aid my navigation. I asked Dan Timms how things were going and he said 'all OK' and that Hutchings and Roberts were loosely formatted astern of us. I switched off my formation lights as we were nearing the French coast. We must have been too far south, because I saw some small boats below and some buildings to starboard, it looked like a marina. I turned to port, climbed and went out into the main basin, turned west to be back in the main shipping lane and got down to an indicated 200 feet and dropped a mine. I headed out to sea and back home, and found that due to the loss of weight after dropping the mine, I had climbed to 300 feet. I looked to the starboard bow and saw some gun flashes from the point ahead, I believe it was Cap de Le Havre. I decided to go a bit lower to get under radar, and descending slowly I hit the sea at an indicated 150 feet. I released the dinghy, Sid Winder pulled it in by the rope and we all climbed in.

"We started paddling but soon gave up as it was futile and just settled down in the dinghy. We drifted, and then the dinghy capsized. Sid Winder and I climbed back in and Dan Timms was hanging on to a line. We pulled him to the side of the dinghy but failed to get him in, so I jumped back into the sea. Sid Winder pulled from the inside of the dinghy and we managed to get Dan back in. We three were done in and lay in the bottom of the dinghy. We must have dozed –

ove left: Sgt Peter Green 102 Squadron
~~klington Sep '44. *Green*

~~t: Warrant Officer Peter Green. *Green*

ove right: Sgt George Cook joined 49
~~adron at Scampton, Lincolnshire in 1941
~~ Hampden wireless operator and com-
~~ed thirty-two operations including the
~~ two thousand-bomber raids. *Cook*

Inset: Flying Officer George Cook.

Below: Newly enlisted airmen at 21 Initial
Training Wing at Torquay in 1943. Of the fifty
recruits in the group, statistically fewer than
half would survive to the end of the war. *Green*

*NB: All photos in this section author's collec-
tion except where credited.*

Above: Mike Nicholson [front row, left] was a Liberator pilot on 358 Squadron in the Far East u
to the end of the Pacific War. Here is seen here with his crew prior to a supply-dropping
operation. *Nicholson*

Far left: Pilot officer Mike
Nicholson.

Left: Master Navigator Bill
Whiter enlisted in 1942 and
trained at 70 OTU on the
Baltimore before joining 18
Squadron to fly the Boston ir
the Mediterranean. On retur
the UK he went to 203 Squac
at Stradishall on Lancasters a
subsequently had a very long
post-war career.

tours on Coastal Command Wellingtons with 172 and 179 Squadrons. *Rickard family*

Above right: Sgt Ron Williams flew seventeen operations as a Wellington wireless operator with 150 Squadron in Tunisia and Italy. *Stuart Williams*

: Flight Lieutenant Jim Lord and his 550 adron Lancaster crew. *Elliott*

ove left: Flight Lieutenant 'Ricky' Rickard ing his observer training in an Anson at 33 Navigation School, Mount Hope, Canada 941. He went on to complete operational

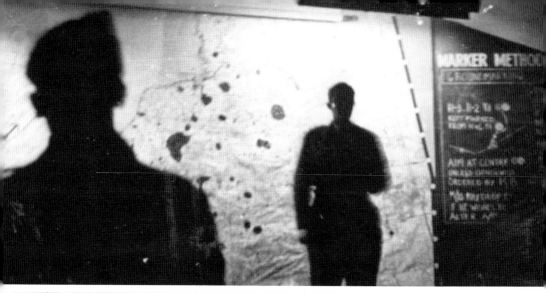

Top: A crew briefing in progress at North Killingholme. 550 Squadron was the only unit based there during its brief two-year existence. *John Elliott via 550 Squadron Association*

Above left: The operations planning section at North Killingholme, Yorkshire, home to the Lancasters of 550 Squadron. The coming night's operation is being planned ahead of crew briefing. *John Elliott via 550 Squadron Association*

Above right: Commander Jack Routley RN flew Martlets with 805 Squadron in the Western Desert and later commanded 885 Squadron aboard HMS *Ruler* and HMS *Indefatigable* during the closing stages of the Pacific War.

Above middle: Air Commodore James Coward was with 19 Squadron at Duxford when it received the RAF's first Spitfires. Shot down and seriously injured during the Battle of Britain, he joined Churchill's staff at Chequers while recovering.

Right: Wing Commander Jack Rose CMG MBE DFC flew Hurricanes in France and the Battle Britain with 32 Squadron, scoring three victories. By 1943 he had converted to Typhoons and commanded 184 Squadron, later taking over 113 Squadron in Burma.

Above: 550 Squadron Lancaster ED562 BQ-G 'We Dood It' with Flight Lieutenant Jim Lord DFC and his air and ground crew on completion of their thirty operations in September 1944. *Elliott*

Middle: The intelligence room at North Killingholme, where the bomber crews could study the latest information on possible targets and enemy defences. *John Elliott via 550 Squadron Association*

Bottom left: Warrant Officer Les G K Giddings served as a Halifax flight engineer with 102 Squadron at Pocklington, Yorkshire. He was shot down by a night fighter on his eighth operation over Leipzig on 19 February 1944 and taken prisoner.

Bottom right: Flight Lieutenant Doug Turner DFC. Selected for 618 Squadron formed to attack the battleship *Tirpitz* using Mosquitoes carrying the 'Highball' bouncing bomb, an operation which was cancelled as too risky. Doug later had great success on anti-submarine Mosquito operations, sinking U-boat *U-976*.

Above: Navigator Andrew Barron [rear row, left] completed a full tour with 223 Squadron [100 Group] flying Liberators out of Oulton, Norfolk and his crew is seen here with Liberator TS530 6G-G 'Gremlin Heaven'. He later joined 196 Squadron at Shepherds Grove with Stirlings. *Barron*

Middle: Bob Clarke was an engine fitter with Fairfield Aviation at Elstree, Hertfordshire, where he worked on modification and repair programmes for the Lysander [as seen here] and Wellington. *Clarke*

Bottom: Flying Officer Alan 'Tommy' Thomsett flew forty-and-a-half operations in Wellingtons with 192 Squadron, which was part of 100 Group. His usual aircraft was LP345 DT-G 'Gertie the Land Girl' in the background of this shot with his crew. Tommy is the third from the right. *Thomsett*

Above: A group of Lavochkin La 5 and La 7 pilots from 2 GuIAP in Belorussia in 1945. Benedikt Kardopoltsev is on the extreme right. *Kardopoltsev via Oleg Korytov*

Middle: Major Vasili Kubarev mainly flew the Yak 9, accumulating over 300 sorties and forty-six aerial victories. He is seen here among a group of nine Heroes of the Soviet Union at Lubertzy in October 1943. *Kubarev via Oleg Korytov*

Bottom: Yakolev Yak 7/9 pilots of 12 IAP KBF [12th Red Bannered Fighter Aviation Regiment of Red Bannered Baltic Sea Fleet]. Among them is Vladimir Tikhomirov. *Tikhomirov via Oleg Korytov*

Top left: Tim Elkington volunteered for the programme to operate Hurricanes from Catapult Aircraft Merchantman [CAM] ships to help protect the Arctic convoys. Hurricane I P3544 LU-V belonged to the Merchant Ship Fighter Unit based at Speke, Liverpool for trials and training. *Elkington*

Inset: Wing Commander Tim Elkington. Flying Hurricanes with 1 Squadron at Tangmere in 1940, on 15 August he shot down an Me 109 over the Channel, but the following day he was himself shot down. He also flew Hurricanes to Russia off HMS *Argus* in 1941 and later went on to 67 Squadron. *Elkington*

Above right: Tim Elkington's log book for September 1941, recording the flight from HMS *Argus* to Vaenga, and the start of operations in Russia. *Elkington*

Middle right: Hurricane W9115 KE-H was also flown by the Merchant Ship Fighter Unit. *Elkington*

Bottom: A group of 134 Squadron Hurricane pilots awaiting the call to action at Vaenga, Russia, in the autumn of 1941. On the far right is Flight Lieutenant Neil Cameron, who later became marshal of the Royal Air Force. *Flg Off B J Daventry via Tim Elkington*

p: 151 Wing Hurricanes at
enga, winter 1940. *Flg Off B J
venntry via Tim Elkington*

ove: Sergeant John Whitaker
ned 38 Squadron at Marham in
38, the only unit to fly the
irey Hendon. He went on to
ve in the Middle East in ground
es with 211 and 55 Blenheim
uadrons, then 6 Heavy Mobile
T Unit. *Whitaker*

ght: John Whitaker first served
a wireless operator and was
otographed not long after he
rted his service. *Whitaker*

Top left: Giacomo Metellini is presented with the Medaglia d'Argento al Valor Militare by Benito Mussolini on 24 June 1942 during fighter operations from San Pietro, Sicily. *Metellini*

Top right: In the spring of 1939 Giacomo Metellini flew the Fiat CR 32 with 'Legionaria Aviation', the 102nd Squadron of 10 Group 'Baleari', to defend the Balearic Islands during the Spanish Civil War. *Metellini*

Above left: Giacomo Metellini in Treviso, 2008. *Metellini*

Above right: Wg Cdr Lucian Brett Ercolani DSO and bar DFC. Flew twenty operations in Wellingtons with 214 Squadron at Stradishall, Suffolk and later commanded 99 Squadron at Jessore, with Wellingtons and later Liberators. He also commanded 355 and 159 Liberator squadrons.

Below: A Reggiane Re 2001 of 2 Stormo being serviced on the island of Pantellaria, Sicily during the campaign against the Malta convoys. *Metellini*

Above left: Warrant Officer Eric Burke was a navigator with 13 Squadron in Italy on Baltimores Bostons in 1945. *Burke*

Above right: Boston IV BZ548 J was the regular aircraft flown by Eric Burke and his crew during ? tour on 13 Squadron, and was photographed at Aviano. *Burke*

?ow: Lancaster I R5868 PO-S, now in the RAF Museum at Hendon, when serving with 467 ?adron RAF Waddington. Les Weeks and his crew pose for the camera; pilot Flg Off Russ ?iams is standing on the far left and Les Weeks is standing fourth from the left. *Weeks*

?t: Warrant Officer Les C Weeks was a Lancaster navigator on 467 Squadron RAAF at ?ddington, Lincolnshire and 83 Squadron Pathfinder Force, Coningsby, Lincolnshire. He com-?ed his tour of thirty operations between June and December 1944.

Above: Hauptmann Heinz Rökker and his crew in front of their NJG2 Junkers Ju 88G at Twente, Holland in March 1945. From left: Carlos Nugent [radar-funker], Heinz Rökker [pilot], Franz Fra [1. Wart – 1st mechanic], Hans Mattar [bordfunker], Fritz Wefelmeier [beobachter]. *Rökker*

Below left: Lieutenant Benedikt Kardopoltsev spent most of his war service with 2 GuIAP in Belorussia, flying the La 5 and La 7. He claimed six air combat victories in the La 7 including f Fw 190s. *Kardopoltsev via Oleg Korytov*

Below right: Senior Lieutenant Alexei Valyaev flew the Lavochkin La 5 with 180 GuIAP, ending the war with two victories and two probables. *Valyaev via Oleg Korytov*

ove left: Wing Commander Oliver Wells OBE at Oakington, Cambridgeshire in July 1943 while *?*ing with 7 Squadron. He initially flew Stirlings before converting to Lancasters, was shot down *?* his seventh operation and evaded for four months before being captured. *Wells*

? right: Lissett, Yorkshire in the winter of 1944/45 and Wireless Operator Jack Bromfield [left] *?*es for the camera in front of a 158 Squadron Halifax. The others are Canadians Ed Rae [rear *?*ner], Gar Cross [bomb aimer] and Arthur Robertson [pilot]. *Bromfield*

ove right: Bill Musgrave's 237 Squadron Spitfire IX PT957 DV-T 'Tagati' at Rosignano, Italy in April *?*5. Tagati is a South African English word meaning wizard – Bill originated from Rhodesia. *Musgrave*

?ow: Jack Biggs [left] and fellow 17 Squadron Hurricane pilots Bill Dunkley and Basil Rathbone *?*943, taken at landing strip 'Acorn'. *Imperial War Museum C1278*

?et: Flight Lieutenant Jack Biggs trained in the US on the first Arnold Scheme course. Following *?*rricane conversion in the UK he was posted to 17 Squadron in Calcutta in October 1942. The *?* converted to the Spitfire VIII in April 1944 and that autumn Jack was moved to an instructing *?*t in India.

Above from left to right:
Flight Sergeant John King was a Halifax flight engineer with 296 Squadron at Earls Colne, Essex. He then moved to 644 Squadron at Tarrant Rushton, Dorset and then to 47 Squadron at Fairford, Gloucestershire, still on the Halifax; Squadron Leader Michael Wainwright AFC. Flew the Blenheim and Spitfire with 64 Squadron from September 1939. After a period with 102 OTU at Kidlington, Oxford flying Master and Lysander glider tugs, he went back to fighters at 58 OTU Grangemouth on Spitfires; Air Commodore John Ellacombe DFC & Bar. First served with 151 Squadron flying Hurricanes during the fall of France and the Battle

of Britain. Later flew with 253 Squadron, then 151 Squadron where he flew both the Defiant and the Hurricane. He converted to the Mosquito and was active during the Normandy invasion with 487 Squadron; Flying Officer Henry Payne initially trained to fly the Hampden Canada, but on return to England he was sent to 299 Squadron at Shepherds Grove, Suffolk to fly the Stirling. He towed gliders to Arnhem during Operation Market Garden and also flew agent and supply-dropping operations; Flight Sergeant Roy Fensome served as a wireless operator on the Dakota, Halifax and Lancaster mainly on 216 Squadron in the Middle East in 1945.

Bottom: Flying Officer Bill Musgrave flew all his operations on Spitfires with 237 Squadron in Corsica and Italy in 1944 and 1945. Shortly before he died he visited the Battle of Britain memorial on the embankment in London with his wife Margery.

It was very cold – but I remember Sid getting out, stepping over the side and falling flat on his face. I followed suit and fell flat as well. We dragged Dan up the beach. We crawled and dragged him up and away from the sea, came across some barbed wire, where Dan got stuck, eventually got through it and up to a stone promenade on the sea front.

"We came onto the road and started walking, when a German patrol crossed the road ahead of us. We decided to hide and after crossing a bridge took a lane heading inland and to a small farm. Our feet were in a bad way so we decided to hide in a hay loft. We found a ladder and climbed up, and I made a nest for Dan and myself, while Sid made his own. We burrowed into the hay, and pulled it over us. Some time before dawn I heard someone climb up the ladder, look in and go away, so we decided it was time to leave but their feet were too sore, so we went to the farmhouse, found a French housewife there who had four little children, the eldest was about eight or nine. I could speak to the woman in my pigeon French; she gave us some soup and bread and ersatz coffee, and told me we were most unlucky as there were two German garrisons each side of the farm. Then the farmer came and I realised he was up to no good, as he was the one who'd climbed the ladder in the night and had notified the Germans. I don't blame the woman at all. If I'd had four children and was asked to hide enemy fliers, I'd have said 'go to hell'.

"The Germans arrived, German army not Luftwaffe and we were taken to Caen and interrogated by two army officers and then Luftwaffe officers. Dan and Sid were given injections in the buttocks with a 'horse' syringe – and then we were separated. They went to hospital – I went to Caen jail for New Year's Eve with all the drunken Germans, and then off to Stalag Luft in Frankfurt. I was not allowed to wash or dry my clothes.

"Dan and Sid ended up in the drink due to my fault entirely; it was an error of judgement. I should have just gone adjacent to Le Havre – dropped and cleared out. Whilst in 815 I had got away unharmed by flying under AA fire from the cliffs above and thought I could do the same this night. The last thing I asked at the briefing was if there was a difference in barometric pressure between Thorney and Le Havre and was assured there was none. We lost more crews by hitting the sea at night including a CO. I believe three or four aircraft were lost in the same period from Thorney, then the ops were cancelled."

Jimmy Greening flew Barracudas with 822 Squadron from shore bases such as Thorney Island and Manston during 1944 and 1945.

"Returning home from an anti-submarine patrol to Eindhoven, our Barracuda was about to be attacked by an Fw 190 and we dived to just above the surface of the sea, when three Beaufighters spotted the Focke-Wulf and saw it off.   We stayed low and then spotted a small one-man submarine which had been beached, and reported this on return to base. The next aircraft out was tasked to find and photograph it, but was unable to do so.   Consequently, the next day we continued the search. This time we were successful, but came near to disaster.   While flying low and slow with the undercarriage down to enable the observer to get his photos, I had forgotten that I was carrying depth-charges on the wing and we came dangerously close to stalling, only just managing to avoid some coastal defence blocks.   I had no further encounters with the enemy, and one of my chief memories of Manston is being grounded for beating-up the mess on VE night!"

Chapter Six

THE EASTERN FRONT

On each and every attack our valorous Red Army will answer with
three times more powerful blows!

Be a pilot, contribute to the power of the air force!

Long live the powerful aviation of the socialist country!

Head-on deliberate midair collision is a weapon of heroes. Glory to the
Stalin's falcons, threat to the fascist predators!

Soviet propaganda posters

"I have done my best during the past few years to make our air force the
largest and most powerful in the world. The creation of the Greater
German Reich has been made possible largely by the strength and constant
readiness of the air force. Born of the spirit of the German airmen in the
First World War, inspired by its faith in our Führer and commander in
chief, thus stands the German air force today, ready to carry out every
command of the Führer with lightning speed and undreamed of might."

Order of the Day from Göring to the Luftwaffe, August 1939

When Operation Barbarossa, the invasion of Russia, began in 1941, the Germans
had staggering early success against the Soviet air forces, claiming to destroy
approximately 5,000 aircraft in the first week, mostly caught on the ground and
lined-up in neat rows. Soviet and German official records are surprisingly in
close agreement, with for example, a Soviet figure of 1,300 losses on the first day,
versus German claims of 1,100.

As aerial combat developed, the victory scores of leading German pilots such
as Erich Hartmann, Gerhard Barkhorn and Günther Rall were, and still are,
often criticised by both Soviet veterans and historians. Due to the extent of the
large-scale air battles over-claiming was common. German tactics allowed pilots
to concentrate on kill totals, while Soviet tactics demanded the accomplishment
of the mission, so that if a fighter shot down a bomber, but other bombers
reached their target, it was not considered to be a successful sortie. Günther Rall
also considered the opposition to be generally ill-prepared.

"The Russian pilots at the beginning of the war were poor, they had bad
tactics and obsolete aircraft. We triumphed at first because they were
totally unable to defend themselves, and were in complete disarray. We

149

scored victory after victory in the air because they had no strategies or tactics. But they learned very quickly with new equipment, the LaGG, MiG and Yak series, and were then adequate opponents. The LaGG-5 and La-5 were impossible to catch. I chased them at full power but they were always out of range, it was very frustrating.

"There's no doubt they learned very quickly how to fight us, so they were soon serious opponents. They copied our tactical formations, and it became evident to us that they had become very confident and powerful. In contrary to the West, they were rude and crude, controlled by the political commissars!" (*This is an oft-stated belief, although in reality the commissars had almost no controlling power.*)

What is clear from veterans' accounts, is that the outbreak of war was almost completely unexpected. Benedikt Kardopoltsev's unit was certainly taken by surprise, and thrown into chaos for some time.

"We used to live in the tents near our airfield, and one night we were raised by the alarm. We were gathered together and told: 'War has begun!' It was Sunday, five o'clock in the morning. Some were told to help load ammo, some helped technicians to prepare 'planes, some had orders to camouflage 'planes.

"My commander asked: 'Who knows how to use the Degtyaryov machine gun?' I said: 'I'm ready!' He gave me two cadets to carry cartridges and the machine gun: 'Hide about 2 kilometres from us, and if you see some saboteurs, kill them. In about two hours we will relieve you.' One hour passed, two...eventually twelve, and it was getting dark. We were thirsty and hungry, but we had no orders to leave our post. Finally, we just went back to the base, and met our commander, who said: 'Where were you? Were you AWOL?' 'You sent us to the guard post in the morning!' 'Well, yes, I had forgotten.' So we went to the canteen, where there was nothing left, and we ended up going to bed hungry. That was my first day of war.

"When the Germans got closer, we prepared for evacuation. For three days we waited for a train, and when we were losing hope it finally came. Technical staff disassembled our aircraft and we loaded them onto the train, then we went to Azerbaijan. We had to fight for food there, less than three months from the war's beginning, and already there was nothing to eat."

Initially serving as a mechanic, Mikhail Pomorov was later retrained to become a pilot and flew the Yak 9. He summed up some of the hard lessons and difficult times he went through.

"My first flight check was made by Sergey Nikolayevich Aleshin, a pilot of the old school. He made me wear a silk scarf, and when we returned he said, 'What kind of a pilot are you, if after flying with your commander you don't have blood on your scarf? If you are not looking around, you will get killed!' The other thing he said was, 'You have to land by your ass, not head! You have to feel the distance from the ground by your ass. And remember, your butt is the most important gauge in the cockpit. If something goes wrong, you will have this funny feeling down there long before gauges will react.'

"War as a whole was won by village boys, although most of the pilots came from the cities, it was easier to get to an aero club there. Some images still appear in my mind; winter, the coast of the Baltic Sea, and a pilot who was running to the toilet to pee every ten minutes because of stress. Death was very close to us, not even because of the Germans; if the engine failed in the open sea, you were dead! Or the other image, we got drop tanks to escort bombers, and from a certain point we had to drop them, and return home. We could not wait until this moment came!"

Alexei Valyaev had a similarly difficult time at first, and his first encounter with the Luftwaffe showed that the Germans had their share of less-experienced pilots.

"On my first regiment, first IAP *(istrebitel'nyi aviatsionnyi polk – fighter air regiment)*, first flight, first kill. My enemy must have been the same as me – young and inexperienced. He got lost, same as I did, and he got just in front of me, so I shot him down. It was an Fw 190, I flew an La-5; it just appeared in front of me. I was so happy! 'I made it, I made it!' I saw how my shells hit him, the yellow or orange tracers were well visible. He made some wild manoeuvres, and then spun down.

"When I came to 180th GuIAP *(guards fighter air regiment)* I was a wingman and Nikolai Gorev was killed on a bombing mission; he was among the first to be killed in our IAP. They went too far, and while they were absent, clouds covered the airfield. He baled out but pulled the ripcord while he was in the cockpit and got caught by the tail of the falling aeroplane.

"Near Lvov there is a small town – Hodorev. Near that town there was a lake, with a river going out of that lake, but that river ended soon. I was looking at that lake, and it seemed too suspicious to me, 'Why does this river end? Where does the water in this lake come from? We should strafe it.' So I did. I was returning from a mission, and strafed a boat on that lake, and suddenly it blew up. The fireball was far above me. When I turned around the flames were at a height of 220 metres. It burned for several days, as it was a fuel depot, that was a whole lake of fuel. Germans made camouflage this way – a thin layer of water above and a pumping station on the shore.

"An inspector came from Kiev, 'How many kills do you have?' 'Two.' 'You have twelve now.' Everybody from our regiment was given some kills by this inspector. We gathered to discuss this situation, and decided that nothing good would come of it. This inspector was informed from Moscow that High Command would not tolerate it, so we ended up with the same amount of kills that we had before."

Alexei Kukin had a very short war as a MiG 1 pilot with 176 GuIAP before he was invalided out of flying as a result of injuries sustained when he was shot down just a few months after the outbreak of hostilities.

"When the Finnish campaign ended my friend Dmitrii Pikulenko, said 'Who will be next? Germans? I wonder what it will be like to fight them?' We all got the chance to find it out. I made my first combat flight in a MiG 1 on 23 June, and caught a Ju 88 above Leningrad sea port. I shot at them until the enemy gunner hit me back. He damaged a hydraulic line, so that one leg did not come down on the landing and I had to land on one wheel. The engine was damaged, and one bullet went through the windscreen and hit the armoured headrest, barely passing my head. Everything started at 7,000 metres – I noticed a green dot, moving above grey water at 4,000 metres and dived to investigate. I was shooting at him, but I couldn't bring him down. I thought 'Damn! What should I do? I've wasted almost all my ammo, but it will not go down!' The problem was my gun sight was way off. I started aiming tracers, and had to move my head to the side. If I had not done this I would have got a bullet right between my eyes.

"The MiG was great higher up; it was great up to 7,000 metres. If you flew below 1,500 it was a different story. If you had to do a split-S, you needed 1,200 metres of altitude. There was a warning notice in the cockpit that if your aircraft did not recover from spin before your altitude reduced to 2,000 metres, you must bale out. But we flew at any height, spun at any height and recovered. We only had armoured seat backs. When I was shot up by an enemy gunner I looked at the damage done by him, and noticed that there was quite a big space between the engine and cockpit, so I asked an engineer of my squadron to put seat back armour there to protect my chest.

"The commissar of the air corps ordered a strafing sortie. After a few minutes he cancelled this order. So bombs were first loaded, and then unloaded. Of course, taking off with a half loaded aeroplane was forbidden. At this time twenty Me 110s came, and began strafing; they always came in large numbers. Seven of our pilots took off and downed seven '110s. They burned seven of our 'planes on the ground in return. This happened within the first couple of weeks of the war beginning. A search for the guilty person began. The commissar said that he was 'white and fluffy', so Neustruev was found to be responsible for the losses. There was no written order, and you couldn't use someone's words as proof. Ivan eventually got ten years imprisonment for that; with the possibility to clear himself in combat.

"I shot from head-on above at a Ju 88, and saw how the canopy was ripped open by the tracers, but it kept flying. It was a common problem;

Alexei Kukin had a fairly short operational career as an I-16 and MiG 1
pilot with 176 GuIAP before being shot down by a Bf 109 in October 1941
and invalided out of flying. *Kukin via Oleg Korytov*

you were spraying the enemy with bullets like a shower, but the effect on them was not good enough to bring the 'plane down.

"One day I saw that one of our 'planes was under attack. I decided to try and scare the attacker off, but when I left formation, a '109 pilot realised that I was close, and shot at my 'plane from a long distance, well beyond 300 metres. The cabin was completely destroyed, the stick was blown off, and the instrument panel was torn to pieces. Then my 'plane blew up and I was thrown away from it. I was lucky that I did not strap myself in before take-off. The right half of my body was filled with fragments, and they still won't let me sleep. When I was hanging on a parachute, I was looking down, and saw a stream of blue tracers below me. It was that same Messer trying to finish me off! Luckily, a group of our fighters appeared, so I had a chance to land safely." (*On 22 July 1941 Hauptmann Reinhard Seiler from 1./JG54 claimed two victories at 18:05 and 18:08. No location was given, so it is quite possible that he shot Kukin's 'plane down.*)

"The Germans had good 'planes and tactics. I was in a hospital for the first time, and Vasilii Bohoncev was brought to the same ward. We both had burns on our faces and hands. We discussed how we were shot down, and came to a conclusion that it was our tactics at fault. We flew in three-plane formations and had to look after each other in order to avoid collision. It was rather awkward. They flew in pairs, and usually one would appear in front of our flight, we would start chasing him, and the second German would shoot us from behind; then they would change places.

"It was best if you hit the pilot. It was not bad if you hit the engine, or damaged the controls, but you had to hit it precisely. Most commonly we had no time to aim, we had to look around in order not to miss enemy 'planes attacking ourselves, so we just sprayed the enemy planes with bullets hoping that something important would get hit.

"The most difficult opponent was the Fw 189. It had a small cabin, and it was very nimble. On one occasion I was flying towards my base, when near Ropsha I spotted two MiGs chasing an Fw 189. I decided to help. It was trying to slip away at tree-top level. My wingman exchanged places with Dmitrii Pikulenko, and stayed behind, covering us while we two attacked the '189. Finally the pilot climbed a bit, so I fired and hit it. It caught the tree-tops with a wing and fell to the ground. Pikulenko made a strafing run to be sure.

"On my last flight, I went out on a reconnaissance on 23 September 1941. I was caught by Messers and had to fight for my life against six of them. I fought from Gorelovo to Malaya Okhta. I was shot down, and fell with my 'plane onto the railway station at Okhta. I had a broken leg and skull. That's how my life as a pilot ended. I was not suited for flight service anymore, so I was in a PVO fighter regiment from 1943 onwards in the chief of staff post. We saw the war end in Romania, at Karol-1 airfield. How we had looked forward to it. Then we had to live a normal life again."

Ivan Zvyagin also suffered appalling injuries during combat, but in his case he was able to return to flying after he had recovered.

"I made forty-one combat sorties, shot down two enemy 'planes, and everything went well, until on my forty-second mission I was shot down. I almost burned alive. It was nearly at the end of a patrol, and we had about five minutes of patrolling time left. Suddenly, my 'plane disintegrated. I did not think about baling out, I was thrown out of the cockpit and all that I had – boots, pistol, and helmet – were torn off by the wind, but luckily, the parachute opened. I came to and found out that all that I wore was on fire. I landed at a place where the Kuban river joins the sea, and was picked up by civilians who were hiding on the shore, and they took me to the battlefront. Since I was severely burned I was sent to the medical battalion and I spent two months in hospital. My neck would not turn, as it was covered in scars."

Possibly the most famous of all the aircraft types flown by the Soviet air forces was the Il-2 Shturmovik dive-bomber. Mikhael Pomorov said, "I would like to take my hat off in front of a Shturmovik pilot, and I wouldn't sit down until he does." Yuri Khukhrikov flew them in action for some time.

"In July 1941 I graduated from the aviation club, basically because the war started, all graduates were sent to Saratov, where we started flying Tupolev SB-2s. They called it a candle. It was completely unprotected, and besides that, made of duralumin, any bullet or shell fragment caused a fire. Then an order came to retrain for the Il-2; they brought in more than thirty from Kuibyshev. They picked out only the most gifted, so they would teach us as little as possible – there was no fuel to practise with. They sent us to a reserve airfield at Diad'kov, that's where pilots learned combat skills such as bombing and shooting. Senior staff from operational squadrons would visit the training school and choose new pilots – this was known as buying. Shora Parshin came for us – he was an ace. A ground attack pilot, he shot down ten aircraft in an Il. He fought from the first day of the war and to the end, he was an excellent man. We found ourselves in the 566th Ground Attack Aviation Regiment. This regiment was the first to get its own honorary name – *Solnechnogorsk*. It fought at Moscow; almost everyone died. During the war the regiment lost 105 pilots and fifty gunners. Twenty-eight of us came to the division and fifteen were killed. Such were the losses.
"The Il-2 was an excellent aircraft. It carried 600 kilograms of bombs, eight rockets, 300 23mm shells for Via cannon (150 per gun), and 1,800 rounds for each machine gun, 3,600 rounds. The gunner had a 12.7mm Berezin machine gun, ten DAG-10 distance aviation grenades for the protection of the lower rear. If a German appeared, you would press a switch, and a grenade would fall on a parachute and explode 150 metres away. The Il-2 was not at all difficult to handle. The gunner was

necessary; his usefulness is beyond question. The only thing was that we sat on gasoline; a tank under me, a tank in front, a tank between me and the gunner. We were all surrounded by gasoline.

"We finished up in Wittenberg, from where we flew sorties to Koenigsberg and even Danzig. One day a shell hit a wing, but we made it back miraculously – the hole was about a metre in size. If a bullet hits, the burned metal could melt. But I was lucky, the shock wave and fragments hit the gunner. His legs were mangled and communications were disrupted. We landed, I taxied, turned off the engine, and jumped out onto the wing. The gunner, Viktor Shakhaev, was just lying there. Guys ran to us and pulled him out, barely saved his legs. But it turned out that I was also hit. A fragment had scratched the back of my head. They wanted to put me in a hospital, but I refused.

"We always had fighter escorts; very often during the Prussian operation we were escorted by Normandie-Niemen. (*The Free French Groupe de Chasse 'Normandie-Niemen' was formed in December 1942 following a treaty between the Free French authorities and the Soviet Union.*) Usually we bombed the forward positions. I went to reconnoitre on foot once. The infantry commander said, 'You guys don't have to shoot. Fly here and show yourselves. That would be enough. If you bomb, you'll always be welcome guests!' We sank ships in ports, and four times flew against airfields. That was scary business. They were well protected. We also worked on armour concentrations. Against those armies hundreds of aircraft were sent, in order to wipe everything off the face of the earth.

"AA artillery was the most dangerous. At the beginning of the war fighters really made the lives of ground attack pilots difficult. But by the end of the war, it was AA artillery, that too was scary business. Several dozen small calibre AA guns were deployed and would fire into the same spot. All around you were black clouds from medium calibre AA guns. You would fly and not know which of them would hit you. When approaching the front line we spread out at 150-metre intervals, and threw our 'planes from side to side. Then we would get into a circle above the target and start working it. The little ones (fighters) would cover us.

"The number of passes depended on the situation. There could be such intense enemy action that it would only be one pass. You would use everything at once, rockets, guns, bombs. If the enemy action was not that great, then we'd make several passes, four to six times. The leader would snake away, allowing the wingman to catch up. The most vulnerable spot on the Il 2 was the engine. Wings were fine, more or less. If a fuel tank was hit, that wasn't bad either. When approaching the target we opened carbon dioxide canisters, which filled the empty spaces in the fuel tanks. If a bullet pierced the fuselage and hit a fuel tank, the sealer would fill the hole, fuel would not leak out, there would be no vapour, and consequently no fire. We carried 82mm rockets. Of course, we fired them at random. But at the forward positions legitimate targets were everywhere, so heavy was the concentration of forces and vehicles.

"Sometimes we flew three sorties a day. If someone says it wasn't scary they're lying. The moment of expectation was the scariest and most unpleasant. You sat in the cockpit, waiting for a signal rocket, with your legs shaking, and panic setting in. After all, there was no guarantee that you wouldn't be shot down during the mission. When a rocket shot up into the air your head would start looking all over the place, and your panic would cease. Then there was an unpleasant feeling when we approached the target but would not attack it immediately. They would be prepared for us, and fire. After the attack started that was it, the pilot was at work, looking for targets, pushing triggers, rockets, guns, machine guns, pulling the bomb release. I never had to participate in a dogfight, but the rear gunner also saw action; after pulling out from an attack he would fire at ground targets.

"We had twice the Hero of the Soviet Union, Len'ka (Leonid) Beda, we had gone to school together. Len'ka killed 118 of our men at the end of the war. It wasn't his fault, they told him before the mission: 'Bomb that target.' But he had to get there first; maybe thirty minutes. While they were flying there, the situation had changed. We had captured that place, but no one had reported it to him. The group worked the target, and our soldiers died. He returned, they tore off his epaulettes, but immediately investigated, and returned them later.

"There were single occurrences of cowardice. There was one time, when someone was leading a large group of about twenty aircraft, he turned away before reaching the target and the entire group returned to the airfield. A court-martial gave him seven years. But he fought well afterwards – four Orders of the Red Banner. There were sly people as well. One such would gain altitude, and as we attacked, he would just hang there, then descend to 1,000 metres, release the bomb load and get in formation. But we observed everything and warned him: 'Sasha, you do that one more time, we'll shoot you down.' The warning worked. There were no penal ground attack squadrons. They would send offending officers to us, not necessarily pilots. They would fly ten sorties as rear gunners. *(Pilots could be punished by being sent to a ground penal unit, or receiving a prison term. The standard was for punishment to be deferred until the war had ended, with the possibility to be cleared in the interim by meritorious service.)*

"The most intense activity was during ground operations. During pauses between operations we flew anyway and performed tactical missions. Of course, with smaller forces we would be sent to support infantry or to destroy columns on the march. For example, Pokryshkin flew more than 500 sorties. Ground attack pilots' hands are covered in blood up to the elbows. But it was our duty, and I think we did a first class job. We did everything we could well."

Both sides quickly came to respect each others' abilities, especially as the war progressed and experience built up. Leonid Kulakov recounted some of his experiences against Luftwaffe bomber formations.

"The Germans called the glass cabin on the Junkers Ju 88 and the Heinkel He 111 'Totenkopf' – dead head, because if you hit there, then everyone, the entire crew, was dead. I shot up a Junkers in the cabin, and as it began to fall, the results were very clear.

"You go out on a free hunt, you pick off a bunch. How many you can shoot down depends on what your mission was and what kind of aircraft. Let's say you encountered a group of Ju 87s. Of course it's possible to take them down because they sometimes even flew without rear gunners. But if you are talking about fighters, just try it! Try to dogfight with them. You will have to go to extreme lengths just to shoot down one. The Germans, if they saw the escort, would try to climb to avoid confrontation.

"The German pilots were very well trained and they had good tactics. They knew not to engage when you had altitude advantage over them. They would fly off, gain altitude, and then come back to bite you."

Differences in aircraft performance also tended to diminish as the Soviets rapidly developed more capable aircraft and began to receive lease-lend aid from the other allies. At first Nikolay Gerasimovich found himself flying combat sorties with the obsolescent, but still effective, Polikarpov I-16 Rata. He later flew the Hurricane, and encountered a variety of German types with which to draw comparisons.

"The I-16 was complex, exacting in piloting technique, the slightest pull of the stick and it sank into a spin. It came out of it quickly, whether it was a simple or an inverted one. The I-16 was very manoeuvrable, it performed any aerobatics. I loved this fighter. In terms of horizontal manoeuvrability, it was a unique aircraft. The cockpit was small, but that is because the I-16 was itself a small aircraft. If you went straight ahead then the field of vision was not very good but we never went straight ahead on the I-16, 'S-turns', banking left-right constantly. We had sliding hoods on our aircraft in the group, but prior to battle we would constantly open them. There was concern that the hood would jam; if you were shot down and it was necessary to bale out, then you could not release it. Some aircraft had an emergency release, some did not. A lot of heat came from the engine, but our faces used to freeze. To prevent frostbite to the face there were special masks made out of moleskin. But they were practically never used because they would hinder us in combat.

"There was not any armoured glass. The visor was made of ordinary Plexiglas. In a frontal attack the engine shielded us. This was a strong quality of the I-16; it was very good in frontal attacks. The undercarriage was mechanically lowered, it was cable controlled by hand and took forty-three turns of the handle. Sometimes in haste, especially when there was little fuel, you would wind it in the wrong direction and the cables became tangled. So each of us had pliers in the cockpit with which to cut through the cables, and the wheels would fall out themselves, then 'left roll, right roll', and the undercarriage locked and you could land normally.

"We tried to manoeuvre engagements as low as possible, to 1,000 or 2,000 thousand metres. The Germans did not particularly like to climb to altitude either, they tried to keep to 4,000 or 5,000. At this altitude the 'Messer' engine showed its best characteristics. But then the I-16 types 28 and 29 surpassed the Bf 109E. Their speed was the same as the Messer, but in terms of manoeuvrability, including in terms of vertical manoeuvrability, the 'E' was inferior. In combat the difference between their speeds was practically negligible.

"The 'Messer' dived well. The I-16 was worse here, its frontal area was large, and in a dive it did not allow you more than 530 kilometres and hour. But it must be said that in combat it was necessary to disengage, whether them from us or us from them, we always disengaged, as circumstances allowed.

"The Bf 109F...in the vertical was strong. You would just about catch it up and it gave a boost and disengaged. The Fw 190 appeared roughly at the same time as the Bf 109F, at some point in October 1942. It was a very strong fighter. The '190 was completely superior to the I-16, except in terms of horizontal manoeuvrability. But by that time our Yaks had already come on a large scale, and the lend-lease P-40 and P-39. The Bf 109G came in 1943 but the I-16 practically had no battles with them. I had about ten combat sorties and two or three dogfights on the I-16, and then I was converted to the Hurricane."

Olga Lisikova was another pilot who found herself flying obsolete aircraft, in this case the Polikarpov PO.2 / U-2 biplane trainer, which was pressed into use for a variety of operational roles (which even included light bombing).

"I was flying a U-2 (SP-2) medical evacuation aeroplane. It was silver in colour, and had highly visible red crosses on it. When I saw that a German fighter was on my tail, I thought that he would see the red crosses and leave me alone. But the fighter closed up on me. I had several seconds before my life would end. I saw an overhang, and I literally thrust my 'plane under it. The burst that was launched by the fighter passed over my aircraft and cut into the other bank of the river. I pressed the stick and flew lower and lower, flying directly over the water, darting back and forth with the river. I thought that the German pilot must be swearing at me up above; he could not cope with such a small 'insect'.

"I sensed a narrowing of the river and then I spotted a bridge. I had to climb. I knew at this moment I would become a target for him. But it

Hero of the Soviet Union Major Vasili Kubarev. *Kubarev via Oleg Korytov*

was obvious he had damaged my aircraft. I came upon an airfield, Verebye, and set my aircraft down without an approach. People were running up to me from all sides, shouting something and waving. I did not understand. I climbed down from the cabin, looked around, and saw that the Messerschmitt was burning. It had dived on my 'plane and began to pull out, but the aircraft had bottomed out. He did not have sufficient altitude for his pullout, and struck the other bank."

Hero of the Soviet Union Major Vasili Kubarev flew more than 300 operational sorties with the 187th IAP, 653rd (later 65th) GuIAP which included around seventy actual engagements with enemy aircraft. He ended the war with a score of forty-six air-to-air combat victory claims, and served on until 1981 when he retired with the rank of general.

"It was the 653rd Fighter Regiment in the summer of 1941. I shot down my first 'plane while flying the I-15Bis – an Me 109. I had four rockets mounted under the lower wings, and when many enemy 'planes appeared in front of us, I fired all four at once. I managed to shoot down the flight leader. Maybe it was shrapnel, maybe a direct hit. He went into a flat spin and didn't come out of it until he hit the ground. I did not see it myself, but I have been told that no one saw a parachute. The remaining group of Germans turned around and left.

"The zveno formation (*section of three aircraft*) was not successful, it was tying everyone up. But a pair was open for free manoeuvre. While we flew the Bis we used zveno formation. The Bis was weak as a fighter, but it was still possible to catch Germans off guard. We flew what we were given, not what we wanted to fly. The zveno formation was abandoned at the end of 1942.

"There was no difference between our opponents and us. We had weak pilots, so did they. They had aces and we did too. But we were killing without thinking who was a good pilot, and who was bad. Bullets don't care who they kill, any pilot could become a victim. Both the Me and Fw were serious 'planes. Which one was better? As many pilots as there are out there, there are as many opinions. For me they were equal. The threat of your opponent had nothing to do with the 'plane type, it was more a pilot's skill level.

"Both sides shot at parachutists. Germans would bale from 200 metres and our I-16s didn't have time to fire at them. But this is war and a good enemy is a dead enemy. We were supposed to get 1,000 roubles for shooting down a fighter, 1,500 for a bomber and something else for reconnaissance planes. We got it in cash, some drank vodka, and some saved."

THE GERMAN VIEW VERSUS THE RUSSIAN VIEW

In 2007, the transcripts of interviews with both German and Russian pilots who had served on the Eastern Front were passed to each of them for comment, and some very interesting views emerged. The German pilot was Norbert Hannig, who spent all his time on the Eastern Front with JG54, predominantly flying the Fw 190, while the Russian pilot was Vladimir Tikhomirov, who mainly flew the Yak series of fighters.

Firstly, Norbert Hannig's (NH) view of various events and tactics, together with Vladimir Tikhomirov's (VT) comments.

NH – "At pilot training school I had a trainer who came from JG54, at that point the best squadron and the best wing, so I tried to get into this unit. From there on we were sent to Biarritz.

VT – "It is really hard to forget the siege... and to forgive those who made it. I still do not understand how Leningrad could hold for so long... Now I must become wise, since I no longer want to start waving fists after war had ended.

NH – "Biarritz was the last school (*2 Staffel Jagdgruppe West, 2 March 1943 to 26 March 1943*) before time at the front, and there I had again an instructor pilot who came from 54 and I learnt so many things, especially from Wing Commander Trautloft. Trautloft was one of the German officers who was personally keen, not only as a fighter, as an officer, but also as a person. He had a good brain and he could remember everything, especially names.

"We went down to Biarritz and there they asked us, 'where do you want go?' Some wings were assigned to the west and some were assigned to the south, or to the east. I said right away '54'. From then on they assigned me to this wing. I finished the school, and the training, and then I got my assignment.

VT – "If that was common training of Luftwaffe pilots – they had been better trained then I thought...we knew even then that most German pilots were better than our young ones. By the end of war (from mid '44) there were lots of inexperienced Germans, on the other hand. By this time there were two types of Germans – either extremely good ones, or extremely poor pilots, and as war progressed, this differentiation only increased.

NH – "We made the longest trip by rail from Biarritz up to Leningrad, it took eight days. We went from Berlin, over Königsberg, then Riga, and finally up north to Leningrad. The train ended at something around two o'clock; it was night time, snowy and cold. The station was empty and dirty, but there were iron stoves where we could make a fire to warm us. Then we saw the front, the shooting...the flashes and so on. It was the first impression of real fighting that we had. The next morning they picked us up, and brought us to the wing commander, Trautloft. (*The posting to 5 Staffel JG54 lasted from 7 March 1943 to 31 March 1944, at which time the unit was based at Siverskaja. From 1 April 1944 to 20 September 1944 Norbert was a fighter instructor and squadron leader on 2 Staffel Jagdgruppe West at Liegnitz in Silesia, before returned to 5 and 6 Staffels JG54 as squadron leader in Russia from 1*

Lieutenant Colonel Vladimir Tikhomirov flew the Yak 7 and Yak 9 with the Baltic Air Fleet's 121 IAP, achieving a total of thirteen air-to-air victories. *Tikhomirov via Oleg Korytov*

October 1944 to 7 April 1945.)

"We went onto the front in March, but there was not much flying due to the winter. People on our wing got a Russian first lieutenant who came over the front line with his aircraft. He had his fiancée with him and both trained the Germans how to use the snow for making runways in winter. In Germany we shovelled the snow away, but they said, 'no, only clean up half of the snow'. The other half they went over with vehicles and pressed it down. In the springtime very quickly, the snow of the un-pressed side melted and dried and we could still fly from the pressed side, which was icy. So the snow didn't stop flying during the winter.

VT – "That must be Kulakov! My tech Rubanov was his mechanic, and was sent to penal squad for removing armour plate so that his girl could fit in his I-16. We asked him honestly, whether he knew about Kulakov's intentions or not, but he always avoided direct answers.

NH – "In 1942 new pilots still had the full complement of training time which they had to fly. But from the start of '44 they began to shorten the time allowed. I had an instructor in Berlin, and he had only twenty-five hours to train our boys up as fighter pilots. They had flown '109 Emil and they converted to the '190. The Focke-Wulf was a very sturdy aircraft. It had a large undercarriage, a wide undercarriage, whereas the '109 had a small one. It was very quick on the stick, there wasn't much time to react."

VT – "I don't know about landing characteristics, but until the last day we thought of the Me 109 as a more nimble and dangerous opponent. The Fw was a bit more sluggish, maybe? Although, as usual, everything depended on the pilot.

NH – "In the beginning the Russians had the old dopple-decker (Polikarpovs). But then they started out with the Yak 1, the Yak 3 and from the Yak 7 onwards they were more or less equal in all the flying characteristics that ours had. The pilots were are not as well trained because they didn't have the experience, but they entered into so many combats, during '43, and especially during '44, that we were outnumbered one to ten. Sometimes they didn't even see us between all the different Russians.

VT – "Not true, at least for naval aviation. We rarely had groups of more than ten ground attack 'planes plus four to six escort fighters. As far as I remember the Germans would always wait until they had at least a one to one ratio. Not too commonly a pair of 'hunters' could attack, and that was the most difficult attack to repel. What was always good from their point was that they were able to gather together quite fast. I'd say that in 80% of my fights I was at a numerical disadvantage. Speaking of pilots' quality, those who started the war in 1941 were great, those who came later were rather weak. True, but it took about twenty-five to thirty flights for a pilot to become more or less operational.

NH – "You could see they had these bombers surrounded by I don't know how many fighter aircraft. But later, say end of '44 / 45 they laid out the same formations in the air that we did, with the finger four. There was one Russian wing, which painted the aircraft red from the nose down behind the canopy, and a golden star in front of the cabin; Stalin Staffel. Those guys could fly.

VT – "Nevei licard of such a squadron – in our aviation there never was a single squad or regiment with a personal name! A gold star was commonly painted on HSU's planes.

The so-called Stalin Regiment was the 434th IAP, later the 32nd GuIAP, commanded by Vasili Stalin, son of Josef. Vasili claimed one Fw 190.

NH – "Females flew the very light aircraft; they threw the hand grenades out. They didn't fly the fighter aircraft, nor the bombers.

VT – "There were bomb racks on those planes, and they used up to 100 kg bombs, most commonly 10-25 kg bombs. But grenades? No."

NH – "Kiev ran from north to south, and the west side of the river is 50 metres high, and there was to the east much flat country. We got this order to search out, where the Russians were. We found out that we were already on the run and had crossed the river but the enemy was on the right side. The Russians went south and north of Kiev and had circled the town. We got the order to help the ground troops defend the town with only six aircraft!

"The aerodrome was on the edge of the town and surrounded by a railway on one side, and two dams of something around ten metres high on the other, which we had to overcome during take-off. We stood with the six aircraft there and pulled them in the evening into the empty hangars and we went back to the barracks. A Russian T-34 made contact with our building, but we stayed on the third floor and the soldiers ran in the first floor and knocked on the door, but we made no noise, and they got back on the T-34 and went away again.

"I remember my forty-second and final victory before I left JG54. We were at two bases, one was the base near the town, and the other one was between two canals, one military canal to the military harbour and one to the civilian harbour. Right in between that was the place where we were stationed with two squadrons. The Russians tried to bomb us but the frontline was only 40 kilometres out, and as soon as they came close we took off.

"I don't recall any one victory in particular. You got an order, you flew, and either you got contact or you didn't. As soon as you got contact then either he was going down or you. One very large advantage I had was my eyes. I could see movement very far out, and if we had to guard Stukas or bombers it meant seeing them first at all times. When I had Lang (*Leutnant Emil Lang*), he could see an aircraft something around 50 kilometres away, and I could see at least 40 / 45. Depending on that you could then choose what you were going to do. If you didn't have to stay close to the bomber as guard, you could gain height. Then we often tried to overfly them and go down from the top, that way there was a lot more speed, you could fire quickly and then pull up again. That was a tactic which was then used by everybody. (*Known as the yo-yo.*)

VT – "Pretty close to what I remember. I could see a 'plane at about 20 kilometres, but identification was possible only at about 600 metres. On the other hand all unidentified planes were regarded as enemy planes. The problem was we couldn't leave the escorted planes.

NH – "One day two of us were suddenly passed by two Russians in Yak 9s going the other way. I immediately went into a vertical climb, and one of them followed me; both our wingmen left and went home. Our skills were the same, and for about ten minutes I could not get on his tail, and he could not get on mine; so we never fired a shot. Eventually we levelled out and passed by each other, waggled our wings, and he went east and I went west.

"The Il-2 had 1.2 cm armour plate from the front to the rear of the cabin. The oil cooler had shutters they could close off. So we forced them down low so the engine started to overheat and they had to open the shutters. Then we could hit their coolers.

"The Russians had square parachutes, we had round parachutes. I shot one down which went into flames and they both jumped out. Two of us flew round them. We put our gear down, and put our flaps down and circled them. They waved at us and we waved at them, but our fuel was very low so we had to leave. They were going to land in the trees. I can still picture them now, waving at us.

"At instructor's school we had many experienced bomber pilots learning to fly fighters, with Ritterkreuz, Eichenlaub and so on. They flew fighters like they flew bombers, in a straight line to drop their bombs, and then turn round and fly back. It would have been very easy to get on their tail. But it is not easy to tell a superior officer, so I told one to choose the fastest aircraft and I took the slowest. I said we would take off, climb to 3,000 metres, fly away from each other for half a minute, then turn and fly towards each other. I pulled up into the vertical, he tried to follow, but I easily got on his tail.

"At the end their (*Soviet*) technology was as good as ours. Our technical advantage had gone by the end of '43, early '44. The Russians never flew more than fifty operations, then were used for training. (*In fact they flew as long as they could – the same as the Luftwaffe.*) Their conditions in the field were far worse than ours, they were living in tents.

"Kroshinski (*Feldwebel Hans-Joachim Kroshinski*) was a great friend of mine. He was shot down. This guy wanted to make as many kills as possible and he attacked one bomber formation, Pe-2, and started out with the first one, then the second one, then the third one. The fourth one he moved in the airstream and he was pushed up in the top and directly in the line of fire and his aircraft motor burnt. He jumped out and as soon as he cleared the cabin he got the whole oil stream in his face, and he was not wearing goggles so the whole of his face was burnt. Also his left leg was hit. He jumped out and pulled the parachute, and dropped towards the sea. It was in the wintertime and he saw the red of his blood in the snow and he took the cord from his hat, and bound it up. The German infantry saw the parachute coming down, went to him, got him clear and took him with the unit down into the harbour. We were looking for him in a Storch but he'd already gone. He was completely blinded in one eye, and he also went almost completely blind in the other eye after two years.

"Trautloft wrote the first document telling pilots how to aim and how to shoot to kill your opponent. This was not given to everybody however, I got it as instructor in July '44, then handed it over to the units. My eldest brother was a company commander in the infantry in Russia in Orel. My father said at his funeral that he died for 'Volk und Vaterland' (*People and Fatherland*), not for the Führer. That was something that could give you some trouble; a brave thing to do.

VT – "A brave thing would be not to go to Russia. If one wanted to fight there is no real need to bring so much suffering to one's neighbours, and then claim that one was severely kicked. They could have announced that Germany wanted to fight for the homeland, and believe me, there would be a lot of those.

NH – "We tended to have the same technicians throughout the war. When my unit was founded in Austria all the technicians were Austrian. Only the replacements came from Germany. These guys were completely solid and did very well and we never had trouble with them. Our ground crews were shipped from Kurland with our navy to Holstein and went into a British prison-ship.

VT – "On average our 'planes had 100 hours running time, but during winter the darkness could last as long as sixteen hours (it would be light from about nine or ten in the morning until three or four in the evening). We had different methods to start up cold engines.

NH – "I don't know what the Russians did with their aircraft, but we had a cold start procedure; each evening 20% gasoline had been mixed with the oil in the aircraft. After take-off the next morning you had to be airborne for at least twenty minutes to clean the gasoline from the oil. That worked all the time and under the coldest temperatures at night.

VT – "I remember I crashed a Cobra (*P-63*) after the war because of this. The oil was over-mixed with fuel and lacked the necessary characteristics, so the engine simply jammed in mid-air, and I had to belly-land.

"What surprises me in general, is how respectful we were and are towards Germans, and how they show us up as idiots. When I read their memos I think that there were two different wars going on between four different countries."

In a similar vein, Norbert Hannig reviewed and commented on Vladimir Tikhomirov's interview transcript.

VT – "Some of our accidents were caused by overconfidence. Some aircraft, such as Yak or Il-2 would forgive your mistakes, but some, such as MiG-3 and I-16 would not, unless it was some technical failure or a mechanic's mistake. One pilot started a dogfight, and suddenly he shouted: 'I'm hit!' and went home. When he arrived mechanics found some screwdrivers were banging about inside the fuselage in high-G turns, and he had thought that this banging was caused by bullets.

"I drank alcohol once before flying and never tried it again. I missed an enemy fighter and almost missed the landing strip and decided not to risk it in future. I remember one Il-2 pilot who did fly drunk, but sometimes it led to some funny stuff. I had to cover him once on a search and destroy mission in the Gulf of Vyborg. The Il pilot had a task for the day and he was free to choose the time and route of the flight. We took off at midday, and started to fly towards the Finnish border. I could not understand where he was going. I passed in front of him, then I tried to lead him but he was not responding. I was piloting a Yak 7, so I finally shot at him. Then he turned and followed me back.

"When we landed I saw that he and his gunner were totally drunk! We let them sleep for a while, and when they woke up I found out that both of them were sleeping during the flight, and that my shots had woken 'em up. The task was not completed, and in the evening we started once again. We were going over the Baltic Sea, and found a convoy of ships. I saw it first as I was 500 metres higher, and let the Il pilot know. He asked for directions. I oriented him, so he made his attack at the large transport with rockets. It was all ablaze, and I thought that he was going to go home now, but instead he turned around and went in with cannons. When we came home we found a piece of the mast stuck in his wing. Of course he would have seen it if he did not have a hangover.

"To convert when we got new 'planes we simply flew them. All Yaks were relatively the same in piloting, so there were no problems. The only case when our 3rd Squadron was sent into the rear was because until the end of 1943 they were still flying the I-16. Their missions were mostly ground attack or close support for Ils. They were great at close support roles, but to be honest, they did not fly that much during the autumn of 1943. I-16s were slow, but their task was not shooting down the enemy, but to fend it off. Their manoeuvrability was great, and this helped a lot when they had to fire at the enemy and then turn around for the Ils.

"Actually, I-16 kill scores at that period were the greatest for the entire war. When they finally changed to Yaks, their kill to loss ratio became more preferable, but kill scores fell. I do think that some pilots got so used to flying one type of 'plane, that they become a part of its body; you would get a feel for even the slightest change in it. A better, newer 'plane did not always mean you had as much trust in it.

NH – "In 1943 I never met an I-16 in the air.

VT – "My colleague Avenesov had different tasks. He was a reconnaissance crew member, and it meant that he could stay out of the firing range of flak from convoys, while we had to go in all the way. We were sitting at Elbing air base in Eastern Prussia, and when we first came to the canteen, pilots from the front were sitting there. By that time we had quite a lot of decorations, so they started saying stuff like: 'How many asses did you have to lick to get this?' Then, in a few days, an order was given out to use army aviation for intercepting convoys. We found one and set off. When they saw all that flak coming in, they returned to base, and when we got there after the strike they said: 'Oh hell, we do not want medals, we want to live!' Every cargo ship had at least four AA guns, while destroyers had up to twenty. Now imagine what a fur ball they could cause when there was a convoy of five cargo ships covered by four destroyers and a couple of trawlers; and what it looks like when cover is twice as strong!

"Land-based flak was also quite an unpleasant thing. I remember a most difficult one near Königsberg; it was connected to radar, so that a first shot could bring down three to five 'planes. You were looking at the formation of Sturmoviks, and suddenly there was the flash of a huge explosion, and you could see that some 'planes were missing. When this happened the first time I had something bothering me, a feeling that it was not going to end up well. Then I felt an urge to move, and I shouted to my wingman: 'Away from the Ils, FAST!' I pulled my stick back, and then it happened, one shot from all guns at once; the sky was boiling. My 'plane was damaged, some bits of the wing skin were gone, but my wingman was shot down. He did not understand why I was flying away, and stayed to cover them.

"The larger the group was, the less Ils we lost to fighters and more to flak and vice-versa. But usually they would send one or two Ils out front to identify and knock out the flak sites; very difficult and dangerous work. They were acting alone, and had no defence against fighters. Quite a lot depended on tactics.

"We were going after ships in the Gulf of Vyborg, I covered five Ils led by HSU Batievskiy with four Yak-9s. A second flight of five Ils was led by HSU Banifatov, and had independent cover of eight Yaks. Over the radio I heard that the same target was about to be attacked by an army Sturmovik group, and that they were in heavy combat. I asked Batievskiy to increase speed in order to catch up with the army group in front of us. At first he did not understand why I had asked this, but he did catch the group. The Germans raised a lot of fighters in order to cover the ships, and if we came in small waves we would not be able to win the fight. In this case we added firepower to the army group, and although we lost two fighters, all the Ils in my group came back. Banifatov's group lost three Ils and four Yaks because they were not able to catch up in time. We could not help them; I could not leave the planes I was ordered to protect.

"It was relatively easy to protect Ils. Comparing what our friends went through in 1941-42 to what we had, it was a piece of cake. The Germans were mostly wiped out of the skies by Las and LaGGs from other regiments, so that they were not able to concentrate their fighters for mass attacks, but even one fighter in the right place at the right time could cause havoc. People still died and disappeared. Anyone of us could be next, but all of us were ready to give our life for our country and friends. I think that pilots from the other side felt the same, after all, we were all of a similar age.

"If you can see a Yak from front on, you will notice how small the screen was. I read a lot of books written by World War II flyers, and I can say that, according to them they shot the left eye of the enemy pilot with the first bullet, right eye with the second and after that third and fourth bullets tore the ears out! That is not true. The most accessible aiming points in a real fight would be wing, tail, front or rear fuselage. Those who tried to aim for the eyeballs usually had a couple of 20 or 30mm cucumbers up their backsides before they pulled the trigger! I never fired from more than 100 metres, and was able to penetrate the armour.

"I flew strafing runs around ten times. We flew along roads and shot everything we saw. I got a couple of bullet holes and that was it. I can't give details of my results, though. One of our pilots once described a strafing run where he overturned a Tiger by cannon fire. It was nonsense of course, bullets can't do such damage.

"The Il-2 was a soldier! At the end of the war we had lost about one 'plane in every ten sorties, mainly from flak fire, but on 8 May 1945 a flight of two Yaks and one Il-2 was lost due to fighters. One hour after the war ended! If we underestimated German fighters, we died. If you were ready, they died. Germans were no match for us in a dogfight, but were as a hit and run.

"The Messerschmitt was fast and agile. The Fw 190 was shot on sight, if the pilot was not too good. It was too slow and weighed too much. Actually it was heavier than the Il-2. I can't understand how it can be called a 'fighter'. Interceptor of bombers maybe, but fighter... If they jumped us, they had success, but if we saw them first, we were all over them.

"We saw the Fw 190D up close at Marienfeld AB. There were about twenty of them. When they first appeared, everybody was scared. But after a few fights we understood that there was nothing to be afraid of. It burned as well as other 'planes, and was easier to hit. The planes from

Marienburg were taken to the Luberezkaya training facility. The Fw 190 was supposed to be good in a dive, but so what? It flew 5-10 metres above sea level, an Fw dive would be highly appreciated.

NH – "The comments on Me 109 and Fw 190 are wrong. The aircraft structure of the Fw 190 types were more stable, especially the gear during landings and take-offs. The motor was air-cooled, not water like the Me 109, where one single bullet through the cooler forced the pilot to a forced landing. The view from the Fw 190 was much better and the weaponry was more effective. The dogfights changed from circling to 'yo-yo', up and down. We as pilots liked the Fw 190 series more than the Me 109.

VT - "It is difficult to know about German kill scores. We had an Il-2 which crash-landed eleven times. It fell, a German could note it as a kill, and we repaired it the next day, it was flying, we thought of it as battle damaged. But of course everybody lied.

"My most challenging flight was in the autumn of 1944. We were covering Il-2s from the 38th Regiment, when we were jumped by 18 Fw 190s. They attempted an attack on the Il-2s by hitting them from above and behind, but we were on our guard and repelled that attack, and one Fw 190 was damaged by Il-2 rear gunners. Then the bravest German went under the Il-2s to try and get them from below, but went too low; the 'plane broke up like glass. I had no time to see what happened next, we were engaged in a heavy fight. I went head-on with an Fw 190 three or four times, and finally he hit my tail fin with the tip of his prop. No serious damage was done; I did not even notice it in flight, only when on the ground did I see what had happened. I scored a hit then, and saw the enemy pilot going down on his 'chute. He was about 180cm, redhead, freckled. I wanted to take a closer look but had no time.

(Tikhomirov brought down Erich Knoebel from V./JG54 on 21 June 1944, who was listed as missing in action north west of Koivisto. This was the only victory in that encounter, so he may have confused this fight with another.)

NH – "Attacked by eighteen Fw 190s? A squadron had twelve aircraft. Our normal formation was two (Rotte) or four (Schwarm) aircraft. If we had to protect ground troops against attacking Il-2s, we flew with no more than four aircraft. It seems that Russian pilots saw each German aircraft fourfold. We never had so many 'planes available.

VT – "The most common tactic for German attacks was always the same, a high speed manoeuvre with an attempt to extend upwards. That is where we caught them. They dived steeply, and at the same time we started to gain altitude in a shallow climb. At this moment they would start a steep climb, and finally we met at the same altitude with the same speed about 200 metres apart. Now it was time to kill. Their first attack was fruitless, they were too fast to aim correctly and too afraid to dive really low, so our job was not to let them have a second chance. If a dogfight started, we were usually engaged with the Messerschmitts, while the Fws were above, trying to pick out those who were damaged or careless. If we were with Lavochkins, they would attack Fw 190s from out of the sun, and the Messerschmitts would disengage. The problem was that flak from both sides would be shooting in the middle trying to pick anything they could, regardless of the nationality.

"I always respected German pilots; those who didn't care perished. Six of us joined the squadron together; I'm the only survivor. At some point you start to believe that someone else will die and you forget about situational awareness. And that's when you are killed. I was lucky to live through this moment.

"Everybody who came to the squadron was full of ideas that war in the air was something like a knights' tournament. I was the same, but quite soon we were shown that it is not so. Germans attempted to kill all parachutists when they had a chance. I saw once how after a big fight, reinforcements of four Me 109s came, and instead of attacking us (we were low and slow, sitting ducks practically) they started attack runs on the parachutists. What they did not know is that they were their own pilots…We gained speed and altitude, and they refused to fight. We were low on fuel and had to leave the engagement area.

"I was too bad at shooting to waste my ammo on enemy parachutists. It would take more than half of my ammo to kill him. I do know about some cases though. If a pilot goes down onto his territory it is not so bad an idea to kill him; if he baled over our territory, it is better keeping him alive.

NH – "I never heard that Germans attacked or killed parachutists. That was forbidden by order and punished.

VT - "We used to have some fun on a daily basis. We'd be mad in a week without some rest. I remember flying out on an intercept, I noticed a dot ahead and went after it. I almost boiled my engine only to find out that it was some spot on the windscreen. That kept us laughing for a month. On another occasion one of the pilots managed to land a Po-2 on a chimney.

"The Ils defences were decent. A rear gunner with good enough training could kill anything in a 300m radius, and I felt sorry for a German caught in front of one. Three or four rounds of VYa usually disintegrated any fighter, and I saw it with my own eyes. We were protecting Ils and were hit by a couple of Fw 190s. They went below the Sturmoviks, and pulled up in front of them. The flight leader received hits from three Ils simultaneously, in both wings and fuselage. I remember the aftermath of an explosion, and all that was left of it was a tail wheel.

"His wingman got one or two 23mm rounds in the cockpit, and zoomed upwards. I went after him, thinking that he was going to escape, but when I gained on him I saw that up to the wing level there was no cockpit wall, no movable part of the canopy, and a bloody mess was all that was left of the pilot. The 'plane made a couple of loops then spun and went to the bottom of the sea. (*This occurred on 24 October 1944.*)

NH – "The Il-2 had 20mm steel protection around the cockpit and motor. The safest attack was from below and rear, and aiming at the oil cooler, which could be closed with a blind. Closed, the motor temperature climbed and it got overheated and burned. But the Il-2 could shoot down fighter aircraft. One of the best pilots from JG54, Oblt Kittel, was killed that way in Kurland.

VT - "Quite often Ils shot at fighters if they got in front of them, but they did not try to manoeuvre for a kill. It was fun to watch sometimes how a German pilot would start an attack run head-on, and when he saw what he was attacking, he would panic and try to get out of their way, right into our guns.

"I once had a fight with an La-5FN. We were stationed at Lavansaari Island, when the 4th Guards Regiment arrived there. Usual pilot talk started – who flies better, which 'plane was faster and more manoeuvrable. They called us 'whistler' for the sound of the Yak engine, and we called them 'growlers' for the bobbling sound of the ASh-82. There is only one way to solve such an argument. So we were called into the air. 'Who among you, whistlers, can challenge our pilot?' Whistler, in Russian, can be translated also as liar, so this was an insult.

"Regiment Commander Belyaev called me and said, 'Take anybody with you and kick their asses!' The rules were simple: simultaneous take-off, then fly in two circles over the base and then separate in opposite directions for thirty seconds and engage. The winning pilot is the one who stays on the other's tail for at least thirty seconds, as this is more than enough time to aim and kill. Wingmen were to provide top cover against any German attacker.

"We took off, and started to dogfight. He tried to go below me and get me from there, but I performed Nesterov's loop, and we started a horizontal fight. There was no way to win it, same as to lose it, so at one point I broke off into the sun, and waited for him to lose me. Then I positioned myself behind and below him and won. We were circling for fifteen minutes, and I couldn't get out of the cockpit without help. I met with my opponent, and I said, 'Is it clear who is a whistler now?' I was with Smolyaninov, and fought against Arkadiy Selyutin. (*Smolyaninov ended the war with four victories, Selyutin with sixteen.*)

173

"I never claimed as a kill those who did not fall instantly. If it was ablaze, but outside my vision, it was not a kill, it was probable, and they did not count. Some high-ranking pilots, especially at 3rd and 4th GuIAP were shooting their ammo at the enemy five to six kilometres away, and claiming kills. Not often though, usually if one needed one or two more kills to be awarded an HSU Suvorov said: 'There is no reason to take pity on the enemy.' Real fighting pilots did not like to cheat however.

"It was common for a pilot to lose up to five or six kilograms in one flight. We usually wore some warm stuff and sweated severely, and without it sometimes we would get frostbite even in summer during high altitude fights. If we covered Sturmoviks we went low, therefore we would wear only light clothing. But fighting was really tiring, although it rarely lasted for more than two or three minutes.

NH – "I flew more than 250 enemy missions. If I had lost that weight on each flight I would be dead.

VT – "I participated in the relief of Leningrad operation from the start. Ground forces were supposed to start on the 15th. We were assembled at the airfield on the 14th and we were told that we were supposed to do everything to destroy the blockade of Leningrad. We were proud that we would be the first ones to shoot during this operation.

"It was minus 10-15 degrees Celsius. It was misty in the mornings and very cloudy during the whole operation. The most unpleasant thing was ice on the runways. For some reason it would build up on some parts but on others it would be clear. During the whole operation we lost no aircraft to fighters, three to anti-aircraft artillery, and five were damaged during landing. We called this a 'Lezginka dance' since, like hands in this Caucasian dance, put horizontally in the same direction, the gear would collapse to point in one direction. I can't say about other fronts, but in Leningrad no man sat on the ground without flying, even commanding officers. There was a queue if there were not enough 'planes to go round. You lived in this city and you knew what it went through.

"When I arrived the food was a lot better, but those who served in the early years said that it was terrible. Mechanics were fed as workers (given only 250 grams of bread daily, if I'm not mistaken, a full loaf of bread cost a Rembrandt's picture or a half a kilo of 583 gold in the worst days on the black market), and pilots had chocolate daily. Pilots gave their food to ground crew, but after two cases of deaths in the air due to starvation it was forbidden. Each time someone flew to the 'Big Land' (the unoccupied part of Russia) they would load a 'plane to the top with food, even leaving ammo on the ground. Surprisingly, not a single thief appeared on the base.

"Kills were rewarded with money. The procedure was, if you kill, you ask for a confirmation from ground forces, and a special committee goes to the crash site. The confirmation could come from the Il-? flight if they saw where the enemy fell, but not from your flight. Over water, only Il-2s confirmed kills. If confirmed you could get a reward; money for 'plane and sorties. All of us sent the money we earned to the State Defence Fund to help to fight the enemy. Most of us had relatives killed by the invaders.

"The war was the happiest and saddest time. Sad because there was too much anger and grief, and happiest because I was doing what I wanted to do. Only winning counted, I had real friends, though most of them are dead now. We knew what we were trying to do, and why. War for those who fight is a test of what they are made of. It gives you experience which you will never get another way. For civilians war is hell, and for soldiers it is a hard, dirty, stinky and dangerous job.

"When war ends civilians start to say this and that about soldier's actions, some don't have any excuses, but it all must be left in the war. I am in blood up to my elbows, but I'm still proud of what I have done, and would have repeated everything if I had the chance. This is why I can't watch Hollywood films about war. The Americans did not win that war. Their war was with Japan, not Germany. That war they won, not ours. Neither Russians, nor Germans were cretins, which is how they are described. Keep the peace. In time of war do not hesitate, but be a man, not a beast, and when war ends, stop, do not take anger with you, forgive, but forget nothing."

Norbert Hannig (NH) also commented on an interview with Guards Lieutenant Benedikt Kardopoltsev (BK), whose six victories included four Fw 190s, one Me 109 and one Ju 87, all achieved while flying the La 7.

BK – "One day we were gathered together, and our surnames were called out. Those who were called were sent to the combat units, and fifteen of us were left behind: 'You will be returned to your squadron for further training.' Of course we were upset, but we were told: 'You are going to fly the LaGG-3, which had the nickname 'lacquered aviation guaranteed coffin'. LaGGs were transferred to us by wounded pilots who flew them in combat, so it was their expression. They brought us six LaGGs, and as soon as we started to study them, we suddenly found out that it was extremely unstable on the ground, and it had a heavy tendency to roll to the left.

NH – "'Rolled' on take-off and landing is unknown to me or does he mean the 'break out of straight direction' due to the torque effect of the prop? We had that with the Me 109, not the Fw 190 however."

BK - "At the end of 1942 our group began to fly the La-5. I was sent to the 2nd ZAP near Gorkii. The first thing in ZAP was twenty flights by

Lieutenant Benedikt Kardopoltsev spent most of his war service with 2 GuIAP in Belorussia, flying the La 5 and La 7. He is on the left in this 1945 photograph with squadron commander Marchenko. *Kardopoltsev via Oleg Korytov*

each pilot; take-off, landing, aerobatics, and route flights. We were trained for single flights. Every day a Douglas would come – it was the 'merchants' from combat units. I was included in one group of six or seven pilots. One who spoke with us was division commander HSU Noga, he asked us: 'At which speed would you make this manoeuvre?' I answered. He asked other pilots, then turned to the ZAP commander and said: 'Who are you trying to sell to me? They are worthless!'

"But then he turned to us and said: 'Well, I will take you. But! You will fly at any speed, and manoeuvre when needed, not when allowed. How do you fasten yourselves in the cockpit?' We used to fasten waist and shoulder belts, as was written in the instructions. But he said: 'You are not fighters, you are milkmen! Only waist! Otherwise you will be limited in turning your head, and will be shot down soon... Do as I say!'

NH – "The Russian training methods were different from ours. We were fastened by a seat belt with shoulder straps. During take-off we fastened both, after gear in – we released the shoulder straps for the same reason as the Russians.

BK – "The winter of 1943 was snowy, but all went well and in about one week we started to fight. Of the six of us, I was the only one without combat experience. When a dogfight ended I was asked: 'What did you see?' I saw a Focke in front of me, and I trailed him and shot at him. I did not even care that someone could shoot at me, or what my wing leader did. So, I wasted all my ammo, and of course hit nothing. Our main tasks were patrolling the frontline and strafing runs on the railroad. A couple of times I took off to intercept an Fw 189; my first kill was a '189.

NH – "The Russians got paid for shoot downs, well we never got money for that. The attack tactic at the beginning of a dogfight had been the horizontal turn arounds and the advantage was with the guy with the shortest turn radius. That changed to the yo-yo-tactic: dive to the target, fire and leave again at height. The Russians flew 'patrol flights' (Begleitschutz für Bomber) or protection for ground troops and free flying.

BK – "On the evening of 7 November 1943 the commander returned to the airfield, and brought an Me 109 on his tail. The flight chief shouted over the radio: 'Commander, who is behind you? I can't recognise the type.' Messer got slightly behind, and shot him down. His name was Kolzov, HSU. Another one force-landed in German territory. It was Major Bychkov, regiments navigator; the Germans caught him, he was trying to organize aviation for General Vlasov."

Bychkov was captured on 11 December 1943, when he was deputy squadron commander in 482 IAP. He had been in 937 IAP earlier, and in 1942 was sentenced for a crash caused by him, although it was not an obstacle for him to later become a Hero of the Soviet Union. According to the interrogation protocols, he did not admit his guilt, but he was stripped of his rank, awards and discharged from active duty.

BK – "On patrols we could fly for fifty minutes in combat, and more than an hour in economical mode. We would recognise who it was at about 400 metres, but beyond that it was just a 'black spot'. The optimal distance to fire was about 100 metres. We had grades on our sights, and if the enemy got in to these marks you could tell the distance.

NH – "The best firing distance was between 100 and 50 metres. Our aiming device in the Me 109 and Fw 190 had a cross with rings in the sighting mechanism. The cross-point was the aiming point to the target.

The distance to the target could be calculated by the dimension of the target in the circles. The aiming device of the Me 262 was gyro-controlled.

BK – "When we claimed a kill all paper work was the adjutant's responsibility. Of course we had some problems with confirmations. One of my claims was not confirmed. It was almost at the end of war, in Grenau, near Neische. It was a free-for-all. Marchenko took me with him, and he shot one down right by the field. Another Fw 190 was there, so I shot at him, and I saw how it rolled over on the ground, burning. We landed and reported to IAP commander Sobolev: 'Shot down 'planes near our home base, send someone to check, we will show where they fell.' He said: 'You have become impudent! If you shot down all the Luftwaffe, who's still flying them? Do you want more awards?'

"I was shot down on 16 June 1944. Although I was flying an La 7, they still caught us, since we were escorting Ils. Near Shaulai there was a rail station, about 30 kilometres from the frontline, and the Germans unloaded their tanks there. Ils were sent to destroy the station with everything in it. There were four of us on the escort mission and I was on the wing of the deputy squadron commander, Slavgorodskii. The forests were burning there, and Levchenko lost us in this smoke, so there were only two of us left to cover the Ils. Just before the attack, the Ils had to climb to at least 500 metres from the tree-top level. Here my flight leader made a mistake – he stayed slow and low. I saw them first and shouted: 'Commander! Fockes on our right – behind!' I could not even understand where to move – my flight leader was on my left side. There was no chance for me – there were eighteen Fockes against two of us. As soon as I said it, I saw smoky tracers going through my right wing. Immediately I saw flames. I remember I thought: 'So, this is how I'm going to die; my 'plane is on fire, and I'm still sitting in the cockpit.' I can't remember how I opened the cockpit, but it could take time, one or two seconds more – and I thought I would not get enough height, I would be killed. All I can remember after this – I was falling free from the 'plane, back first – was that I took the ring and pulled it. The explosion happened at the same time as I hit the ground and hurt my legs quite severely.

"I landed, picked my parachute up and hid in the bushes. The Germans for some reason left without further fighting. I looked out from the bush and saw a barn and five or six German soldiers with rifles. One came towards me; about 50 metres away from me he turned around and went into the house. They had seen me, and I think he was going for help. I escaped; no-one tried to follow me. At this moment a new wave of Ils arrived. They howled and strafed so fiercely that I ducked and covered myself up, the ammo was blowing up and I was afraid that I would get killed. Suddenly I heard a noise on the footpath. I hid in the bushes, and then saw three soldiers coming towards me. I stood up in front of them, and while they were surprised I ran away. They shouted: 'Halt, Halt!' They shot at me, but hit nothing; that happened on the second day. All in all I walked behind enemy lines for three or four days. I kept walking east. On the fourth day I came upon a motorway with heavy traffic on it. On the other side of the road I saw a field with crops. I decided to cross the road during night time.

"I went to the road and crossed it. The crops on the other side were short, so I had to lie prone and suddenly I noticed a wire. I moved to the left and found the mine with four wires attached to its detonator. It was a minefield. I found a free place and moved forward, then another wire, and another. How did I manage to cross the minefield? Like a fool. There is a saying that fools are lucky, that was me! When I came to our lines, the major who met me did not believe me: 'How did you manage to get through?' Damn, I was lucky!

"Speaking of the Lavochkin; first of all it had better firepower, it was an extremely dynamic 'plane. Las easily caught Messers or Fockes. When I saw the La-5 after the LaGG-3 I fell in love. Although I think that the Yak was easier to fly as it did not require such precision. The canopy was always closed, we could see quite well. There was no rear view mirror either.

NH – "We always flew with the canopy closed, the temperatures in Me 109 and Fw 190 were normal, we had an oxygen mask and used it from 3,000 metres above ground.

BK – "I never felt the exhausts in the cockpit, but when I fired my guns I would smell the burnt gun powder, and it was hot in the 5FN, some pilots even got burnt. We had good armament; three 20mm cannons. We used to have machine guns on the I-16, although those really were only for scratching the surface.

"One day we were sitting at readiness, and a Ju 88 went over our base. We took off. There was a special tube to breathe, as we had no masks at that time, so we started to chase that recce 'plane. At about 8,000 metres I lost consciousness and came back down to 2,500 metres. I had forgotten the oxygen. We had quite a lot of dive-bombing and strafing runs. At the end of war we had an order: 'No flights without bombs.' We used FAB-50 and FAB-100, one under each wing. We used to dive at about 70 degrees. The only one who dived at 90 degrees was Mikhail Ryabzev – he liked it.

"The German pilots were different. During the Orel operation our regiment met the 'Udet' group; those were strong opponents. As soon as such a group would appear at the front they would shoot all the young pilots. By the end of the war we got new 'planes and it became easy, you felt how powerful the La-5 was. If a German got behind you, you just pushed the throttle forward, and you would see the enemy fall away behind you.

"Our pilots shot down a Ju 88, and they baled out, the farmers caught them, and since they tried to escape and shoot at them, the farmers stopped them, using sickles as weapons. Then they tied the Germans up and brought them to our field. I remember our commissar slapped one of them in the face.

"I saw Americans on the ground, they flew B-17s. They were returning from a bombing mission and two engines were damaged. They taxied to a standstill and left the 'plane – the crew consisted of nine men. We had a war to fight, and they were trying to make a luxury hotel out of our dugouts. Then their cargo 'plane came and brought new engines. The Americans threw the damaged engines on the ground and rolled them to the side. It was January and bitterly cold, so they installed a tent over the wings and started heating it up. It took them a couple of weeks to change two engines. Our technicians worked in pairs and changed an engine in one night without any tents and by bare hands. We used to say to each other, 'If the Americans tried the taste of real all-out war they would not last two weeks, they need too much luxury'. When they finished and flew away, our mechanics started to cannibalise the engines they left trying to utilise the spares.

"We were based near Vitebsk, and suddenly just above the air base an Me 110 dropped out of the clouds. Our 'alert-1' flight took off and in one pass they shot the '110 down. But it was actually our Pe-2. In another case Pavel Nepryahin strafed our river crossing.

NH – "Friend or enemy – we knew which aircraft from our forces would be in the area – if none, then the aircraft at any distance must be from the other side. But before shooting you double checked so you knew who it was.

BK - "We were based in Belarus on a very narrow field, and Deputy Commander Pushkin HSU was taking off. For some reason he veered to the side and saw an aircraft shelter in front of him. He jumped over it, but the prop blade of the 'plane in that shelter ripped through the belly of his 'plane, and it fell on the other side of the shelter. At the same time Nepryahin had gone there to relieve himself, and suddenly found a 'plane falling on top of him. We all witnessed how he beat all world records at running, even with his pants around his ankles!

"We had a combat school in Lubertzy. There were Yaks and Las, several Messers and Fockes, and we fought them and each other. Very good practice; I spent about two months there.

"On 7 May '45 I shot down one of the last 'planes; it was our regiment's last combat. I flew with Troshin on my wing, Galich and Zybko. Our tanks were going to Prague and we covered them. We were going to our home base and met four Fw 190s with drop tanks going west. We started turning, but missed a bit in the beginning of the manoeuvre and the Fockes got tactical advantage – they were going towards us but higher than we were flying. I raised the nose of my 'plane and shot, hoping to hit the lower fuselage of the leading 'plane, just behind the engine, in the fuel tank. For some reason the enemy pilot half-rolled and all my three cannons hit the canopy. I saw how it burst open and shiny bits of glass went everywhere; the 'plane went down like a leaf. All the others spread out and started fleeing. Galich and Troshin got two 'planes, and the other managed to escape – we were low on fuel and could not chase him."

ROYAL AIR FORCE IN RUSSIA

Winston Churchill pledged support for Russia following the German invasion, and within a few weeks, the RAF dispatched two squadrons of Hurricanes by sea to Archangel and Murmansk, in order both to provide protection for the vital seaports, and to start training Russian pilots to fly Hurricanes, large numbers of which were to be supplied to the Soviet air forces. Tim Elkington was among the first group of RAF pilots, who sailed with their aircraft aboard HMS *Argus* in August 1941.

"It was a random choice of pilots to make up a new squadron, (134) from a nucleus of 17 Squadron. The wing (151) sailed for Russia in August 1941, twenty-four pilots flying off HMS *Argus* on 7 September. The brief for the take-off makes interesting reading:

1. "*Aircraft will be flown off in flights of six. The first six aircraft will be erected on the flight deck & it is anticipated that the succeeding three flights will be ranged from the hangar & flown off at forty minute intervals after the first flight has left the deck.*

2. *All spectators are to be in the starboard netting. Pilots are to run up their own aircraft when ranged & are to indicate that their aircraft is in all respects ready to take off by raising the left thumb.*

3. *All movements of aircraft on the flight deck are controlled by the flight deck officer who will stand on the port side of the aircraft he is controlling. The executive signal for take-off is the lowering of a green flag.*

4. *On receipt of the executive signal pilots are to release the brakes & carry out a normal runway take-off under high wind conditions but sitting up as high as possible to obtain a good view of the deck immediately on opening the throttle and thereby ensure a take-off run with wheels either side of the centre line.*"

"The remainder, with 550 men, arrived at our destination before us, from Archangel. What times those were, but I never want to fly off a carrier again. Have any of you done a carrier take-off with only 360 feet of deck? *Without* a catapult! It was very frightening when she goes hard-a-star-board to come into wind, and you are looking down into the Arctic Ocean.

"Initially we were on ops. We spent many hours on readiness in the dugout. But not like the Battle of Britain, virtually all our flying was as planned escort to their Pe-2 bombers. Landmarks were tough to find in Russia, just endless woodland and lakes; and a map that came out of a school atlas. The best landmark to use was the sea. If you got lost, fly north till you saw it and then go east till you came to the Kola estuary and there we were.

"The Hurricane IIB was the first twelve-gun Hurricane. However, six were taken out for the carrier take-off and not replaced till some time later. But there were also some eight-gun IIAs supplied. The standard convergence was 250 yards, but several of the grittier pilots, in the Battle of Britain days, had that reduced to 150, with great effect.

"During our time there, our Jack Ross started training a few key Russian pilots who would then instruct the masses. After 22 September, the weather frequently stopped us flying, so we spent a lot of time sitting around, playing chess or bridge or crib, (on the carrier outbound it was mainly Monopoly or 'Liar Dice'). These were good days.

"We spent readiness hours in our dug-outs. The airfield was Vaenga, now Severomorsk – a large expanse of sandy soil, about 500 feet above sea level. Below the 'drome were Upper and Lower Vaenga – primitive with their wooden houses, underground shops and general lack of amenities. Upper Vaenga however, did boast a club where one could eat, dance, see a film or attend a concert. Also, we had the sauna baths – the only bathing facilities north of Murmansk – where the old woman who wandered around beating backsides with birch twigs was quite a character. The basement shops had little to sell, and what they had was of poor quality.

"The townsfolk lived in flats in large, unfinished brick blocks; white-washed in winter, brick red in summer. The hospital stood on a hill to the north of the town. The docks were sizeable. Transport was available in the form of two Humber shooting-brakes, Commers or lifts in the rickety Russian works lorries. Thumbing a lift in poor Russian was hard. Occasionally, only a horse sleigh was going our way, but that was safer than risking the long and dangerous hill into Lower Vaenga on foot.

"Our billet was a comfortable two-storied building with wooden floors and double brick walls, and, except for one awful night, central heating. Water was pumped from a well or a lake and sterilised by our mobile unit.

"Food in our eating place, at least initially, was rich – too rich – but with many good things including caviar, smoked salmon, tinned Finnish ham, champagne, butter, eggs, red wine, pancakes, chocolate and tinned compote of cherries or plums. Tea was in a glass without milk. One third of the men were fed on six months rations that we took with us, and seemed to enjoy them. Cigarettes, rum, whiskey and gin were plentiful, and games and gramophones were provided Like my fellow pilots, I know all the words of the Ink Spots' songs!

"To reach Murmansk, fifteen miles or so to the south, in winter, was by a most dangerous road, it was possibly the size of Bournemouth without its suburbs. Houses and shops were similar to those in Vaenga, but with more brick. The Hotel Arctica seemed to be the only reasonable feeding place, but prices and conditions were abominable! The House of Culture was the only theatre, roughly finished, with a room upstairs for dancing. We went there on Sundays for a show, drink and a dance.

"Girls? Well, the only ones who might stir the imagination were our three translators. Anna was the blonde with the sweet singing voice and streamlined figure who worked with the engineer officer. Bella was the 'Merlin Girl' on account of her spinner-like bosoms. Fat in face, with a good voice for modern music, she worked on translating technical publications. Mira was the dark gypsy girl who was so far from her loved one in Moscow. She instructed the Russians in aircraft handling. Sadly, I am told that all their lives ended in misfortune. I am not sure whether or not it was *that* Anna – she wore a .38 on her hip – but, as I walked off the floor with her after a pleasant evening dancing in Murmansk, she was intercepted by her husband – who also wore a .38. No argument, but I still have her handkerchief!

"The only unusual event was taking off whilst the airfield was being bombed. We had no early warning system, but that was the last time they came over. We were operating at the top of the world, and by God it felt like it. Very unforgiving territory and weather. One of the boys did get his hands on the Ilyushin Il-6 but my only trip was in the U-2, a clapped out air ambulance.

"The Russians couldn't have been friendlier. As for their flying skills, I was only in touch with one or two. They were all much more experienced and much older than us, and found it hard to take our advice. The main two were Captain Safonov, a meticulous pilot, and Kuharenko, an absolute mad-cap! I flew with I-16 ace Boris Safonov in late 1941, and escorted his general (Kuznetsov) on his first flight in the Hurricane. Unlike Boris, I only claimed half a Ju 88 in the month that we were operational. I also flew with Captain Kuharenko in the Y-2. They were the first two Russians to convert to Hurricanes.

"We had a regular issue of tins of fifty ciggies – free. And Guinness was a 'medical supply'. Good for the blood? I bought a cow-skin wool-lined ear-flap hat on the one occasion we got to THE shop in Vaenga. So we must have been able to get cash somehow. They eventually got some to us on a convoy which wasn't sunk. In return, we had the invidious task of censoring outgoing mail.

"When we finally left the country we, the advance party, marched eight miles at night along the treacherous Murmansk road to the Rosta oiling jetty on the Kola estuary, to embark in fleet minesweepers HMS

Hussar and two others, en route to Archangel. It was a nightmare of a night but only one broken arm to show for it, although we were all dead tired and hungry. Our ship almost missed the jetty in the dark, but we finally got aboard. My kitbags, decades later, were still black with oil.

"At Archangel we were stuck in the ice for three days, living on hard-tack. There was a woman ice-breaker captain – large and frightening! On board, I had the pleasure of meeting General Gromov, who signed my log book. Finally home in *Empire Baffin*, while the others in HMS *Kenya* and her destroyers beat us home, leaving us one day to the mercy of the *Tirpitz* because it was too dangerous for them to stay around. Our ship, on its maiden voyage, went in for a refit on its return because of ice damage on the home journey."

General Major Nikolay Golodnikov was one of the Russian pilots trained to fly the Hurricanes at that time, converting from the Polikarpov I-16.

"The English from 151 Wing gave us their Hurricanes, so these were the ones that we trained on. Those English fought well. There were two types of Hurricanes, with eight and twelve machine guns. Other than this they were practically indistinguishable. Then aircraft began to come from England, in boxes. It appeared these were the Hurricanes that were for the Sahara as they were in desert yellow camouflage.

"We had documentation in English and English instructors. Although the instructor just sat in the cockpit showing us all the instruments on the spot and not to everybody, only to the first group. This group then had to show what they had learnt to all the others. We were given girl-translators to help us; they translated everything for us. Although, as it turned out, the English had a Major Rook. He spoke Russian altogether decently in so far as he had graduated from our Kacha air school. But he only started talking at the farewell banquet and during the whole time of training spoke English. Our squadron commander, Kovalenko trained with him. However often he would try to persuade him, 'Why are you wriggling out of it, you understand everything?', he did not manage it. Rook once flew on the I-16 and climbed out soaking. He said, 'Let the Russians fly it!' (*Squadron Leader Anthony Rook was OC 81 Squadron at Vaenga in 1941/42.*)

"In total, five days was spent on conversion. We studied the general layout: 'Here is the engine, here we pour the fuel, here the oil' etc. I talked a bit, had a sit in the cockpit, and taxied a couple of times and then to take off. I made three flights and that was it, I had converted. As we used to say, 'If you want to live then you will land'. Safonov was the first to take off, he sat for about four hours in the cockpit, while his hands got used to it, then he took off with the others behind him. There was no special selection for training, we trained by squadron.

"My first impression was: 'hump-back!' Such a 'hump-back' cannot be a good fighter! My impression did not change subsequently. The

Wing Commander Tim Elkington was among the first group of pilots to fly 134 Squadron Hurricanes off HMS *Argus* to Russia in August 1941. Here he is seen shortly after arrival at Vaenga. *Elkington*

wings particularly surprised me. They were very fat. The Hurricane's wings were fatter than those of the Pe-2. It was simpler to control than the I-16; it did not cause any difficulties to either get familiarised with it or to pilot it. The cockpit was of course larger; the field of vision in front was very good. To the side and, in particular behind, it was bad. The hood reminded me of an I-16 – there were a lot of partitions and it moved backwards. It deeply hindered the field of vision to the side due to the partitions; wherever you poked your nose you would come up against a partition. Initially, prior to battle, we would open it to improve the field of vision. Later, when we adapted to it, we began to leave it closed so as not to lose speed. The hood locked with two side locks.

"The control column surprised me. It was like on a bomber. On top there was such a fat 'ring' (Baranka – a ring shaped bun), while inside it there were two triggers, with small levers. In order to employ all the weapons it was necessary to operate it with two hands. At the base the column only went forwards and backwards, while it 'broke' left to right in the middle. From this point the cables went to the ailerons. There was armoured glass and a back armour plate as well. They were reliable."

Tim Elkington commented: "Control column? Nonsense! A button for the guns and a lever for the brakes. You would NEVER have your hand off the throttle." Golodnikov continued:

"All the instruments were, of course, in pounds and feet. But we adapted quickly to it. We had precisely the same instrument panel layout on the UT-2, although naturally it was in metric. So for anybody who flew UT-2 it was easy. We had experienced pilots so you could ask them, 'What is this instrument?' And he would say to you, 'Don't pay any attention to it. You will never need this instrument. Here is your altitude, engine speed, barometer, oil pressure, temperature – that is enough.' The boost was also in pounds on a scale from minus 4 to plus 12.

"On the Hurricane there were ultra short wave radio sets, six-channel ones. They were reliable and good stations. The only thing that was bad was the fact that the microphone was in the oxygen mask. The mask itself and the microphone were heavy and hindered combat. If you pulled up the mask more strongly then it was tight, if you loosened it, then during g-force the mask came down. The transmitter was simplex-duplex so it was possible to move the switch to 'receive-transmit' with the button and it was also possible with your voice, you started speaking and the transmitter switched itself on. You chose the mode yourself; a special button-switch in the cockpit was either on voice control or on the button. So at the beginning everybody went onto voice control. Sometimes in combat somebody would swear, 'Ah you pest! I will get you now!' the transmitter switched on, the pilot stopped hearing and it was not possible to pass the necessary command to the others. So later on, on all aircraft we had to change over the control of the portable transmitter to the button.

"The machine guns were 7.7mm. In terms of reliability it was similar to the ShKAS, initially they often jammed with dust. We stuck all the holes along the edge of the wing with percale fabric; you opened fire and shot along the percale; then they began to work reliably. When firing from a distance of 150 to 300 metres they had little effective. On the initiative of the group commander, Safonov, at our group mobile aircraft repair factory they began to fit our weapons on the Hurricanes. We had an innovator, Boris Sobolevsky, a weapons engineer and it was he who dealt with this. There were either two ShVAKs in each wing, or a ShVAK and a BK. Then the English, as a matter of form, lodged grievances. They said, 'How is this happening, without our permission?' Rubbish. Everybody understood that they had simply decided to insure themselves, just in case.

"My squadron commander was Aleksandr Andreyevich Kovalenko,Ø who became one of the first Heroes of the Soviet Union. He was a typical Ukrainian: calm and calculating. I was his supporting aircraft. In 1942 there was a large raid on Murmansk and we went up as a group of six. So they said to us on the radio, 'A group of '109s!' I told him, 'I see the '109s!' And he replied calmly, 'Good. Well lads, let's go and strike them.' Then over the radio we hear, 'A group of '87s! You are being switched to the '87s!' Again he said calmly, 'Well lads, let's go and get to the '87s!' We discovered them on the approach to Murmansk, there were about twenty of them or more. At great speed we attacked from below. I saw Kovalenko position his Hurricane almost vertical and with slide and he struck from about 50 metres with one burst on the Stuka, using his twelve machine guns. Then he dropped to the side, I also dropped and saw that the Junkers was splitting up, the tail in one direction, the rest of it in the other. Kovalenko had cut right through the Junkers before my very eyes saying simply, 'I've almost used up all the rounds'. Then we were told from the radio intercept station that the

Germans had yelled, 'We're surrounded by Soviet fighters! They are destroying us!' In that battle, together with the other group of six that tied up the 'Messers' we shot down eight aircraft.

"The ShKAS, in terms of rapid firing, was a unique machine gun. From close range, from about 50 metres, it was possible to saw off a wing with a battery from four ShKAS. At such proximity you fire long, do not save rounds, and do not give a damn about scatter. It was possible to knock both the tail and the wing off, literally cut it off. Incidentally, it was specifically on the Hurricane that I shot down my first one, a '109. The English weapons were still on. I was a support aircraft at that point, and he attacked the lead aircraft, I chopped him, literally from about 15 to 20 metres. The English began to fit cannons on the Hurricanes a lot later than us. They used our successful experience."

Tim Elkington – "Cannons? We had them in 601 Squadron in mid 1941." Golodnikov again:

"The engine was good, powerful and quite reliable; it operated very cleanly. What is more there were branch exhausts with flash eliminators. This was very convenient; it did not dazzle the pilot's eyes. In this sense our machines were significantly worse. During negative g-force the engine choked. There was no compensatory small tank. This is very bad because any manoeuvre should be completed with positive g-force. We quickly became familiar with this characteristic, but initially in the heat of the battle, we would forget it. Later with experience we would not allow this since a sharp weakening of the thrust alters the manoeuvre unexpectedly for you, and in battle this is very dangerous.

"The airframe was poor, and very heavy. The engine could not endure prolonged operation at maximum rate, it would quickly fail. The Hurricane had a very light tail. We were based on sandy, insufficiently compacted aerodromes. A technician or motor mechanic had to sit on the tail; we had to taxi with a passenger technician by the name of Rudenko. He once flew in a circuit still on the tail. He sat with his back forwards and did not manage to leap off, so he punctured the duraluminium of the fin with his hands, seized hold of it and held on. The pilot landed the aircraft with him like this. There were instances of them falling from the tail and dying.

"The propeller was interesting, it had variable pitch but with wooden blades. The pitch was changed by hand, with levers and thrusts. It did not present difficulties. In the squadron there was one propeller technician to four aircraft for servicing the propellers.

"I had to get used to flying the Hurricane. I liked the I-16 more. In fact, I did not like the Hurricane; I did not have any affinity with it. It resembled a pterodactyl, with a fat profile. The acceleration performance was very bad. At maximum speed it was likely quicker than the I-16, but while it was picking up speed a lot of things could happen. It did not lag when applying rudder, but everything somehow happened smoothly and slowly.

"With the I-16 you just applied the rudder and it immediately turned, with a jerk, but this 'hump back' was very slow. Its lift was good, so the rate of lift was comparable with the I-16. The horizontal manoeuvrability was very good. If a group of four went up in a circle it was not possible to break it; the Germans could not get but its vertical manoeuvrability was very bad, because the profile was fat. On the whole we tried to wage battle on the horizontal, the take-off of the Hurricane was short, once again due to the fat wings. In terms of performance the Hurricane was slightly inferior to the Bf 109E, primarily on the vertical, whilst it was not inferior on the horizontal. Then the Bf 109F came, the Hurricane began to be deeply inferior, but we fought on. The Hurricane burned quickly and well, like a matchstick.

"I preferred the I-16 of course, the one that I fought on – the type 28. But there was no choice. I made around twenty combat sorties on the Hurricane and had around three or four dogfights. Then I converted to the P-40."

Tim Elkington's final comment on this view of the Hurricane and its challenges was: "Fascinating, well observed."

Chapter Seven

MEDITERRANEAN &
FAR EAST THEATRES

Took a Blenheim to Valona
Every morning just at nine;
Same old aircraft, same old aircrew,
Same old height and same old time.

'Do four runs down' said the CO
And make everyone do well.
If you do you'll get a medal,
If you don't I'll give you hell.

Over Corfu weather clearing
And the sun begins to shine,
42s and G50s
All awaiting on the line.

On the way back same old fighters
And the gravy getting low.
How we wish we could see Eleusis
Through the snowstorm down below.

Oh group captain, our group captain,
Sitting coy at HQ,
How we wish that you could sample
'Musso' chucking muck at me!

How I wish I were at HQ
Drinking coffee by the score.
Then I wouldn't have to push of
To Valona any more.

To the tune of 'Clementine'
Flying Officer Derek Walker, 30 Squadron Italy 1941

THE MEDITERRANEAN THEATRE

FIGHTERS

The Mediterranean theatre, including the siege of Malta, the campaigns in Greece, the to-and-fro of the desert war in North Africa and the eventual allied invasions of southern France and Italy, included substantial British, German, Italian and United States air forces. Italian air force General B A Giacomo Metellini flew many combat missions in the region as a fighter pilot, starting in the Western Desert in support of the Axis powers' attempts to reach Egypt and capture the vital Suez Canal.

"At the beginning of 1940 we began to fly the new Fiat G 50 (6 *Stormo* '*Diavolo Rossi*', 2 *Gruppo Caccia*), with a low wing and retractable undercarriage, all-metal, but still equipped with a radial engine and an open cockpit. Our unit was one of the first to be equipped with the 'modern' G 50; it was up to us, therefore, to test the aircraft in the field in order to find any weak points or areas for improvement. The engine was poor; the aeroplane did not shine in performance; it was rather heavy, slow and not very manoeuvrable. The principal defect was that as you were coming in to land, the 'plane had a tendency to rock from side to side, and drop the left wing, so you had to come in at high speed. I didn't like it at all, no-one liked to fly the G 50.

"At the end of 1940 we received the unexpected order to transfer to North Africa. The operations were mainly ground attacks on enemy units. They were not particularly intense actions: the anti-aircraft reaction, in fact, was mainly small-calibre return fire, even if most times, it did not succeed in anything.

"From 25 May 1941 we began escorts to German and Italian Stuka Ju 87s on Tobruk. We were there to protect the bombers during missions against the port and the ships. The Stuka was lightly armed and dropped its bombs at a low altitude, at which moment it presented an easy target for English fighters. We had to follow the Stuka in the dive, so that at the moment of pulling out we could protect them from the fighters. They were risky missions, not only for the presence of enemy fighters, but more because Tobruk was well defended by anti-aircraft batteries and we were their target. The pull-out was quite high g, at least 3g, so we had to pull everything. The problem was the gunfire. As we were diving down 'puk-puk-puk' we could see these balls of fire flying past.

"As we were short of aeroplanes, in January 1941 I volunteered to try and retrieve damaged aircraft which had been left behind during our retreats. I formed a team of pilots and mechanics, who flew to these abandoned airfields to repair the aircraft and fly back if possible. These 'planes were very badly damaged, mainly because of the effect of the sand on the engine. The first 'planes we sent were the G 50 and the CR 42, without filters. So the airfields in Africa were filled with abandoned 'planes which were not really recoverable. Obviously it was quite dangerous because the British were coming, the Italians leaving, the aircraft not working. They were dangerous aircraft that could fail at any moment. In less than ten days we managed to rescue more than forty 'planes."

Of all the air battles that raged over and around the Mediterranean, perhaps the best known are the bitter struggles by the Axis powers to defeat Malta, and the valiant efforts of the allied defenders to protect both the island itself, and the convoys bringing the vital supplies through the straits of Gibraltar. Giacomo Metellini soon found himself embroiled in this long-running phase of the Mediterranean air war.

"On 3 May 1942 we received an order to transfer to the airfield at Saint Peter di Caltagirone, in Sicily, in order to participate in operations on Malta, ahead of its imminent invasion. There were two kinds of missions; mostly free fighting, go there, look for Spitfires and try to get them. Secondly, escorting the bombers attacking the island, Ju 88s at first.

"We had to face the Spitfires from the Maltese bases head-on, therefore we adopted tactics of extreme mobility in order not to be caught, with the enemy getting on our tail to attack us. Unfortunately, we did not always succeed in having the upper hand, and the root cause of that was the fact that the English, thanks to their interception radar, were aware of all our movements once we left Sicily, while we had to wait for our base to transmit to us how much they could understand from the English communications. The English knew we were coming, knew exactly when we were scrambled, got up to 25,000 feet and just waited for us.

"The escort missions were particularly risky as they consisted of flying beside the bombers. The English were more numerous than us. With the sun on their backs, they were thrown towards us and, aiming at everyone, they made a fast pass. For us it was difficult to counter this type of attack because, when we sighted the Spitfires, they had by now completed their nose-dive attack and, taking advantage of all the speed acquired during the dive, they continued their descent below us. Following them in the dive was not considered, since they were much faster, and we would have had to abandon the escort of the aircraft that we were called to protect. When you were doing your free fighting, at least you were given more freedom of movement. So from that point of view, I preferred it.

"With experience we devised new tactics and, instead of flying alongside the bombers to escort them, we began to fly around them, wrapping them with a formation similar to a sphere. Without leaving the protection zones, we therefore prevented an enemy surprise attack. This tactic of extreme mobility became a very effective one because, when engaging the opposing fighters, the possibility was given to the bombers to carry out their mission and return to base.

"The 2nd Fighter Group was based on three squadriglia – flights, 150th, 152nd and 358th (*by now flying the Reggiane RE 2001*); my squadriglia was the 152nd. The group strength was about thirty aeroplanes. Normally we only flew in flights, unless there was a big attack.

Apart from the offensive missions on Malta we also carried out search and rescue missions escorting seaplanes that tried to recover pilots who had parachuted into the sea.

"When we carried out free fighting over Malta the actions were tough and sometimes inconclusive. It was very difficult, the first time we had been in real combat with many aeroplanes at the same time. Until then I had never had occasion to meet with enemy aircraft, although you knew what it meant to carry out operations over enemy territory, given my experience in Africa. However in Africa I had not had to defend myself from enemies who had got on my tail to try and shoot me down, in a faster and better armed aeroplane, which the Spitfire was.

"The British and the Germans were more disciplined than us, and adopted tactics with formations of at least two or four aeroplanes that had the task of protecting each other. Once the fight began, it became a free for all, whereas the British and the Germans were more disciplined, they'd say 'no, I'm not leaving you'. The combats never did last long, a few minutes at the most, also our limited duration did not allow much fuel for the combat and return. We only had twenty minutes over Malta. At a certain point we had to try to disengage, and sometimes we were followed on the way back by a Spitfire that, thanks to their much closer base, had greater duration and could fly and fight over a longer time, get back, refuel, and get back up. It was important never to relax your concentration, being prepared for the unexpected, continuously to watch all around.

"Once returning from a patrol mission, by now far away from Malta, I looked behind my back and saw with surprise, three-quarters behind me a Spitfire, very close and just about to open fire. Instinctively I turned upside down and pulled through towards the sea. The dive was such that just at the moment of pulling out, I blacked out. When I came round, the aircraft was still pulling out, and I was flying very close to the sea! I was able to take control and climb. Luckily, no Spitfire was following; he was so surprised by my manoeuvre that he had decided not to follow. In combat with English pilots you also needed good fortune, or you were gone.

"I had my first combat success on 2 July 1942. I was engaged in a very furious battle circling the island. In a moment, I saw a Spitfire in a very fast pass directly in front of me, in a dive and showing the underside. I opened fire, one short burst, without the time to follow its fate. Other pilots of my group confirmed that they had seen the aircraft crash into the sea. I hope from my point of view (and I'm sure I speak for all the Italian pilots who flew over the island), only to have brought down the 'plane and not the pilot, that he was able to launch himself free by parachute and was saved from the sea.

In that same month, numbers of RAF Spitfire Vs were flown off the aircraft carrier HMS *Eagle* in the western Mediterranean to reinforce the Malta defences;

later hatches being flown off from other carriers, including HMS *Furious*. Flight Lieutenant Rod Smith was a Royal Canadian Air Force pilot who took part in this operation. He flew operationally with 126 Squadron in the defence of Malta, and later with 412 (Spitfire) Squadron in Europe, finally accounting for thirteen air-to-air combat victories.

> "I took off from HMS *Eagle* after a 500 foot run, at dawn, and was the second one off. I flew in the first batch of eight en route to Luqa, Malta, a trip of 710 miles. We saw Algeria, and made a landfall at Tunisia, passing over Tunis. We changed tanks in sight of Pantelleria, and landed still a group after three hours and fifteen minutes in the air with lots of petrol left. My brother Jerry was at Luqa – it was a small world! (*Pilot Officer Jerry Smith served with his brother on 126 Squadron, but went missing during a patrol they flew together on from Malta on 10 August 1942.*)
>
> "Straight away we were flying patrols, and on 13 August during a convoy patrol near Linosa, we spotted a formation of SM 79s. I dived down and at a height of 800 feet I gave one of them a four-second burst and its starboard engine caught fire. It crashed into the sea in a mass of flames."

Geoffrey Wellum also found himself ferrying Spitfires to the island, and recalled that the whole idea of flying off from a carrier deck was somewhat challenging.

> "The whole thing was a sort of shambles really. When we looked at our Spitfires, we found we had very old fashioned airscrews on them that only gave you twenty-six-fifty revs on take-off and we wanted 3,000. We eventually got new airscrews and then some bright spark said: 'Well why don't you put down twenty-five degrees of flap?' I said, 'You can't. In the Spitfire the flaps are either fully up or fully down', and so what they did was, they made wedges of wood of 25 degrees and you got an expendable airman to stand under each flap, you put the flap right down, 'Ready?' 'Yes, right' put the wedge in, flap up, 25 degrees.
>
> "I went down to my aeroplane to get it ready and found an airman taking all the ammunition out. I said 'Hold on a minute, mate. What's all this about?' He said, 'Cigarettes'. So I said, 'Right, well, fair enough. Cigarettes – I bet they go off pretty well!' They were short of cigarettes in Malta, and they're very much lighter than ammunition. But because we had 90-gallon overload tanks to get us from the Balearics into Malta via North Africa, we had to save every bit of weight we could. I was the first of eight so my take-off run was cut down anyway and I needed all the help I could get. But once the ship pulled, 32 knots of wind went over the deck, and once you let the brakes off under full power you had complete faith. It was no problem taking off at all once you got the aeroplane ready to do it."

Perhaps the most famous of all the Malta convoys was code named 'Pedestal', and this became a priority target for Giacomo Metellini and his Italian air force compatriots.

"On 12 August 1942, 'The Battle of Middle August' (*Operation Herkules, the planned Axis invasion of Malta on 15 August*) against the Pedestal convoy began. We were immediately called with ten RE 2001s of my group and some Macchi 202s, to escort SM 79 torpedo bombers (the famous Cursed Hunchback). We left in the direction of the convoy that we caught up to the south-west of La Galite islands, 150 kilometres south of Sardinia. We engaged in combat with Sea Hurricanes that had taken off from aircraft carriers. There was a lot of confusion, aeroplanes of several types in the sky, and blasts of anti-aircraft fire came at you from the crews defending the ships. Our group brought down three Hurricanes and damaged eight. There were no losses on our part and we returned to our base in Sardinia.

"The next day, after take-off our group was to assemble with MC 202s to carry out an escort mission for SM 79s. The assembly point was over the airfield at Castelvetrano, in Sicily. The RE 2001s of my group had to take formation alongside the torpedo bombers for close escort; one section of three aircraft on the left, with me in the lead formation, and the others on the right. In the confusion of the departure and the subsequent assembly, waiting for the torpedo bombers, only my section was ready to act as an escort. The bombers went on circling, waiting for the other section. So the bomber leader decided, with much courage, with good appreciation of the danger, to set out towards the enemy convoy. Me, with my two wingmen, also knowing the fate to which we were headed, decided to accompany them, promising myself to make all possible efforts to save the lives of these brave ones. Hurricanes and other aircraft flying from the aircraft carriers, were waiting for us as soon as we arrived over the target.

"The torpedo bombers made the best possible attack, then turned away, but all did not return to base. My two companions and I did our best to protect those that risked more than we did. You hit many enemy aircraft without following their fates. Our RE 2001s were doing the best they could, but the enemy was too numerous. I saw an SM 79 low over the sea, running towards the target, trying to avoid hits from the anti-aircraft fire in order to bring itself to the best distance to drop its torpedo. I saw a Hurricane trying to get on its tail. I headed towards the enemy aeroplane and began to fire, but one of the two machine guns jammed. I had to stop my attack for three or four seconds in order to clear the jammed machine gun. That was sufficient time for me to be hit by one long burst from the opposing fighter. There were numerous hits in the fuselage and on the wings, and I was fortunate not to be wounded. At first I did not notice the bullet that pierced my canopy, then I noticed the bullet hole – it had penetrated at the height of my head. The round had only missed me by some centimetres: my head was a little tilted forward in the action to recharge my machine guns, and the blow of the enemy made me miss my breath!

"I realised that not only the canopy had been hit: the engine did not work too well and all the temperatures were starting to rise quickly. I had to make a decision in a hurry: to try to return to base, knowing that the distance to cover, about eighty miles and twenty minutes, could be fatal if the engine failed. It was about six in the afternoon, so I had to think about the risk of coming down and waiting for rescue, possibly not coming, because it was night. The other choice was to jump out by parachute while I was still close to the enemy convoy, hoping that one of the ships would see me and pick me up, thinking I was an English pilot. The aircraft still seemed to be controllable, therefore I decided to risk a return. I was not convinced that if I jumped I would be sighted by one of the ships and that it would stop to find me, with the risk that it would be hit by one of our aeroplanes.

"I decided to go back home, and I flew away and aimed for the southern coast of Sardinia, this being the closest goal. I could not risk flying for a long time with an engine that was losing power more and more and getting hotter and hotter. I realised that the only way to make it was to take advantage of the minimum power still available to climb a little and then throttle back to carry out a long glide in order to cool it. I was quite high and began this system of long glides and then slow climbs. Every five minutes approximately, I radioed my position saying that, if they did not hear from me every five minutes, it meant that I had parachuted into the sea. But there was nobody at the other end listening to me, because my radio had been hit, but I didn't know.

"After a flight of approximately twenty minutes, which to me seemed like a lifetime, I was able to reach the base at Elmas in Sicily, with temperatures red-hot and a failing engine. The technician, as soon as he saw the aircraft, immediately declared it out of use. Of the two wingmen, one was shot down while the other succeeded in returning to base. Those twenty minutes of flight as I returned towards Sicily were the longest of my life."

Co-operation between the German and Italian air forces was surprisingly limited during operations against Malta, as Giacomo Metellini explained.

"In order to try to intercept the Spitfires before they attacked our bombers over Malta, we sometimes flew an indirect escort, with MC 202s that flew high over us. The Germans did not want to act as an escort with their Bf 109Gs because, they said, they confused our RE 2001s with the Spitfire because of the similar wing shape. Therefore, when Macchis were engaged in other missions, we were by ourselves. Our activities in cooperation with the Germans were limited to escorting Ju 88s. Other actions were escort missions to German rescue seaplanes for pilots who had come down in the sea, not only Italian ones, but also Dornier floatplanes.

"During a combat I got hit a couple of times. I did not notice it at first, it was only when I got back to base and released my parachute, that something fell to the ground. I picked it up and, to my surprise I found that it was a 7.69mm round. I had not been aware of the hit, and the bullet had been stopped inside my parachute after having entered the fuselage through the tail of the aircraft, and it had crossed behind the seat and, had finally finished its race in the parachute. I have always thought that in air war, fortune counted more than ability, without which however, the probability of death increases considerably.

"Once engaged in visual contact, we were able to defend ourselves quite easily and, in aerial combats we could hope to out-turn the opposition, thanks to the ability of the pilots and the aerodynamic characteristics of the Re 2001. It was in fact a much more manoeuvrable aircraft and turned tighter than the Spitfire, therefore we could remove ourselves from trouble easily enough when an enemy got on our tail. If it had had a more powerful engine, and had been better armed, we would have been in a better position for combat, especially in the early phase of the conflict, when the veterans of the Battle of Britain were not physically present on the island – pilots who had already served in combat on other fronts (for example in Africa), some with many victories already. The ability of our newly qualified pilots often put us in difficulty. The enemy pilots were very, very good, with a very good aeroplane, so they were tough opponents."

The Fleet Air Arm was also very active throughout the Mediterranean, not only embarked on carriers, but also – and rather less well known – operating from forward airstrips in the Western Desert. After a period of ferrying replacement aircraft across Africa, Jack Routley flew the Grumman Martlet with 805 Squadron from 1941 to 1943.

"On arrival in the Middle East I was used as a ferry pilot, and flew Hurricanes from Takoradi to the Middle East. Takoradi is on the Gold Coast, and there was an RAF airfield where they assembled aircraft there that were shipped to West Africa; the Mediterranean was untenable at the time. People like me were selected to fly them up across to the Middle East.

"By October of 1941 we were flying from Dekheila near Alexandria. I flew whatever aircraft there were, including Fulmars, Swordfish and Gladiators. I had five hours in Martlets and was whisked off to 805 Squadron in the desert. We were fairly mobile, we moved as the land battle waxed and waned, and we had tents and equipment and stuff for aircraft maintenance, but we could pack up and move whenever we needed to. Rommel came forward to El Alamein in 1942, and we got out of the desert then and went to Port Said. There was a crummy airfield there, El Gamil, 'lovely El Gamil' as we called it.

"A couple of Me 109s attacked our airstrip, but they must have been learner pilots because they fired at the runway. We had no anti-aircraft protection at these strips, and they just flew up the runway and fired some bullets into the sand, avoiding all the tents where we were, under the table at that moment, and the aircraft that were lined up somewhere, and the rest of the tents with the rest of the people in. They just strafed the runway and disappeared. We subsequently had an RAF regiment with Bofors guns to protect us.

"We were a lone squadron on our own, and we were dictated to move when the land warfare thought that was a good idea. The RAF prohibited us from doing anything else but shipping patrols but they didn't want us to mess about with the ground war. But occasionally on return from a shipping patrol, we would just clear our guns when we happened to see something up the desert road; that was how we came to do some ground strafing. The air force was very pleased when we did this too, on the odd occasion.

"Flying as a wingman to Bob Waltham, my first convoy protection mission, I met our Italian friends in their SM 79s. We were providing combat air patrol fighter cover for a group of ships with destroyers and frigates en route from Alexandria to Tobruk. We were over the convoy at 4,000 feet below the cloud layer, controlled by one of the escorts, and the SM 79s, two of them, flew in low over the water, under the radar screen and attacked the convoy. They were not seen until they were spotted by spotters on the surface ships. Then all hell broke loose, the ships put up a barrage of anti-aircraft fire, and the controller advised us to dive through this lot and take on the '79s. We did this and got in a burst of fire just before they dropped their torpedoes, but drop their torpedoes they did, striking one of the large transports. We followed them, continuing to fire, initially both at the lead aircraft, and then we split and took one each. I did see where the fire was going – splashes in the sea showed this, and smoke was coming from the port engine. Return fire was coming from the gunners of the SM.79.

"Then we were directed to return over the convoy to help cover a damaged tanker, and we were welcomed back with a burst of friendly fire from the convoy. Our claim was that both SM 79s were damaged, one so severely that it was unlikely to have returned to base. We did not see the aircraft ditch because of being recalled. Those Italians were good aviators, they did the job, and they got away. I took off my hat to those guys; they had no escort but they persisted through the escorts in the convoy, and there was a fair amount of flak flying around, and they were undeterred. They flew very low down, right down on the water. (*This engagement took place at 4 p.m. on 23rd November 1941, while 805 Squadron was operating from Sidi Haneish. Jack shared a claim with Sub Lieutenant R W M Walsh for one probably damaged and one possibly damaged.*)

"A pair of us attacked a German transport column on the desert road heading east. We were returning from a shipping patrol and had dog-legged westwards on the way back. We strafed them setting trucks ablaze and we could see troops being bowled over as they set-up gun tripods to return fire. I had cannon shell damage on the rear of my air-craft, and this led to loss of rudder control. I headed out to sea low over the water to return to Dekheila, where the damage could be fixed. It was possible to turn in a very wide arc using ailerons. I kept an eagle-eye behind me in case there were enemy fighters around, I would have been an easy prey. I landed safely back at Dekheila and they repaired the dam-age, and I returned in a day or two to the squadron. (*This happened on 27 June 1942, somewhere between Sidi Barrani and Mersa Matruh.*)

"We had a tame chameleon, which sat on the bar and zapped the flies that were around. He sat on the CO's shoulder in his Martlet, fly-ing out of the desert back to El Gamil, and he had a wonderful time there, because there were not only flies, but cockroaches as well, and he got a very high protein diet from these cockroaches on the bar. Poor Charlie, he passed away eventually from a surfeit of cockroaches.

"Conditions in the desert were pretty primitive of course; sand pen-etrated everywhere, including the aircraft. Although we had radial engines, that were not as sensitive to sand intrusion as the Hurricanes and the Seafires, still we did have engine problems. I had several occa-sions where it was necessary to return from patrols early because of engine problems; I had one hairy take-off where things weren't working very successfully. It coughed and spluttered a bit just about as I was leaving the ground, and it didn't have the thrust that it was expected to have. It was a bit hair-raising as to whether I was going to make it.

"The worst moment for me, was when we'd flown to Nairobi, to have our aircraft overhauled. There was an aircraft carrier in Durban needing some replacement Martlets, and six of us were used as ferry pilots to fly them down from Nairobi, in late December '42. We flew three legs, about seven hours, to a primitive airstrip in N'Dola in north-ern Rhodesia, refuelled and took off on New Year's Eve for Salisbury. One aircraft had a mechanical problem, and we all had to land back at N'Dola, to keep the group together.

"The aircraft was fixed, and by late afternoon we took off again for Salisbury, and after about three hours of flying, by early evening we were confronted by a solid, black, wall of severe thunderstorms. It was lit by sheets of lightning, and it was too late and we had insufficient fuel to turn back, and there were no other alternative airfields in that area. In the thunderstorm there was extreme turbulence, heavy rain, crashing thunder and fierce lightning flashes. All communication with the desti-nation airfield and the other aircraft was lost.

"We looked for somewhere to force-land. It was farming country and there were some sizeable fields there, but the formation had split up by then and we were on our own to find somewhere to land. After blundering around in the dark for a while, I chose a field in what turned out to be a village called Bindura, and I put the Martlet down in this field without damage; others did so too in nearby fields. A couple were damaged, but there were no personnel injuries. We just sat it out on the ground until the weather had passed. The local South Africans were very hospitable to us, and we'd dropped in during New Year's Eve straight out of the sky. So of course the booze was flowing and we had a great party. The next day we dusted off the flyable aircraft and flew them into Salisbury.

"I was invited to stay on at the naval air repair yard as a Martlet test pilot. I had an engine failure in a Martlet while I was at pretty good altitude near the airfield and I was badly positioned relative to the runway and wind conditions. I did have radio communication with the tower, and asked them if they would clear the runway, and I would try and put this down on it, but I would have to land down-wind, because I couldn't get round to the other end. So I did a gliding performance from a few thousand feet down to the approach to the runway, and kept up quite a bit of speed. When I could see that I was going to make the runway comfortably, I cranked the wheels down and then after crossing the boundary and aligning with the runway, I was able to use the flaps and check off some of the speed. I still landed at fairly high speed, and one of the advantages of a tailwheel was that it got me down the runway quite a long way, and it was quite a long runway fortunately. I got to the end, and just had enough urge to turn off the runway towards a parking area where the Grumman Martlets were nicely lined-up ready for the next test-flight.

"We had a Grumman technical representative there called Bill Kempenfelt, and he bounced out of the hangar – he'd been on the telephone to air traffic while all this was going on – and he remonstrated saying: 'You've parked out of line, now we're going to have to tow the damn thing in!' He was a great character, and it was a very successful ending to what could have been a fairly hairy story.

"The Martlet was not a match for the Me 109 that the Luftwaffe had in the desert; that was a more manoeuvrable and a higher performance aircraft. Nevertheless, I was pleased to have the Martlet compared with things like the Roc. Or the Fulmar for that matter, that was a very low performing aircraft too."

In September 1943, the Italian forces capitulated to the allies, and many pilots were given the opportunity to change sides and continue fighting for the allied cause. However, Giacomo Metellini decided against changing sides, and instead headed for a neutral third country.

"On 9 September 1943 I found myself at Sarzana, with the rank of captain, as commander of 152 Squadron, when the news of the armistice reached us over the radio. Uncertainty resulted, and I waited to decide what to do, hoping that the allies would free Italy quickly, then, as the months passed, and seeing that the situation was getting worse, I asked to resign, but it was not accepted. I was not comfortable in joining the allies, they were my enemies for two years. I didn't like the Germans, especially as they started to take prisoners. So I decided to escape to Switzerland, and they interned me. I walked; I knew how to get there, so I smuggled myself with the guys who were smuggling contraband."

Further on towards the end of the war, Bill Musgrave was flying Spitfires from Corsica, and soon became involved in the invasion of southern France. There were also some unfortunate incidents when using the Spitfires as fighter-bombers.

"We got to 237 Squadron in Corsica (Poretta); onto Spitfire Mk IXs. Rome was still in the hands of the Germans, and from Corsica we could cover everything, we could almost get to Bologna, we could certainly get to Florence. The Germans knew bloody well that the invasion was due in France, and I think at least 75% of their squadrons had pulled out for France, so it was quite a rare thing to see a German aircraft in the sky.

"Most of our work was ground-strafing and bomber escorts; the bombers coming mainly from Sardinia, American 12th Air Force B-25s and Marauders. We were on the eastern coast in Corsica up until the end of July, so nearly four months. Then we moved over to the west coast to get ready for the invasion of southern France; we went to Calvi. The invasion of southern France was a complete walk-over, at the start our role was beach-head cover, strafing radar stations and any troops we could find. But that was over in a few days, and we landed up at an airfield in southern France (*Cuers on 27 August*). We very badly damaged a radar station near Hyères. On the way back we sighted two submarines, one making an immediate crash dive. The next day we saw a Fortress blown up in mid-air by flak – it was a hell of a sight.

"We were moved to Rosignano and finished the war there. That's when we went onto dive-bombing, mainly bridges, and the odd stores building. A lot of squadrons did the same, especially those operating on the east coast. They were dive-bombing in liaison with the army, what they called the cab-rank. The army would pick out the target and down they'd go. A famous RAF pilot, 'Cocky' Dundas was flying one day, leading a dive-bombing exercise, dropped his bombs and pulled out of the dive and watched the others coming in. He watched one Spitfire and it suddenly just blew up. It was put down to a fluke hit by an ack-ack shell on the bomb. We carried a 500 pound bomb and two 250s.

"A short time later, he was on another dive-bombing mission, and the same thing happened again to one of his flight commanders. You could understand a flight of Spitfires approaching a target, doing a steady 250-300 miles an hour, you can expect them to be hit then, but to be hit in a dive doing about 400 or 500 miles an hour is a bit much. They investigated and found that there was a batch of bad fuses. One of my chaps was killed like that.

"We also had one chap, he couldn't hold a pee for long. On the long trips, what do you do? He took off his flying boot and then poured it out the window; he was great. All our rooms had a balcony, and one night I noticed this chap getting out of bed, and he went onto the balcony; the next thing we saw he walked in through the door. He'd jumped over the balcony, crashed through a bundle of telephone cables which broke his fall, landed on the ground, had a pee..."

BOMBERS

At the outset of the air war, much of the RAF equipment in-theatre was seriously outdated. Stephen Hall was an air gunner on 216 Squadron, which was still flying the Bristol Bombay bomber/transport.

"Suddenly, 10 June 1940 peace turns to war. (*Italy enters the war.*) Frantic activity, the squadron is put on operational duties. It was so easy to distinguish each and every target long before we got there. Tobruk never failed to fascinate me with its colourful display, plus the flaming onions, consisting of strings of seven or eight yellow fireballs like large footballs, reaching a few thousand feet. Derna and Bomba had very light defences, but Benghazi, what a reception, it was amazing. I used to look back (I could do no other, I was in the rear turret) and wonder how anyone could fly through it and get away with it.

"On one memorable occasion we were committed and suddenly, just above us, one of C Flight dropped a flare. How we survived the concentrated barrage, one will never know. Just when we thought we were clear, bang! wallop! crash! There were two gaping holes, and my parachute harness was torn, a shell had blown the tail wheel in, and gone out the rear end and hadn't exploded.

"A typical raid: crews notified, briefing, service aircraft, taxi to bomb-loading area, then depending if fortunate or unfortunate, the armourers have been notified of the type of bombs, you load up, and when completed, taxi back to the refuelling dump. Top-up, leave the aircraft at dispersal point, and have lunch. After lunch, take-off and fly to desert airfield, maybe two hours or so flying away, land, top-up with petrol, have tea and await take-off time, this naturally will depend on if the raid is short or long distance. Take-off, complete the raid, land, visit the intelligence tent, have a meal, refuel, return to base, where the whole system starts again. After three continuous raids, one becomes very weary from lack of sleep, it was pure luck we never crashed on landing.

"On a Tobruk raid, being the first over the target area, I reported the presence of an unfriendly guest. Skipper told me to hold my fire, and I dived for cloud cover, mission completed and reported the fact to the intelligence officer, who was not a bit convinced. The number two aircraft lands with the same story, only this time with a few holes to help convince the still doubting officer. Number three proved an unbelievable fiasco, they landed peppered and scorched on the tail. They had been shot-up, the engine caught fire, and the skipper gave the bale out. Jock, the rear gunner, is not quite sure of the message, and proceeds to midship. There standing at the open door is the midship gunner, parachute clipped on and in his left hand a mug and irons. Jock, seeing this, about turns, races back to the tail, tries to crash out through the Perspex dome without releasing the catches and dazes himself.

"Meanwhile, the WOp stops the midship gunner from jumping, and Jock is quietly soothed back to normality. At the same time, the night fighter has formatted under the starboard wing, the second pilot is entangled with the two sandbags carried in the nose. He's trying to get his revolver out in an attempt to shoot at the fighter. After a little while, the fighter pilot gives a thumbs-up and peels away. You may well imagine the dog's life that crew got; unbelievable but very true.

"The reason for the two sandbags in the nose: Flying Officer Chisholm was flying over the TransJordan at 10,000 feet, and found his aircraft going into a loop, which took both him and his second pilot all their strength eventually to regain control. At around the same time, we were watching another Bombay, which was coming in to land from a major overhaul test flight. We saw the flaps coming down and suddenly its tail came up and it plunged into the ground, killing everyone on board. Investigation revealed that when the fuel tanks became empty, the centre of gravity moved, causing this sudden diving and loops. Once the tanks had equalised, the aircraft behaved itself.

"We had taken stores to the Fleet Air Arm base at Alexandria and were awoken early next morning to fly back to Helio, immediately briefed to do a support raid with the navy. Racks were fitted in the cabin to carry 160 fragmentation bombs, the correct way using a five-bomb-at-a-time rack. This is all right in practice, but flying to and fro over the target would last hours, so an extra man was carried. Over the target area, the pilot opened the front escape hatch, the extra man used the flare chute, the fitter/AG the main door, the WOp at his wireless and myself in the rear turret. Once over the target, the skipper would show the green light that was all clear to start unloading. Each person picked out a bomb, pulled the pin, and either dropped it through the hatch, down the flare chute or out the main door and magic, flashes on the ground.

"The operation of landing 250 miles inside enemy territory (9 *July* '42) was a most cheeky affair. The Fleet Air Arm had sighted a large convoy making for Tobruk, but they hadn't the range, so the surprise element was adopted. We were to land on a satellite airstrip near Sollum. The Albacores (826 *Squadron Dekheila*) were given a one-and-a-half-hour start, and we all landed together. I signed out a Thompson sub-machine gun and Peacock, my fitter, was a nutter, his comforting words were, could he have the gun if I was injured or killed?

"Our aircraft carried members of a Scottish regiment who on landing fanned out and set up defence positions. The rest of the passengers

202

unloaded petrol and helped refuel the Fleet Air Arm aircraft, then at a predetermined time they took off for home. I must say even though we saw enemy aircraft landing on the main strip, they weren't a bit concerned about our using the airstrip code word 'Chocolate'.

"One morning started like any other. We marched to the hangar, went to my aircraft to find it had 'destroyed' written on it in chalk – 'mine's the same', 'so is mine'. Everyone was puzzled. The refuelling doors had the same, what twit had been mucking about? Back for breakfast, who are those blokes? Don't know. By ten o'clock all hell was let loose. The CO's office had been entered and those blokes just went mad. The squadron was fallen in with a pep talk, all crews would sleep in the aircraft with rifles and fixed bayonets. What had actually happened was Major Stirling (the 'Phantom Major'), who pioneered the SAS in the Middle East, had used our squadron for training."

Eric Barfoot was rather more fortunate, and flew Wellingtons with 70 Squadron against various targets throughout the Mediterranean. On one occasion he experienced the indignity of being shot at by his own side, fortunately without coming to harm.

"After leaving OTU, I was due to go to 3 Group, but the co-pilot ahead of me had some sort of dose, so I was pulled forward and that saved my life. He became CO of 70 Squadron, and the first fifteen ops I did with him was from Kabrit. We couldn't reach all the way along to the target down near the Suez, so we had to fly up to an advanced landing ground.

"In one of the raids we were led to Rhodes, and as we went along there was St. Elmo's Fire flashes around the guns and the cockpit, which frightened me to death, but no harm done. We got to this place over Rhodes, and we had to bomb the airfield, which was behind the port. As we got to the port we could see the flak going up, 'Wham!' a poor squadron got that. We got to the airfield round the back so we didn't go through it, we went round it. We were bombing the airfield and were attacked by a CR 42. We got back to Egypt and met some navy chaps in Alex, apparently there was nobody bombing the port, it was the navy shelling them. The Ities thought we were over there when shooting at us, it was a pretty safe journey.

"We did thirty-seven ops altogether. The only time we were really hurt was when we were coming in to land after an op from Benghazi, and as we approached back from the target, we saw an aircraft with its lights on, going round and round, getting a green light from the ground. I had never heard any voice on the RT, because it didn't work. But they gave this thing a green light and round and round it went. We got a red and suddenly we got a green. In we went, and this thing was an intruder, a Ju 88. It crept up behind us, and let us have it when we were at about 500 feet but he didn't do much damage. Both our own gunners and the army gunners on the ground, all knew it was a Ju 88, but the army still had to ask, 'When can we open fire?', and were told 'No, it is a Beaufighter in distress'. Well it was us that was in distress, but the army gunners opened up and shot one of our elevators off. We scooted along the ground, but we all got out safely.

"On another occasion the squadron leader asked me to take a Wimpey up, at night, for an air test. She had a full load of fuel and when I landed back at Abu Sueir, I was told to take her round again. I opened up and she lumbered off down the runway; the speed crept up to 80, then began to drop again. I was running out of runway, so there was nothing for it but to yank her off the ground and pull the undercart up. The engines were on full boost and flat out and she staggered along at about 50 feet and would not build up any speed, so a turn was out of the question. Then I noticed that she was still on full flap! The selector was in the correct mid-position, so I guessed we had a faulty valve.

"The tallest tree in Egypt was dead ahead, so I shut my eyes and pulled back on the control column, and we missed. I tried to bring the flaps up slowly, a little at a time, but nothing happened, so I tried to make a very wide and shallow turn at 60 to get back to the runway. Suddenly, the flaps came up and as always, she sank. With only about 100 feet between me and the desert she thumped in tail first and skated along on her belly. I was OK and clambered out safely as she caught fire, and then all her ammo started exploding; the next day all that you could recognise were the engines. The MO came out to find me and offered me a fag, but my hand was shaking too much to take it."

Wireless operator/air gunner Sergeant Tommy Turnbull crewed Blenheims of 45 Squadron, later moving on to 52 Squadron with the same type. He too came to grief on more than one occasion, and his description of these events showed just how perilous the desert environment could be.

"Moving from one desert landing ground to another, I had the misfortune to crash twice in a short space of time. The Germans were pressing in all round Tobruk; we used to bomb their tanks and motor transport then land inside the defences, re-bomb, then attack again on the way back to base. On one of these raids, it got dark before we refuelled. There were no night flying facilities, so we just pointed in what we thought was a clear route for take-off – we were wrong. We hit a pile of oil drums, just as the aircraft left the ground. We seemed to be flung into the air, and we started shuddering. I used the Aldis lamp to shine on the tailplane; one side was damaged very badly, and the rudder seemed to be half missing. The pilot had difficulty holding a course and maintaining what height we had. We jettisoned our bombs over the sea, finally made a landfall, and crashed in. Although the aircraft broke up and we were covered in dust and somewhat bruised, we got away with it.

"Returning from a raid on Derna, we pranged again, we simply flew into the ground. It was dark and I think we were all a bit tired. I heard the pilot asking the navigator to cover some light or other, which was dazzling him and obstructing his view of the instruments. Then there was a grinding sound as our prop-tips churned up an inch or two of desert. A sudden jerking of the aircraft, a strange silence as we rose skyward for a second or two, flopped back down again, skidded forward, breaking up in clouds of dust. I was bounced about inside until we came to a halt. I tried to open the hatch, but it was jammed; I was dreading the wreck catching fire. Then I crawled through a hole in the side that I hadn't seen at first. The pilot and navigator were both clambering down the wing when I emerged."

Fellow wireless operator, John Whitaker (although by this time he had been grounded), also served with the Middle East Blenheim squadrons. During this period he came across the American bomber forces who undertook one of the most daring raids of the war – the attack on Germany's vital oilfields in Ploesti, Romania.

"I was posted to 211 Squadron. This was made up of short-nosed Blenheims probably cast-offs from the UK. As with every unit I joined in the RAF, they were a great crowd, keen as mustard to keep their aircraft flying, not so easy in the dusty atmosphere of Egypt. As I had been grounded I was put in charge of all things electrical, no great chore.

"We had one bad incident. While on a night flight in clear conditions an aircraft just flew into the ground for no reason that was ever established. The aircraft broke into two pieces at its weakest point, the gun turret, and the wireless operator (who was also the gunner) was thrown out and landed unconscious on the ground where he lay all night until found next morning by an Egyptian Camel Corps team who brought him to the hospital. Although badly injured he survived and made a full recovery, although he refused to fly again in Blenheims. The pilot and bomb-aimer were killed.

"Early in 1940 I was posted to 55 Squadron, on short-nosed Blenheims again. We moved up to Amriya, near Alexandria, and waited for Mussolini to declare war. Then we were off to Fuka, part way between Alamein and Mersa Matruh where we hung around until December when Wavell made his brilliant strike. The squadron did very little flying as bombers are not much good in desert warfare, for if you don't make a direct hit the bomb just blows a lot of sand around. When the push started in December we were off, our aircraft harrying the Italians but not really contributing much.

"I was on Benina airfield, with the Americans, when the raids on the Ploesti oilfields happened. They were a wing of B-24 Liberators, and we got on very well with them. We were always friendly with the Americans, and it was given an additional boost because all their units were 'dry', so we gave them whisky and in return they gave us cigarettes.

Warrant Officer Eric Burke served as a navigator with 13 Squadron in Italy in 1944/45. Here his usual Boston IV BZ531 leads a vic of three on an operation from Aviano against German troop concentrations. *Burke*

It was common knowledge shortly before the Ploesti raid that the wing was to be part of the attack. They were not afraid, but were understandably nervous as it was known that Ploesti was heavily defended.

"We watched the aircraft take off and thought nothing of it, but much later when they started coming back, it was noticeable that they came in ones and twos, and for a long time people kept peering towards the north until it was obvious that those who were still missing had been lost. I never realised the scale of the casualties until much later."

By the time navigator Eric Burke came on the scene, the Blenheim had been replaced on operations by more modern American equipment, and the war had shifted its main focus to Italy.

"I was posted to 13 Squadron; it would have been in January '45 that we started ops. We were converting from Baltimores to Bostons, and we started operating mostly over the Po Valley. We were in support of the 8th Army basically. The army used to set out oil drums in the shapes of letters, L, E or something, and give us courses to bomb. We did recces, we were light-armed reconnaissance people, at comparatively low-level, bombing and strafing troops and MT columns, and going for bridges. Getting towards the end of the war, but to me it was quite a tough three months. We did about twenty-seven ops as far as I remember.

"One night we were flying one of these army co-ops, climbing to a higher height than normal, and we stalled. We recovered, but we still had a bomb load aboard. So the pilot pulled up and said, 'sorry about that folks, we'll go up again', at which stage, the gunner called up: 'he's gone!' (The wireless operator was sat in a hatch at the back.) The pilot was usually quick on the uptake, and he said: 'what do you mean, he's gone?' 'He's baled out'. So we had to drop our bombs in the Adriatic. We came back, and the gunner was quite upset, so we said to him, 'you go to bed, we'll talk about this in the morning'. We then found out that Bill had come down, lost a flying boot on the way, but he came down luckily on our side of the bomb line. The army picked him up and he returned to us the next day."

THE GERMAN VIEW

Prior to establishing great success as a night fighter pilot defending his homeland, Heinz Rökker flew the Ju 88 in the Mediterranean.

"I started action in 1942 in Africa, against Malta and North Africa, Sicily, and Crete. We came back to Belgium, then once more to Sicily in 1943, and then we came back, Rommel was defeated at that time.

"I was shot down once, in Africa. I shot down a Wellington and one motor was burning, so we flew very slowly and I had too much speed and so I flew past them and he fired with the front turret with two machine guns. Two motors were hit and I was hit and my observer hurt his leg. I saw that the temperature was too high on one of the motors and stopped it. We were very near the ground because I came from 1,000 metres to 200 or 300 metres and so I tried to fly with one motor. Then the other motor began to go higher, and because we were very low we could not jump out. It was very dangerous, so I decided to belly land and all was good.

"My first shoot-down was a Beaufort, in daylight – the only one. They were en route to Messina to drop torpedoes and we were en route from Sicily to Crete. We had a very new Ju 88. We were flying at 1,000 metres and the weather was good, we looked down and then two 'planes came across our route. We suddenly saw the roundel and we got down and in the same moment they dropped their torpedoes. I shot too early – I made four or five attacks but I didn't hit anything, but he hit me with his two guns. I could not shoot because I had a problem with my electric gun equipment, only one gun was firing, and at the same moment he touched the water. He broke free but the motor caught fire and so he touched down on the water and they came out, three men, in dinghies.

"We circled them and my radio operator got contact with an E-boat. He told them we had shot down an English aeroplane in the water. They could see where we were and they said we should stay there until they came. I had twenty-five holes in my 'plane, one of them could have been in the wrong place, then it would have been likely that I joined them in the water!

"We lost all our 'planes in Africa. There was an English commando raid, they came in the night and destroyed all our machines. So we had to fly in a Condor 200 from Tobruk. Only our chief could fly with my aeroplane because I landed when it was all over and it was the only aeroplane that was left.

"We had to land many times in the desert. Maintenance in the desert was a problem, with the sand and everything, sand got everywhere. Tobruk was in our hands, the English had to retreat from there, and so there was a big stock of English food. It was the first time I ever ate peaches in tins."

FAR EAST OPERATIONS

The surprise Japanese attack on the United States Navy base at Pearl Harbor in Hawaii on 7 December 1941, finally brought America fully into the war. US Navy storekeeper chief (SKC) Alfred Rodrigues was about to eat his breakfast when the attack started.

"We heard all these explosions and rushed outside to see aircraft attacking the harbour. We knew they were Japanese because we could see the red discs on them and they were flying so low you could see the pilots' faces. I got hold of a machine gun and started shooting back at them. We could see them attacking the B-17s landing after their flight from the States. I never did get to finish my eggs and bacon!"

However, the Americans were by no means alone in fighting the Far East campaign. As had happened in Europe in 1940, initially the Japanese had great success, and rapidly advanced across the Pacific, and the RAF was called upon to help defend India and Ceylon from possible invasion. Jack Biggs at first flew Hurricanes in the defence of Calcutta, operating from an improvised airstrip close to the centre of the city, before moving on to Ceylon.

"When we got to Bombay they said, 'You're posted to Calcutta'... to 17 Squadron, and here's how you get there'. So we walked, and you remember the old-fashioned topees we used to have, sun helmets. We walked up into Red Road, and the ground crew said they had never seen such a sight! Talk about 'Weary Willie' and 'Tired Tim' in the Comic Cuts. We were so raw to be out there, but we did as we were told, we wore the sun-helmets.

"M C Cotton – 'Bush' Cotton – Australian squadron leader (*DFC*), nice chap, he took over the squadron. On the Red Road you had concrete balustrades as it was a cambered road, so you had to plop down the middle; if you didn't you were off. Only our squadron and 136 were allowed to land there. At the end of it you had the Maidan, which was a big grass strip that used to run behind the back of Queen Victoria's monument, where we used to hang our parachutes to dry. Sometimes we used the grass strip if it was dry, but if it was wet we used the road. You literally came down Old Court House Street, you had buildings on either side, and you did your approach and landed on Red Road. It was only about 600 yards from Chowringi which is the main thoroughfare of Calcutta.

"When we were not on immediate readiness, you had fifteen or thirty minutes stand-by or you had set-down, so you were clear, you could do what you liked. That's how they kept the squadron, on immediate readiness in which case your parachute was in the 'plane for you to jump in, and you had them on the end of the road so you could take-off quickly, there was no use trying to taxi them out. We were the aerial defence of Calcutta.

"This was about October '42, and they'd just lost Rangoon, so we didn't have the upper hand. If they wanted any assistance to do any sweeps on the Arakan, the CO or the flight commander, would say, 'You, you and you, take the Hurricanes', four of you or six of you, a detachment, we'd fly to Chittagong and across the Bay of Bengal. Then we'd refuel and go down the Arakan to Ramry and Cox's Bazaar and places like that, and do what was needed to try and shoot up the Japs. When you got to Chittagong a big Sikh major would give you the bomb-line, tell you where it was. When you got there probably it was somewhere completely different, and you ended up shooting your own troops up, which happened quite often, because it was so hit and miss.

"We used to be on night readiness for the Japs coming in to Calcutta. We'd go down to a forward grass strip, and we were scrambled from there. I got scrambled one night, and I was number two because I was only a lowly sergeant pilot – my number one didn't take off, and I took off on my own; I had to because we'd been scrambled, but he couldn't get going. I got vectored onto this thing, and I kept doing what the controller was telling me to do, I was scared to death. I saw this thing ahead and I thought, 'I think I've got it', and he saw me at the same time. He scarpered, and I thought: 'Thank Christ for that!' Firing guns at night is no fun! It makes a hell of a lot of flashes and you go blind for a few seconds. Then the Japs did come and bomb Calcutta. But I was on sick leave, because I'd contracted dysentery. That's why I missed the bombing; perhaps they wouldn't have bombed if I'd been there? When I got back Calcutta was an empty city – the people had all left. I had friends who had watches in the repairers and they were still there because everyone fled to the hills, they were terrified.

"We used to have a rest from the Red Road, and go to Alipore, which was a big concrete runway. Again, we used to go to a forward strip for our night readiness, because they thought we could probably catch them before they got to the city. During the monsoons they used to put metal planking down and say, 'Come in, don't worry, you'll be all right'. It looks as though you've got six inches of water, which you had, but you had something solid underneath. Then we went up to Agartala, up on the Assam border, Imphal way, and from there we used to do sweeps.

"Going out on the boat, we had this sergeant major, and he gave us talks. 'You air force boys, you pilot types, don't you worry, you've got nothing to fear from those Japs. Their eyesight is so poor, they won't even know you're there.' I was down at Chittagong once, and the Japs came over the end of the bloody runway doing slow rolls! Because the advanced warning system was so pathetic, nobody knew they were there. I thought: 'Oh, they're the blokes who can't see!'

"We used to do weather recces on our own, 'cause with two you were running the risk of hitting each other in the cloud. When it was your turn, you just hoped to God it would be a nice day. The last one, I must have got up to about 25,000 feet, and there wasn't a break at all. So I just came down, and that's when you had to remember where your railway lines were, because you had no ruddy idea, you didn't do any dead-reckoning and say, 'I've done 300 miles at so-and-so...' You just came down and then you got back to the unit, and thought 'Oh God I'm a clever bloody pilot, I've found a way home'.

"Tex Barrick was flight commander and we were doing a sweep, down Ramry and Cox's Bazaar. We were shooting up troops, and we got them on the latrines, which was rather gratifying. Poor souls, I don't think they appreciated it. Tex had one that went up in the breech, we had cannons, and it blew his top panels out. Of course that made flying a bit of a problem, so I took him into Cox's Bazaar and I landed at about 120 to make sure he didn't stall.

"The Japs used to put trip wires across the rivers; just about the height they expected you to be flying, so they wanted you to fly into them. And they had a lighthouse there with remote-controlled guns. They had no men there, but you'd approach this just off the end of Ramry, and suddenly there'd be bullets flying past your head, and it was this lighthouse with machine guns set up in it; remote controlled by somebody down the bottom. They were crafty people; very brave too. A couple of times we were sent up to chase some Dinahs away, but mostly we were ground-strafing because we had a 20mm cannon, and they were formidable when you were hitting enemy ground units.

"They said we were going down for the defence of Ceylon to Trincomalee, China Bay. It was a grass strip again, then we were posted down to Vavuniya, which is in the middle of Ceylon. We were on the unit with 135 Squadron, and they said, 'You're both here, and you're going to change your aircraft, and it's a toss-up whether you get Thunderbolts or Spitfires.' I don't know whether the two COs tossed up or not, but 'Bush' Cotton got the Spitfires, and the other squadron got the Thunderbolts – that was in April '44.

"One day we went on a sweep with Bradbury and Shorty Miller, a Canadian. Bradbury was an Australian, and Fred Pepper and myself were Englishmen. We went in two twos, I was with Shorty Miller. We attacked a gun emplacement down the Irrawaddy. Bradbury went in, and suddenly Fred went straight in; we never knew what happened to him, he just fell out of the sky. We got back to base and the CO asked: 'What's happened?' and we said, 'Fred Pepper's not with us anymore'. Fred had left his money, as we all did, and we all got pissed on Fred's money. Because that was the way you did it, otherwise you'd never take off again.

"Flying a Spitfire at night was tough, actually it's not flying it at night, it's landing it that's the problem. You didn't have any of those beautiful runway lights, they used to run down with a torch and light them, and then as soon as you'd landed they'd run down and put them out! That was those gooseneck things; it was primitive stuff, but I wouldn't have missed it for anything, it was really most enjoyable.

"We escorted Sir Bertram Ramsey the admiral of the fleet, C-in-C Far East. He was on the *Queen Elizabeth* and we flew by him with our Spitfires, and they had some Beaufighters as well. We came in and landed, and a Beaufighter spun in on circuit, just off the edge of the field. Because Rowdy and I had been on this escort, the CO said, 'Would you like to go to the funeral of the Beaufighter boys?' So we went to represent the squadron. They had AC2s and LACs carrying the coffin, and they buried them the next day. The coffin seeped, and all the gunge came down this poor airman's bush shirt. I felt so sorry for the lad, it was disgusting really. How the hell he ever got over it I don't know.

"By then they'd built a runway at China Bay, because the Yanks came in with their Superforts, and they took over the mess. We used to eat in their mess rather than ours 'cause the food was far better. One day we lost a pilot, he was an American. One of the bearers brought in his Christmas cards, and the caption inside said 'don't worry, it may never happen'. He'd hit a kite hawk taking off on the Red Road, a simple way of going, just piled in. That brought a lump to the old throat you know, you think 'that could happen to me'.

"I did an air test in an aeroplane, it had been into maintenance. All you did was just stall it and make sure that the wings didn't fall off; you couldn't do any more. The CO wanted to have a Balbo, a twelve-squadron formation. We often had them, but obviously not everybody could fly so having done my air test, I didn't get the chance. Willie Buchan took the aircraft up that I'd tested, they did a break right, and poor old Willie spun in – he baled out. He could have been a bit too enthusiastic on his break, but then again you can do a high-speed stall. It's only a question of losing your flying ability, whether it's a high-speed or a low-speed; if you lose it, you lose it."

Sergeant Charlie Browning also flew Hurricanes, this time with 42 Squadron at Ondaw in Burma.

"I joined up in '42, but eventually by early '45 I was on the squadron. It's always extremely difficult if you have to go to war, but the best part is when you're winning, and right at the end."

Having flown both the Hurricane and later on the Spitfire with the same unit, Jack Biggs was very clear which of the two he liked the best.

"I preferred the Hurricane to the Spitfire. She was such a lovely old thing, she wouldn't misbehave and you could be as rough as you wanted, she'd never let you down. She wasn't fickle; the Spitty could be on occasions, you had to make sure that for one thing you turned all the way into the deck, rather than come in with the oleo down and over-heating, and you had to taxi like nobody's business. But the Hurricane, you didn't have an oleo sticking down in front of your air intake or radiator, it was purely and simply a well-designed aircraft, that had the radiator in the middle.

"I think when Charlie Browning talked about his first take-off, he about summed it up. It's just like he said, your head in the 'office' and you haven't got a clue what you're doing and you're pulling back on the stick. They were so fast by comparison with what we'd flown. To be tootling along at about 180 miles an hour and not knowing what you're doing, it was a bit disconcerting.

"It lent itself to its duties – it was a gun platform and an absolutely wonderful aircraft to fly. I liked the fact that when you stalled it, it behaved so beautifully. There might be a little bit of a wing wobble, but for the most part it would come straight down. But the Spitty sometimes, when you were stalling, she could probably flick a wing on you, and you'd get yourself in a spin if you weren't careful."

Tim Elkington too, arrived in theatre, but too late to get involved in any meaningful operations. He mainly flew Spitfires, plus the occasional Mustang and Thunderbolt.

"We had the aircraft but no real task set for us. Thus most flights were just flights of fancy, there were no comparative or operational trials. Except for the P-47, where we did dive-bombing, gun and napalm trials. My canopy shattered one day whilst over Everest and I was in shirt-sleeves! The best use of some aircraft (P-47 and P-51) was taking me down to Trincomalee to visit my WRNS girlfriend. I got down there one afternoon, got a room, unpacked, only to find she had left for the hills. So re-pack, re-start (fortunately) and off into the wild blue yonder en route to Ratmalana, although there was just one problem, it was getting dark. Where the hell are the lighting switches? I had never flown it at night before. I climbed higher and higher to keep the sun as illumination. I finally found them, but the radio failed and I was alone up there in the dark without a friend. Or any idea of how to get down. At last – CONTACT! I was way out into the ocean, but got down, into a mail van, and up to the hills overnight, where I camped on the Queen's Hotel floor until dawn."

Jack Rose also encountered the Thunderbolt very late in the war, while he was officer commanding 113 Squadron in Burma; he was not impressed by it.

"Right towards the end, about May, we were down in Burma at Kwetnge, and we flew the Hurricanes back to Wangjing in the Imphal valley and got rid of them. Then the first Thunderbolts came and compared to the Hurricanes, they looked like huge sort of flying dustbins! The AOC was there to see the first one come in and the American colonel pilot said, 'Would you like to fly it?' However he didn't want to, so he got in it and just had a look around. When he got out he was asked by the colonel what he thought of it, and he said: 'Well it's a marvellous piece of machinery but I can't see it superseding the aircraft!'"

The Burma campaign also made substantial use of transport aircraft and supply-dropping bombers in supporting army operations deep in the jungle. Pete Jackson was one such crewman.

"I was an air gunner on 194 Squadron during the Battle for Burma, also paratroop jump master on the invasion of Rangoon. When war ended I was attached to 232 Squadron (Liberator and C-54), repatriating POWs back home to Australia via the Cocos Islands."

Mike Nicholson trained to fly the Liberator in Canada, then found himself flying one out to the Far East to join in the supply operations.

"We collected a brand new Liberator from Montreal to fly it out to the Far East. We flew first to Gander in Newfoundland via Goose Bay. I was twenty-three years old, and in charge of a crew of ten. The longest leg we flew was fourteen-and-a-half hours. We set off for the Azores, eleven-and-a-half hours in 10/10ths cloud and I was told to let down by the Canadian navigator. I said, 'Are you sure? I can't see a thing.' We broke cloud 200 feet above the sea and went straight into Lajes, Azores.
"We arrived on 358 Squadron at Jessore. I remember the fruit bats, and the vultures who would appear every three days or so and overeat. In the mess there was a fan in the ceiling and a rope going out through a hole in the wall to a punkah-wallah, the original 'electric' fan. We used to play the gramophone endlessly, and I am always taken straight back there whenever I hear the Ink Spots, the Mills Brothers, Paper Doll and Myra Hess.

"Our duties were to drop supplies to the Chindits at drop zones (DZs) in the jungle. We also supplied the Chinese, flying over the hump to Kunming (Ledo Road, 1,000 miles long, was built by the Americans and abandoned after the war). We dropped propaganda leaflets in seventeen languages, so we had to be careful to drop the right ones to the right people, the language changing as we went south. We also dropped the occasional Frenchman into Saigon, French Indo China. On long night flights our wireless operator could pick up Californian commercial radio 7,000 miles away as we flew home after a drop.

"The ground crew were led by Wing Commander Blackburn, the engineering officer. I don't know what he did, but he tinkered with the carburettors and transformed the Liberator. With bomb loads of 3,000 to 8,000 pounds we had a range between 1,800 and 3,000 miles; fully loaded you had nine tons of fuel. The engines were very reliable, even though they were so complex – there was a danger of them blowing up if you let the turbos overspeed.

"On operations we usually flew at 18,000 feet maximum. The navigator warned when we were approaching the DZ, usually in steep jungle valleys surrounded by mountains, so we reduced height until we were flying just above the trees. Dakotas were better at it then us because they were more manoeuvrable. The DZ was a clearing with either a smoke or sheet indicator. The navigator handed over to the bomb aimer for guidance; flaps down, open up the engines, down to 200 feet, bomb doors open. Package away, flaps up slowly otherwise you'll sink, and you're only at 200 feet, then climb up – will you be able to turn in time? And repeat at the same place.

"During the build-up of the south east monsoon, one chap flew right into the centre of a storm and lost 1,500 feet altitude and didn't know which way up he was. They were impossible to avoid, and lasted for up to fourteen hours. We had torrential rain and lightning and only UV lights lit the control panel. The storms buffeted the 'plane and you could see the wings flexing – it had marvellous wings. We would get St. Elmo's Fire coming off the props.

"Our longest trips were sixteen hours, and landing in the dark was pretty tricky. You'd let down through the storm, put the landing lights on and look out for the flarepath. They just had simple paraffin flares, and the runway was awash from all the monsoon rain. Check for drift against the side wind, flaps down, open up the engines and kick it straight just before touchdown, but don't brake too soon! Taxi back in, press the oil dilution for four minutes then shut down. All is calm.

"Rats got into the food on the camp, then into the aircraft. One aircraft lost two engines after the rats had chewed through the electrics. On one occasion I took off with a full load and had no airspeed indication because the pitot cover had been left on. We got back down OK, and the marvellous engineering officer came racing out in his jeep to meet us, took off the pitot cover and put it in his pocket. We never heard any more about it

"We did not have an Elsan on board, and one of our crew was particularly smelly, so we always made him go before he got on board. If you had to use the tube, it came out by the rear turret and sprayed all over it, obscuring the gunner's vision. You had to warn him so that he could turn the turret to one side."

Navigator Flying Officer David Johnson was also part of the Liberator force at this time.

"As the Japs had retreated south through Burma and Thailand towards Singapore, it was too far for the Liberators to bomb them from their bases in the Bengal area, so 99 and 356 Squadrons were moved to the Cocos Islands, only just over 1,000 miles from Singapore, from where they could go and get back. We then went to Kolar to do a thirteen hours refresher and familiarisation course, although I think by then we were pretty well familiar! Our next move was to collect another Liberator to deliver to 99 Squadron and to complete our posting to 356 Squadron on the Cocos Islands. By then, the war was nearly over and our main occupation was to locate and drop supplies to the army on the ground in the Singapore/Sumatra area, and subsequently the aircraft had panniers fitted in the bomb bay, with not very comfortable seats to form part of the ferry service for the less fit army POWs from Singapore/Cocos/Ceylon/Bombay to get them back to the UK as quickly as possible.

"In November 1945, 356 Squadron was disbanded and I navigated a Liberator to Cawnpore in India, which was the collection point under lease-lend where there were hundreds of American aircraft, most of which were just bulldozed."

Less well known was the unsung activity of second-line units. Squadron Leader Jack Parry commanded 221 Group Communications Flight, which was formed in Calcutta in early April 1942 and based at Dum Dum airfield.

"This was when the whole of the RAF in Burma finally evacuated Magwe (the Burma Oil Company's oil fields in the Irrawaddy) and retreated to India, where the group had been reformed in Alipore, Calcutta. We had arrived with seven or eight Tiger Moths, a Curtiss Wright P22 Falcon and a Yale – and to add to these the flight acquired a motley assortment of civilian light aircraft, plus a Dominie, Anson, Harvard, two or three Lysanders and a non-operational Hurricane IIb. We were also given our 'flagship', a nearly new Lockheed 12A, as the AOC's aircraft.

"Our duties consisted of carrying army and air force VIPs, ranging from the GOC-in-C (Lord Wavell) and the AOC–in–C (India), all over eastern India and to operational areas on the Burma front. In eighteen months I landed at no less than fifty-five airfields/landing grounds in over twenty different types of aircraft. Maintenance of the menagerie by our ground crews, British and Burmese, was magnificent, much of it in primitive conditions and with lots of improvisation. In September '42 we were designated air HQ (Bengal) communications unit, having grown too big for our boots as a squadron. In about February 1943 AHQ (Bengal) moved from Calcutta to Barrackpore some twenty-five miles north of the city, and our unit was shifted to the Barrackpore race-course, from which we flew for about four months before returning to Dum Dum.

"I managed to fly unscathed slap bang through the middle of a balloon barrage covering the Kidderpore docks, Calcutta. I was bringing back two army officers in the Yale from Ranchi to Calcutta. It was getting dark, the sun was setting behind us, and I was losing height and musing at what a pretty sight the Hooghly river looked, as a bright silver streak in the dusk, when there was a squeak from behind me, 'See the balloons?' I hadn't – and too late to take evasive action, I could only duck down a bit, hope and keep straight. Seconds seemed like minutes as balloons shot by overhead and cables whizzed past our wingtips. My passengers' remarks when we landed were more polite than I expected – perhaps they were too scared to say any more. Strong though a Yale is, I wouldn't have put much money on it as a wire-cutter.

"We received a request for an RAF staff officer to be taken to Chittagong; we kept one of the DH Moths ready with a BVAF (*Burma volunteer air force*) pilot. On arrival of the officer we discovered that he was a group captain, had a double-barrelled name and he was an officer of RFC vintage. He considered it degrading to be flown to Chittagong by a BVAF pilot of PO rank, particularly in an aircraft such as a Moth, and insisted that he would take the aircraft and fly it himself to Chittagong. Although we were to provide an air transportation service and not to hire aircraft, we reluctantly provided him with a Tiger Moth after taking into full consideration his rank as a group captain.

"So off he flew, but by late afternoon there was no sign of his return. Then we received a signal from him, 'Slight accident, aircraft OK. Send a propeller. Flying back.' In the evening before closing down for the day another signal came in, 'Send tyres and wheels too'. That night a third signal was received, 'Send undercarriage. Aircraft OK. Flying back.' Next morning while we were deliberating whether to send another aircraft to pick up the group captain from Chittagong and/or arrange a ground party to bring back the aircraft to Dum Dum by rail, yet another signal came in. This time it stated, 'Send tail wing unit complete with rudder. Aircraft OK.' So instead of sending all the spares we sent another Tiger Moth to retrieve the groupie and arranged for a ground party to bring back the aircraft by rail.

"One day LAC Bibby, my clerk, told me that he had never flown in an aircraft and was unhappy about it. If the war were to terminate and he had to go back to Epping where his home was, he did not want his friends and relations to know that he had never taken a flight in an aircraft. I therefore informed Sgt Goldsworthy about Bibby's plight and asked him if at any time he was putting an aircraft on air test, to allow LAC Bibby to take a flip. 'Goldy' remembered the request and one afternoon when they were about to air test the Zlin, Bibby went for a flight. I was in the orderly room below the grandstand of the Barrackpore racecourse when I heard the Zlin taking off from the strip between the race-track rails. Very soon afterwards I heard the crash tender and the ambulance racing along and the hue and cry of personnel in high pursuit. I ran out and saw the Zlin rocking on a tree-top at the far end of the race-track. Soon Bibby appeared with no injury, followed by Sgt Crombie, the pilot of the Zlin, also unhurt but looking very dejected. Bibby however was smiling and looking very pleased with himself. Sgt Crombie said that he pulled up a little too late to clear the big tall tree. Bibby said he now had something to tell his relatives and friends in the pubs at Epping; he had not only flown in an aircraft but had the rare distinction of climbing down a tall tree without having to climb up the tree first."

FLEET AIR ARM

Substantial Fleet Air Arm forces operated throughout the Pacific war from a sizeable fleet of aircraft carriers. Having survived his Martlet flying in the Western Desert, Jack Routley returned home to convert to the far more capable Hellcat, ready for service in the Far East.

"885 was the Hellcat squadron in the escort carrier, HMS *Ruler* in the Far East. We formed up in Ballyhalbert in Northern Ireland in 1944. I took command of the squadron in October/November, and we worked up. Our carrier came by, we did our deck-landings, and we shipped out to the Far East. By the time we got there we had twelve Hellcats and four Avengers. We didn't know until we left Colombo where we were going, and we were relieved and pleased to hear it was Sydney. After two or three months everybody was rusty, and we had a ship full of aircraft but we couldn't do any flying en route. So we had to do a work-up in the Sydney area. Then we headed out for the forward area and we operated in and out of the Leyte Gulf, which was halfway between Sydney and the operating area.

"The Japanese didn't offer the opportunity for combat. They didn't take any action against us; we were providing fighter cover and anti-submarine for the fleet train, which was the logistics support organisation to the forward area. The fleet train included escort carriers, destroyers, hospital ships, oil tankers, naval stores tankers, and things like that. It brought everything from personnel, to mail, to avgas, and would rendezvous with the striking fleet during replenishment periods. The Japanese were getting heavily beaten-up by the Americans anyway; most of their naval stuff had disappeared.

"By that time, I had done a spell at the navy fighter school, which was at Henstridge near Yeovilton, and I did the RAF Central Gunnery School course at Sutton Bridge, which was a sort of 'Top Gun' course during World War Two. They had all the aces gathered together to guide us, Al Deere, 'Sailor' Malan, Johnny Checketts, people like that, and it was very intensive Spitfire air-to-air firing and air-to-ground, air tactics and fighter leader, and we did ground school work at night on ballistics and interceptions. Excellent value, and I emerged from that and my experience as an instructor, flying Spitfires at the navy fighter school, and reckoned I could take on anything the enemy offered. From that moment I never saw another enemy aircraft!

Wg Cdr Al Deere DSO OBE DFC and bar flew with 54, 601 and 611 Squadrons and ended the war with seventeen victories; Gp Capt Adolph 'Sailor' Malan DSO and bar DFC and bar was Fighter Command's highest scoring pilot with twenty-seven victories while flying with 74 Squadron and as Biggin Hill wing leader; Wg Cdr John Checketts DSO DFC flew with 611 and 485 Squadrons and 142 Wing, with a final score of fourteen victories.

"The first series of operations during our time there, was against a group of islands called the Sakishima Group; it was during the time that the Americans were sorting Okinawa. They were concerned that the Sakishima Islands could be used as a staging post for the Japanese to interfere with Okinawa. So the British Pacific Fleet was targeting the area. We covered five replenishment periods during that time, the fleet would attack for several days, then withdraw to a replenishment area 300 or 400 miles away to seaward of the mainland, and they would stay for two or three days, and top-up with personnel and stores. The air-crew could be rested because we provided the air cover for fighter and anti-submarine protection while they were refuelling. That would have been a memorable time if the Japanese had had the resources.

"We went on to the attack where the British Pacific Fleet was part of the combined fleet with the US fleet, for operations against the Japanese mainland. Not to be forgotten was the Kamikaze threat, which was a very major concern, and the Japanese made good use of this. Against the American wooden-decked carrier it was a very grave threat. The British carriers had steel armour-plated decks so Kamikaze attacks against British carriers would tend not to be too disruptive. They bounced off or, on occasion, they hit the island and were swept over the side with minor casualties, but flying was able to be resumed fairly soon afterwards.

"The Hellcat was a really good carrier aircraft; the Martlet had a narrow-track undercarriage and tended to ground-loop on landing on a runway unless you were alert. It was OK for flight-deck operations, but narrow-track undercarriages were not things that I was very fond of; even in the Seafire, that tended to bounce around a bit. The pros for the Hellcat were performance; it was an absolutely wonderful carrier aircraft. It had a big wide undercarriage, and it sat down contentedly on a deck when you arrived. It had the performance to out-perform the Zero, it had speed and altitude advantage. I don't know about manoeuvrability, maybe the Zero was a more manoeuvrable aircraft; I'm not sure. So the Hellcat was good value, it had six .5 calibre machine guns, rocket rails, and could carry 500lb bombs; it was a versatile aircraft and a good one for the theatre."

Jim Langford was also in theatre at this time, but in his case he was part of the Fleet Air Arm's bombing force, which extended its operations right into the Japanese homeland.

"We joined 820 Squadron Grumman Avengers, and we waited for HMS *Indefatigable* to come back from her first set of operations against the Japanese. We eventually joined her, went up to Japan, dropped bombs on aerodromes, shipping, and the last raid the British Pacific Fleet did was on the day the war finished, 15 August. 820 Squadron lost one observer, and the Seafire squadron (887) lost one of their pilots on the last day of the war.

"The Pacific Fleet stayed up there, and we had been about 100 miles off the coast when they dropped the bomb on Hiroshima. And then we came back to Australia, did a goodwill tour of Australia and New Zealand, and then eventually took passage on a ship home to arrive back in March '46."

Chapter Eight

NIGHT FIGHTERS!

Thee would I salute in the threshing of thy wings
My heart foretells me triumph in thy name
Onward, proud eagle, to thee the cloud must yield

From *The Prussian Border-Eagle* by Theodor Körner
Inscribed on the gravestone of Heinz Wolfgang Schnaufer

"Gentlemen, we are no longer on the offensive; rather we shall find ourselves for the next one-and-a-half to two years on the defensive. Now these facts are becoming apparent to those in the highest positions of the Luftwaffe, and are being taken into account in their calculations. Naturally this will mean that we must now have many more fighters, and as many as we possibly can of the 110 and 410 'destroyer' types."

Generalfeldmarschall Erhard Milch, speaking in Berlin in July 1943

ROYAL AIR FORCE

In the early stages of the war, the RAF's own night fighter force was very much in its infancy, relying on such types as the Blenheim I, with fairly primitive airborne interception (AI) equipment. Later, single-engine types such as the Hurricane and the Defiant came into use, the latter type especially finding its nocturnal niche after a disastrous baptism of fire as a day fighter during the Battle of Britain. Blenheims were subsequently replaced by Beaufighters and Havocs, but the ultimate RAF night fighter of the war was without question the Mosquito.

Michael Wainwright was among the pilots who experienced the shortcomings of the Blenheim at first hand, flying the type with 64 Squadron from Church Fenton in Yorkshire during the winter of 1939/40.

"The Blenheim wasn't meant to be a night fighter although we had radar in the back, AI gear it was called. All we had was four machine guns under the belly. Those were Mark I and we started to use Mark IV; that was amazing because your normal flying was 87 octane fuel but with the Mark IV, you took off with 100 octane fuel and then you switched over to 87 once you got up in the air. It was a very nice aeroplane and I could take the dog up in it as well and keep him out of mischief! Yes, it was a nice aeroplane but no bloody good for fighting a war."

Aircraftman R M Jones was a fitter based at St. Athan, but sent on working parties around the country to install AI equipment.

> "AI was first fitted to short-nosed Blenheims. I was in a work party which travelled to Gravesend, and later Middle Wallop, to fit up the aircraft of 604 Squadron. When that squadron converted to AI Beaufighters, Flt Lt 'Cat's Eyes' Cunningham gained the first night victories. (*Gp Capt John Cunningham DSO and two bars OBE DFC and bar ended the war with twenty victories with 604 and 85 Squadrons*). The AI programme was now stepped up and Beaufighters were flown in from Filton to a special installation flight at St. Athan to be modified before being ferried to the squadrons. At one stage they arrived only in undercoat paint after a heavy raid at Filton which badly damaged the paint shop."

Before the advent of really effective AI radar, other means had to be found to locate enemy aircraft and guide the fighters onto them. Perhaps the most strange was the fitting of powerful searchlights to Havoc aircraft, intended to illuminate German bombers for accompanying single-engine fighters to attack. Tim Elkington flew Hurricanes on a number of such occasions.

> "We worked with the Turbinlite Havocs where we took off in close formation with them at night, viewing an illuminated white-painted strip on their starboard wing. When they got a radar contact, we'd drop down below them, accelerate and then they would illuminate with their x-million candlepower searchlight. We were supposed to see the enemy! The best victory was when the enemy pilot thought that it was a ground searchlight, got disoriented and spun in."

John Ellacombe flew both Hurricanes and Defiants in concert with Turbinlite Havocs when serving with 151 Squadron from Wittering.

> "We had Turbinlite Havocs with a big light in the nose, and the Hurricane would take off first then as the Havoc took off, the Hurricane would come down. Squadron Leader Charles Wynn was leading the pilot in the Havoc and he got a vector onto an aircraft and as we got close to this one, an aircraft flew over the top of us, it was a Dornier, so I cuddled up behind him, fired and hit him a lot. He started to dive and I followed him down. I had to pull up because I was afraid I was going to crash into the sea and I reckoned he crashed into the beach on the coast of Lincolnshire. I couldn't claim it as a destroyed because I didn't actually see it because I was heading back.
> "I also flew the Defiant, a nice aeroplane, good manoeuvrability, but not quite fast enough. It had the same engine as the Hurricane but of course you had an extra man and the four-gun turret; you didn't have any guns at the front. I had a very good navigator who flew with me several times, Sergeant Stewart, and about six times we formatted onto

what I thought were bombers, and Stewart would say, 'Don't shoot, sir, it's a Wellington', and I never managed to get onto a German."

ON THE RECEIVING END

Of all the weapons ranged against them, the one that many of the RAF bomber crews feared the most was the night fighter, lurking unseen in the darkness. The range of armament and increasingly sophisticated radar and counter-measures meant that almost right to the end of the war the Luftwaffe's Nachtjagd remained a force to be reckoned with. Henry Payne's Stirling was attacked by a lone night fighter as he returned to base over East Anglia.

"As we got back to base, my gunner asked for permission to unload his guns, then suddenly he screamed out; 'Corkscrew for Christ's sake!' Which I did, exceedingly quickly, but I didn't know which way to go, and damn great cannon shells came past my cockpit within inches. An Me 410 had apparently got right under my tail and had followed us all the way to England totally undetected. Just as we were being attacked, one of 196 Squadron's Stirlings was shot down, and he was on fire on the runway. (*This was on 21 February 1945, the Stirling shot down was LK126 captained by Flt Lt Campbell.*)

"So we flew around for about ten minutes, with occasional scraps with this damn '410, he kept attacking us, but my gunner was awake, and gave me the right instructions, and we could out-manoeuvre him easily. Eventually we got a message to go to Foulsham. We landed, most unwelcome, because they were all getting ready for a peaceful day, and the Stirlings descended upon them."

Les Weeks too, suffered a late attack on his 83 Squadron Lancaster on the way back to Coningsby from a raid.

"Just once we had an encounter with a night fighter. We got all the way to the target and bombed, and coming back we'd almost got to the English Channel, and 'bom-bom-bom', machine gun. It woke the two gunners up, and that was the only time they used their guns in anger. It knocked a chunk out of one of the tail fins."

Not so fortunate was Jack Bromfield (JB), shot down on his twelfth operational sortie, a raid on Hannover, on the night of 5 January 1945. The attacking aircraft was a Junkers Ju 88G belonging to II./NJG.2 based at Twente in Holland, and flown by Hauptmann Heinz Rökker (HR), who claimed two aircraft shot down that night, and survived the war with a total of sixty-four victories.

In July 2004, Jack and Heinz met for the first time. Both men felt the same, that they were doing their duty and that it was the aircraft and materials that were the targets, not the people. This was a common view from many of the veterans; the majority said that they were trying to shoot down the aeroplane, not kill the pilot and crew. When asked how he felt on meeting Heinz for the first time, Jack simply said "Wonderful!"

Jack gave more details of that fateful night:

"My job was to listen out for transmissions at set times; recall, diversions, any information. Normally you'd hear nothing, just a long dash and a time signal, and in between those ten-minute segments, you were given a section of the 1155 dial to search. What you were listening for was: 'Achtung Nachtjäger, Achtung Nachtjäger.' What you would do then is tune your transmitter exactly to the frequency you were listening on, throw a little switch and press the key, and your set was then connected to a carbon mike in the starboard outer engine. So he'd just get engine noises on that frequency, and he'd go somewhere else.

"We had taken off at 5 o'clock and around two hours later we were about thirty miles north west of Hannover on the run-in to the target, having turned on course over Wilhelmshaven. The first I knew about the attack was when we were hit and there was a ruddy great bang in the fuselage. The tail gunner saw the fighter first and called out, 'port go' and the skipper said, 'rolling, coming up starboard and resuming course' and threw her into a violent diving turn to try and throw the fighter off. As we came back up we were hit again from below and it started a fire in the crew rest area.

"The escape hatch by my seat was jammed at first, but I eventually got shoved in the back and it fell away, taking me with it. I knew it was a Ju 88 that had got us, because I heard Jumo engines as I was dangling under my 'chute. Our bombing height had been 20,000 feet and after the first attack we were down to about 14,000 feet."

Heinz described his view of a typical such encounter with a bomber and the tactics the night fighter force used:

"The first four-engine bomber that we saw, we couldn't tell in the night what type it was, whether it was a Lancaster or a Halifax. A Stirling you could see but not those two-tailed, and so we always said, four-engined 'plane. The first I shot down over Berlin, two of them in 1943, December or so. I cannot remember all my successes, there are too many.

"We couldn't say exactly where we shot down the bomber. It could be that there was a discrepancy of 50 kilometres. It is dark, and you cannot see aeroplanes under you, the only thing you can see is the target burning. You can see something under the 'planes, but you could see them only as a shadow. Everybody, including night fighters, had to look out for the enemy, called Wilde Sau. Zahme Sau: you had to try to come into the bomber stream and situate yourself in it. But we started far from the bomber stream. They told us where we should be able to see it, but it was not easy to find because you were coming up from underneath the bomber stream.

Wilde Sau (Wild Boar) and Zahme Sau (Tame Boar) were tactics allow-ing single and groups of night fighters to roam freely amongst the bomber stream with minimum control from the ground.

"We flew only single, we had no contact with others. I always had the same crew. For example, my 'funker (*Bordfunker*) – radio operator, – I was with him from the beginning until the end. Almost all shoot downs we did together, he was always my crew. It was not our target to kill people in the 'plane, for us it was the 'plane we shot down. We were surprised after the war that so many crews didn't live. It was not so easy for the crew to jump out."

Jack Bromfield took up this point:

"The Halifax was much easier than the Lancaster. Where the pilot sat in the Halifax, I sat underneath, and the hatch was under my feet, so the pilot, myself, the navigator and the bomb aimer could all go out of that hatch, with plenty of time for the others to go out of the rear door. The rear gunner, if his turret was still working, could just turn it through 90 degrees and roll backwards. Much easier than the Lanc to get out. In the Lanc they were all through the back door. There was a hatch in the front, but some guys had to come over the main wing spar, which was very high; but the others would go out of the rear door, which was on the starboard side as opposed to the port on the Hally. They had a lad-der to get in there, which meant that the door was level with the tailplane, which I thought wasn't as good.

"Only the flight engineer, George Dacey, did not survive and we think he did not get out at all (he has no known grave, and is commem-orated on the RAF memorial at Runnymede). The tail gunner had found himself a fighter pilot's parachute that he sat on, to save him having to go back into the fuselage, climb over the elevator bar, find his parachute and then get out of the rear door. He just turned his turret and rolled out backwards. Just the other day I cut myself shaving right on the cheekbone. At first I thought the foil had gone on my razor, but it was a tiny piece of Perspex from that last op, that had been just under the skin for all those years.

HR – "The bombers had a good chance to catch us because when we put on our radar they could find us.

JB – "The same worked for us. We had Monica (*a tail-warning radar*) which told you if there was an aircraft there. But it also told him (*the night fighter*) that there was another aircraft present! There were always measures and counter-measures, and counter-counter-meas-ures.

NIGHT FIGHTERS!

HR – "The bomber had no chance to escape.

JB – "Most of the time we didn't even know you were there. We always knew Heinz, when you were coming, because the flak stopped.

HR – "You couldn't see us. English crews told me they didn't know that we had Schräge Musik. Did you know of it?

Schräge Musik was a system of fixed, upward-firing cannons installed in the night fighters to allow them to approach from underneath the bombers unseen by the rear gunners.

JB – "Yes, I knew. We didn't understand a great deal about it.

HR – "During the war?

JB – "Yes, I only knew what it was, I didn't know what it did. How often did you come across Mosquitoes and Beaufighters?

HR – "I never saw them, only the one I shot down. It was landing and at that time in Belgium and France there were some airfields where the English landed and also the Americans. He was landing there and he had his lights on and so I could see him. I couldn't say now what air-field it was; I said at the time it was St. Trond. I could only shoot the aircraft down when landing, not in the air as it was faster than we were.
    "A piece of the Mosquito got in my motor and the motor didn't work, so I tried to land at Twente, but there was fog and I couldn't touch down there, and so they said I must fly to Diepholz. The water was very very hot, and so I couldn't fly for a long time. I made a normal landing and suddenly saw another 'plane was belly landing next to me, and at the same moment they turned the lights out, as they thought it was my 'plane. Our enemy was the long-range night fighter – Mosquito and Beaufighter.

JB – "If you had Schräge Musik near the cockpit, did you also have for-ward-firing cannons built-in?

HR – "Yes, but it wasn't dangerous for us. We could fly under the Lancaster or Halifax and he couldn't see us; all was black and so we could fly five minutes or ten minutes with him. The pilots sometimes made quick manoeuvres and we stayed with him until he was level.

JB – "Did you always fly the Ju 88 or did you also fly the Me 110?"

HR – "Yes, most of the time, I only spent a short time with the Me 110. The first success, Lancaster or a Halifax, I had with Me 110, was over

Berlin; the only one with that type. We came back to Germany from Sicily and there we changed from the Ju 88 to '110. It was ordered for some crews to go to Glize-Rijen in Holland. Some crews who were there had already some success with the aircraft, and we were told we should try them in the Himmelbett. I had only one flight there in a Himmelbett, in Gorilla I think. It was an ordinary night flight, not for attack but for exercise, and there we were given '110 for these exercises, but only four or five crews.

Himmelbett was the original night fighter control system, which restricted aircraft to patrolling in defined areas and flying as directed from the ground. Each area had a code name, such as 'Gorilla'.

"They gave us the order to fly to Berlin when there was an attack, because we couldn't fly in these Himmelbetts because there was Window. (*Bundles of foil strips thrown out by the bombers to confuse the enemy radar.*) And so began the Wilde Sau and Zahme Sau. Later on we came together with the whole group, and they tried the '110. Then we were in Kassel. We went there, only some of our group, not a Staffel, just four or five – a flight. We had the order to go to Kassel and there we got the Ju 88, and the other part of the group, they were at Parchim, came back to Kassel and they got also the Ju 88.

JB – "Which did you prefer, did you think the Ju 88 was better?

HR – "Yes, better, it was a very safe aeroplane. I think I could fly it now! It was so good to me I had no problems with the machine, ever."

Peter Spoden, a fellow Nachtjäger, agreed with this view:

"I liked the Ju 88 more than the '110. Not all night fighters felt the same. In my opinion, the Ju 88 had certain advantages. Firstly, we were four in the cockpit and had contact. We could help each other when wounded, and were not separated like in the '110. Secondly, we had two radio-operators, one for radar, and one for navigation. With eight eyes you see more! The engine handling (one lever) was better than in the '110, and the Ju 88 was better with one engine out. The emergency exit, which was below, was better than the difficulty of jumping out in the '110.

"Of course, I would have loved the Me 262 NJ version. I moved to the '88 in early summer 1944 from Me 110 G-4 to Junkers 88 G-1, and later on G-4. We always had one 'plane and one crew. I lost my flight logs when becoming a POW; it was a crazy time, and thank God so long ago."

HR – "The ground crew were very good, they had much experience, since 1940, and with me. Some new men came but from 1940 till the end of the war, they gained much experience.

JB – "Also, if you don't keep the same men all the time, you've probably got to weed out one or two bad ones, but if you keep the same men, that's when you get *esprit de corps*. I found our ground crews were second to none.

Heinz – "From the middle of 1944 to the end of the war I always had the same aeroplane, and the same ground man. He had the duty to make it fit, and had pride in keeping it ready. Prinz Wittgenstein was our commander of the Geschwader. I only met him once, during his role, but we had heard of his great heart and how he only thought of shooting down the enemy. He took off when nobody else would.

Major Prinz Heinrich zu Sayn-Wittgenstein scored eighty-three night fighter victories before being killed in action attacking his fifth Lancaster of the night over Magdeburg on 21 January 1944, possibly falling victim to a Mosquito.

Peter Spoden also came across other outstanding night fighter pilots:

"After the night missions we landed at the NJ-airports nearby and I met Herrmann, Schnaufer, Sayn-Wittgenstein and others just for a short talk and returned after refuelling at our home bases. After the war we met at different fighter reunions.

Oberst Hajo Herrmann was the instigator of the Wilde Sau tactics; Major Heinz-Wolfgang Schnaufer was the top scoring night fighter pilot, surviving the war with 121 victories.

"Oberst Herrmann was an outstanding officer; I admired his attitude. A highly experienced officer and excellent bomber pilot, Hajo Herrmann, the sort of old campaigner that wars have produced since the dawn of time. He had advised Göring and the senior echelons of the Luftwaffe that in addition to the twin-engined night fighters, singled-engined Me 109s and Fw 190s should go into action above the burning targets. This, then, was Wilde Sau, which often enough put the fear of death into us twin-engine men by their pilots' wild manoeuvring. Both systems would cause the RAF great trouble during the next months."

HR - "Towards the end of the war we were running out of gasoline. We had enough machines, and enough gasoline until 1945. But only some crews were allowed to take off. Crews who had success were allowed to fly. Three or four machines would fly only; we had twelve in our gruppe. We still had new crews coming in. Younger crews had flying, starting, landing, and flying in the night, rather than the day. They had not much experience; because there was no gasoline to allow them to practise therefore we had many losses from these young crews. We had so many Ju 88s in the last part of the war, but all were destroyed.

"Fighters were led by radar from the ground, to the enemy all over the coast. Himmelbett was Kammhuber's idea and his work; but when the big bomber stream came it was not so effective. It was only a little piece of the ground, a 50 kilometre box, and it was only one fighter. Gorilla – they all had different names for different areas. Then came Window, and when Window was dropped you could not follow the bomber to the target. (*General Josef Kammhuber was the first commander of the night fighter force, and the instigator of the Himmelbett system of ground control.*)

JB – "We threw out little strips like tinsel, they were wrapped in very poor quality cardboard, with a piece of string which went in and out of the side and when you opened the hatch, the string pulled the cardboard and they all fluttered out. But you had to have a piece of plywood or something to put over the hole, because if not, they all came back again. At one time they used to drop them out of the flare chute, then they discovered it was much more effective for the wireless operator to do it.

HR – "We had radar for night fighters. It was Lichtenstein and then came SN2. It was not so effective because we were not leading from the ground, we led with our eyes. We looked to where there were bomb bursts, before they were at the target, so we could see where the bomber stream was. When an aircraft went down, it was visible from about 100 kilometres away, when it was burning in the air it meant we could see where the enemy's flight was."

Peter Spoden again:

"When flying Himmelbett we used code names with the ground controller. However, in Zahme and Wilde Sau we were on our own. The ground people gave all night fighters the directions of the bomber stream, which very often was wrong. But we saw the 'abschuss', intense flak-fire and 'christbaum' (*flares*), and followed those with our own SN2 and Naxos radar until contact. During an attack we did not talk except for intercom with our own crew.

"In the old Luftwaffe the procedure with claims was quite difficult and very strict (at least with the night fighters). As pilot you had to make a written report about how the shooting happened, time, type of enemy aircraft, how much ammunition was used, kind of attack (Schräge Musik etc.), witnesses and most important: exact time and location where the enemy aircraft crashed. The radio-operator made a fix with radio-bearings which was not always possible in the heat of the fight.

"All this went to the RLM (Reichsluftfahrtminister) for checking, and after in the above case, seven months later I got a record and an acknowledgement of the claim. This did not work anymore at the end of the war. Most RAF bombers crashed over Germany or occupied country, so identification was not difficult. Of course in some cases there was over-claiming. As a night fighter you got the Iron Cross when you had at least four successes. The Ehrenpokal you got with ten, the Golden Cross with fifteen and the Ritterkreuz with twenty-five. Crazy times. If you weren't dead already!"

OPERATION GISELA, MARCH 1945

In a last desperate attempt to stem the endless bombing raids, the Luftwaffe launched a large force of night fighters against English airfields to seek out and attack bombers at their most vulnerable, as they were in the circuit to land after a raid. Heinz Rökker took part in the operation, which was code named Gisela.

"At the latest by early 1943, German long-range intruding over Great Britain should have been built up again, because it was a well known fact that the British operational aerodromes were fully lit up during their take-off and landing procedures. Furthermore, during the assembling process of the bomber stream, the bomber crews, against regulation, often switched on their navigational lights for fear of collision. To hunt them under these conditions would have been the ultimate dream of the German long-range intruders.

"At the end of the war they said we should fly over England because there was no defence from the English. Many of the flyers put on their lights and so we could see them and when they landed we tried to find them. I saw one with lights, and I tried to shoot him down. But the distance was too great. Because I could see them very well and was beneath them, I fired a burst, but was behind, and too low. At the same moment he switched off his lights. I could not see him anymore and so I could not get him.

"We stayed over England for one hour. Twice I went, and we had ten bombs. We threw the bombs on the airfield, they were lit but there was no flak, nothing. I was flying over Norwich, Grimsby and Lincoln; I'm not certain though, the English people didn't tell me where I was! We would fly very low over the sea, because you couldn't be got at with radar. It was very dangerous to fly 100 metres over the sea. You always thought you would hit the water. But we had a very good method to see the height, at short distance. We could see the foam, but to see the aircraft at 50 metres, 100 metres or even 20 metres, that was special. When we saw the coast we climbed and then flew at 1,000 metres and saw nothing, no flak, no night fighters. Finally I dropped the bombs on an airfield that was lit up. I fired forward with my cannons and all was lit at that time, so we shot at the light; then, the lights went out.

"We saw the town was full of light and we saw a tram; we were not so high! In the far distance another German night fighter shot down one

English 'plane. I couldn't see properly, because you saw tracer from underneath and going up and you saw when it was burning. But I didn't observe an aeroplane, it was probably Lancaster or Halifax I think."

THE FINAL WORD

The following was written by Heinz Rökker in 2000, and eloquently summarised the whole night war experience from the German viewpoint.

"The evening sun sets low on the western horizon and shoots rays of light through dark clouds, a sign for the experienced flier that the weather will worsen. For us, this is familiar. The British usually time their raids so their take-off and landing conditions are favourable, whereas we German night fighters struggle with bad weather over our hunting grounds. That is exactly the case tonight.

"After our meal in the officers' mess at approximately 18:00 hours, we head to the gefechtsstand (*operations room*) for a briefing. First Met gives us the weather forecast for Holland, Belgium and northern Germany, warning us of heavy thunderstorms, and he gives us special information for tonight regarding flak-defended areas, searchlight positions, radio frequencies and tonight's possible targets (set by the high command at the town of Stade, sixty miles west of Hamburg). Afterwards, the crews retire to their readiness rooms, and the officers remain in the operations room, where the ground-control officers – and many radar girls – wait for the enemy bombers to appear on their screens.

"Now begins a time of increasing nervous tension. In a way, the attackers are better off, as they have definite orders when to take off, where to fly, etc. The defenders have to wait, wait and wait. And this tension rises to a peak and then fades again. The telephone rings, but the call is unimportant.

"To understand the pressure we live with at this stage of the war, consider the following facts: most of us are still flying the Bf 110, which is heavily armed but slow. Readiness is absolutely for experienced crews only, (just Oberleutnant Schmidt and me). From the summer of 1944, there was an alarming shortage of fuel, and under doubtful weather conditions, we did not expect the younger crews to have any success.

"My crew, Bordfunker (wireless/radar operator) 'Schani' Pinter (an Austrian) and our so-called 'third man' Emil Mathan have already arrived at the hangar by crew truck. The 1.Wart (first mechanic) has checked our 'plane (G9+ES), and it is ready for flight. We squeeze ourselves into the cockpit, fasten our parachutes and seatbelts and wait for further orders. Fortunately, the rain has stopped and the thunderstorms have moved away to the east. Will we be ordered to take off? Or is this just another false alarm?

"24:00 hours and we are still waiting. The weather has deteriorated; from time to time, lightning flashes light up the night and are followed by thunder and heavy rain. Suddenly, the 'phone rings again;

Oberleutnant Schmidt answers it. Immediately we can see from his face that something is happening, 'Erhohte Bereitschaft' (readiness). We quickly put on our flight suits and wait for the order to rush to our aircraft in the hangars. A couple of minutes later, the order comes through.

"Suddenly, at 00:13 hours, the sleeping airfield comes to life. A white flash rises into the sky to indicate, 'Start befehl' – our order to take off. At the same time, the loudspeaker in the hangar announces the order: 'Start befehl each Funkfeuer Quelle' – take-off to radio beacon 'quelle' (fountain) – the code word for the letter 'Q', situated 150 miles west of Hamburg. My technician closes the roof of the canopy; I start the engines. Taxiing to the departure point must be done in absolute darkness, there are no identification lights or taxiway markings. In case intruders are patrolling the area, we sometimes have to take off without the runway being lit by the flare path. At such times, a dim light at the end of the runway guides us in the proper direction.

"The first one airborne is Oberleutnant Schmidt. When I see the sparks coming from his exhaust pipes, I know he is away and it is my turn. When I push the throttles forward, my 'plane immediately roars down the runway and into the night. I am surrounded by absolute darkness. We are in clouds with our course set for 70 degrees; we climb at full power and are shaken by the ever-increasing storm clouds around us. Lightning occasionally illuminates the cockpit in a ghostly, pale colour. All of a sudden, a mauve light flickers on our aerials and propeller tips, 'Elmsfeuer' – St. Elmo's Fire.

"My aircraft, 'ES', becomes increasingly difficult to fly as the grip of ice takes over, and we are tossed like a toy by the forces of nature. 'Sitzbereitschaft für spitzenbesatzungen' (cockpits start to lose altitude). After several agonising minutes, we break free into a shaft of clear air. The ice loosens its grip, slips away, and we are now safe and can fly freely again to 21,000 feet. The hunt begins.

"Shaken up and down, I am concerned as we are slower and inferior in every way to the Mosquito, and are sometimes slower than the four-engine Lancasters without their bomb load. The Heinkel He 219, equal to the Mosquito, is supplied to only twenty to thirty crews. Far superior to all allied aircraft is the new, jet-powered Arado 234. *(A night fighter version of the Arado was proposed, but it came too late and was used only as a reconnaissance aircraft at altitudes of over 30,000 feet during the last three months of the war.)* Furthermore, radio communication and radar (ground/air, board/board and the airborne radar) are often completely jammed by specially equipped RAF bombers that fly in the formations.

"To overcome the jamming, the German controllers sometimes use other methods to pass information about the anticipated target to pilots. Radio stations transmit music typical of the area that the controllers thought were to be bombed. For example: Viennese waltzes if Austria (then part of Germany) was suspected; shanties for Hamburg; carnival songs for the Rhineland; typical Bavarian melodies for Munich and operettas from well-known Berlin composers for Berlin.

"Thus, little information about the bomber formation's course, altitude or main target (there are always diversionary raids) was available to us. Furthermore, the increasingly effective action of the Mosquito intruders, with their superior radar and flying performance, coupled with poor weather and inexperienced crews, contribute to many of our losses. All this while facing defeat within the foreseeable future! In spite of it all, the crews' morale remains high; nobody speaks about the terrible end. Everybody secretly hopes for the 'wonder weapons' promised by our political leaders.

"We do not hate the British or the Americans; these boys are doing their duty just as we are. Neither side can change the political situation, so we have to carry on with our job to prevent as many allied bombers as possible from destroying our cities and killing our people.

"When we reach radio beacon 'Q' the first RAF pathfinders are dropping their target indicators. We see cascades of red, green and white flares marking the aiming point. They light up the area and descend slowly on little parachutes. We call them 'christbaume' (Christmas trees). From now on, it doesn't take long for the terrible spectacle to begin! Thirty miles away, we can see the first explosions on the ground in Hamburg, and they're followed by widespread fires. These eventually combine into one enormous fire that covers entire suburbs with a disastrous firestorm. The updraft brings wind velocities of 120 miles an hour, and the firestorm consumes everything in its path; there is no chance at all!

"Soon, we see the first kills by night fighters and flak: Lancasters, Halifaxes and our own comrades go down as orange-coloured torches, descending in steep dives to explode on impact with the ground. We see the parachutes of the lucky men who manage to bale out; there are not many. Searchlights move all over the night sky, looking like pale arms of an octopus in search of prey. In addition, explosions of anti-aircraft shells at all altitudes make life difficult for friend and foe. Over the city are many aircraft from both sides, and there are collisions.

"Altogether, it is an inferno-hell for everybody. We night fighters can easily be seen by enemy bombers' gunners and by the marauding British night fighters, and we are hit by our own flak. We have to be cautious to avoid colliding with other aircraft, as all around us are at least fifty to eighty four-engine bombers and a similar number of night fighters. Bombs, incendiaries and target indicators fall between us. The fires send up their light to 20,000 feet. It is as bright as day; you could read a newspaper! The smell of smoke fills our cockpit.

"While the raid is in full swing, I see a Halifax and follow it into the darkness. I slowly close into position under it so I can use my Schräge Musik, two 20mm MG/FF upward-firing cannon. I am almost in firing position when a nearby aircraft catches fire and lights up the sky for me, a dangerous situation, so I quickly move to the darker side and wait. After a couple of minutes, I close in again and aim between its two port engines where the fuel tanks are. A short burst of cannon fire causes a small bluish flame, but the bomber immediately goes into a steep dive and crashes in an explosion twenty miles west of Hamburg. We see two of the crew bale out.

"Later, Schani has a blip on his cathode-ray tube; he takes over and guides me. 'Marie 800 (*distance 800 metres*), a bit higher, left, left, straight now, Marie 500, straight ahead, a bit higher and to the right, now you should be able to see him!' And so it is, another Halifax flying home, straight and level, no evasive actions. Again I close into the same position and fire. This time, the tanks in the right wing immediately catch fire, which quickly extends along the fuselage to behind the tail. We can clearly recognize the code letters 'W-BM' on the camouflage-coloured Halifax (*433 Sqn Skipton-on-Swale*). The burning aircraft flies onward for another two minutes, and again, only two crewmen bale out. Eventually, as if in agony, the Halifax turns slowly upside down and falls to the ground. It crashes at 01:28.

"We are right in the middle of the returning bomber formation and look for our next victim. Again, Schani sees a blip on his screen, so we start the chase for the third time, however, we are having trouble closing the distance. I give my 'ES' full power. There are some polar lights in the north that enable me to see the bomber quite early: another Halifax, recognisable by its bluish exhaust glow (the Lancaster's exhaust glow looks orange). This time, I close in from astern and then give a burst from my two forward-firing Mk 108 30mm cannon. Its right wing immediately bursts into flames, and I notice the code 'EQ-P' (*408 Sqn Linton-on-Ouse*). The Halifax inclines to the left and slowly goes down.

"Suddenly, something unexpected happens: diving away, the brave British rear gunner gives me a burst from his four Brownings, and my 'plane is hit in the right engine, which immediately catches fire. To watch the bomber go down, I had to lower my left wing, and that saved my life. The bullets passed over my head and into my right engine. While the burning Halifax goes down (at 01:36), I try to extinguish the fire. Unlike the British, we have no fire extinguishers. The only means of putting out the fire is a steep dive with a strong relative wind that we hope will extinguish the flames. Thank God, it works!

"Our altitude is now 6,000 feet; I shut down the engine and manage to feather the propeller. Only now do we realise that our chase has brought us far out over the North Sea. We have no Mae Wests nor dinghies and only one engine left to take us home. To fly with one engine is not usually a problem for the Bf 110, as long as we don't have to climb. I set a heading of 180 degrees to reach the Dutch coast to the south, and I'm very cautious to avoid the heavy flak-defended areas around Bremen and Bremerhaven on one side and the East Frisian Islands on the other side on my return flight.

"Schani calls the tower at Twente, still 150 miles away. Luckily, they hear us, faintly, but they warn us that an intruder Mosquito is patrolling the area. This could be fatal for us, but I must take the chance, as no airfields are nearby with a runway long enough to allow a single-engine landing by night; the only other suitable airfields Leeuwarden (Holland) and Wittmundhaven are fogged in. When the intruders are on patrol, all lights on the airfield are dimmed to an absolute minimum. But because of our emergency, these restrictions are now ignored and all help is given to us. The runway is fully lit, and the flak searchlights form a 'dome' that is visible for quite a distance as a white patch on top of the clouds. This gives us absolute priority for communications and landing, and the fire brigades and medical personnel are prepared to rush to the site of a crash.

"By now, we are flying at 5,000 feet, partly in the clouds and with a speed of only 180 miles an hour. It is not at all easy because our artificial horizon is out of order; the dead engine powered it. Again, we are lucky, as after about forty-five minutes, the tower radios that the Mosquito has left the area. I prepare for an instrument landing, and my only remaining problem – to avoid an additional circuit – is to meet the main beam of our ILS at a point and altitude at which we usually begin our approach. To fly another circuit with the Bf 110 at low altitude and on one engine is not a good idea.

"Fortunately, I manage to hit the main beam at the favourable height of 600 feet. Still in the clouds, I lower the flaps and landing gear. At 150 feet, I break free of the clouds and realise that I am short of the runway. So I start the right engine again, but it immediately begins to shoot sparks and flames, so I turn it off; it does, however, give me the necessary few metres I need to reach the airfield and cross the 200 yards to the runway, where we land safely. Our blood pressures go back to normal!

"Now, fifty-six years later, I sit in Hamburg airport on a warm summer evening after thunderstorms have passed over the city. I watch as airliners take off and follow the traffic with the tower over the intercom. My memories go back to a time when Lancasters and Halifaxes took off from their airfields in England to bring their deadly loads to Germany. Fortunately, this belongs in the past; the allies and Germans have become partners and, in many cases, even friends. But we should not forget to honour the brave airmen on both sides, who did their duties and were not as lucky to survive as we were."

Chapter Nine

TRANSPORTS

O'er the barren hills of China
By the yellow Yang't'ze,
Over brooding, jungled Burma
From the mountains to the sea,
O'er the rugged Himalayas
From Assam to Yunnan-Yi;
There's an epic being written –
Written by the A. T. C.

To a struggling, gallant nation
Goes a giant helping hand –
'Oil – oil for the lamps of China' –
Guns for every soldier's hand.

From this sunny, steaming valley
Climbing upward to the sun –
'Cross earth's mightiest natural barrier
Wings destruction – ton by ton.

Mid the stirring tales of valour,
Deeds of daring – Men who jump
Into danger – May we mention
Just a bit about the 'Hump'?

When you're four miles nearer Heaven
And the sky is thick and black
And the thunder-heads are building
All the way to Hell and back.

Cyclones screaming 'cross the ridges
Like a dying banshee's wail –
And your props are gleaming crescents
Framed by devil's fire and hail.
Down below just matted jungle,
Towering, wind-swept mountain crags –
Lurking death to the careless pilot
Who forgot to check his mags.

High above in the seething darkness,

HEROES ALL

Raging elements hold sway.
Snow and sleet and slashing lightning,
Jarring down-drafts all the way.

To a pilot's straining senses
As he hunches o'er the wheel –
Vertigo! – Believe those gyros
For you cannot fly by feel.

Compass spinning like a dervish –
Radios dead – and – frozen loop –
Thudding ice against the cowlings
As you plough on thru the soup.

Air-speed dropping – low fuel pressure,
R. P. M. all shot to Hell –
Engines popping – temperature rising,
Everything just going swell.

Then at last – a hole beneath you
And an airfield's welcome light.
Down you roar upon the runway–
Vicious cross-wind from the right.

"Home to bed and welcome slumber
Then – O death, where is thy blight?
By the shoulder rudely shaken
"Sir – you've just been called for flight!"

Flying Officer C R Call [10]

Among the unsung heroes of the air war, the transport squadrons had a vital role keeping the front lines supplied with men and materials, frequently flying in extreme conditions. From basic passenger work, through VIP transport, supply dropping and glider towing, the usually unarmed transports were constantly in demand. Supreme commander allied forces in Europe, General Dwight D Eisenhower famously said: "The Jeep, the Dakota, and the landing craft were the three tools that won the war."

ROYAL AIR FORCE

Jack Parry, who did a great deal of communications flying in the Far East, summed up the value of the transport squadrons to the overall war effort.

"Dakota squadrons did sterling work throughout the whole Burma campaign. During March/April 1942, after all RAF fighters and bombers had been withdrawn from Burma, Daks continued to evacuate civilians (and some 'lost' troops) from Upper Burma – Magwe, Mandalay, Lashio, Shwebo, Myitkyina, Fort Hertz – many of whom would otherwise have become casualties on the walk out to India. I remember, on 3 April 1942 at Shwebo, watching a Dak come in at last light, land on the only possible strip – a 500-yard fairway of the golf course – load up sixty-one passengers (I counted) mainly Indians, plus a few pets, and take off in the dark for Chittagong or Calcutta with about twice as normal civilian load. When the Chindit operations under Brigadier Wingate started, his forces were entirely dependent on supply dropping by the Dakota squadrons.

"One day in January 1945 we received orders from AHQ Bengal Command for the AOC's Lockheed 12 to be made ready for a VIP to take off at 13:00 the next day; for security reasons they never mentioned names or rank. After an hour or two another call came in from AHQ saying that another VIP would be travelling as well and that both could use the same aircraft, as both were departing at the same time.

"The next morning we had everything ready and shipshape. A VIP came at 12:55 right on the dot and was driven straight to the waiting aircraft. He was Lord Wavell, the C-in-C. Flt Lt Isaacs the pilot waited for the other VIP, Lord Wavell looked puzzled and asked why the aircraft was not taking off; he was informed that there was another passenger to come, as we had a request for two VIPs. At about 13:05 the second VIP arrived. He was a brigadier, and we told him to hurry up and bundled him into the aircraft without ceremony but he was not pleased about it. Only on entering the aircraft did he realise why we were hurrying him. Lord Wavell seated in the front part of the aircraft turned round and growled: 'Come on, hurry up, you.' The brigadier, who was probably looking forward to an enjoyable flight in a VIP aircraft, took his seat meekly at the rear and was still and silent as a tomb."

Sergeant Jack Wade trained as a WOp/AG and much to his surprise, found himself posted to transport work rather than the expected tour on Bomber Command.

"I joined Transport Command when I was posted to Bramcote on 1 Course 105 (Transport) OTU, in July 1943. We were breaking new ground because no one previously had specifically trained for Transport Command. I don't think any of us had even heard of Transport Command and when we saw the Wellington 1Cs in dispersal we happily thought that we were destined for Lancs and couldn't understand why there were no straight AGs around. When the news broke that we were for transport training a deputation marched down to Squadron Leader Brookes, the O/C flying, demanding that we be reposted to what we considered to be our rightful place in Bomber Command. We were rather young, very naïve, and bearing in mind the casualty rate among the 1943 generation of aircrew in Bomber Command, I rather think our collective guardian angel was working at full throttle that day. In any case, Squadron Leader Brookes made Captain Bligh look like a benevolent vicar when it came to dealing with what he considered to be almost mutiny and we left a bit subdued."

Sergeant Stephen Hall was awarded the Distinguished Flying Medal (DFM) in December 1942 for his work with 216 Squadron in Egypt, which was not untypical of transport units at that time, many of which were still flying obsolete aeroplanes.

"I joined B Flight 216 (Bomber Transport) Squadron RAF Heliopolis, Egypt, 18 March 1939, and was allocated to Vickers Valentia KR2341. The crew was first and second pilot, wireless op, fitter aircraft, rigger aircraft, the squadron being unique as each aircraft was self supporting, needing only further technical assistance for major/minor inspection.

"We had reveille at 4.30 a.m. awoken by Abdul with a cup of char. The first parade was 5 a.m., march to the hangar, carry out usual maintenance, return for breakfast at 7 a.m. The second parade at 8.30 a.m., continue duties until lunch (Tiffin), then the rest of the time was yours, so you could sleep, swim, go to Helio, Cairo. The station food was good, being supplemented by an extra ration system costing ten ackers per person. An aircraft was always conveniently flying to Palestine near the weekend for the purpose of obtaining fruit.

"The Gold Coast route was pioneered following much the same way that Imperial Airways used; Heliopolis, Wadi Halfa, a dual stop near the second cataract on the Nile where the Empire flying boats could land, plus an airstrip. There was a transit hotel there, which later was taken over by the service. Then the next stop Khartoum, Sudan, we had a small ground staff resident to give extra technical assistance if and when needed. The route followed El Obeid or El Fasher, Fort Laury, French Equatorial Africa, Kano, Lagos and finally Takoradi. We gradually built up these stops with supplies, oil and fuel.

"My first early flying incident happened when we, that is Flg Off Chisholm, skipper I/C, and I were leaving Khartoum, Takoradi bound, carrying on board in addition to supplies, three bottles of whiskey for our flight commander P G Chichester, together with some government chaps. The take-off was okay and flying uneventful until we ran into a terrific electrical storm, which forced our skipper to land. This was accomplished safely, our only problem was the sandy soil, as we were unable to taxi. We were fortuitous in having an Arabic-speaking passenger who negotiated with the tribal chiefs to help in preparing a take-off run, and by the means of wireless, an okay was given for the presentation of a cow, which seemed the protocol way of thanking for help. Our water supply ran out and we were forced to use the local water, which had to be boiled and quinine tablets added, and as a further safety precaution, the end product laced with whiskey. Despite the hardships, etc., it was not the joyous of greetings when the flight commander had no whiskey. It is safe to say the life-saving liquid was thoroughly enjoyed at night around the campfire – sorry Sir. I'm sure we are now forgiven.

"I was working with another rigger, in the hangar. Someone called 'tea up', passing our fitter working on the auxiliary engine. I said 'tea up', and he made some comment like, 'I'll have another go at starting this engine and be in'. I had just reached the annex door when there were shouts of: 'Fire!' Looking round, I saw the flames racing along the wing. The usual panic, still burning, our aircraft was pushed out together with the other aircraft, which in turn had caught fire. What had happened was that the fitter had had trouble starting the auxiliary engine, which is housed in the starboard nacelle, and is used for pumping up the air bottles, which in turn start the main engines. With his persistence to get the thing started, the petrol fumes had built up to such an extent that they finally ignited. About this time, the squadron was being re-equipped with Bristol Bombays, a truly vast improvement in speed, armament and payload. Our own crews brought them out; I believe one aircraft was lost, landing by night in Gibraltar harbour."

Flight Sergeant H Dennis was also in the Middle East at this time, but in his case his unit had already received rather more modern equipment.

"I served with 267 Squadron from 1940 to 1942 in the Middle East, flying Hudsons and Dakotas. The squadron commanders when I was with them were Wing Commander Wynne-Eyton and Squadron Leader Stracey-Smyth, whom I saw killed with seven passengers when they took off from Bilbeis, which was about twenty miles from Cairo on the Suez Road. After take-off he shot the 'drome up, which was a saying in those days. He came down too low and his wingtip caught the sergeants' mess tent, and that was the end of Stracey-Smyth DFC, plus the passengers, who were going on rest leave to Palestine.

"One incident concerned Wynne-Eyton when, after taking off on a test flight, one of his wheels came off, and having no wireless operator on board, it was quite obvious they could not get in touch with him. There were red Very lights all over the landing strip, so in the end all the available squadron staff lay on the ground and spelled out: 'WHEEL OFF', which did the trick, and he made a perfect belly flop after getting rid of all his fuel. There was an Me 110 which Wynne-Eyton used to fly at Heliopolis."

Wing Commander Charles Sandford Wynne-Eyton AFC commanded 267 Squadron from August 1940 until July 1942, and again from October 1942 until February 1943. The 'Me 110' referred to was actually a Bf 109F, flown by the unit between February and June '42, following capture in Cyrenaica during Operation Crusader. Wing Commander John Patrick Stracey-Smyth DFC, commanded the squadron from August to October 1942; he was awarded the DFC while flying Hudsons with 224 Squadron at Leuchars in 1940.

George McLannahan was also a 267 Squadron pilot, and outlined some of the schedules that developed as the Mediterranean war turned in favour of the allies.

"I was with 267 Squadron, 249 Wing and HQ 216 Group from mid 1943 until September '45. My crew was the first Dakota to arrive in Rome in 1944 while we were based at Bari. We were doing alternate fortnights on schedules around Italy and the Med, and night ops into Yugoslavia and North Italy."

In Britain 24 Squadron spent the entire war flying an extraordinary variety of aircraft from Hendon, primarily flying mail, passengers and VIPs around the various theatres of war, including scheduled services to the Mediterranean. Bob Clark witnessed an unexpected arrival at Elstree.

"At 9 a.m. a Hudson, *Spirit of Belgrade* (a presentation aircraft) made an emergency landing, having flown from Gibraltar. Passengers were General Wavell C-in-C India and Peirse – chief of Far East Bomber Command. General Sir Alan Brooke turned up later by car to meet them."

Flight Lieutenant Fred Harrison was a pilot on the same unit.

"I was based at Hendon from '42 to '46 with 24 Squadron. The squadron mainly flew VIPs using Hudson, Dakota, Flamingo, etc. With the Hudson we flew the Malta run with supplies and passengers, the route being Portreath (for fuel), Gibraltar, then seven trips to Malta and back to Gibraltar, then return home for service.

"Due to enemy activity and using unarmed aircraft (no 'chutes either), all flying was done by night. Once we were attacked by a Ju 88 some miles from Malta. After the siege of Malta was over, we were equipped with Dakotas supplying the armed forces after D-Day. Later we ran the air routes to the Near and Far East carrying passengers."

A system of staging posts was established along the routes to the Middle East and Far East to handle transport and other aircraft in transit. Norman Didwell was a member of the ground crew at 44 Staging Post.

"One afternoon at Sharjah they said there was an aircraft coming in from Comm Flight Delhi (*air headquarters India communications flight*); it was an emergency. A Wellington had come in, and I was working on it, they'd lost a lot of fabric on the starboard wing between the engine and the fuselage. When the Dakota finally arrived, the station commander at Sharjah was there with his jeep to meet it, so there was obviously a big-wig on there. It was Field Marshal Wavell, with his entourage. To put these VIPs up they'd got the old Imperial Airways fort in Sharjah as that was the only main building there. The second pilot was Flight Lieutenant David Niven, and the pilot was Wing Commander Withers (*possibly Wing Commander Harold Robert Withers OBE*), known as Googie, 'cause of Googie Withers the actress.

"Both engines were pouring out oil. We found out that somebody at Comm Flight Delhi had boobed, they'd both done over their hours. It had to be a double engine change, so they sent a Comm Flight from, I think, 216 Squadron, either from Cairo West, or it might have been at Heliopolis at the time, down to pick him up the next day. (*216 Squadron was based at Cairo West from November 1942 until July 1945.*)

"We had to take the engines out with shear legs, we had no Coles crane there. Two new Pratt and Whitney engines had to be flown up from India, from the MU (maintenance unit) at Karachi, (*317 MU*), or from the MU in Cairo (*109 MU*). The only place we could work was near the fort, at night, with Leigh lights as all they had was a generator. We were working on this Wimpy, and old Wavell came out with his RAF liaison officer. I'd been there eight months, Ted Prouch had been there eight months, Sergeant Grant had been there about twelve months. Anyway, he said, 'Take these chaps' names and service numbers'. We wondered what was going to happen. 'You're working hard, I won't detain you any longer', he said, 'rather primitive isn't it, rather primitive'. Wing Commander Withers and the flight lieutenant were there the next morning, they never went to Cairo and we had quite a long chat. Then the Dak was ready for an air test. So Wing Commander Withers said: 'Would you lads like to come up on an air test?' 'You'd better get something to cover the seats,' he said. We went up and down the Gulf for about an hour, so I actually flew in the aircraft of Field Marshal Wavell.

"At Amman landing strip we had an old Arab foreman who remembered Lawrence of Arabia, and he had fought in the Arab Revolt. On the staging posts we serviced Wimpys, Spits, Hurricanes, Liberators, Dakotas, Hudsons, Halifaxes, Corsairs, Barracudas, Flying Forts, Mitchells, Mossies, Blenheims, Beaufighters, Beauforts, Lancasters, Albacores, Fulmars, DH 86, Oxfords, Ansons, Kittyhawks and many more. When I was at Habbaniya, we had as many as forty aircraft in the same evening, and 40 Staging Post at Habbaniya only had about fifty officers and men, it was all go. We had one Wellesley; it was flown by a Polish warrant officer and was used for carrying the mail; I used to service it."

Roy Fensome was a WOp with 216 Group Squadron and 216 Group

Communications Flight/Special Transport Flight, flying general transport work in the Middle East.

"I was posted to Helwan, the Cairo airport, where I was crewed up with a special unit that used converted Lancasters, Dakotas, and Halifaxes, where we used to take VIPs, equipment, engines, special forces, all over the Middle East. 216 Group Transport Command, it was a part of that set-up. In total I did 500 hours and had not seen any real action except engine failures. This mostly occurred with undercarriages that malfunctioned.

"We used Lancasters most of the time that I was there. We went as far as Mauripur on the coast of India with special forces people. We had two goes at that because on the way out there, one of the engines packed up, and we lost a bit of height, and so we had to go back and get the engine done and go off again with no mishap. The skipper told me to send out an SOS, which I did. But the engineer did a good job because he managed to get some power out of it, and then we went back to base, and I cancelled the SOS.

"We had a full crew as if we were going on a mission, but of course we didn't get attacked or anything like that. It was just a matter of getting from A to B, delivering the stuff and coming back."

Following a lengthy period as a fighter pilot, Michael Wainwright was given command of the West Africa communications squadron, and was shocked by what he found.

"I went to one of 45 Group's out-stations in Accra, and my job was an honest job to start with, to organise facilities on Ascension Island for aeroplanes that were being ferried to make the build-up of aircraft for the attack on Japan. There was a flight, which was getting in a hell of state and it was commanded by a major from the South African Air Force. We had fifteen Dakotas, and only about seven were flyable, and they were cannibalising the others. I said: 'Look, you've got far too many aeroplanes, you're only going to have ten.' I kept the seven that were working reasonably well, and I got three new ones, brand new, out of Kemble. I really built up what was in effect an airline; it functioned as an airline. Those aeroplanes were flying all the time; they didn't stand on the ground. I built up a route which went from Accra to Gibraltar. And from Accra to Lagos, to Kano, to Khartoum, to Cairo; every day. Quite fun, I enjoyed that."

Squadron Leader Ray Glass started flying late in the war as a pilot on the consolidated RY-3, a transport variant of the B-24 Liberator with a large single fin.

"After VE-Day, I joined 1332 HCU at Riccall for a captain's course on Liberator IIIs and VIs with converted bomb bays for troop carrying to the Far East in canvas type 'deck chair' seats with their knees interlocking.

"I then joined 232 Squadron at Holmsley South. After they moved overseas, I returned to Riccall to convert onto one of the only two Liberator Express RY-3s, a single fin version in the UK. This was indeed a luxury job with forward-facing padded PVC 'deck chair' type seats for thirty-three passengers and galley. We flew these to Dorval via Reykjavik, Iceland and Goose Bay, Labrador. In spite of our attempts to join the squadron there, flying a route to Sydney, Australia via the Pacific (losing and gaining a day each way) we had to return to the UK. I then joined 59 (Broken Wheel) Squadron Waterbeach to continue trooping to Mauripur, India until demobbed.

"During the 1332 HCU captain's course, the final passing out cross-country (Orkneys, Faroes, Reykjavik, Rockall, Riccall) were like an international marathon – we crossed a cold front. The second pilot was flying with 'George' in, I was in the RY-3 galley having some hot soup and bully beef sandwiches with lovely thick crusty bread (I can still taste it now!), when the engine note changed and the aircraft lurched. I wondered what was going on, dashed up front, found the starboard outer had iced up and we had turned 180 degrees and lost a few thousand feet. This was fortunate in a way, we had dropped below the icing level and were able to restart the outer and regain our course and height after passing through the front. The old 'butterflies' and 'twittering rings' subsided and we enjoyed the sight of Reykjavik all lit up after all the blacked out towns of Europe. Another cross-country route was dubbed 'Riccall, Rockall, F-all, Riccall'.

"On the trip with the RY-3 to Canada the radio 'blew up' and we had to return to Prestwick in low cloud, so requested a GCA (ground control approach) but the crew had been stood down and attempted an SBA (standard blind approach) on R/T bearings which nearly ended in disaster; breaking cloud and almost touching the tops of trees, we gave it the 'gun' and climbed to a safe height. Flying control in the meantime had dug out the GCA crew who did a magnificent job, I was able to put the nosewheel on the runway centre line.

"After changing the radio we were asked to do a mail run to Reykjavik as the regular kite had gone u/s. This fitted in nicely with the weather pattern over the Atlantic, as we would miss some bad weather with an overnight stop. Not anticipating the length of time we actually had to stay – on the way we lost the gyro compass and the magnetic compass was most noticeably sluggish in these latitudes. On fitting a new gyro at Reykjavik, we burnt out a magneto swinging the damn thing. We had to wait almost a month for a new one to be flown out from Montreal. The RY-3 Twin Wasps had the mags on the front of the engine and the American base in Iceland and the UK had none of this type. In the meantime my fiancée was doing her nut as to what had become of me. Although I had written, the post only went when the mail run arrived, and the first question that the ground crew asked when we landed at Reykjavik was, 'have you any mail?' and a cheer went up when the answer was 'yes'.

"In Iceland in November, recollections were of short days, the sun, when visible, would rise about 10 a.m. and set about 2 p.m. We were billeted in the Winston Churchill Transit Mess, double-glazed and double-doored, most comfortable but when you went through the doors, the cold and wind took your breath away until you acclimatised.

"After flight testing the new mag, the weather for the crossing was good and at last we were airborne and on our way to Goose Bay passing Greenland away to starboard on the horizon – it looked green too – or was it wishful thinking! On approaching Goose Bay the radio op received a message that their bearings were putting us too far north; my navigator had been taking sun shots and reckoned we were on course. We were flying above a layer of stratus clouds and we felt that their bearings were being 'bent' by snow. On picking up the homing beacon we were spot on course and crossed the coast on track. The next shock was finding the runway not ploughed but steam rolled with snow. We approached with some hesitation and the touchdown was the smoothest I'd ever made, the pressed snow made it so, and braking very gently. On being directed to a hangar, I was about to shut down when the doors slid open and I was beckoned to taxi straight in. Another first – never taxied inside a hangar before, taboo in the RAF. The ground crew had not seen an RY-3 before and had taken bets as to whether the single fin would go in, it did and the next surprise – the hangar was centrally heated. We celebrated the crossing with rum and coke. Next morning we took off in a snow storm, having been assured that Dorval was clear. After handing over to the second pilot, I fell asleep and awoke to brilliant sunshine, flying up the St. Lawrence River."

Among the roles for which transport flying became best known, particularly in the European theatre, was glider towing, mainly using converted bomber types such as the Albemarle, Halifax, and Stirling. John King was involved in this work with several Halifax units.

"We went to Earls Colne, towing the Hamilcar and Horsa glider, dropping paratroops, and we got there just after the Rhine Crossing."

Eric Barfoot flew Dakotas with 216 and 267 Squadrons in the Far East, mainly supplying ground forces deep in the jungles of Burma, but encounters with the Japanese were not their only worries.

"The most frightening thing ever to happen to me was nothing to do with shooting, or anything like that, but it was in a Dakota over the Arakans in Burma. We were returning empty after a supply drop and we flew into a fissure between the clouds at about 7,500 feet. The fissure closed in on us, and that meant we had to make a steep climbing turn into the cloud. Suddenly there was a huge thump and all the instruments went haywire, so I really had no idea which way up we were, I had lost all sense of attitude and direction. I told the crew to put their 'chutes on, and one of them offered me mine, but as I reached out for it we were amazed to find ourselves suddenly pop out of the top of the cloud into bright sunshine, and flying almost level! We had been carried up to 12,500 feet in the space of about thirty seconds. It took me a couple of days to get over that one, helped along by copious amounts of whisky."

SPECIAL OPERATIONS

Among the highest risk flying of all were the clandestine operations into occupied France and the Low Countries, at night, to deliver and collect special operations executive (SOE) agents, and to keep the French Resistance supplied. Particularly associated with Tempsford in Bedfordshire and its associated Gibraltar Farm, the following extract is taken from the operations record book (ORB) for 138 Squadron for the night of 8/9 December 1941, when the squadron was operating forward from Stradishall in Suffolk; the aircraft involved was a Lysander, and the mission was to collect a Belgian air force captain.

"22.10 aircraft airborne on Operation Stoat, captained by Flt Lt Murphy. Course set for Abbeville and unable to pinpoint on French coast, course altered on ETA at 23:00. Course set for Neufchâteau at 23:50. Ground covered in snow, making woods stand out clearly and pinpoint made over aerodrome at Neufchâteau. This was circled until 00:40 hours, when a light was seen south of aerodrome. Another light was seen at 00:45 hours, showing a steady beam. The first light continued to flash, and throttle of aircraft closed twice over and it was therefore concluded this agent was being chased, so it was therefore decided to land.

"Flare path was approached – some 20 yards short of the light. Landing light was used and the ground dipped down very sharply in front of aircraft, so the pilot took off again. Pilot then decided to land on eastern side of aerodrome and pilot remained where he was as soon as aircraft stopped moving, with revolver ready. At 00:55 there was an explosion, which I thought had been my revolver firing, but this was not the case and it was due to enemy approaching and being belligerent. Aircraft then took off at 01:00, and course was set to base. Landed at 03:20."

Flight Lieutenant (later wing commander) Alan Michael 'Sticky' Murphy DFC DSO and two bars, in fact received a neck wound during the enemy activity, and the Lysander returned with over thirty bullet holes in it.

HEROES ALL

LUFTWAFFE

The Luftwaffe's transport force reached its height during the campaigns in Russia, Crete, and North Africa, suffering huge losses in all three. Heinz Rökker had good reason to be thankful for the Luftwaffe's transport force during the retreat of Rommel's Afrika Corps from Libya. With very few serviceable combat aircraft remaining, he found himself being flown out in an Fw 200 Condor. Primarily a maritime patrol aircraft, a number of Condors were pressed into use as transports in both the Mediterranean and eastern theatres (see page 208).

SOVIET AIR FORCES

Having won acceptance from her male contemporaries, Olga Lisikova was soon in the thick of the action dropping paratroops on the Eastern Front, initially using the Lisunov Li 2, which was a licence-built Dakota. Some of the aircraft she flew had some measure of self-defence capability.

"I flew the C-47; I was the only female pilot. As soon as the lend-lease agreement was concluded, we almost immediately received the C-47, because it was accomplishing a very critical mission. The aircraft was intended for delivery of parachutists. It had special seats and girders for parachute lines. The Germans were moving a large number of Russian captives by train and we had to deliver a group of good, strong officers from special operations to prevent them. This was a very complicated mission, because we had to drop them in a very confined space. I put the aircraft in a 70 degree banking turn so that the parachutists would fall to the same point.

"Because I was a Leningrader, I was most interested in missions that supported Leningrad. Our commander knew this and frequently assigned me such missions, as many as 100. I was flying to Leningrad from the very beginning, on some of my first flights. When the order came out to create a Moscow special purpose aviation group (MAGON), they really meant 'special purpose'. Its primary use was not for hauling provisions to Leningrad; it was believed they would quickly relieve the blockade. The aviation group was able to move 100 tons of cargo in a day, but its main purpose was to transport 30,000 highly qualified workers in the tank industry. Later they used us as they needed to, as a 'cork for every bottle'. They assembled aircraft from many Aeroflot subunits: Uzbek, Turkmen, Novosibirsk, Minsk, Ukraine, and so on. All these aircraft were concentrated at Vnukovo.

"We flew to Leningrad only at low level and in groups of no less than seven aircraft; nine was the best number. They mounted ShKAS machine guns on our aircraft, and on top was a turret where they mounted the UBT (machine gun). Our aircraft used a flight route over Lake Ladoga,

246

where fascist fighters patrolled. When they came down on us, our gunners commenced defensive fire. In order to hit a target, a fighter had to approach within 400 metres, or they would miss. This defensive fire prevented the German fighters from getting that close. Although we did not shoot them down, we did not allow them to kill us at will.

"19 November 1941 was the most difficult day for our aviation group. Rzhevka, at that time was called Smolnyy airfield and was still closed, and we were flying to Komendantskiy airfield, at Novaya Derevnya. The Germans were very close. Fighters were escorting us, but the fighters had landed before all of our aircraft were on the ground. Two German fighters shot down Misha Zhukov, the first aircraft in the landing circuit, and everyone on that aircraft was killed. Kireev's aircraft was second to land. He was the chief pilot for Vyacheslav Molotov (Soviet minister of foreign affairs), who two days later was to fly to the United States to sign the lend-lease agreement. He was sitting in the right seat, permitting Zhuravlev to fly the aircraft. Kireev was killed outright; the wounded flight engineer was able to lower the landing gear. He died two hours later. Seriously wounded, Zhuravlev landed the aircraft, but his entire crew was in a critical condition; all of them were evacuated to a hospital.

"I think during the fifth flight, two aircraft fell behind, Kostya Bukhanov was flying one of them. They were shot down, but managed to land in a damaged condition; they saved almost all of their passengers, only two died. Then there was Ibrahim Zhanteev, on 30 November 1941. He fell back from the group that was going to Leningrad. The Germans intercepted him right away and shot him down, but he managed to turn and land on the water. But it was 200 metres to the shore, and the depth there was eight metres. He had passengers on board, the children of the workers of Lenenergiya (the Leningrad power utility). There were forty to fifty people in all, and the Messers strafed those who made it out of the sinking 'plane in several passes. Our forces did not find a single survivor. In general the fascists knew full well who we were transporting. Their reconnaissance aircraft were circling our airfield the whole time."

Chapter Ten

THEY ALSO SERVED

If I only had wings!
Oh, what a difference it would make to things.
All day long I'd be in the sky,
Up on high,
Talking to the birdies as they passed me by.
How the fellows would stare,
To see me roaring past them thro' the air,
Never tiring of the thrill it brings,
If I only had wings!
I'd be so fearless and bold
That when the stories of my deeds were told,
You'd see my picture in the papers,
And they would proudly say
'The RAF and me we had another good day'
If I only had wings!
One little pair of those elusive things
You would never hear me complain again –
If I only had wings!
If I only had wings!

S Collins and R Aldrich [11]

Inevitably it was the aircrew that received all the attention during the war, and have continued to do so in the many histories of aerial warfare written since then. While this is understandable, it is important to recognise the vital part played by all the supporting tradesmen; the ground crew, clerks, cooks, medical staff and all the others who played their part in keeping the aircraft in the air.

GROUND CREW

Frequently called upon to work very long hours in all weathers, the fitters and riggers who toiled to repair battle-damaged aircraft and keep them ready for operations receive a lot of well-earned praise from their aircrew. As Tim Elkington said when talking about his own ground crew: "Without the NCOs we would be nowhere. They were – and are – the backbone of any organisation."
Fellow fighter pilot Geoffrey Wellum agreed:

"Backing us up of course were the ground crews. The flight sergeants on the flight line being absolute stalwarts. Senior NCOs with years of experience – rising to the occasion at the very height of the battle more often

248

than not in danger of air attack when everything was called for. Ruling the roost with the total devotion and sense of where their duty lay. They truly were the salt of the earth. Make no mistake, without them, the Battle of Britain could not even have been fought let alone won."

Jack Bromfield had the same feelings about his bomber ground crew.

"The ground crews don't get the praise they really deserve. It was tough when a crew didn't come back because it was their aeroplane, not the guys that were flying it; it was the ground crew's aeroplane that had gone missing."

Vasili Kubarev echoed these sentiments, focussing on some of the issues with aeroplanes that suffered in the rush to produce them as quickly as possible.

"Very often 'planes that came from the factories were of bad quality. Our mechanics were given a day to look through the entire structure of the 'plane, tighten up what needed to be tightened, then we did a test flight. The remaining defects would then be fixed by the mechanics; they knew 'planes very well, and therefore the repair quality was good. The techs' work was excellent. I would build a monument to them. There was a saying: 'Heroes would get a monument placed in their motherland, but there should be a monument for his mechanics, right next to it.'

In the Soviet air forces, the mechanics were frequently at the end of the queue for food rations as Leonid Kulakov recounts.

"The mechanic prepares the aircraft; one cannot forget the conditions in which they worked. When we returned from a sortie, they fed us. But my technician, the flight technician, was not even permitted to take an extra piece of bread; they were swollen from hunger. If you gave them bread, they would not accept it: 'It's inappropriate. We can't.' He couldn't even rotate the inertial starter on the Kittyhawk, as he didn't have the strength. We snuck bread from the cafeteria but the technicians would not take it from us."

Norman Didwell served initially with Bomber Command before being moved overseas to help men at the Middle East staging post.

"I went to 99 Squadron at Mildenhall in May 1939, and did all the odd jobs you get when you're a sprog on a squadron. On Saturday 2 September 1939, there were some modifications to be done on the Wellingtons, so we knew war was coming.
    "Chiefy Darling in B Flight said: 'Right lads, drop everything you're doing, gather round the flight commander's office.' Squadron Leader Catt, known affectionately as 'Pussy', said, 'Go over to your billets, get all your kit, and get back here within half an hour.' We thought, 'it

Colonel Leonid Kulakov (left) with his 103 GuIAP P-40 Kittyhawk at Kovalevo, west of Moscow. *Kulakov via Oleg Korytov*

looks like the balloons are going to go up, we shall be going to France'. Anyway, we all assembled there, some came over in the aircraft, some, like myself, came by coach. So where did they fly into? Newmarket Heath race course, not more than ten miles as the crow flies. I don't think some of them even dragged their undercarriage up.

"After the fifth aircraft landed, a bloke came running down, waving a stick, 'You can't put these aeroplanes here, go, go!' The CO said, 'There's a signal from the War Office, to take over this location, and to operate my squadron from here. I want all the keys for that building.' He wouldn't hand over all the keys, and some of us were sleeping under the canopy (of the grandstand) in the outside as it were. The rain blew in, we got soaked. Somebody must have blown the whistle and immediately they were ordered to open up everything, because we had to be put under cover. This old b****r, the clerk of the course wouldn't allow anyone to be given the key to the kitchen. So we had a field kitchen, the old cook and his assistant had to do it out in the open.

"Some of the officers were married, and had to move out of married quarters in Mildenhall and get digs in the town; such as Kirby-Green, who was one of the fifty officers shot. (*Squadron Leader T G Kirby-Green was shot down in a 40 Squadron Wellington on 16 October 1941, was twenty-first out of the tunnel in the Great Escape, and was murdered 29 March 1944.*) The others had to sleep in the grandstand, until they ruled the aircrew weren't getting enough sleep, we had eighteen aircraft, doing the daily run-ups and that. So they moved them into the Jockey Club headquarters.

"We had Mark I Wellingtons, and within a few days of war being declared on the Sunday morning, we got new aircraft, Mark IAs with the dustbin turret. Most of the air gunners were ground crew in those days. They were ground crew wireless operators, ground crew fitters, riggers, and what have you, we even had an air gunner cook. He eventually went as a sergeant pilot. They'd go on ops, come back and the next night they'd be on guard! There was no such thing as sergeant air gunners until 1940, and they had to make these people up and give them a bit of extra money. An AC2 flight rigger got the equivalent of three old shillings a day, and sixpence a day air gunners pay, if they were qualified; some of them were still under-training air gunners, so they didn't get paid that. You are talking in today's money about 15p a day to risk their lives for their country.

"I then got posted on a quick course to Morecambe – a six-week course to qualify as a full rigger, but I learned more on 99 Squadron than I did on the course. Most of the ground crew on 99, especially being a new, modern aircraft, the Wellington, were ex-Halton apprentices. Thirty-second, thirty-third entry from Halton, apprentices were just finishing their three years in '38 early '39, and they were sent to the new Wellington squadrons; I learned a lot from these blokes.

"I was at Boscombe Down for a few months on an Air Ministry proving flight. We were experimenting night flying with a Spitfire and a Hurricane. We were trying to cover the exhaust pots; they tried all kinds of gadgets. (*Presumed to refer to CFS handling flight which moved from Upavon to Boscombe Down at the same time as Norman.*) There were all sorts at Boscombe Down; there was a Manchester, there was an early Lanc – and that had a dustbin turret (*probably second prototype DG595*). There was one Mosquito there with radial engines in. (*There is no record of a Mosquito with radial engines. It is possible that what Norman saw was the Gloster F.9/37 prototype, which was certainly at Boscombe Down at that time.*)

"I upset the station warrant officer one night. One of the kites came back, it was wet, it got stuck in the mud, and we had to dig the b****r out. As were walking back the station warrant officer came round the corner of the block, 'Hey you! What the hell'. Oh dear, he went off alarming about how filthy and scruffy we looked. Squadron Leader Bragg gave him a bollocking, but we all got posted overseas."

In the USAAF 8th Air Force in England, 'Punchy' Powell had a close relationship with his crew chief.

> "My crew chief was Bob Lyons, a really fine person. At the first of our 352nd reunions, his wife said to mine, 'I don't really understand something. My Bob was an enlisted man. Your Bob was a pilot and officer. Why do they have such a close relationship? I thought officers and enlisted men didn't really associate with each other.' My wife replied, 'Grace, my Bob says that your Bob, his crew chief, got him through the war. I think that's the reason. They have great respect for each other.'"

A small number of ground crew, such as Mikhail Pomorov, subsequently retrained as aircrew.

> "I used to service the regiment commander's 'planes; he had a MiG-1 and UTI-4. He used to train on a daily basis in this double-seater – he expected to be sent in to action. Usually we used to put a sandbag into the front cabin for centre of gravity. I asked him, if he could take me into the air instead of this bag. So at least once a week I was in the air. At first I couldn't understand what he was doing, but in time, by May 1942 I was able to land an I-16 by myself. I was already dreaming about going to flight school."

MAINTENANCE UNITS

Away from operational units were the second-line maintenance and repair organisations for both aircraft and equipment. Mechanics were similarly hard-worked, as one 'erk' who served his time on engine overhauls at St. Athan recalled.

> "It was dark and wet when I arrived at St. Athan; it always seemed to be that way! The workshops where the Merlins were overhauled were dark and dirty; the men who stripped the engines waded about in oil, and I was allotted the task of cleaning the cylinder blocks and crankcases in a big paraffin tank which sprayed constantly and had a Desoutter air gun with a wire brush. The noise and smell were horrible – they haunt me now – I hated it and so did the others.
> "Eventually after two months or so, we had some new arrivals and I managed a move, but only on to valves, inlets and exhausts – hundreds and thousands of them. I'd clean them with a scraper and emery cloth in a pedestal drill till I was fed up, then re-cut the seats."

Another of the vital support activities was fire and rescue, and C J Robbins served in this role at a station with a very wide range of activities going on.

> "I was posted into Kemble around 1942, as the station fire officer. This

and Filton, formed 44 Group based at Gloucester. Together with 45 Group at Dorval, Canada, this set up was Ferry Command, with a main function of putting aircrews into new aircraft to fly them across the 'pond'. It was also engaged with an OAPU at Kemble (overseas aircraft preparation unit) and an OADU at Filton (overseas aircraft despatch unit) testing aircraft for specialised overseas duty, mainly in the Med. Kemble was a fascinating place to be, as it had not only the flight testing for 44 Group, but a massive MU testing Spitfires and Lancasters, plus others, with a huge air park, which enabled a 'penguin' like me, to do quite a lot of familiarisation flying, both station commanders being keen on rescue."

FLIGHT TESTING

Flight testing was not only required at the factories, but also at maintenance units on freshly repaired and overhauled aircraft. Wing Commander Hunter McGiffin was a test pilot involved in trials with the modified Coastal Command Whitley aircraft.

"I flew an Anson from Christchurch to St. Athan to ferry boffins, and flew a Whitley back to Christchurch. I carried out an airworthiness test on a Whitley fitted with new aerials and four days later took this aircraft to Boscombe Down, where they said it was unsafe as the centre of gravity was too far aft. This was due to a professor fitting a long cylinder in the fuselage, which he had hoped would detect a submerged submarine.

"The centre of gravity problem was put right, and we carried out a three-hour trial with a submarine with some squadron leader observers and the professor on board. It transpired that the device only worked if the aircraft was within 150 feet of the submarine, so the idea was scrapped!"

Warrant Officer Norman Tayler was one of a small team of test pilots at St. Athan before being posted away successfully to complete a tour of operations in Bomber Command.

"I was a test pilot at 19 Maintenance Unit (MU) St. Athan. The unit handled large numbers of aircraft, which involved working seven days a week, particularly during the Battle of Britain period. On any one day I would test up to eight different types, which made for very interesting flying, particularly as we received no instruction on a new type, with the exception of the Stirling (three hours – two landings) in August 1940 at Boscombe Down. Although I trained as a fighter pilot on Hawker Furies in 1937-38, I ended up as a heavy bomber pilot on Stirlings with no OTU training, and no night flying since basic. I left 19 MU on a direct posting to 7 Squadron on 12 September 1941."

Pilot Reg Viney, who described his experiences with 271 Squadron ferrying troops out of France in 1940, had previously been involved in some flying trials.

"I took a Harrow up to Farnborough for experimental purposes. The landing area was then long and narrow, grass and with a crosswind. Being 'green', I eventually landed into wind at about the tenth attempt, the whole establishment by now having turned out to see the fun. A three-ton magnet was put underneath, the idea being to fly over the North Sea and blow up magnetic mines. It didn't half upset the compass – not to mention losing the pilot aircraft due to the usual sea mist – I couldn't fly for laughing!"

This was probably Harrow II K6998 which first flew as a minesweeper on 5 December 1939 and continued on trials until returned to 271 Squadron on 28 June 1940.

INSTRUCTING

'What did you do in the war, Daddy?
How did you help us to win?'
'Circuits and bumps and turns, laddy,
And how to get out of a spin.'

Woe and alack and misery me! I trundle round in the sky,
And instead of machine-gunning Nazis I'm teaching young hopefuls to
fly;
Thus is my service rewarded, my years of experience paid,
Never a Hun have I followed right down nor ever gone out on a raid.

They don't even let us go crazy, we have to be safe and sedate,
So it's nix on inverted approaches, they stir up the CFI's hate.
For it's oh! such a naughty example, and what will the AOC think!
But we never got posted to fighters – we just get a spell on the Link.

So it's circuits and bumps from morning till noon, and instrument-fly-
ing till tea.
'Hold her off, give her bank, put your undercart down, you're skid-
ding, you're slipping' – that's me.
And as soon as you've finished with one course, like a flash up another
one bobs,
And there's four more to show round the cockpit and four more to try
out the knobs.

But sometimes we read in the papers of the deeds that old pupils have
done,

And we're proud to have seen their beginnings and shown them the
way to the sun;
So if you find the money and turn out the 'planes we'll give all we
know to the men
Till they cluster the sky with their triumphs and burn out the beast
from his den.

Anon [12]

For many aircrew, a rest from operations actually meant a lot of hard work as an
instructor, bringing on new crews. Jack Biggs was posted as an instructor after a
long period of operational flying with 17 Squadron in India and Ceylon.

"The CO or the adj called me in and said, 'We've got to make a posting
Jack, and you're about the longest serving one here. We're going to send
you up to India for an instructor's course.' 'Thank you very much.' I
think they had one Hurricane left on the squadron, so I flew that down
to Colombo airport, Ratmalana. Then I got a Dakota up to Delhi, and
caught the train from Delhi up to Ambala, which was about 200 miles.
"That was October '44. Then I was posted to Empire Flying
Training School; flew Cornells, Oxfords, Tiger Moths, and the Harvard.
I was then a qualified flying instructor to go on Harvards, and I stayed
at Ambala where there was 1 SFTS (India), and I taught the Indians to
fly them. That again was good fun, I wouldn't have missed it, and I
grew to love the aircraft funnily enough.
"The instructing went on until I left in '45. I got posted to Bombay,
and caught the *Duchess of Richmond* home, and got back to this country in March '46. Then I went to Seend, which was a Spitty OTU (56
OTU). I went there as a part-time gunnery instructor and assistant
accounts officer, and I spent my time writing de-mob references, even
though I'd never met any of them! The accountant said: 'Just put some
nice platitudes in.' I mean unless they'd got a crime sheet that long or
something! 'This airman has been a trustworthy and competent...' And
that's what I did, with the odd trip in a Harvard and a bit of gunnery
instructing.
"After about 1,000 hours, I started to get a bit cocky, I think. At
Seend, I got another instructor and said, 'Come on, let's grab a couple
of students and do some formation flying.' I was touching his wingtip
with mine. It was perfectly safe, you were both doing 115 knots, so it
was no problem at all. Then I nudged his aileron with my wingtip."

Pete Brothers was also sent away instructing on two separate occasions.

"I went to a Hurricane OTU, Aston Down (55 OTU) 18 December
1940, for a rest; then detached from there to Central Flying School.
Better not do well on this course, or they'll make you a bloody instruc-

tor and that's it for the rest of the war; that will be no fun. Got through the course, and was posted back to the OTU, but hadn't got a job. Dennis David had taken over my flight, so I was sort of supernumerary. (*Dennis David retired as a group captain in May 1967.*) This lasted about a month or so, then they said: 'You're now a squadron leader, you've got to form 457 Squadron at Baginton.'

"After 457 I was sent down on rest, transferred to Spitfire OTU near Shawbury (*61 OTU Rednal*) where the station commander was not exactly an old friend of mine. When Don Finlay was a wing commander engineer, and I was a wing commander flying, I had said, 'You know, what you need to do Don, is get a few pints of Scotch inside you and make yourself into an ordinary chap.' And there he was, my station commander at Rednal. I just had my Spit from Tangmere; when I left the wing I had it re-allocated to the OTU, and it was my Spitfire, with 'PB' on it. I then had it re-allocated to Rednal, flew it up there and was greeted by Finlay, who looked at my aircraft and said: 'We haven't got enough aircraft on this unit for every pilot to have his own machine.' Stupidly, I said: 'I fully realise that sir, that's why I've taken the precaution of bringing my Spit,' which did not go down well!

"I had a briefing from the AOC that there'd been too many training accidents at Rednal, and I was the wing commander, and I was to sort it out. One day, the weather was bloody awful, so I stopped flying. Twenty minutes later, a Spitfire took off, so I rang up the tower and asked: 'What aircraft's that?' 'Oh it's from the gunnery squadron sir.' I rang up the gunnery squadron and said, 'What the hell are you up to? No flying, not for pupils.' 'The CO's just been round sir, and asked why we weren't flying and asked us to get cracking.' So I got air traffic to get that aircraft on the ground – fast; and they did.

"Don Finlay walked in and asked: 'Who ordered that aircraft to land?' I said, 'I did; I'm wing commander flying. As long as I'm here I shall be wing commander flying, and I shall decide when people shall fly and when they won't.' He said: 'There's nothing wrong with the weather, I can fly in it.' I said: 'Of course you can, so can I, but it's not good enough for a chap who's only done half-an-hour in a Spitfire.' He stormed out of the office, slammed the door. From then on, he never spoke to me."

James Coward finally got back to flying after a lengthy period of convalescence on Winston Churchill's staff at Chequers, but much to his disgust he was not allowed to return to operations.

"After losing my leg and being posted to Churchill's staff, I finally got back to flying after eighteen months. It was very difficult getting away once you started working for Churchill, he hated having new faces around.

"I started off on Spitfires, to get into practice for commanding a squadron at an OTU. (*Hullavington in January 1942, then 52 OTU at Aston Down.*) Then I was posted as CFI at an aerodrome up in Scotland flying Typhoons and Hurricanes. (*55 OTU Annan.*) I couldn't get a squadron, because my medical category was home service only, because the leg was giving me problems.

"So I got a delivery squadron at Croydon. (*On 23 November 1943 he took over as OC 1 ADU at Croydon.*) Every day was spent flying aircraft around the countryside and organising others to do it; various squadrons having aircraft refitted and flown to OTUs, or other units or factories somewhere. It was quite interesting. I flew different aircraft every day, I flew Mosquitoes, Meteors, and all the main marks of Spitfires."

Somewhat differently, Michael Wainwright found himself being employed as an instructor at an air armament school, and then training army glider pilots at 4 Glider Training School at Kidlington, near Oxford.

"They sent us to do the airborne division pilots in the army at Kidlington, then they moved us over to Shobdon. We flew Hotspur gliders to teach the airborne boys who were going to have to operate the big gliders and we towed them with a Mark II Master, we also towed them with a Lysander, which was a nice aeroplane. You had to claim some money for new shoes from the air force, which sympathetically they did, because the Lysander had a horrible habit of leaking somewhere and it always leaked over your left shoe.

"You had to go up to about 2,000 feet to give the guy time, because when they did actually cast off, (we had an understanding with various farmers all over the place for fields that we could go into) they could learn how to assess their height and know how long it was going to take them to get down, and they'd muck around, try to get down on the field. You'd have to get them down in a big enough field so you could go later on and pull them out. Some of the fields were a bit marginal in size but he had to get up enough speed and you'd have to go with a bloody rope as well, so that was a bit awkward. With a Lysander you'd climb at 500 feet a minute, and you'd still keep your tow rope on; he'd cast off and there you were flying around with this bloody rope dangling behind you to go down and pick him up. That was another dodgy business.

"I also spent some time at 2 Air Armament School at Acklington; there was a strange variety of aeroplanes there. We had the Hawker Audax, and you flew them for people who were going to be rear gunners. There they were, trying to fire things with a bloody Lewis gun, can you believe it? We were in no fit state to go to war. We had Overstrands too for training bombers. We had two types of aircraft there; one was a Sidestrand that had an open front cockpit, and the other had a glasshouse cockpit. Lovely, beautiful things; but they were rich man's toys really. I used to loop the loop in an Overstrand!"

PHOTOGRAPHIC RECONNAISSANCE

Some of the bravest were the photo-reconnaissance pilots, flying unarmed and alone, often for very long periods of time over enemy territory, totally reliant on their speed and altitude for protection. Clive Knowles flew eighty-one operational sorties in Blenheims and Spitfires with 140 Squadron, mainly from RAF Benson. Some examples from his logbook give a flavour of the sort of work he was called upon to do, with a number of operations being abandoned due to the presence of contrails to give him away.

"11.10.41 Spitfire R7116, photos at 500 feet, twenty minutes instrument flying, three-and-a-quarter hours.

6.11.41 Spitfire L1000, low obliques at 200 feet, one hour and forty minutes.

7.11.41 Spitfire X4907, photos at 28,000 feet, two hours.

23.11.41 Spitfire R7142, Ops – Cherbourg mosaic, high, 21,000 feet, successful. One-and-a-half hours.

12.12.41 Spitfire X4907, Ops – Port-en-Bessin, low, successful. Film NBG (*No Bloody Good*). One hour and fifty minutes.

5.1.42 Spitfire R6910, Ops - Ijmuiden. Low, successful. Chased a Do 217 but lost it in a hailstorm. Also saw a convoy off the Hook. One-and-three-quarters hours.

20.2.42 Spitfire R7116, Ops – St. Brieuc. High, successful. Photos obtained from 24,000 feet. 10/10ths over England. Refuelled Boscombe Down. Two-and-a-half hours.

9.3.42 Spitfire R7028, Ops – Scheldt. High, successful. Photos from 25,000 feet. Intercepted by PRU type. One hour fifty-five minutes.

10.4.42 Spitfire X4492, Ops – Channel Islands. High, successful. Three runs made over Jersey. Chased by a Hun on the way home. One-and-three-quarter hours.

8.5.42 Blenheim R5805, Ops – Abbeville, Le Tréport 8,000 feet, successful. Two runs. Interrupted by an Me 110 over the Somme. Sgt Brown fired at same. No ack-ack and only one searchlight.

17.8.42 Spitfire BP922, Ops/68 – St. Malo-Dinan-Domfront-Flers-Argentan. High, successful. Reported shot down near St. Malo by Huns. Returned having seen damn all. Two hours and fifty minutes."

Spitfire pilot Peter Fahy explained how secretive the role of the photo-reconnaissance pilot was, and described some typical sorties.

"I ended up on photographic reconnaissance unit, PRU. When I got to Benson near Oxford, I was told if anybody asked me what PRU stands for, you replied, pilots' rest unit, because photo reconnaissance was a secret. You kept quiet about it, never tell anybody what those blue Spitfires do, and why they were blue, we were told. PRU was quite good to be on. The Spitfire had petrol in the wings instead of guns, and cameras behind the pilot's head, and you could take photographs of what our friends in Germany were up to. After PRU, eventually I was posted to OTU to teach young chaps to fly Spitfires. (57 and 61 OTUs at Eshott and Keevil) They were about twenty years old, and I was all of twenty-two, and they looked upon me as their uncle, and sometimes they called me Sir (it's the power!).

"In early '44 I was posted to 16 Squadron (Spitfire XI Northolt) and it was tasked with photography of the 23rd Army, and a tour was sixty trips. Photographic reconnaissance was very high or very low, and not very often in between. You flew around at 1,500 feet, which was the best for spotting light ack-ack, and my German friends had quite a lot of ack-ack, and a marvellous supply of shells of all colours, and I did get very frightened. I remember one low-level trip along the banks of the Rhine/Waal, including Emmerich-Weisel bridges a week or two before Arnhem – some flak! Another one was a fairly hairy trip to get low-level obliques of defences and troop concentrations on the Dutch/German borders. I went down to zero feet to get below the flak and didn't see the high-tension wires until I'd passed under them! As one gets older, the nonchalance of youth is recalled with surprise and gratitude!

"On a lot of trips you got your photographs and you got this country with a lot of people so hostile towards us, wanting to stop us getting back, and that was the most frightening, especially if you had unwisely drunk a lot of beer the night before; His Majesty did not provide a loo in a Spitfire! If you did, and your heater wasn't working, which it quite often wasn't, you were cold and when you did it, it evaporated and froze inside your cockpit. You spent the rest of the trip chipping your own stuff off, trying to see where you were going – it wasn't pleasant.

"I found the Spitfire wonderful to fly, especially on PRU, which was a bit faster and could fly a bit higher, and I had some very good cameras. To be able to fly at 40,000 feet comfortably was something, especially over Germany and perhaps taking a look at Berlin and seeing all those lovely lakes and green fields and thinking how stupid the war was, and then turning for home and knowing it would not let you down. It wasn't pressurised; you didn't stay at 40,000 feet for too long, otherwise you might get bends, but you could get up to 44 – waffled a bit. It was the Spitfire for me.

"Quite often from high level you would only know the area, you wouldn't be able to distinguish what you were supposed to be photographing. At times you wouldn't be told what the target was in case you were shot down, then you couldn't reveal what you were photographing. I remember particularly, radar sites which at one time were secret, and quite often photography for them was at low level, which could be very unpleasant. It was a matter of luck when you were at the top of the list, you took what came to you, whether it was high level or low level. All I remember was that when I crossed enemy territory, I always looked forward to returning home.

"Eventually I started to go deaf, and the C in C, who didn't really have much of a sense of humour, said: 'Fahy, you're deaf.' It was like a charge. 'So you can join the admin department in the stores', and I said, 'No thank you, if I can't fly Spitfires, I don't want to be here at all. The C in C was shocked, 'What? You don't want to have a career in the air force?' I think I upset him."

Squadron Leader Jimmy Taylor was a contemporary of Peter Fahy's on 16 Squadron.

"On 16 Squadron we had six or seven pink Spitfires from April to December 1944, but I don't think we carried out more than a dozen low-level sorties in them. I didn't like the LF.IX; its engine was rough, the guns were not loaded, and it didn't have the same feel of elegant cooperation that a PR.XI provided. Mainly though, our XIs could carry an oblique camera together with vertical ones, so the IX scored only because its pink was more concealing than an XI's blue against low clouds. Strangely, some of our flight mechanics swear we never had them on 16 Squadron! The reason is that they never serviced them, as we had no armourers to maintain the guns. So they went to the only unit in 34 Wing that had armourers, which was 69 Squadron, flying Wellingtons at night at 800 feet over the German lines."

AIR TRANSPORT AUXILIARY (ATA)

The taxi Anson's piled with flying kit,
Each ferry pilot cons his morning chit,
When from the weather office comes the cry
That to the west black clouds bestride the sky.
Then out 'Met's' head is thrust from the windows wide
This dark portent to ponder or deride;

THEY ALSO SERVED

'Tis dull, 'tis dark, the cloud's precipitating,
No weather this for us to aviate in!
But one more bold by far than all the rest
Out to the runway taxies, gazes west,
Raises an eyebrow, casts his eyes about,
Wriggles his corns, his shoulder blades, his snout.
Instinct at work – will it be wet or fine?
What does this flying-weather seer divine?
He turns about and trundles back to 'Met'
To tell him that it really will be wet.

Anonymous ATA pilot [13]

The ATA had its origins in 1938 with a plan to employ civilians with flying licences to fly light aircraft in the event of hostilities. It subsequently emerged as a major organisation to ferry aircraft of all types between factories, maintenance units and squadrons, thus relieving service pilots from the work. The verse above makes reference to the ubiquitous Avro Anson, the aircraft of choice within ATA when ferrying their pilots between jobs.

ATA had its headquarters at White Waltham near Maidenhead in Berkshire, with a network of ferry pools at various other locations throughout the British Isles. Joe Dorrington described the training he went through and some of the many types of aircraft he was called upon to deliver.

"I was based at Haddenham most of the time. (*5 [Training] Ferry Pool*). I began on Maggies. When we started the first thing they did was see if you could fly. So we were off to a little field called Barton-le-Clay (*24 Elementary Flying Training School*). Once you'd soloed there, the next thing was you did your cross-countries.

"There were about twenty routes you had to go on, and it was pretty good really, because it taught you the way round, it taught you where the balloons were, and if the wind is in the west and you want to go round the far side of Birmingham, and if the wind is in the east you want to see where you're going, that sort of thing. That lasted six weeks or so, because often you'd be marooned for two or three days somewhere. I got stuck at Honeybourne, just by the Chilterns; couldn't go over the hills because the clouds were right down. I wandered into flying control to see if I could spend the night. 'Oh yes, we'll put you up in the local pub.' Got the local transport, and I was there for three or four days.

"I then went on to Harvards. Before we started we had quite a bit of time in class with retractable undercarriages, variable and fixed propellers and all that sort of thing. That got us onto Proctors as well, I did quite a bit of flying on Proctors. The girls were not keen on Proctors; because they felt safer when they had the instructor sitting in the cockpit behind them, but in this they sat alongside.

261

"Then I had a go at Spits. There was one old Spit at Haddenham, and then you got your wings after that. Then posted away as a taxi pilot, I had a month at Ratcliffe, by Leicester, (6 *Ferry Pool*) then I was at Whitchurch, in Bristol (2 *Ferry Pool*). It was quite good, they'd give you anything if you had the chance. You spent a lot of time in the air, but the senior pilot flew the thing. So you'd get in an Anson, full of pilots, and drop off one after the other until you were the last man in. Then you flew it to somewhere else to start picking up and you sat in the back seat while a few of you were kicked out and you came back again. Did a bit more ferrying at the pool at Haddenham. Then had a 'class 3' as they called it, which was twin-engine things. I'd just passed that and my father died, so I went home again.

"We just had the pilot's notes and a ferry pilot's book, that was the be-all and end-all, and you always carried it in your flying overalls. It would tell you, roughly speaking, what to do. When you got Spitfires, and all the different marks, it was pretty complex because you had to remember that a Merlin rotated one way, and you'd got to trim the rudder one way to take off, and the Griffon rotated the other way. If you were in any doubt, you just looked it up in your book. The only twins I flew were Oxfords. Just trained on Oxfords at White Waltham, then off I went.

"I did frighten myself once; the first ever Mustang I had with an Allison engine. It had been put down at Greenham Common because it was overheating, and I had to pick it up and go down to Llandow. It was one of those ones where the roof of the cabin rolls over, hinged on its edge. I got it nicely going, and looked round all the dials and things. The temperature was right in the red towards the far end. I had a quick look round and could not find any jettison thing anywhere, so I thought, 'well I'm stuck with it anyway'.

"I went round for a bit and it didn't seem to get much worse, so I thought I must put it down. Of course, as soon as I landed the airflow ceased and it was right up hard against the stop, so I swung off the runway and stopped everything. I got onto flying control and said it was very, very hot. They said: 'You can taxi it somewhere if you want to, but it's your concern if it blows up or seizes or something.'

"The only one I ever bent, I think I liked least of all, was the Barracuda. It was like a brick. Once you started coming down, you'd got a hell of a job to start going back up again. It was all right when you'd got the wheels up, but it took a lot of doing to get back up again if you made a mess of it. It was a high-wing thing, miles to climb up; the high-wing parallel to your line of sight. This particular one, I was taxiing round to dispersal in some trees. They waved me to swing round, and I pointed to the trees – a bit close – 'oh no, come on'. I swung it round, and sure as hell, crunch, it hit the tree. That was a bit embarrassing; pilot's fault of course, I should have taken a lot more care.

"The one I enjoyed most of all, was the Spit V; they were very nice to fly. I knew nothing about fighting of course, but for pleasure, the earlier Spit was the best one to fly. They were getting very heavy by the time they got to XIVs. I had a four-hour-forty-five-minute trip in a Queen Bee from Kirkbride. I reckon that was a penance for breaking the 'Barra. There was a headwind, and the trains were passing me all the way there; bloody cold! The only good thing about it is that the Queen Bee is still flying, and the owners kindly gave me a flight in it at Henlow, fifty-nine years to the day.

"I once flew a Moth Minor. I had no handling notes for that at all, nobody had ever heard of it. Monoplane, single cockpit, and unfortunately, it wasn't meant for a parachute. So where you sat there was a little curved bit of Perspex, and that was a very draughty old thing.

"The Hurricane was much more roomy than the Spit, but not so nice to fly. When you had a four-cannon Hurricane, you could not trim it to straight and level; it was like a porpoise going along all the time, very sick-making. One time I was taking Hurricanes from the factory at Langley up to Silloth, and ones that had been stood out in the sand hills for two years, back to Witney to be broken up. You had to be careful, 'cause you could stick your fingers through the canvas. They were 'one flight only' jobs.

"I knew Lettice Curtis, a formidable lady. There were quite a few ladies in the ATA. In the ab initio people it was roughly fifty-fifty. And then about a dozen WAAFs or so, I believe, they came in, well after me.

"We didn't show off much, we were more conscientious. The only real weakness was that if anything we were all for pressing on to get home for a party at night. In ATA, in no time at all you were taking Moth Minors and Tigers down from Castle Bromwich to Llandow, when I hadn't even got my wings even then. Once you'd done your cross-countries, then you could have a go at taking them. The training was very good really, and you emphasised the need to get down instead of pressing on just for the sake of it, which some of the Americans were pretty keen on, they didn't like stopping for anything."

ROYAL AIR FORCE FERRY PILOTS

Carrying out a similar role to the ATA, RAF Ferry Command (which became Transport Command in 1943) was responsible for bringing newly built aircraft from the factories in Canada and the United States across the Atlantic to Britain, a frequently hazardous job in extremes of weather, flying long duration trips over a very unforgiving sea. Flight Lieutenant Cyril Jackson was a navigator at the time.

"I served on 45 Atlantic Transport Group (Dorval, Montreal) from October 1943 to September 1945, and on 231 Squadron also at Montreal, from September 1945 to January 1946. One of the things I remember was that we always got bacon and beans at Reykjavik, not too good in unpressurised aircraft at 9,000 feet! The CO there had two Dachshunds, and they claimed the two fireside chairs, and I still have two of them at home. I just fell for them in a big way. The civilian aircrew with whom we flew with burnt the furniture in the stove pots."

Jack Wade found that the aircraft he was called upon to ferry were not always in the best of condition.

"I ended up at Blida near Algiers, with 3 Ferry Unit. We delivered, collected, and air-tested all types from Harvards to Liberators, including the odd-looking Walrus (dry landing only). The bases of Oujda and Blida were nominal, we flew into Italy, France, Greece, Egypt, West Africa, and most of the Med Islands, Malta, Gib, Sardinia etc., going wherever the job took us. Since you might take a Wimp to Foggia and bring back a Mosquito, most crews evolved into a pilot/WOp or pilot/nav set-up, although if you stuck to the heavier stuff the crew remained as a threesome.

"The aircraft could be fairly new out from the UK, or a patched up fly-back to the knacker's yard at an MU. The first job we had was to take three 'has-been' Wimp 1Cs from Heliopolis to Blida. Pinching bits from the other two, the three wireless ops got one complete set in our Wimpey, and my job was to get the QDMs and flash them by Aldis to the other two layabouts in their aircraft. We finally ran into a sand storm south of Mersa Matruh and we never heard from them again. We lost our port engine cowling climbing over the Atlas Mountains prior to letting down into Blida and arrived looking like something from an Oxfam shop. Considering what they had to work with and some of the conditions in which they did their job, I don't think anyone can give the erks too much credit. The cynical flight sergeant with his standard remark, 'It'll clear itself in the air sarge', or the other gem, 'It was all right on air test yesterday', was more of a cartoon character than a reality, although he did sometimes exist."

Wireless operator Flight Lieutenant Norman Nava spent long hours ferrying aircraft to many far-flung corners of the world.

"I was with 45 Group from July 1944 to July 1945, after several tours of flying operations with Coastal Command. I flew as radio operator in a wide variety of aircraft and to many destinations around the world, east as far as India and west as far as Australia. In that time I helped to deliver Liberators, Mitchells, Dakotas and Canadian-built Lancasters, to various theatres of war. Other transport flights included Hudsons, Coronados, Mosquitoes, Skymasters and Privateers.

"Deliveries included one as far east as Allahabad, India, and one as far as Sydney, Australia. It took fifty-eight flying hours to India and seventy-two hours to Australia. The return from the latter, despite our priority, was five weeks later. There was an Atlantic crossing in a Liberator with a Polish crew, with faulty navigation. It took twelve hours and ten minutes from Gander, Newfoundland, to Prestwick, Scotland. I insisted they flew my radio bearing, and as we landed at Prestwick, two engines cut-out due to petrol shortage.

"A Mosquito 'beat-up' Dorval airfield to boost morale after a number of Mosquito losses on delivery. And during a return flight in a Coronado flying boat, I spent the whole time in the tail-galley cooking eggs and bacon for the other passengers. Then there was the gold smuggling that went on between the USA/Canada and Africa/India. Hughie Green, who did his war flying from Montreal, produced a theatre show there with the personnel of Transport Command."

Reg Baynham spent much of his time on flying boats, including flying schedules across the Atlantic to take ferry crews back to North America to collect more new deliveries.

"My entire flying career was as a pilot with Transport Command, including a little-known spell operating Coronado flying boats on the North Atlantic routes. Although I had many interesting episodes on Dakotas in France, Germany and the Far East, my outstanding memories are of flying boats on the North Atlantic. Many times have I looked down at the thousands of square miles of heaving sea (and sometimes ice flows) and just hoped the fans would keep turning.

"Most flying boat captains were civilian, and vastly experienced with thousands of hours. Andre Chatel (my skipper) was Free French and an ex French naval flying boat captain, some other civvy skippers were ex airliners.

"Flt Lt Marshall and crew were posted to Transport Command, from Coastal Command, to make one UK delivery of a Catalina on 27 March '44. Having made a few trips, I was aboard as check pilot. It was supposed to be a rest from operational patrols for them. During the long night we hit severe icing conditions and could not get beneath it. On using the prop de-icers, lumps of ice were flung off and windows broken. We finally made it to Greenock, with no aerials and everyone frozen.

"On the night of 14/15 August 1944 with twenty-five passengers on board a Coronado, from Reykjavik to Goose Bay, the number three engine caught fire. We shut-off the fuel and dived, and managed to extinguish it. The cause turned out to be loose holding down studs on one cylinder, it was probably sabotage! Another such case was found after

265

a Catalina test flight and equipment check, at Elizabeth City, North Carolina in 1944. On attempting to pump fuel from internal to wing tanks, wires to the electric pump were found to be cut and taped over.

"I was in a Martin Mariner in November 1943 at Elizabeth City. At the start of the take-off run, on Pasquotank Inlet, the rear hatch burst open, flooding the aircraft. We managed to secure the bulkhead door, and taxied half a mile to beach the aircraft, just before it was due to sink."

CIVILIAN CONTRACTORS

Bob Clarke described in great detail the little known activity of the many civilian contractors involved in the repair and modification of service aircraft, many of which had not previously been in the aviation business at all.

"I commenced work as an aero engine fitter in 1941 at Elstree when it was taken over by Fairfield Aviation Company from Croydon. Fairfields were bombed out at Croydon in August 1940 and moved to Elstree with their main plant in a part of the Odhams Press factory a few miles away at Watford. Elstree airfield was rather derelict at the time, but later a concrete runway was constructed and covered with wood chips and dyed green (a slippery surface which caused at least two Wellingtons to overshoot), also there were dummy hedges on wheels to give the impression from the air of small plots. The conditions were very basic to begin with, very few facilities.

"I first worked on the Master, and later outside on flights, priming engines, inhibiting engines, filling tanks, conducting flow tests, and generally preparing for test flight and delivery. I used to accompany Flight Lieutenant 'Timber' Woods on test flights and sometimes go with him and an inspector to do a final check on a nearby airfield (Handley Page's at Radlett), to pick up a damaged Wellington to fly back to Elstree.

"While repairing and modifying Lysanders for special duties we commenced work on Wellingtons. They were stripped down, re-assembled, and sprayed etc., in the Odhams factory, then dispatched to the field on a long Queen Mary low-loader, to have engines installed and final adjustments made. If an aircraft was capable of being repaired and overhauled at Elstree, it was flown in, or picked up at Radlett, which had a longer runway.

"When we took on the Wellingtons (the first three arrived in April 1943), the conditions improved dramatically; the runway and apron laid, and the big hangar built (this was in 1942), which contained a canteen, a first aid room and toilets. The two original hangars remained, but a fire and ambulance station were constructed, also an instrument house and armoury. The apology for a control tower, formerly our only contact with the outside world by 'phone remained, and was still in use when I left, but the only contact with aircraft was still the use of the Very pistol.

"We were fortunate that, in spite of near misses, no bomb fell on the field that I can recall. The nearest I came to being a casualty was when an electrician accidentally pressed a fire button on a Lysander, and bullets came flying out of the spats, just clearing me and punching holes in the roof of the small hangar; they may still be there!

"Fairfields also had a mobile group of riggers, engineers, electricians, etc., that used to travel around to various airfields where they were needed. These mobile gangs had the motto 'Ubend'um, Wemend'um' on the backs of their jerseys. A member of the field group would sometimes join them, and there was frequent switching of staff between factory and field."

During their time at Elstree, or Aldenham as it was then known, Fairfield's handled a total of 473 Wellingtons and 1,217 Lysanders. In addition Blenheims were handled in the early days, and the first of sixty-seven Masters arrived in 1941.

Chapter Eleven

D-DAY TO VJ-DAY

In pre-dawn dark, set cockpit lighting dim,
Ten seconds now – count down to 'engines start',
The first faint flush beyond the eastern rim,
Ere D-Day dawns we're primed to play our part.

Our Spitfires' task – top cover for the troops
Who at first light will land on Norman soil,
To carry with them all the Free World's hopes:
The Nazis' plan to rule the world we'll foil.

Peter Fahy

NORMANDY

The allied landings in Normandy on D-Day, 6 June 1944, were accompanied by a vast array of supporting aircraft, including fighters patrolling the beachheads, light, medium and heavy bombers attacking targets both close to the landing area and much further inland, and gliders and tugs landing troops to attack and hold key points such as bridges.

Jack Rose was airborne that morning in his 184 Squadron Typhoon from Westhampnett in West Sussex, but at the first attempt his aircraft suffered a technical problem and he was forced to turn back. He subsequently made one of the early landings at the hastily prepared landing grounds in Normandy.

"I flew on D-Day and it really was a magnificent sight, the invasion forces stretching as far as you could see. Unfortunately, on the first sortie I tried everything I could but I couldn't get my wheels locked down, so I came back and had another sortie later on in the day.

"The first landing was after about six days, on B1, B2, B3 and so on (*initially landings were made on emergency landing strips, then refuelling and re-arming strips, then semi-permanent advanced landing grounds, which were given B numbers*), they kept building as they went along. Obviously, pre-preparation must have been pretty forceful. But the Typhoon air intake was a huge one in the middle of the radiator and there had been plenty of experience in the desert of having air filters but what happened was, you'd be taking off in pairs on these strips, and the ground had been bulldozed and what was left were shiny firm surfaces pierced all over the place by pools of fine sand.

"The first pair took off fine, no problems, but if you wanted to get eight in the air, you either had to wait until the dust settled which would take forever, or you just had to swallow it. It was highly invasive, very fine, abrasive dust and the sleeve-valve engines were completely ruined. So, all the Typhoon squadrons from our group were withdrawn, air filters built and then we went back to Normandy. Meanwhile, the fort was being held by the back-up group who were operating out of England so they didn't have to land on these strips.

"One landing strip was close to Caen, and once or twice, the Germans, who were still in Caen, used anti-aircraft against us as we were taking off and landing. On one of the other strips when I took off, a piece of the expanded metal (*square mesh track*) ripped one of my tyres. When we came back from the sortie, before I landed, I put my undercarriage down and asked somebody to look at it, then I knew I only had one tyre and just the hub on the other side. The undercarriage was widely spaced and very solidly built so I landed tilted over on the one tyre/wheel. It descended onto the stub on the other side and dug in; all it did was swivel round a few times and that was it, luckily there was no damage to the aircraft.

"The only time I saw a German fighter was when I was on the ground waiting to take off and a '109 came from the beach travelling north to south. It wasn't all that high – I suppose about 4 or 5,000 feet – low enough to see it was a '109, and he was flying straight and level and it was covered by anti-aircraft, you could see it come to grief."

'Punchy' Powell flew his 352nd Fighter Group P-51 from Bodney in Norfolk, no less than three times on D-Day.

"On D-Day, the first mission we flew was at about 02:00. The 486th Squadron was the first off, and the number two man in the second flight, being unable to see his leader well enough to line up properly, lined up at a slight angle. On take-off, Bob Frascotti, flying Umbriago, flew into the second storey of the new tower under construction just outside my squadron's pilot room. We were being briefed for our take-off scheduled about thirty minutes later. The 'plane exploded, ammo was going off and there were moments of panic; our immediate reaction was to think we were under attack. The other two squadrons took off by the light of Frascotti's burning aircraft.

"The first mission was to join several hundred others to put up a wall of fighters from the deck to 20,000 feet to keep any German fighters from getting to the beaches. Each group and squadron had an assigned sector and altitude to patrol and we stayed to the limit of our endurance, then returned to Bodney to refuel and rearm. For the second and third missions we were split into smaller units and assigned a sector and told that anything moving toward the beaches on the roads would be fair game. We shot-up trains, trucks, buses, troops, and motorcycle dispatch riders, whatever. The French had been warned to stay off the roads. This was all low-level strafing and we suffered some losses to ground fire and accidents."

Mosquito pilot John Ellacombe and his navigator Bob Peel were also in action on the day, flying with 487 Squadron which had been forward deployed to Gravesend in Kent. They continued to harass the retreating German armies up to the notorious Falaise Gap.

"The skies were fairly crowded; there was a lot of attacking the beaches, but we were patrolling railway lines and roads looking for stuff coming up with reinforcements. I didn't fire my guns, we just flew up and down that area. It was very funny because we weren't told it was D-Day, we were only told there was a big operation. They were all so terrified if somebody was shot down, they would have said 'Oh, we're about to attack', but it was very exciting when we suddenly realised: 'That was it!'

"We were told by the SAS that a lot of fuel trains were pulled up in Châtelleraut – we were the first down there. We were airborne in fifteen minutes, flying at very low level; we never had a shot fired at us as the radar never picked us up – and we bombed as we came in. There were four trains lined up in the station, we bombed them and as we turned away, we could see all the flames. That was one of the most successful sorties we flew.

"We had a lot of sorties at night, attacking, blowing the lines and following routes where we would go down to see where all the trains were going and shoot those up or bomb the lines. We were told again by the SAS that a German SS division was moving into Poitiers and into the old French barracks and would be there at six o'clock in the evening. Twenty-four Mosquitoes arrived there; we understood that we killed about 1,000 of them.

"We flew so low we would go underneath the high-tension cables and lift over the hedges and the German radar never picked us up. It was an ideal aeroplane; it used to fly at about 240/250 miles an hour, which was quite fast. During the German retreat at the Falaise gap in the dusk and full moon, we were attacking them. It was an unbelievable slaughter; we would bomb a road, there were two lots of traffic all going the same way, and having bombed the road and stopped the traffic, we would go down and you could actually see your 20mm shells exploding on men as they were running; the devastation was simply fantastic."

The action was not all one-sided however. Heinz Rökker described how, despite being caught on the hop, and already suffering from fuel shortages, the night fighters were still able to cause a lot of damage to the bomber streams.

"The night after D-Day we were at Châteaudun, and we took gasoline from the other 'planes and I took it from the leader. I was leader of a squadron, he was leader of the group and we were the only two who started. Not high, about 1,000 metres, I had seen five or six enemy at the same time, and I could shoot them down, as I was beneath them.

There was no return fire, they didn't see me. I got six in one flight."

Pete Brothers became involved in operations planning as the campaign progressed, and was then sent to Exeter to set up a new fighter wing for operations on the continent.

"I did a few months at 10 Group, planning operations for the next day. I was acting group captain ops, and at midnight every night, we had a telephone conference with the other groups. Who should walk in, about two o'clock in the morning, but the SASO, Reggie Pine, and he said: 'What's going on tomorrow?' We replied: 'Oh, the Warmwell wing is redeploying to Manston at first light, refuelling, then it's crossing the Belgian coast at nought feet.'

"Dear old Steele, AOC, said: 'Right, Exeter. Six squadrons, all at odds, go and make them into a wing.' There was a Spitfire Squadron at Exeter, two squadrons at Culmhead, one squadron of Spits at Bolt Head. Harrowbeer had a Spit squadron and a Typhoon squadron. I moved the Spit squadron from Exeter to Culmhead, so I'd got three Spit squadrons there, and we started operating. Every now and again, I'd go down and see how Bolt Head were getting on. They couldn't join the wing, their Spit 12s ran out of oomph at about 14,000 feet, they were strictly low-level.

"I said ,'We need to split it up. Leave me with the Spit squadrons at Culmhead, and make it Culmhead wing, and put the Spit 12s, 9s and the Typhoons together for a separate wing.' Then I had mine until the war got out of reach, although with our Spit 7s we had a wonderful time. We went down to the Swiss frontier and back with no trouble. That's when I got my last '190. We chased them for miles and I caught up with one as his ideas of evasion were drifts and turns. I thought: 'Oh you poor kid, you don't know what it's all about.' I was horrified, I put a cannon shell smack into his cockpit, I didn't mean that. I wanted just to shoot him down and him bale out. I felt very sad about that, and have done ever since; he'd hardly learned to fly."

As operations on the continent built up, the 2nd Tactical Air Force (TAF) became the primary command structure for RAF operations. Substantial use was made of light bombers such as the Boston against the retreating German armies, as 88 Squadron observer, Jack Booth recalled.

"My pilot, Squadron Leader Tom James said, 'We've got a base in France, Vitry-en-Artois, three Bostons going over first, as much personal kit as you can get in. Then Dakotas will fly bedding and everything.' On 29 November we took off at 08:00 to soften Dunkirk up and quieten them down a bit. Over Deventer we were hit by 105mm flak, and shrapnel came through half-inch armour plating, through my parachute, and finished up in my right leg. We had our rudder controls shot away, and belly-tank go up; we were going down in flames. We put down in a field near Eindhoven.

"I finished at the end of March; I had done forty-two sorties. Sometimes they'd give the code word to bomb anything that you thought appropriate, like road convoys. We used to go line astern and cut across the road at 45 degrees to drop bombs. The idea was to make a crater behind and in front; by bombing crossways, you stood a better chance. Nearly all the pilots, once they'd dropped the bombs, would turn to avoid the flak especially in rail trucks, and allow the gunners to have a go at them.

"We were in two vics of three, four, five and six flying lower than one, two and three. Once, we were number four and were nearly bombed by number three when our pilot had flown ahead and got underneath them. We shouted: 'Get back! Get back!' Later, we'd just got on the aircraft, and this same pilot came along. We took off in pairs, and about six miles out from the end of the runway, straight ahead, there were brickworks. We showed no sign of turning; wondering, 'When are we going to turn?' I shouted: 'Turn! Turn!' We banked at very low level with four 500-pounders on board, and just missed the brickworks. We got back and both gunners were very ashen looking. The pilot came over to them, dropped his trousers and said: 'There you are, stick it up my a*** as well. Sorry about that chaps.'"

SUPPORT FOR THE GROUND FORCES

Bomber Command and USAAF heavies were increasingly used for daylight operations against targets in the invasion area. Ted Milligan and his 460 Squadron Lancaster crew from Binbrook also came across the debacle at Falaise.

"On 14 August we were on another daylight attacking the retreating Germans in the Falaise area. The weather was brilliant, and there was lots of smoke over the target. We bombed from just 2,000 feet, and Jerries were seen to be breaking all records on bicycles going east and south."

John Torrans was involved in a confused bombing operation which could so easily have ended in disaster for him.

"On 30 June the target was Villers Bocage, a daylight trip. We were deputy master bomber. There was cloud over the French coast up to 28,000 feet and our captain decided to get below it. We broke cloud at 8,000 feet and the captain called the main force down for their bombing run, but they appeared to have gone deaf or switched their R/T off. About 15% of them carried out these instructions and the remainder stayed at around 20,000 feet. Consequently, it was as the Yanks would say, an 'ass tightening sensation' to be on the bombing run with bombs, and incendiaries, etc., falling all around us. Fortunately none hit."

Stirling pilot Henry Payne took gliders to Arnhem for Operation Market Garden, and did the same for the Rhine crossing, Operation Varsity. The 299 Squadron operations record book for Arnhem relates:

"18.9.44. Operation Market 'D + 1' final briefing was held at 08:30. Last minute changes resulted in the same route (as before) being taken. The squadron put up twenty-two combinations (*including Pilot Officer Payne*) and once again Wing Commander Davis led the station. The take-off was very good and less than a minute was required for each combination. Again it was noticeable that a tremendous effort was being made by this group and 46 Group. The sky near Aldeburgh seemed full of aircraft and gliders and troop-carrying Dakotas. Fighter cover was again given and little opposition was experienced. Group intelligence reports later confirmed that losses were negligible and the operation from our standpoint was very successful." [14]

Henry takes up the story:

"At Arnhem I took a glider out, a Horsa, and dropped it. Mine was quite an uneventful trip. 196 Squadron, our sister squadron, however, they had a hell of a rough time, but 299 wasn't too bad.

"I did several trips to Norway taking troops there and getting the German army out. We also went to Stavanger and Copenhagen, where the army were our passengers, armed to the teeth. We landed, they hopped out, we got down under the wings while they rounded up the Germans occupying the aerodrome.

"We did trips to Germany landing on bomb-cratered aerodromes, to bring back prisoners of war. I used to bring twenty-five or so very weary looking skeletons, and when we got them to Ford, there was a big reception there."

"Another trip was to pick up twenty of the crack French paratroop regiment, to take them down to near Marseilles, where we were going to land to take over the aerodromes in southern France. But we dropped them from 70 feet instead of 700 feet, because the altimeters were all wrong, the barometric pressures had changed, and the poor devils got broken collarbones, broken legs, it was a total disaster. We were thoroughly ashamed but there was nothing we could do."

Sergeant John Perfect was one member of the Glider Pilot Regiment who landed at Arnhem. He survived to enjoy a long post-war career as a school teacher.

"I volunteered for the army as soon as I reached eighteen and trained as a glider pilot. I landed a Horsa at Arnhem during the abortive

Operation Market Garden, and luckily managed to avoid capture and got back to our lines. I subsequently flew again on the Rhine crossing do, and went back to Arnhem on the sixtieth anniversary."

Sergeant Raymond 'Tich' Rayner of the Oxfordshire and Buckinghamshire Light Infantry, 6th Airborne Division, was one of the men aboard the No. 4 glider that landed in the vicinity of Pegasus Bridge in the early morning of D-Day.

"We took off from Tarrant Rushton and were cast off and were over-weight to get to Pegasus Bridge so we had to land on another bridge which we found. We came in about ten miles away from our objective, and we were fired on before we landed. Machine guns were pushing out tracer bullets, going past the glider but luckily never hit anything at all, never hit the pilots."

Bob Rees was employed as a transport pilot with 271 Squadron at Down Ampney, and support for the army included casualty evacuation.

"I was a Dakota pilot mostly. 46 Group squadrons were trained for air assault with the Glider Pilot Regiment, the air landing brigades and the parachute brigades; with the RASC air despatch for supply by air; with casualty evacuation as air ambulances; with the staging posts for general transport work – freight, passengers, ex POWs and so forth. 271 Squadron kept its Harrows and Sparrows as ambulances until most were destroyed on the ground in December '44 and January '45. There were also 'Hendon Mods' and Ansons, held as reserves for ambulance work."

DEFENCE OF THE REICH

In the latter stages of the war as Germany became increasingly desperate to regain some measure of air supremacy against the vast allied bomber formations, advanced fighters and other types were hurriedly developed and pressed into service. It was however, a case of too little, too late. Bob Clarke's diary revealed how people at home started to see the effects when the V-1 campaign began.

"*June 16*
Rumours of a radio-controlled aircraft. BBC announce that pilotless 'planes loaded with explosive are coming over.

"*June 19*
The flying bombs coming in all night. They are coming over the coast about every ten minutes for hours on end. Our bombers are attacking the launching sites, and we're re-positioning the ack-ack batteries.

"June 21
Constant alerts, Londoners flocking to the tubes, trains in chaos as flood gates under River Thames closed."

John Torrans' squadron was soon involved in attacks on the V-1 launch sites in northern France, but the Germans put up intense flak barrages in an effort to defend them.

"During a raid on the Foret-du-Croc on 20 July, Squadron Leader Foulsham was flying the Oboe aircraft. We were flying to starboard of him at about 6,000 feet, when his aircraft was hit by anti-aircraft fire. Fuel and smoke started to emit from the port wing trailing edge. We called him on R/T to inform him of this damage. There was a large flash and an explosion and the aircraft just disintegrated, and all that was left was a large black cloud – there were no survivors."

The only jet aircraft to enter service on the allied side was the Gloster Meteor, which first flew with 616 Squadron in July 1944 before moving to Belgium in February 1945. Squadron Leader Dennis Barry was one of the first pilots to convert to fly the new type.

"On 24 April we went to Fairwood Common, where the squadron was allocated an Oxford on which to practice two-wheel landings in preparation to enable us to fly a new type of aircraft, which had a tricycle undercarriage.
    "D-Day 6 June, I, with three other pilots, was seconded to Farnborough (*meteor training flight*) for instruction on the Meteor, which involved a different flying technique. On 27 July we were posted to Manston as the first jet squadron."

Although it never saw aerial combat with a German jet, the Meteor achieved considerable success against the V-1 menace on so-called Diver patrols. These encounters were fraught with danger, since the V-1s were liable to explode in mid-air with considerable force, and avoiding the debris cloud was something of a challenge for the successful pilot! Warrant Officer Sid Woodacre was serving on 616 Squadron when it exchanged its Spitfires for Meteors at Culmhead, before moving forward to Manston.

"We didn't know how they worked, but we were expected to fly them. The CO just gathered us around, pointed out the controls and we took it from there. The secrecy was terrific. Our side of the airfield was completely cordoned off and surrounded by military police. Very senior RAF officers would arrive to see the new 'planes and promptly be told to push off by military police sergeants. We thought it was hilarious. All sorts of dire penalties were threatened if anything was ever said about the Meteor outside our own circle. It was, in fact, a very easy 'plane to fly.

"I was among the first to shoot down a V-1. This was on 17 August 1944, when I encountered one south of Canterbury and engaged it at some 400 miles an hour. I saw it explode harmlessly in fields below me, but the blast was enough to throw my Meteor about, even at 1,500 feet.

"If you were unlucky enough to hit the bomb itself, it would blow up and you could be in considerable danger. One of our pilots (*Flg Off Dixie Dean*) put his wing tip under the wing tip of a flying bomb, and the airflow disturbed the gyros, toppled it, turned it over, and it went into the ground."

Sid's combat report reads as follows:

"While on anti-Diver patrol under Biggin Hill control, I saw a Diver coming in south of Dover and intercepted it three miles south of Canterbury. A Mustang was seen 700-1,000 yards astern of the Diver but this did not fire. I had no difficulty in overtaking both the Mustang and Diver and then attacked and fired three short bursts at 200 yards. Strikes were seen on starboard wing of Diver, which rolled over and went down and was seen to explode on ground ten miles south of Faversham."

Heinz Rökker saw Meteors attacking his station, but by this time there was little the Luftwaffe could do to oppose them.

"We saw their jet aeroplanes, Meteor, at the end of the war. They attacked, four there were. I was very surprised, because I thought we had the only jets."

James Coward on first learning about the existence of German jet aircraft.

"When word got around that the Germans had a jet 'plane, it didn't have much impact, people didn't know what it meant. People in the air force realised that it was going to be pretty good, but pilots weren't worried about it."

The Me 262 was a superior aircraft to the Meteor in terms of its performance, but by the time it entered service, allied bombing raids were having a serious effect on its production. Norbert Hannig described some of the efforts that the Germans went to in order to protect the factories.

"They built big hangars in Fürstenfeldbruck. They dug out the sand and built a cone 35 metres high, 110 metres long, and six metres steel then they put concrete over the sand, dug the sand out and then had the factory. They built two corridors, the lowest one was the factory, the next one was the catapult for the aircraft. They opened the doors, pushed them out, and on top of it they built rooms for the personnel. After the war the Americans tried to destroy it. They collected all the ammunition they had found, put it in and packed everything with mud and dirt. Then they ignited the whole thing but they couldn't destroy it."

Norbert also recalled his own transfer to fly the Me 262.

"This engineer had one Me 262 in the hangar and I asked him, 'What do I have to do to start the engine?' and he showed me. 'Press this button down; wait until this shows up here'…then a big flame came out. We learnt enough! *(Norbert arrived at Lechfeld on 8 April 1945 and then moved to JV44 at Munich-Riem, followed by 1 Staffel JG7 at Prague-Rusin, until taken prisoner by the Americans on 9 May 1945.)*

"I never had any problems flying the aircraft. Lager Lechfeld is on the Lech river, going direct north-south to the Alps. The first flight from there I went along the river to the south. I had to examine the cockpit for the instruments, and Lechfeld was already green in the middle of April; the grass and trees were flourishing. I looked down and suddenly everything was white! I was now over Switzerland. I had to return very quickly. It was something amazing, the speed was shown in kilometres, 200/180 nose up, 200/220 gear up, 240 gear in, then landing flaps coming up and then 250, 350, 450, 650 and there still was more.

"For landing they told us: 'if you move the throttle too fast, the engine may quit'. So very slowly and the speed starting to go away, they had no speed brakes on the '262, so all you had to do was throttle back and keep them steady and as soon as you were down to 400, gear out. The gear then was the speed brake but then the nose went down, so you had to watch that you kept it up. The landing was the same as with the '190, there was no great difference. But the advantage was the front wheel, you could see where you were going.

"I had no air fighting in the '262. We caught some aircraft in the air but landed without fighting, and I flew ground missions. From the north came the Russian troops and we tried to catch their aircraft on the ground and we were sent out to attack them. It was three 30mm cannons against troops, it was like hell. We just ripped up everything. At that time it was the best aircraft. The Fw 190 and Me 262 were both very reliable and the technicians were well trained and I never had trouble with the aircraft. I was in Adolf Galland's wing only for eight days in Munich-Riem.

"The Fw 190 Dora was used only in the Reich. We had them as protection for the Me 262 because you had to go very long, and very straight ahead to gain speed. If you got speed then OK, but to gain speed you must go a long way, and the Americans were up in the sky at all times and waited until somebody was on the move. We had a command structure, but there was not much to command any more. Sometimes you got a line to a higher command but they didn't know what to do with you."

Flight Lieutenant Rod Smith of 401 Squadron shared in the destruction of an Me 262 on 5 October 1944, while flying a Spitfire IX.

"While leading the squadron on a routine patrol over Nijmegen bridge at 14,000 feet, an Me 262 was sighted 500 feet below, in front and coming head-on. We attacked, and the Hun turned and dived down towards the bridge, half-rolling at very high speed. Flg Off Mackay and Flt Lt Everard damaged him first with a few strikes; I then attacked him with three others. He zoomed, and Flt Lt Davenport and I cut him off and fired simultaneously. I fired an approximately eight-second burst, 350 yards astern, with small deflection, and his starboard jet unit caught fire. I turned down to starboard, and he turned down behind me. I am uncertain as to whether he attacked. He fell in flames just south west of Nijmegen, and although the pilot came clear before it hit the ground, he was killed."

The most radical high-performance aircraft put into service by the Luftwaffe was the Me 163 Komet rocket-powered fighter, although it's success was limited. Jack Bromfield saw one attack his bomber formation.

"I saw a Messerschmitt 163 Komet climb up and there was a Lancaster, we were only 200 yards apart. We saw this thing go up, you could see the trail from the rocket. I thought we were the prime target, he's coming for us. But he picked on the wrong man, instead of picking on us – we only had .303 machine guns. The Lancaster had the rose turret with .5s and hit him at 600 yards, and he just blew up. Lucky to hit him; coming straight down at you there's no deflection. Had he picked on us it might have been different. The effective range of our machine guns was only 400 yards."

The only other jet-powered aircraft to enter service was the Arado Ar 234, used both as a light bomber and as a reconnaissance aircraft, albeit in quite small numbers. Bill Musgrave tried in vain to intercept these in his Spitfire as they flew reconnaissance missions over the Italian Front.

"At Falconara we were doing stand-by duty; we had four aircraft down at one end of the runway, all pilots ready. We were scrambled several times, nothing much but that was the time I saw the Ar 234s. (*Arado Ar 234 reconnaissance machines operated in small numbers from northern Italy by Kommando Sommer during March 1945.*) We could see the vapour trail. A Spit could climb pretty fast, but they were up at 36,000 feet."

The V-2 threat also had to be tackled through major bombing efforts against the production and launch facilities. 'Punchy' Powell flew his longest, and final mission of the war against one such target.

"We were escorting bombers to Peenemünde to bomb the plants producing the V-2 rockets. We flew out mostly over water along the Frisian Islands up towards Norway/Sweden and across Denmark, then over Peenemünde. I logged six hours and fifteen minutes on that flight and landed on fumes."

In addition to the jets, the Luftwaffe also began to receive the Focke-Wulf Ta 152, a highly advanced development of the Fw 190D. It was one of the fastest piston-engined fighters ever produced, but in insufficient numbers to make any significant impact. Knight's Cross holder Oberfeldwebel Willi Reschke had flown the Me 109 and Fw 190 including service with Wilde Sau units JG301 and JG302 and thought very highly of the Ta 152 when JG301 started to receive them in January 1945.

"I flew in the defence of the Reich. At first I flew the Me 109 and later moved to the Fw 190. The Me 109 had a very high boost pressure and had better performance than the Fw 190 above 5,000 metres. The Fw 190s were themselves very easy to fly and were aerodynamically superior to the Me 109 up to 5,000 metres. At heights above 5,000 metres, the performance dropped off, as well as the vertical speed. During that time I was shot down twice in an Me 109, the first time by a P-51 during the first combat flight, and the second time during take-off at Neubiberg near Munich. The other six aircraft I was shot down in were during defence against four-motor aircraft.

Willi was first shot down on 24 August 1944 while flying Me 109 G-6 White 10, just after claiming a B-24 near Neuhaus. On the second occasion on 29 August, he was attacked by another Me 109, and had to force-land near Ungarisch-Brod.

"The Ta 152 was far superior to the Me 109 and the Fw 190 in all domains. We could take off within 300 metres, the acceleration was so great that the pilot was pressed firmly into the seat. It was a bit difficult to manage the first take-off. The rate of climb was a fantastic 15 metres per second up to 7,000 meters and the maximum altitude was 14,000 metres, which was not reachable by any other aircraft. The performance achieved was brand new, with a speed of 750 kilometres an hour, and the increased wing span, by five metres, allowed very sharp turns.

"Due to the small number of aircraft, only the staff schwarm of JG 301 was equipped with the Ta 152, and in all the meetings with opposing fighters I never had any problems. The air combat at 50 metres against the Tempest, or the Yak 9 was, in comparison to preceding aircraft, quite easy to handle. The Ta 152 was the best life insurance you could have in the last weeks of the war."

On 14 April 1945, Willi shot down Tempest V SN141/SA-U of 486 Squadron,

Hopsten, flown by Warrant Officer O J Mitchell, who was killed. His last victories were two Yak 9s on 24 April 1945, three minutes apart. In total he flew about seventy missions and scored twenty-seven victories.

The Luftwaffe night fighter force continued to be dominated by the Me 110 and Ju 88, with small numbers of more advanced types including a variant of the Me 262 and the Heinkel He 219. Of the established types, both Heinz Rökker and Peter Spoden preferred the Ju 88, as Peter explained.

> "I never got to fly the He 219. I flew the Me 110 from 1943 to 1944, and the Ju 88 from summer 1944 to the end. I preferred the '88, it had more power and four crew-members but other fellows like Schnaufer and Johnen stayed with the '110. A few 219s were in NJG 1 in the Netherlands and we heard in the last months that she was quite good, nose-wheel, pretty fast and had ejection seats."

Hauptmann Wilhelm Johnen KC flew with NJGs 1, 5 and 6 and ended the war with thirty-three victories.

THE GERMAN SURRENDER

The final operations by Bomber Command took place on the night of 2/3 May 1945 and the final loss suffered was a 199 Squadron Halifax shot down by Oberleutnant Fritz Brandts of NJG.3. The scale of air operations had already declined significantly as the Luftwaffe ran out of petrol, pilots and bases, with many aircrew flying their last operations in April. For the Germans, the emotions were a mixture of relief that it was all over, but despair for the fate of the country they had fought so hard to defend.

Heinz Rökker:

> "My last flight was on 15 April, it was an attack coming from the north. We got the order to start and we had the direction but after half an hour we got the order to land. In the meantime the bombing was finished. We were only a short range from England to here and we thought they would fly to another town, so we saw nothing.
>
> "When peace was declared I was in Schleswig-Holstein in the north of Germany, English soldiers were there and we had no problems with them. We were on our airfield and they landed there, Lancaster and some other aeroplanes. The first time we had seen such a machine on the ground."

Norbert Hannig:

> "Our wing commanders said on 8 May, 'We got the order that the war is over'. Each pilot could get his aircraft and fly back home, so you got

an Me 262 as a last present. I came back from the last mission and got my luggage from the barracks. As I returned to my aircraft there was another guy sitting in and he said: 'There is a motorcycle, it's mine, you can have it, OK?' I had no choice, I set off west on the motorcycle, but the roads were so jammed with troops and vehicles that I could not make much progress. I came to an airfield and decided to try and find a 'plane. There was a row of Storches and they all had the keys in them. I had not flown one before but I got in, started up and took off heading west. My last flight was with a Fieseler Storch on the 9th, flying west to surrender to the Americans."

Peter Spoden:

"Herbert Lütje was Geschwaderkommodore in NJG 6. He told me to defend the airport at Munich-Schleissheim in a ground battle against US troops on 28 April 1945, which I did not. It was the best decision I ever made."

For the victorious allied forces, initial euphoria soon gave way to concerns about how to cope with occupying a devastated country, and thoughts about what the future might hold for airmen who had only ever known war in their adult lives up to that point.

Alexei Valyaev:

"On 19 April '45 I made my last sortie; we blew up a fuel depot. I heard shooting from the aerodrome. I ran outside, and saw soldiers, that were shooting in the air. 'What are you doing?' 'Commander! Haven't you heard? We won! The war is over!' So I also started shooting! Victory!"

Benedikt Kardopoltsev:

"When we got to Germany, for about a week there was some roughness going on – people avenging the deaths of their relatives or comrades and so on, but then everybody relaxed. There is no sense making war on children and old people. In Poland it was completely different. We came as friends, but they met us like enemies. In Germany people would come looking for jobs, and we would feed them in our canteen – it was not allowed, but why not, after all?

"In the middle of the night we heard shooting. We shouted: 'What happened?' War has ended!' So we started saluting ourselves. In the morning we were gathered together and told that shooting with handguns was understandable, but our mechanics had started up the engines on fighters and started saluting with cannons, and that was intolerable!"

Grigory Avenesov:

"My life was not too happy after the war. I had to leave flying for teaching in the military navy academy in Leningrad. War was clear and easy, and life is difficult! But war is so stupid, it should never happen again. I do not understand what happens nowadays, why are there so many wars still going on?"

Mikhail Pomorov:

"We were at Kölberg, in Polish territory; here the war ended. It was something inexpressible. At four o'clock in the morning I was in my room with Boris Nazarov, he was supposed to fly with Dmitry Shabashov on a mission. When we heard about the war's end, he jumped through the window and started shooting, 'War is over!' Boris flew and was killed on 9 May. Germans were fleeing with their goods to Switzerland and Denmark, but did not miss a chance to shoot at our 'planes, even though the war was over."

Yuri Khukhrikov:

"The last two sorties were on 8 May. The first sortie was at 10:00, and the second around 14:00, to the Zemland peninsula. They refuelled us for the third sortie. We taxied, and waited for the order. The chief of staff Nikolai Ivanovich Borkov ran to us, 'Lura, taxi back. It's over!' We turned off our engines. The war was over! I had flown eighty-four sorties."

The RAF was already involved in flying food into the continent, especially Operation Manna for the Dutch people, and returning liberated POWs to the UK. Bob Rees:

"In my log for 8 May: 'VE-Day announced. Europe 'en Fete'; 575 Squadron still airborne.' For myself and many others, 8 May did not mean that we could quit. Take off, 07:00 with nursing orderly as one of the crew. To Blackbushe, then to B.152 (Fassbürg) with jeep and American paratroops. In the afternoon we were at B.156 (Lüneburg Heath) and went from there to B.56 (Brussels) with fifteen casualties, sixteen ex POWs and three passengers (a full load). A night-stop at Brussels. We went on to B.154 (Rheinsehlen) with navy freight – three tons of Irish stew. On the following day back to B.56 with ex POWs; then to B.106 and back to Blackbushe with captured enemy radar, plus escorts, landing at night, and back to Broadwell in the early hours of 10 May.

"On the 11th the round was resumed, with serum for the Dutch, Irish stew for the navy, passengers and freight from place to place, until in the early hours of the 13th, back to wing with thirty-one ex POWs.

At wing they were led off to be dusted with DDT. There were two WVS women standing by, one said· 'Oh, look at those poor men, how they must have suffered. Their hair has gone quite white!'"

Bill Musgrave:

"After finishing on the squadron I was posted to Desert Air Force training flight in Sinello. We had Mustangs, Spits and Kittyhawks; I was on the Spitfire flight. I was there for about two to three months, and the war packed up. We were told to fly our Spitfires out to Brindisi and leave them there. As soon as we switched the engines off, oxy-acetylene onto the wings and cut them off. Seeing some of the Spits flown by famous pilots, a number of German emblems on them, it was tough."

Eric Burke:

"I was on leave in Florence on VE-Day. We moved up to Aviano, and spent some time there that summer. At the end of that they said you're either going to Palestine, where there was a bit of trouble, or to Greece. There was a civil war pending in the Balkans. In the event we went to Greece for about a year, then most of us came home for de-mob."

There was obvious relief for the many thousands of servicemen still held in POW camps, some of whom had been behind the wire for over five years. Norm Rosholt:

"We woke up one morning and our guards were gone. They went west to be captured by the allies rather than the Russians. The camp sent out a search party to find the Russians and tell them that there were 10,000 hungry prisoners. The Russians herded their meat on the hoof and they cut out 500 animals and herded them over to a peninsula in the Baltic Sea. They had cows, horses, pigs, goats, sheep and anything they could contain. We ate well, no steaks but plenty of hash. We also found a warehouse full of Red Cross parcels, at least a million.
        "After ten days the 8th Air Force flew in and hauled us to Rouen in France for delousing and clean clothes. After spending a month at Lucky Strike on the coast of France we boarded a ship for home."

THE JAPANESE SURRENDER

The war against Japan continued for a further three months after VE-Day, before the two atom bomb attacks precipitated the Japanese surrender. As in Europe, the air forces soon changed to relief flying and the repatriation of prisoners. Jack Routley was present in Tokyo Bay for the formalities.

"The atom-bombing of Hiroshima and Nagasaki led to the Japanese surrender. We were in Tokyo Bay for the surrender ceremony in USS *Missouri* on 2 September. There was a large contingent of American battleships, aircraft carriers, cruisers and destroyers. There was the British Pacific Fleet containing Australian, Canadian and New Zealand cruisers and destroyers. That was a mighty armada in Tokyo Bay, which was there by MacArthur's intent, to show these guys what they were up against, in case they were thinking of having another go. I've never seen so much ironmongery.

"We had to return to the lease-lend agreement, the Hellcats that we had in our squadron. Our aircraft had to be ditched in deep waters, and so they were unceremoniously dumped somewhere off Australia. The aircraft carrier was returned to the United States and made into saucepans or something."

Jimmy Greening:

"On 2 June 1945 the squadron moved to Maydown in Northern Ireland to prepare for service in the Pacific with the Tiger Force, and while we were there we suffered our only loss during my time, when a Barracuda had engine failure and ditched in the north-east Atlantic while searching for rogue U-boats. Fortunately, the crew managed to get into their dinghy and we were successful in locating them and directing a lifeboat-carrying Warwick to them.

"I was sent to 758(B) Squadron, the Naval Advanced Instrument Flying School at Hinstock in mid July 1945 as a prelude to what I hoped would be twin conversion – I had my eye on the coming Sea Hornet. In fact I only did four days flying in Oxfords and went back to Maydown, since the squadron was embarking for Trincomalee in Ceylon for the planned attack on Singapore. While on embarkation leave, the atomic bombs were dropped, so their ship never sailed."

Norman Wilson:

"In September 1945 we carried press members to Singapore. On our arrival at Seletar flying boat station, and being possibly the very first there, we were transported ashore by a Japanese crew boat. The banks of the base were lined with allied prisoners who had been released from such places as Changi jail. We had little food on board but gladly distributed it. A Japanese officer wanted to surrender his Samurai sword to me. Stupidly I refused it and told him to report to the docks where Lord Mountbatten would shortly arrive.

"The task of the press was to photograph the first aircraft (a Liberator) arriving following the surrender, and the arrival of the Royal Navy bringing Lord Mountbatten to take the official surrender ceremony on 12 September. We participated in the flypast for that occasion.

284

Over the next period we flew many officials into Singapore and, very satisfyingly, ex prisoners back to Ceylon for medical attention."

John Caird:

"We were put into service dropping supplies to the POW camps dotted throughout Indo China and Burma, and to supply the allied prisoners who had suffered under the Japanese. On one camp they had been told to clear a strip so we could drop supplies and apparently had worked day and night for three days to do that. They waved excitedly as we went low and pushed out the sacks of supplies. One could only imagine how glad they were to get some food and medical supplies."

Lancaster WOp Harry Brent:

"VJ-Day came and we were given leave. Paddy said goodbye after an almighty and tearful night out, and the old crew split up. I was to help form a squadron for Transport Command, our bomb aimer was now training as a steward on Yorks. The gunners were said to be scraping spuds somewhere and we were all alone and feeling like the condemned."

Bill Musgrave:

"I came back to Cairo where we had to await our next move. So waiting to fly back, and on 15 August it was VJ-Day and it was my twenty-first birthday. We had a Rhodesian club in Cairo; it was quite a party!"

AFTER THE WAR

There still remained a host of tasks to complete before any substantial rundown of the allied air arms could get underway. John King was involved in flying troops to Norway, which still contained a substantial German military presence.

"We were called to briefing and told the only place in Europe that wasn't controlled by the allies was Norway. The Germans were still in control. So the whole of 38 Group was tasked with taking troops there, to land at every airport in Norway to take control so that more troops could be flown in.

"With all the Germans and all the troops there, there would be no accommodation for the aircrew, we would have to sleep in the aircraft. We went over Oslo down low, to tell the people that we were on our way. That was quite an experience, seeing the people in the street waving, we could even see the German soldiers standing in the street.

"We got to Gardermoen, landed, and were met by Germans. The skipper said, 'Fancy a trip to Oslo? I've been having a snoop round and I found a shed. There was a wagon in there, full of petrol, keys in it, it looked as though someone was ready to make a getaway. If we nick it we'll take a drive into Oslo.' So we did; people were cheering us and waving and shaking hands as we drove through, and the Germans were standing there watching. We got to this hotel, we walked into the dining room, and it was full of German officers and their girlfriends; all in their dress uniforms. It was the main hotel for the German officers. There were all different colours; black, SS, Luftwaffe and the place went as though someone had switched it off when we walked in, in scruffy battledress. Everybody was looking at us and we knew they were talking about us.

"We asked the waiter who they were. He said: 'That lot down there in the corner in civvies, you don't want to get mixed with them, they're the Gestapo and secret police.' He brought us a meal. There was a piece of steak with vegetables; we asked what it was, and he told us: 'Whale meat, that's all we've got. There's no other meat, the Germans have taken it all.' When we got up, the whole place went quiet again. As we came out a jeep pulled up, an army officer jumped out, and said, 'What the hell are you doing in there? That's off limits. It's German officers, no-one's allowed in there, even I can't go in. For Christ's sake get out of here, get back to Gardermoen, before anybody sees you.'"

For many others the end of hostilities brought about an abrupt change to their lives. Some simply ceased training, many aircrew were moved to non-flying tasks while they waited their turn for demobilisation, which frequently meant a loss of rank. The simultaneous release back into civilian life of very large numbers of servicemen was not feasible, and many found they had to wait many months or even years for their 'number to come up'. After release, the problem than was deciding what to do with the rest of their lives.

Bill Musgrave:

"Got back early September, and we were demobbed by October. But what was tragic towards the end, the new chaps who were coming through just recently qualified, some of the pilots recently appointed as pilot officers, they arrived and they were told, 'sorry, your career in the RAF has finished. What do you want to do? Do you want to be a bottle-washer or what?' That was terribly sad and that shouldn't have been allowed. They were just chucked out."

Henry Payne:

"I vowed to my wife, while the war was on I would not marry her while I was flying. I said I've seen enough widows created and I wasn't going to leave another one. I did go for an interview as a test pilot in 1947 with Geoffrey de Havilland, and I was accepted and offered a job, but my wife said: 'No, you're not!' So I went back to engineering.

"It was agreed at the end of the war that we would meet once a year as a crew. We had reunions for twenty-five years, but they've all gone now; I suppose the skipper should be the last to leave the ship! We had a very good crew, they were wonderful."

Peter Green:

"When I finished my tour, it was January '45; they didn't want any aircrew. I went on flying control at Westwood, Peterborough, (7 *SFTS Anson, Master, Harvard, Spitfire*) I went to Calveley from there, in Cheshire. (*11 P[AFU] Harvards*) It was nice there, a lovely part of the country, flying Harvards, with French and Belgian pilots. Then I finished up for demob at Kirton-in-Lindsey in Lincolnshire."

John Caird:

"It was going to be very difficult to adapt to civilian life after all these years. No-one can really appreciate how we felt. Nice to be home, but then what? Whilst I had been away, my prewar friends had either been killed, got married, or left the area."

Jack Biggs:

"I had a very pleasant career in the air force, it wasn't mundane. Some of these bomber people, they only knew their immediate crew, they didn't know a lot more about the rest on the station. But when you're on a singles unit, you know most of the pilots, you were all together. So you were more of a family on a singles unit."

Ted Mercer:

"In the end I was on 44 Squadron as squadron instructor, and we were mucking about doing nothing in particular; taking ground crew around looking at the Ruhr, going to Italy to take troops back. I opted for another instructor's course at Finningley (*Bomber Command Instructors' School*), hoping that I would be an instructor on Lancs again. But no, it was back to the Wimpy and I finished up at Silverstone (*17 OTU*), but it did me a little bit of good because I got my instructor's category regraded up to A2, which helped me later in civil flying, which I did until I retired at the age of eighty."

Jack Booth:

"I finished on the squadron, and went up to Kirkham on a crash equipment course; I was posted to Riccall after that. (*1332 CU Yorks and*

Stirlings). I spent most of my time playing table tennis in the hangar. Someone came up to me and said, 'the adjutant needs to see you, you're posted'. When I got back I said, 'Anybody know where 229 Group is?' One chap said, 'Last time I heard of 229 Group that was in Delhi in India'. I said, 'Don't be so bloody stupid, I've just come back from France!' He was right though. In a very short while I was out there and I finished up at Dum-Dum in India. I was supernumerary for a while, and then I ran the station for a couple of months until we got another equipment officer out from England. I came back the hard way, on a Yankee Liberty ship."

Jack Bromfield:

"After the Russians had liberated the camp, this horde of B-17s appeared and that's what I flew home in. I landed at Ford, near Littlehampton. They took us to the railway station, under guard; because they were frightened we might scarper; they locked us in the carriages where you couldn't get the windows down.

"We got into Cosford and there were WAAFs who looked after us. Everybody was lousy, we were all standing there scratching like chimpanzees! They took us to a big hangar; we were supposed to chuck all our clothing in an incinerator. Well, no way were they having my operational battledress, which had been with me for so long; I just bundled it up. I'd still got the pants on that I was shot down in; I hadn't changed, I hadn't had a bath or a shower. I went to work in that old battledress until about 1950.

"We were sent home on eight weeks leave, on double rations, and extra eggs and milk; they looked after us well. We were sent on a POW repatriation course at Wittering. There was a chap there who had terrible nightmares every night. He'd been on Stirlings and I think there must have been a fire, we all felt really sorry for him.

"I had to report to Melksham, 12 School of Technical Training. I did about six weeks training there and they taught us to drive; that was hilarious. All these ex aircrew blokes on night convoys and all these three-tonners parked up outside the pubs. I finished at the beginning of '47, just after New Year's. I'd had a year and a bit swanning around in this truck. By that time my WO was through. I didn't think I'd get it, because an edict came out telling us all to strip down to sergeant. The groupie was an RFC pilot, and he said: 'You earned that, you leave it where it is.' So I got demobbed as a WO.

"It's all such a long time ago now. Our mid-upper gunner, Gerry Marion, is still alive in Canada and we keep in touch from time to time. The other day he came on the 'phone and said to me 'you sound just the same now as you did on the intercom'."

Pete Brothers:

> "I did a speaking tour in the States with Günther Rall, 'Dolfo' Galland and 'Mackie' Steinhoff. Mackie was the chap who had his eyelids burnt off flying an Me 262. He was brought to Halton a couple of years after the war, and they grafted new eyelids on for him, so he was deeply grateful to the RAF. Mackie, I reckoned, was one of the few brains, of the German air force. Dear old Dolfo Galland was a bloody good aviator, yes no question, but he knew he was, which was sad. But Günther was a nice, quiet, relaxed chap, I liked Günther.
>
> "At the end of the war we sent an Anson over to Germany to grab some of their leading lights, including a Stuka chap, Rudel. (*Oberst Hans Ulrich Rudel, the highest number of operations of any Stuka pilot.*) He'd got half a left leg still swathed in bloody bandages. He insisted on walking around with a crutch, going round the peri-track every morning to keep fit. He said: 'I want you to put your two finest fighter pilots at 2,000 feet over Tangmere airfield, and give me a Spitfire, and I will shoot them both down and fly home.' Talk about arrogance!"

Wing Commander Branse Burbridge DFC and bar, DSO and bar, US DFC was the RAF's top scoring night fighter pilot, gaining twenty-one victories in ten months flying Havocs and Mosquitoes with 85 Squadron. A deeply religious man, Branse had struggled with his conscience before deciding that the war was a just cause. When he left the service in 1945, both he and his navigator Bill Skelton entered the Christian ministry.

> "I feel all of us were confronted with a sense of, 'What are we going to do now?' after the war. We wanted to get into something worthwhile or something we were doing before the war took place."

The final words come from Leonid Kulakov, who summed up the feeling of the vast majority of aircrew of both sides towards their opponents.

> "If I met a German today who I fought against at Leningrad, of course I would talk to him. Why not? He was following orders. Back then, I would not have lifted a hand, of course because he was an enemy. In regards to their pilots, we did not have a bad opinion of them. We thought of them as professionals. Why? Because they frequently shot us down. Those who were not watchful they shot down."

HEROES ALL

The moon is full, the night air keen
It was the time when people sleep
As I stroll past the village inn, a light shines from within
Through the frosted glass I peer
My old eyes see young men in flying gear
They're laughing, joking, these were the Lancaster crews of yesteryear
Having fun over their glass of beer
My heart beats fast, there's Bud, Danny – many others from the past
I tap the window almost breaking the glass
No ghostly figure gives me even a glance, they're all enjoying their
songs and dance.
My steps continue towards the village church
Where later these young airmen will go to sleep, in peace, within their
keep
Now I've returned the circle's complete, each day I visit their beds so
neat
I'm very old, now alone, time is short
Was it only yesterday that we were comrades all?
For me now death is no fear
One evening as you pass the inn, glance through the window
You may see Danny, Bud, and me, and the boys within having fun
Over a glass of beer
Later back to the church we'll go
Singing the songs we used to know
Then I will be happy to join them in their keep
Enjoying a long and peaceful sleep.

Derrick 'Dixie' Dean
In memory of the crews of 207 Squadron Bottesford, and those now rest-
ing in the grounds of St. Mary's Church

REFERENCES

[1] www.hazzardonsport.com

[2] *Laurels for Prinz Wittgenstein* Werner P Roell, Independent Books, 1994.

[3] *Royal Air Force St. Athan, A History 1938-1988*, S J Bond, Service Publishing Services, 1988

[4] *Airborne For The Duration* Eric Barfoot, The Book Guild, 2004.

[5] *Ghost Stations*, Bruce Barrymore Halpenny, Merlin Books, 1986

[6] *Echoes in the Sky – An Anthology of Aviation Verse From Two World Wars* Ronald Dixon Blandford Press, 1982.

[7] *Speech by Winston Churchill to the House of Commons 21 August 1940*

[8] www.raf.mod.uk

[9] *Echoes in the Sky – An Anthology of Aviation Verse From Two World Wars* Ibid.

[10] *Over The Hump*, 2nd Lieutenant J D Broughel

[11] *Echoes in the Sky – An Anthology of Aviation Verse From Two World Wars* Ibid.

[12] *Echoes in the Sky – An Anthology of Aviation Verse From Two World Wars* Ibid.

[13] *Echoes in the Sky – An Anthology of Aviation Verse From Two World Wars* Ibid.

[14] 299 Squadron website

ABBREVIATIONS

AA	Anti-Aircraft
AB	Air Base
AC	Aircraftman
AC2	Aircraftman Second Class
ACM	Air Chief Marshal
ACRC	AirCrew Reception Centre
AE	Air Efficiency Award
AFC	Air Force Cross
AFCE	Automatic Flight Control Equipment
AFU	Advanced Flying Unit
AHQ	Air Headquarters
AI	Airborne Interception
Air Com	Air Commodore
AM	Air Medal
AMO	Aircraft Maintenance Order
ANS	Air Navigation School
AOC	Air Officer Commanding
AOC-in-C	Air Officer Commanding in Chief
ASV	Air to Surface Vessel
ATA	Air Transport Auxiliary
ATC	Air Training Corps
AVM	Air Vice-Marshal
AWOL	Absent Without Leave
BG	Bomb Group
B&GS	Bombing and Gunnery School
BPD	Base Personnel Depot
BVAF	Burma Volunteer Air Force
CAM	Catapult Aircraft Merchantman
Capt	Captain
CB	Companion of the Bath
CBE	Commander of the British Empire
CDR	Commander
CFI	Chief Flying Instructor
CFS	Central Flying School
C-in-C	Commander in Chief
CO	Commanding Officer
COL	Colonel
Cpl	Corporal
CU	Conversion Unit
DATS	Dominion Air Training Scheme
DDT	Dichlorodiphenyltrichloroethane (an insecticide)
DFC	Distinguished Flying Cross
DFM	Distinguished Flying Medal
DI	Daily Inspection
DR	Dead Reckoning
DSO	Distinguished Service Order
DZ	Drop Zone

ABBREVIATIONS

EATS	Empire Air Training Scheme
EFTS	Elementary Flying Training School
ENT	Elementary Navigation Training
ERFTS	Elementary and Reserve Flying Training School
ETA	Estimated Time of Arrival
ETO	European Theatre of Operations
FAA	Fleet Air Arm
FAB	Fugasnaya Aviatsionnaya Bomba
FG	Fighter Group
Flg Off	Flying Officer
Flt Lt	Flight Lieutenant
Flt Sgt	Flight Sergeant
FRAeS	Fellow of the Royal Aeronautical Society
FS	Fighter Squadron
FTS	Flying Training School
Fw	Feldwebel
GCA	Ground Controlled Approach
Gp Capt	Group Captain
GuIAP	Guards Fighter Air Regiment
HCU	Heavy Conversion Unit
HF	High Frequency
Hg	Mercury
HM	His Majesty's
HMS	His Majesty's Ship
Hptmn	Hauptmann
HQ	Headquarters
HSU	Hero of the Soviet Union
IAD	Istrebitel'nyi Aviatsionnyi Diviziya (Fighter Air Division)
IAP	Istrebitel'nyi Aviatsionnyi Polk (Fighter Air Regiment)
IAS	Indicated Air Speed
ID	Identification
IFF	Identification Friend or Foe
ITW	Initial Training Wing
JG	Jagdgeschwader
(J)LG	Jagd Lehrgeschwader
JV	Jagdverband
KBF	Red Banner Baltic Fleet
KC	Knight's Cross
KCB	Knight Commander of the Order of the Bath
LAC	Leading Aircraftman
LDV	Local Defence Volunteers
LoM	Legion of Merit
Lt	Lieutenant
MAVM	Medaglia d'Argento al Valor Militare
MBE	Member of the British Empire
MBVA	Medaglia di Bronzo al Valore Aeronautico
MBVM	Medaglie di Bronzo al Valor Militare
MF	Medium Frequency
Mm	Millimetre
MO	Medical Officer

293

Mph	Miles per Hour
MT	Motor Transport
MU	Maintenance Unit
NAAFI	Navy Army and Air Force Institutes
NCO	Non-Commissioned Officer
NFT	Night Flying Test
NJG	Nachtjagdgeschwader
OADU	Overseas Aircraft Despatch Unit
OAPU	Overseas Aircraft Preparation Unit
OBE	Order of the British Empire
Oberst	Oberstleutnant
Oblt	Oberleutnant
Ofw	Oberfeldwebel
OL	Order of Lenin
OPW	Order of the Patriotic War
ORB	Operations Record Book
ORB	Order of the Red Banner
ORS	Order of the Red Star
OTU	Operational Training Unit
(P)AFU	Pilot Advanced Flying Unit
PFF	Pathfinder Force
PH	Purple Heart
Plt Off	Pilot Officer
PNB	Pilot / Navigator / Air Bomber
PO	Pilot Officer
POW	Prisoner of War
PRU	Photographic Reconnaissance Unit
PVO	Provito Vozdushnaya Oborona
RAAF	Royal Australian Air Force
RAF	Royal Air Force
RASC	Royal Army Service Corps
RCAF	Royal Canadian Air Force
RCN	Royal Canadian Navy
RCN(R)	Royal Canadian Navy Reserve
RFC	Royal Flying Corps
RFU	Refresher Flying Unit
RLM	Reichsluftfahrtminister
RM	Royal Marines
RNZNVR	Royal New Zealand Navy Volunteer Reserve
Rpm	Revolutions per minute
RRAF	Royal Rhodesian Air Force
R/T	Radio Telephony
RTU	Replacement Training Unit
RW	Receiving Wings
SA	Sturmabteilung
SAS	Special Air Service
SBA	Standard Beam Approach
SFTS	Service Flying Training School
Sgt	Sergeant
ShKAS	Shpitalny-Komaritski Aviatsionni Skorostrelny

ABBREVIATIONS

SKC	Storekeeper Chief
SOE	Special Operations Executive
SofTT	School of Technical Training
Sqn	Squadron
Sqn Ldr	Squadron Leader
SP	Service Police
SS	Schutzstaffel
SS	Silver Star
S/Sgt	Staff Sergeant
Sub Lt	Sub Lieutenant
TAF	Tactical Air Force
Uffz	Unteroffizier
US	United States
U/S	Unserviceable
USAAF	United States Army Air Force
USAF	United States Air Force
USN	United States Navy
USS	United States Ship
U/T	Under Training
VE	Victory in Europe
VIP	Very Important Person
VJ	Victory in Japan
VR	Volunteer Reserve
VVS	Voenno-Vozdushnie Sili (Soviet Air Force)
WAAF	Womens' Auxiliary Air Force
Wg Cdr	Wing Commander
WO	Warrant Officer
WOM	Wireless Operator Mechanic
WOp/AG	Wireless Operator / Air Gunner
WRNS	Womens' Royal Naval Service
W/T	Wireless Telegraphy
WVS	Womens' Voluntary Service
ZAP	Zapasnnoy Aviatsionni Polk (Reserve Air Regiment)

SELECT BIBLIOGRAPHY

2nd Tactical Air Force Christopher Shores & Chris Thomas Classic Publications, 2004

Aces High Christopher Shores & Clive Williams Grub Street, 1994

Action Stations various authors

Airborne For The Duration Eric Barfoot DFC Book Guild Ltd, 2004

A Real Good War Sam Halpert Phoenix, 2001

Ausbildung und Einsatz eines Nachtjagers im II. Weltkrieg Heinz Rökker

Combat Codes Vic Flintham & Andrew Thomas Pen and Sword, 2008

Confounding the Reich Martin W Bowman & Tom Cushing Patrick Stevens Ltd, 2008

Each Tenacious – A History of No. 99 Squadron Squadron Leader A G Edgerley 1993

Echoes in the Sky – An Anthology of Aviation Verse From Two World Wars Ronald Dixon Blandford Press, 1982

Enemy in the Dark Peter Spoden Cerberus Publishing Ltd 2003

Footprints on the Sands of Time Oliver Clutton-Brock Grub Street, 2003

Ghost Stations Bruce Barrymore Halpenny Merlin Books, 1986

History of the German Night Fighter Force Gebhard Aders Crécy Publishing, 1992

Honour the Air Forces Michael Maton Token Publishing, 2004

Jagdgeschwader 301/302 "Wilde Sau" Willi Reschke Schiffer, 2004

Luftwaffe Fighter Ace Norbert Hannig Grub Street, 2006

Malta: The Spitfire Year Christopher Shores & Brian Cull, with Nicola Malizia Grub Street Publishing, 1992

Men of the Battle of Britain Kenneth G Wynn Gliddon Books, 1989

Nachtjagd War Diaries Dr Theo E W Boiten & Roderick J Mackenzie Red Kite, 2008

Observers and Navigators and Other Non-pilot Aircrew in the RFX, RNAS and RAF: Wing Commander C G Jefford MBE BA RAF (Ret'd) The Crowood Press, 2001

RAF Bomber Command Losses W R Chorley Midland Publishing 1998

RAF Flying Training and Support Units since 1912 Ray Sturtivant Air Britain Historians Ltd, 2007

RAF Squadrons Wing Commander C G Jefford MBE BA RAF (Ret'd) The Crowood Press, 2001

Royal Air Force St. Athan, A History 1938-1988 S J Bond Services Publishing, 1989

Stalin's Falcons Tomas Polak & Christopher Shores Grub Street Publishing, 1998

Stars & Bars Frank Olynyk Grub Street Publishing, 1995

The Battle of France Then and Now Peter D Cornwell After the Battle, 2008

The Bomber Command War Diaries Martin Middlebrook & Chris Everitt   Midland Publishing, 1998

The K File – The Royal Air Force of the 1930s James J Halley MBE Air Britain Historians Ltd, 1996

The Rise and Fall of the German Air Force Air Ministry, 1948

The Source Book of the RAF Ken Delve Airlife Publishing Ltd, 1994

The Squadrons of the Fleet Air Arm Ray Sturtivant & Theo Balance Air Britain Historians Ltd, 1994

The Squadrons of the Royal Air Force & Commonwealth James J Halley MBE Air Britain Historians Ltd, 1989

War Prizes Phil Butler Midland Publishing, 2006

Wings & A Prayer Gillian R Warson, 2007

INDEX

PLACE NAMES
Abbeville, France: 245, 258
Abbotsford, British Columbia: 29
Abbotsinch, Renfrewshire: 54
Abingdon, Berkshire: 137
Aboukir, Egypt: 135
Abu Sueir, Egypt: 204
Accra, Gold Coast: 242
Acklington, Northumberland: 77, 257
Addu Attol, Maldives: 135
Adriatic Sea: 207
Agartala, India: 210
Alberta, Canada: 29
Alboran, Morocco: 141
Aldeburgh, Suffolk: 273
Aldenham, Hertfordshire: 267
Aldergrove, Antrim: 30
Alexandria, Egypt: 146, 196, 197, 202, 205
Alipore, India: 209, 215
Allahabad, India: 265
Alness, Ross and Cromarty: 134
Alten Fjord, Norway: 117
Ambala, India: 255
Amman, Jordan: 241
Amriya, Egypt: 205
Angle, Pembrokeshire: 41
Annan, Dumfriesshire: 31, 257
Arakan, Burma: 209
Arbroath, Angus: 54, 55
Arcadia, Florida: 12-13
Archangel, Russia: 51, 181, 182, 184
Arctic Circle: 139
Arctic Ocean: 182
Arnhem, Holland: 2, 259, 273, 274
Ascension Island: 242
Ashbourne, Derbyshire: 27
Aston Down, Gloucestershire: 256, 257
Atcham, Shropshire: 86
Atlantic Ocean: 12, 137, 140, 142, 243, 265
Aunay-sur-Odon, France: 101
Aviano, Italy; 50, 206, 283
Aylesbury, Buckinghamshire: 9
Azores: 213, 214
Azov, Russia: 51
Babbacombe, Devon: 5, 12
Baginton, Warwickshire: 78, 256
Bahrain, Persian Gulf: 135
Balashov, Russia: 19
Balearic Islands: 61
Ballyhalbert, County Down: 80, 217
Baltic Sea: 131, 143, 151, 168, 283
Bari, Italy: 240

Barrackpore, India: 217
Barth, Germany: 131
Barton-le-Clay, Bedfordshire: 261
Bassingbourn, Cambridgeshire: 111-114
Bataysk, Russia: 19
Bayeaux, France: 126
Bay of Bengal: 209
Bay of Biscay: 140, 142
Beachy Head, Kent: 80, 106
Bedford, Bedfordshire: 8
Beelitz, Germany: 16
Belorussia: 18, 176
Belsen, Germany: 130
Belvedere, Rhodesia: 47
Benghazi, Libya: 201, 203
Benina, Libya: 206
Benson, Oxfordshire: 29, 258, 259
Berlin, Germany: 16, 50, 95, 107, 108, 111, 114, 131, 162, 164, 223, 226, 232, 260
Bernburg, Germany: 44
Biarritz, France: 162
Bicester, Oxfordshire: 44
Biferno, Italy: 115
Biggin Hill, Kent: 2, 28, 59, 62, 63, 218, 276
Bilbeis, Egypt: 239
Binbrook, Lincolnshire: 40, 272
Bishop Rock, Isles of Scilly: 140
Bishop's Court, County Down: 36
Blackbushe, Hampshire: 282, 283
Blackpool, Lancashire: 10, 11
Black Sea: 144, 145
Bletchley, Buckinghamshire: 4
Blida, Algeria: 264
Bologna, Italy: 200
Bolt Head, Devon: 271
Bodney, Norfolk: 21, 86, 87, 269, 270
Bordeaux, France: 66
Boscombe Down, Wiltshire: 41, 251, 253, 254, 258
Bottesford, Leicestershire: 40, 290
Bournemouth, Hampshire: 30
Bramcote, Warwickshire: 142, 237
Brawdy, Pembrokeshire: 122
Bremen, Germany: 234
Brennan, Germany: 131
Bridgnorth, Shropshire: 8
Brindisi, Italy: 283
Broadwell, Oxfordshire: 283
Brough, Yorkshire: 23, 47
Brussels, Belgium: 127, 282, 283
Bulawayo, Rhodesia: 11, 32
Bushey, Hertfordshire: 103
Bushey Hall, Hertfordshire: 89

Caen, France: 147, 269
Cairo West, Egypt: 47, 135, 239, 241, 243, 285
Calcutta, India: 12, 208-210, 215, 216, 237
Caledonian Canal, Scotland: 118
Calveley, Cheshire: 287
Calvi, Corsica: 200
Cambridge, Cambridgeshire: 4, 75
Canary Islands: 141
Canterbury, Kent: 276
Cap de Le Havre, France: 146
Cap Griz Nez, France: 66
Cape Town, South Africa: 55
Cap Finisterre, France: 140
Capua, Italy: 19, 48
Carberry, Canada: 24
Cardiff, Glamorgan: 68
Cardington, Bedfordshire: 1, 8, 10, 12
Carew Cheriton, Pembrokeshire: 134
Carnaby, Yorkshire: 102, 103
Caron, Saskatchewan: 24
Casablanca, Morocco: 141
Castle Bromwich, Warwickshire: 263
Castle Camps, Cambridgeshire: 83
Castelvetrano, Sicily: 194
Cawnpore, India: 215
Charlottetown, Canada: 24
Châteaudun, France: 271
Châtellerault, France: 270
Chequers, Buckinghamshire: 10, 257
China Bay, Ceylon: 210, 211
Chittagong, East Bengal: 209, 210, 216, 217, 237
Chivenor, Devon: 9, 138, 140
Christchurch, Hampshire: 137, 253
Church Fenton, Yorkshire: 220
Cocos Islands: 135, 213, 215
Colney Heath, Hertfordshire: 104
Cologne, Germany: 94, 100, 122
Colombo, Ceylon: 217, 255
Coltishall, Norfolk: 77
Coningsby, Lincolnshire: 92, 93, 99, 101, 222
Copenhagen, Denmark: 273
Corsica: 11
Cosford, Shropshire: 67, 288
Cottesmore, Rutland: 93
Coventry, Warwickshire: 4
Cox's Bazaar, Bengal: 209, 210
Crail, Fife: 55, 56
Cranwell, Lincolnshire: 2, 10, 34, 35, 134

Craig Field, Alabama: 25
Crete, Greece: 146, 207, 246
Cross City, Florida: 57
Croydon, Surrey: 103, 119, 257, 266
Cuers, France; 200
Culmhead, Somerset: 2, 271, 275
Cyrenaica, Libya: 240
Dale Mabry Field, Florida: 56
Dalton, Yorkshire: 38, 41
Danzig, Poland: 156
Dar-es-Salaam, Tanzania: 135
Dar Sibena, Morocco: 141
Debden, Essex: 28, 87
Dekheila, Egypt: 196, 198, 203
Delhi, India: 240, 241, 255, 288
Deopham Green, Norfolk: 20, 21
Derna, Libya: 201, 205
Desford, Leicestershire: 29
Deventer, Holland: 272
Devil's Dyke, Cambridgeshire: 109
Diad'kov, Russia: 155
Diego Garcia, Solomon Islands: 135
Diepholz, Germany: 129, 130, 225
Dieppe, France: 82, 83
Dishforth, Yorkshire: 41
Doncaster, Yorkshire: 4, 65, 66
Dorval, Canada: 243, 264, 265
Dover, Kent: 76, 77, 276
Down Ampney, Wiltshire: 274
Dresden, Germany: 122, 123
Duisburg, Germany: 93, 94, 110
Dum Dum, India: 215-217, 288
Dunholme Lodge, Lincolnshire: 5, 94
Dunkirk, France: 28, 60, 66, 67, 272
Durban, South Africa: 11, 55, 198
Düsseldorf, Germany: 93
Duxford, Cambridgeshire: 10, 59, 75
Earls Colne, Essex: 42, 244
East Haven, Tayside: 55, 56
Edinburgh, Midlothian: 7
Eindhoven, Holland: 147, 272
El Alamein, Egypt: 197
El Aouina, Tunis: 30
El Ballah, Egypt: 39
Elbing, Prussia: 169
El Fasher, Sudan: 238
El Gamil, Egypt: 197, 198
El Obeid, Sudan: 238
Elizabeth City, North Carolina: 266
Elmas, Sicily: 195
Elmdon, Warwickshire: 54

Elstree, Hertfordshire: 103, 116, 240, 266, 267
Emmerich-Weisel bridges, Germany: 259
English Channel: 66, 70, 76, 79, 81, 100, 102, 106, 222
Epping, Essex: 217
Errol, Perthshire: 55
Eshott, Northumberland: 259
Essen, Germany: 16, 94
Euston, London: 4
Evanton, Ross and Cromarty: 35
Exeter, Devon: 271
Ezel, Latvia: 144
Fairford, Gloucestershire: 42
Fairwood Common, Glamorgan: 275
Falaise, France: 270, 272
Falconara, Italy: 278
Fallingbostel, Germany: 130
Farnborough, Hampshire: 254, 275
Faroe Islands, Denmark: 138, 139
Fassbürg, Germany: 282
Faversham, Kent: 276
Filton, Gloucestershire: 221, 253
Finchley, London: 98
Finmere, Buckinghamshire: 44
Finningley, Yorkshire: 4, 287
Firth of Forth, East Lothian: 137
Fiskerton, Lincolnshire: 4
Florence, Italy: 200, 283
Foggia, Italy: 264
Ford, Hampshire: 119, 288
Fort Hertz, Burma: 237
Fort Laury, French Equatorial Africa: 238
Foulsham, Norfolk: 118, 120, 222
Frankfurt, Germany: 122, 125, 126
Frisian Islands, Germany: 119, 234, 279
Fuka, Egypt: 205
Fürstenfeldbruck, Germany: 277
Gander, Canada: 213, 265
Gardermoen, Norway: 286
Gardner Field, Bakersfield: 56
Gatow, Berlin: 50
Ghedi, Italy: 50
Giancalis, Egypt: 47
Gibraltar: 9, 134, 140, 141, 191, 240, 242, 264
Gibraltar Farm, Bedfordshire: 245
Gillingham, Kent: 13
Gilze-Rijen, Holland: 115, 226
Gloucester, Gloucestershire: 253
Goose Bay, Canada: 213, 243, 244, 266
Gorelovo, Russia: 154

Gorkii, Russia: 176
Gosport, Hampshire: 13
Gourock, Renfrewshire: 12
Grangemouth, Stirling: 68
Grantham, Lincolnshire: 30
Graveley, Huntingdonshire: 6
Gravesend, Kent: 221, 270
Greenham Common, Berkshire: 262
Greenock, Renfrewshire: 266
Grenau, Germany: 178
Grimsby, Lincolnshire: 95, 229
Guinea Fowl, Rhodesia: 26
Gulf of Mexico: 26
Habbaniya, Iraq: 135, 241
Haddenham, Oxfordshire: 261, 262
Hague, The, Holland: 63
Halfpenny Green, Staffordshire: 34
Halifax, Nova Scotia: 12, 27
Halse / Huls, Germany: 97
Halton, Buckinghamshire: 48, 109, 251, 289
Hamble, Hampshire: 34
Hamburg, Germany: 111, 131, 232, 234
Hannover, Germany: 125, 222, 223
Harrowbeer, Devon: 271
Hartford Bridge, Hampshire: 44
Hastings, Sussex: 5
Havel, Germany: 50
Hawarden, Flintshire: 33
Heaton Park, Lancashire: 27, 40, 47
Heligoland Bight, Germany: 99, 109
Heliopolis, Egypt: 202, 238, 241, 264
Helsinki, Finland: 143
Helwan, Egypt: 242
Hemswell, Lincolnshire: 34
Hendon, Middlesex: 107, 240
Henlow, Bedfordshire: 2, 263
Henstridge, Dorset: 218
Heydekrug, Germany: 130
High Wycombe, Buckinghamshire: 9
Hinstock, Shropshire: 284
Hiroshima, Japan: 219, 284
Hixon, Staffordshire: 40
Hohemark, Germany: 126
Holmsley South, Hampshire: 243
Holstein, Germany: 167
Honeybourne, Worcestershire: 29, 261
Horsham St. Faith, Norfolk: 99
Hornchurch, Essex: 65, 143

INDEX

Hullavington, Wiltshire: 257
Hyères, France: 200
Ibsley, Hampshire: 80
Induna, Rhodesia: 26
Irish Sea: 138
Isle of Man: 79
Isle of Wight, Hampshire: 71
Ismailia, Egypt: 30, 32
Jerusalem, Palestine: 30
Jessore, East Bengal: 214
John O'Groats, Caithness: 138
Julik, Germany: 95
Kabrit, Egypt: 203
Kama, Russia: 52
Kano, Nigeria: 238, 243
Karachi, India: 135, 241
Karinhall, Berlin, Germany: 92
Karol, Romania: 154
Kassel, Germany: 107, 114, 126, 226
Keevil, Wiltshire: 259
Kelai, Maldives: 135
Kemble, Gloucestershire: 242, 253
Kenley, Surrey: 6, 66, 79, 80
Khanko Peninsula, Finland: 53
Khartoum, Sudan: 30, 238, 243
Kidlington, Oxfordshire: 257
Kiev, Ukraine: 151, 165
Kirkbride, Cumberland: 263
Kirkham, Lancashire: 288
Kirton-in-Lindsey, Lincolnshire: 287
Kisumu, Kenya: 29
Koggala, Ceylon: 6, 135
Kogul, Russia: 144
Kola Estuary, Russia: 182, 184
Kolar, India: 215
Kölberg, Poland: 282
Komendantskiy, Russia: 247
Königsberg, Germany: 156, 169
Kovalevo, Russia: 18, 250
Kronstadt, Russia: 144
Kuibyshev, Russia: 155
Kumalo, Rhodesia: 26
Kunming, Burma: 214
Kurland, Russia: 167, 173
Kwetnge, Burma: 213
La Galite Islands, Tunisia: 194
Lagos, Nigeria: 238, 242
Lajes, Azores: 214
Lake Annecy, France: 100
Lake Ladoga, Russia: 246
Lake Ontario, Canada: 45
Lake Victoria, Africa: 29
La Linea, Spain: 141
Lancashire Aero Club: 3

Langley, Buckinghamshire: 263
Lashio, Burma: 237
Lavansaari Island, Gulf of Finland: 173
Lechfeld, Germany: 277
Leeds, Yorkshire: 6
Lee-on-Solent, Hampshire: 146
Leeuwarden, Holland: 234
Le Havre, France: 126, 146-148
Leipzig, Germany: 107
Leningrad, Russia: 19, 52, 152, 162, 174, 246, 247, 282, 289
Leninsk-Kuznetskii, Russia: 19
Leuchars, Fife: 30, 117, 240
Leuna, Germany: 112
Leyte Gulf, Philippines: 217
Libava, Latvia: 144
Liegnitz, Silesia: 163
Lille, France: 64, 127
Limavady, Londonderry: 30
Limburg, Holland: 93
Lincoln, Lincolnshire: 115, 229
Linton-on-Ouse, Yorkshire: 40, 41, 105, 233
Lissett, Yorkshire: 4, 95
Little Brickhill, Buckinghamshire: 4
Little Staughton, Bedfordshire: 126
Liverpool, Lancashire: 11
Llandow, Glamorgan: 262, 263
Loch Striven, Firth of Clyde: 117
Locking, Somerset: 41
London, England: 4, 5, 10
London Colney, Hertfordshire: 103
Lord's Cricket Ground, London: 5, 47
Lorient, France: 140
Luberezkaya, Russia: 171
Lubertzy, Russia: 180
Ludford Magna, Lincolnshire: 94
Lugansk, Russia: 18
Luke Field, Arizona: 56
Lüneberg Heath, Germany: 282
Luqa, Malta: 193
Madley, Herefordshire: 36, 38
Magdeburg, Germany: 111, 227
Malaya Okhta, Russia: 154
Malta: 190-194, 207, 240, 264
Mandalay, Burma: 237
Mannheim, Germany: 85, 99
Manston, Kent: 63, 67, 102, 148, 271, 275
Marham, Norfolk: 2
Marienfeld, Germany: 171
Marseilles, France: 273
Martlesham Heath, Suffolk: 67, 77
Mauripur, India: 242, 243

Maydown, Londonderry: 284
Melksham, Wiltshire: 288
Mersa Matruh, Egypt: 190, 205, 264
Merseburg, Germany: 111, 112
Merville, France: 63-65
Messina, Italy: 207
Middle Wallop, Hampshire: 80, 221
Milan, Italy: 100
Mildenhall, Suffolk: 250
Minsk, Russia: 246
Mitteland Canal, Germany: 128
Moffatt, Rhodesia: 47
Möhne, Germany: 118
Mombasa, Kenya: 3, 135, 136
Montgomery, Alabama: 25
Montreal, Quebec: 213, 244, 265
Moorsele, France: 63
Moosburg, Germany: 127
Morecambe, Lancashire: 251
Moreton-in-Marsh, Gloucestershire: 33, 36-38, 40
Moscow, Russia: 51, 52, 155, 247
Mount Farm, Oxfordshire: 84
Mount Hope, Ontario: 45
Mulheim, Germany: 95
Mull of Galloway, Dumfries: 37
Munich, Germany: 232, 279
Munich-Riem, Germany: 277, 278
Munich-Schleissheim, Germany: 281
Munster, Germany: 102
Murmansk, Russia: 181, 183, 186
Myitkyina, Burma: 237
Nagasaki, Japan: 284
Nairobi, Kenya: 198
Nancy, France: 87
Naples, Italy: 19
N'Dola, Rhodesia: 198
Needham Market, Suffolk: 106
Neepawa, Canada: 27
Netheravon, Wiltshire: 54
Neubiberg, Germany: 279
Neufchâteau, France: 245
Newhaven, Sussex: 83
Newmarket, Suffolk: 73, 74, 109, 116, 250
Newquay, Cornwall: 5
Nijmegen Bridge, Holland: 278
Normandy, France: 268, 269
Northampton, Northamptonshire: 8
North Coates, Lincolnshire: 137
North Killingholme, Lincolnshire: 33, 34, 105, 106
Northolt, Middlesex: 29, 259

North Sea: 16, 37, 46, 54, 67, 104, 114, 120, 137, 142, 234, 254
North Weald, Essex: 72
Norwich, Norfolk: 229
Novosibirsk, Russia: 246
Nuremberg, Germany: 3, 104, 120
Oakington, Cambridgeshire: 126
Obuhovo, Russia: 53
Odiham, Hampshire: 68
Okinawa, Japan: 218
Ondaw, Burma: 212
Orel, Russia: 167, 179
Oujda, Morocco: 264
Oulton, Norfolk: 120-122
Oxnard, California: 56
Padgate, Lancashire: 1
Paestum, Italy: 28
Paignton, Devon: 12
Pamanzi, Mayotte: 135
Pantelleria, Sicily: 193
Parchim, Germany: 114, 226
Paris, France: 106, 127
Patricia Bay, Victoria: 27
Pearl Harbor, Hawaii: 21, 25, 208
Peenemünde, Germany: 102, 279
Pegasus Bridge: 43, 274
Pembrey, Carmarthen: 28
Pembroke Dock, Pembrokeshire: 41
Penrhos, Caernarvonshire: 43
Peplow, Shropshire: 33
Perth, Western Australia: 135
Pikeville, Kentucky: 21
Ploesti, Romania: 205, 206
Pocklington, Yorkshire: 42, 103, 107
Poitiers, France: 270
Poretta, Corsica: 200
Portreath, Cornwall: 140, 240
Port Said, Egypt: 39, 197
Po Valley, Italy: 206
Prague, Czechoslovakia: 181
Prague-Rusin, Czechoslovakia: 277
Prestwick, Ayrshire: 34, 35, 243, 265
Pütnitz, Germany: 17
Radlett, Hertfordshire: 118, 266
Ramry, Burma: 209, 210
Rangoon, Burma: 126, 209, 213
Ratcliffe, Leicestershire: 262
Ratmalana, Ceylon: 213, 255
Reading, Berkshire: 8
Redhill, Surrey: 79
Rednal, Shropshire: 256
Red Road, Calcutta: 208-211
Regent's Park, London: 5, 8

Reims, France: 127
Rennes, France: 33, 99
Revigny, France: 106
Reykjavik, Iceland: 243, 244, 264, 266
Rheinsehlen, Germany: 283
Rhine, Germany: 244, 273
Rhodes, Greece: 203
Rhyl, Denbighshire: 37
Riccall, Yorkshire: 42, 243, 287
Riga, Latvia: 162
Rome, Italy: 200, 240
Ronaldsway, Isle of Man: 55
Ropsha, Russia: 154
Rosignano, Italy: 200
Rouen, France: 282
Ruhr, Germany: 99, 117, 122, 287
Runnymede, Surrey: 99, 224
St. Athan, Glamorgan: 2, 39, 40-43, 48, 67, 68, 221, 252, 253
St. Eval, Cornwall: 137
St. John's Wood, London: 5, 8, 11
St. Nazaire, France: 119, 142
St. Peter di Caltagirone, Sicily: 191
St. Romain, France: 126
St. Sebastian, Spain: 119
St. Trond, Belgium: 225
Sagan, Germany: 130
Sahara, North Africa: 141
Saigon, Vietnam: 214
Sakishima Group, Japan: 218
Salerno, Italy: 28
Salisbury, Rhodesia: 198, 199
Saltby, Leicestershire: 42
Sandtoft, Lincolnshire: 33, 103
Santa Ana, California: 56
Saratov, Russia: 155
Sardinia: 194, 195, 200, 264
Sarzana, Italy: 199
Scampton, Lincolnshire: 4, 6, 7, 92, 96, 100
Scapa Flow, Orkney: 139
Scarborough, Yorkshire: 8
Schleswig-Holstein, Germany: 281
Seend, Wiltshire: 255
Seletar, Singapore: 284
Seychelles: 136
Shandur, Egypt: 28
Sharjah, Persian Gulf: 241
Shaulai, Russia: 178
Shawbury, Shropshire: 44
Sheffield, Yorkshire: 4, 98
Shepherd's Grove, Suffolk: 120
Shobdon, Herefordshire: 257
Shwebo, Burma: 237
Sicily: 191, 207, 225
Sidi Haneish, Egypt: 198

Silloth, Cumberland: 30, 263
Silverstone, Northamptonshire: 287
Sinello, Italy: 283
Siverskaja, Russia: 163
Skipton-on-Swale, Yorkshire: 233
Skitten, Caithness: 117, 139
Slavgorodskii, Russia: 178
Sleap, Shropshire: 103
Smolnyy, Russia: 247
Sobolev, Russia: 178
Soesterberg, Holland: 83, 85
Sollum, Egypt: 203
South China Sea: 137
Speke, Lancashire: 143
Stade, Germany: 230
Stag Lane, Middlesex: 14
Stavanger, Norway: 273
Steeple Morden, Cambridgeshire: 87
Stoke-on-Trent, Staffordshire: 114
Stockton-on-Tees, Durham: 46
Stradishall, Suffolk: 26, 43, 94, 245
Stratford-on-Avon, Warwickshire: 5
Sudetenland, Germany: 16
Suez Canal, Egypt: 55, 190
Sutton Bridge, Lincolnshire: 10, 60, 117, 218
Swanton Morley, Norfolk: 27
Sydney, Australia: 217, 243, 265
Taganrog, Russia: 51
Takoradi, Gold Coast: 146, 196, 238
Tallinn, Estonia: 143-144
Tambov, Russia: 19
Tangier, Morocco: 14
Tangmere, Sussex: 2, 80-82, 256, 289
Tarrant Rushton, Dorset: 42, 274
Tempsford, Bedfordshire: 245
Tenby, Pembrokeshire: 68
Ternhill, Shropshire: 68
Thorn/Toruń, Poland: 130
Thornaby, Yorkshire: 23, 46, 137
Thorney Island, Hampshire: 14, 81, 146-148
Thornhill, Rhodesia: 26
Tiree, Hebrides: 30
Tobruk, Libya: 190, 197, 201-204, 208
Tokyo Bay, Japan: 284
Topcliffe, Yorkshire: 38
Toronto, Canada: 12, 13
Torquay, Devon: 5, 6, 9
Trieste, Italy: 20
Trincomalee, Ceylon: 211, 213, 284

INDEX

Trossy St. Maximin, France: 103
Tunis, Tunisia: 30, 193
Turkmen, Russia: 246
Turnhouse, Midlothian: 143
Twente, Holland: 223, 225, 234
Upavon, Wiltshire: 251
Upper Heyford, Oxfordshire: 35, 44, 96
Uxbridge, Middlesex: 1-3, 6, 68
Uzbek, Russia: 246
Vaenga, Russia: 182, 184, 185
Valley, Anglesey: 68
Vavuniya, Ceylon: 210
Verebye, Russia: 161
Vienna, Austria: 49
Villers Bocage, France: 272
Vitebsk, Russia: 180
Vitry-en-Artois, France: 44, 272
Vnukovo, Russia: 246
Vyborg Gulf, Russia: 168, 170
Waddington, Lincolnshire: 101
Wadi Halfa, Egypt: 238
Wangjing, Burma: 213
Warmwell, Dorset: 28, 271
Waterbeach, Cambridgeshire: 108, 243
Watford, Hertfordshire: 103, 266
Watton, Norfolk: 30, 31
Werder/Havel, Berlin: 16, 50
Werneuchen, Berlin: 50
Western Desert: 146, 190, 196, 217
West Freugh, Wigtownshire: 35
Westhampnett, Sussex: 268
West Kirby, Lancashire: 12
Westwood, Cambridgeshire: 287
Whitchurch, Somerset: 262
Whitley Bay, Northumberland: 7
White Waltham, Berkshire: 261, 262
Wick, Caithness: 138, 139
Wigsley, Nottinghamshire: 104
Wilhelmshaven, Germany: 223
Wilmslow, Cheshire: 10, 67
Witney, Oxfordshire: 263
Wittenberg, Germany: 156
Wittering, Northamptonshire: 67, 221, 288
Wittmundhaven, Germany: 234
Woodbridge, Suffolk: 102, 103
Woodford, Cheshire: 3
Worthy Down, Hampshire: 54
Wunsdorf, Germany: 85
Wyton, Huntingdonshire: 5
Yatesbury, Wiltshire: 34, 35
Yeysk, Russia: 51
Zemland Peninsula, Germany: 282

PERSONNEL

Adelhütte, Oblt Hans: 16, 18
Aldrich, R: 248
Allison, WO William: 43
Arabia, Lawrence of: 241
Arnold, General Hap: 11
Avanesov, Col Grigory: 53, 143-145, 169, 282
Ayres, Flt Sgt N S: 122
Bader, Gp Capt Sir Douglas: 74, 77
Baldwin, Air Vice-Marshal Jack: 109
Barfoot, Flt Lt Eric: 5, 203, 204, 245
Barkhorn, Major Gerhard: 149
Barron, Flg Off Andrew: 120-122
Barry, Sqn Ldr Dennis: 80, 275
Baynham, Reg: 265
Beamish, Gp Capt Victor: 71, 72
Bennett, Sqn Ldr P D S: 99
Biggs, Flt Lt Jack: 11, 24-26, 30, 31, 208-212, 255, 256, 287
Black, Sgt: 97
Blackburn, Wg Cdr: 214
Blair, John Willy: 72
Bohoncev, Vasilii: 154
Booth, Flg Off Jack: 44, 271, 272, 288
Borkov, Nikolai: 282
Bow, Sgt: 99
Bradbury: 211
Bragg, Sqn Ldr: 251
Brandt, Oblt Fritz: 280
Brent, Harry: 285
Bromfield, WO Jack: 4, 8, 35-38, 91, 92, 94, 95, 104, 110, 111, 123-125, 127, 128, 131, 222-228, 249, 278, 288, 289
Brooke, General Sir Alan: 240
Brookes, Sqn Ldr: 238
Brothers, Air Com Pete: 2, 3, 23, 33, 59, 62, 63, 70, 71, 77-80, 256, 271, 289
Brown, Sgt: 259
Browning, Sgt Charlie: 32, 212
Brubaker, Capt Welden: 113
Buchan, Willie: 212
Burbridge, Wg Cdr Branse: 289
Burke, Flt Sgt Eric: 11, 47, 206, 207, 283
Burrell, Sgt William: 93
Busbridge, Flt Lt Dennis: 30
Butler, Sgt Eric: 93
Caird, Flt Lt John: 6, 285, 287
Caldecotte, Fred: 116
Call, Flg Off C R: 236
Campbell, Flt Lt: 222
Carter, Flg Off Peter: 63

Catt, Sqn Ldr R G E: 250
Chatel, Andre: 265
Checketts, Wg Cdr John: 210
Chichester, Flt Lt, P G: 238
Chisholm, Flg Off: 202, 238
Churchill, Winston: 10, 69, 74, 91, 181, 244, 257
Clarke, Bob: 103, 116, 240, 266, 267, 274, 275
Clarke, Flt Lt Eric: 95-99
Coleman, Cpt John: 87
Collins, S: 248
Cook, Flg Off George: 6, 7, 34, 92, 93, 134, 135
Coombes, Bill: 62
Cotton, Henry: 44
Cotton, Sqn Ldr Monty: 209, 211
Coward, Air Com James: 10, 59, 60-62, 67, 74-78, 256, 276
Coward, Noel: 90
Cowley, Flt Sgt Creighton: 44
Craig, AC2 'Lofty': 109
Cross, Sqn Ldr I K P: 109, 110
Crossley, Wg Cdr Michael: 76
Culley, Sgt A L: 104
Cunningham, Gp Capt John: 221
Curtis, Flt Lt Des: 142
Curtis, Lettice: 264
D'Annunzio, Gabriel: 49
Dacey, Sgt George: 224
Darling, Flt Sgt: 250
Davey, Wg Cdr Dennis: 31
David, Gp Capt Dennis: 256
Davies, Flt Sgt G B: 104
Davis, Wg Cdr Peter: 273
Dean, Derrick: 290
Dean, Flg Off Dixie: 276
Deans, Flt Sgt Dixie: 130
Deere, Wg Cdr Al: 218
Dennis, Flt Sgt H: 239, 240
Didwell, Cpl Norman: 73, 108-110, 116, 241, 241, 249-252
Dixon-Wright Wg Cdr, F W: 109
Dodd, John: 48
Dorrington, 3rd Officer Joe: 8, 261-263
Dowding, ACM Hugh: 77, 78
Drozdov, Vladimir: 52
Dundas, Gp Capt Hugh: 200
Eaton, Flg Off John: 100
Eisenhower, General Dwight D: 236
Elkington, Wg Cdr Tim: 81, 82, 181-188, 212, 213, 221, 249
Ellacombe, Air Com John: 72, 73, 82, 83, 221, 222, 270
Elliott, Flg Off John: 33, 34, 105-107

Ercolani, Wg Cdr Lucian: 94
Eschwege, Hptmn S von: 64
Evans, Sub Lt Idwal: 146-148
Everard, Flt Lt: 278
Fahy, Sqn Ldr Peter: 1, 29, 259, 260
Fensome, Flt Sgt Roy: 38, 39, 242
Finley, Wg Cdr Donald: 256
Finucane, Wg Cdr Brendan 'Paddy': 79, 80
Fitt, Flt Sgt Vernon: 103
Foulsham, Sqn Ldr: 275
Frascotti, Bob: 269
Gadsby, Flt Sgt Jack: 96
Galland, Generalleutnant Adolf: 278, 289
Gaughran, WO, W: 126
Gerasimovich, General Major Nikolay: 51, 158, 159
Gibson, Flg Off: 136
Giddings, WO Les: 107, 108, 128-131
Glass, Sqn Ldr Ray: 242
Goldsworthy, Sgt: 217
Golodnikov, General Major Nikolay: 184-188
Gordon, Sqn Ldr Pete: 72
Gorev, Nikolai: 151
Göring, Reichsmarshall Hermann: 92, 149, 227
Grandy, Flg Off: 23
Grant, Sgt: 241
Green, Hughie: 265
Green, Sgt H T: 104
Green, WO Peter: 9, 42, 102, 103, 287
Greening, Lt Jimmy: 13, 14, 55, 147, 284
Grisman, Plt Off W J: 110
Hager, Oblt Johannes: 122
Hall, Sgt Stephen: 201, 238, 239
Hall, Sgt W: 104
Hall, Sub Lt: 83
Halpert, Capt Sam: 111-113
Hammond, Plt Off Ken: 33
Hannig, Gisele: 122, 123
Hannig, Leutnant Norbert: 15, 16, 50, 162-180, 277, 278, 281
Harris, Capt 'Skirts': 146
Harris, Sgt G E: 43, 44
Harrison, Flt Lt Fred: 240
Harrison, Sgt W: 104
Hartmann, Major Eric: 149
Hawker, WO E J: 126
Herrmann, Oberst Hajo: 227
Hetherington, Flt Lt: 109
Hill, Sqn Ldr: 126
Hitler, Adolf: 3, 16

Hogben, Sgt Harry: 7, 43
Holt, Sgt M H: 99
How, Eric: 67
Hunt, Hannah: 69
Hutchinson, Wg Cdr C G: 117
Hymans, Sgt: 54
Isaacs, Flt Lt: 237
Jackson, Flt Lt Cyril: 264
Jackson, Pete: 213
James, Sqn Ldr Thomas: 272
Jensen, Henry: 114
John, Sgt Dai: 46
Johnen, Hptmn Wilhelm : 280
Johnson, Flg Off David: 215
Jones, AC R M: 221
Kammhuber, Generalleutnant Josef: 228
Kardopoltsev, Guards Lt Benedikt: 19, 51, 150, 175-181, 281, 282
Kempenfelt, Bill: 199
Kent, Flt Sgt Harry: 39, 40
Khukhrikov, Yuri: 155, 282
King, Flg Off R V: 126
King, Flt Sgt John: 42, 43, 244, 285, 286
Kirby-Green, Sqn Ldr Tom: 110, 251
Kittel, Oblt Otto: 173
Klette, Major Immanuel: 112
Knoebel, Uffz Erich: 171
Knowles, Sqn Ldr Clive: 83-85, 258, 259
Korner, Theodor: 220
Kovalenko, Sqn Commander Aleksandr: 184, 186, 187
Kroshinski, Fw Hans-Joachim: 166
Kubarev, Major Vasili: 160, 161, 249
Kuharenko, Capt: 183
Kukin, Alexei: 152-155
Kulakov, Col Leonid: 18, 158, 164, 249, 250, 289
Kuznetsov, General Fyodor: 183
Laing, Jamie: 86
Lang, Leutnant Emil: 166
Langford, Sub Lt Jim: 14, 55, 56, 219
Leigh-Mallory, ACM Sir Trafford: 67, 78, 82
Lisikova, Guards Senior Lt Olga: 19, 52, 159-161, 246, 247
Liversuch, Sgt Raymond: 43
Liversuch, Sgt Ronald: 43, 67
Lord, Flt Lt David: 2
Lord, Flt Lt Jim: 33, 34, 105, 106
Loton, Wg Cdr A G: 23
Lütje, Oblt Herbert: 281
Lyons, Sgt Bob: 252

McGiffin, Wg Cdr Hunter: 137, 253
McKee, Wg Cdr Andrew: 109
McLannahan, George: 240
MacArthur, General Douglas: 284
Mackay, Flg Off: 278
Malan, Gp Capt Adolph: 218
Marchenko, Capt Ivan: 176, 178
Marion, WO Gerry: 125, 127, 288
Marshall, Flt Lt: 265
Mathan, Emil: 230
Mattinson, Flt Sgt Frank: 47, 48
Mercer, Flt Lt Ted: 5, 94, 287, 288
Metellini, General Giacomo: 19, 48-50, 60, 61, 190, 194-196, 200
Milch, Generalfeldmarschall Erhard: 220
Miller, 'Shorty': 211
Milligan, Flg Off Ted: 40, 103, 272
Milne, Sgt Sidney: 44
Mitchell, WO O J: 280
Moll, Sqn Ldr Jan: 31
Mollison, Jim: 45
Molotov, Vyacheslav: 53, 247
Mossop, Sgt Bill: 97, 99
Mountbatten, Lord Louis: 284
Murphy, Wg Cdr Alan: 245, 246
Musgrave, Flg Off Bill: 11, 26, 29, 30, 200, 201, 278, 279, 283, 285, 286
Mussolini, Benito: 205
Nava, Flt Lt Norman: 265
Nepryahin, Pavel: 180
Nicholson, Flg Off Mike: 5, 27-29, 213-215
Niven, Flt Lt David: 241
Nordmann, Oblt Karl-Gottfried: 65
North, Flt Lt Harold: 78
Notley, Plt Off Lyall: 103
O'Dell, Flt Sgt Bob: 40, 41, 105, 106
Olivier, Lt Laurence: 54
O'Sullivan, J: 138
Park, ACM Sir Keith: 66
Parry, Sqn Ldr Jack: 215-217, 236
Parton, Sgt L W: 109
Patton, General George: 127
Payne, Flg Off Henry: 27, 28, 222, 273, 274, 287
Pead, Sgt I F W: 104
Peel, Bob: 270
Pepper, Plt Off Fred: 211
Perfect, Sgt John: 274
Petrie-Andrews, Flt Lt Joe: 6, 29, 110
Pickard, Gp Capt Percy: 109
Pikulenko, Dmitrii: 152, 154

INDEX

Pino, Reginald: 271
Pinkham, Fl Lt Philip: 74
Pinter, 'Schani': 230, 233
Pomorov, Mikhail: 52, 53, 151, 155-158, 252, 282
Powell, Lt Robert: 21, 56, 57, 85-89, 252, 269, 270, 279
Rall, Generalleutnant Günther: 16, 149, 150, 289
Ramsey, Sir Bertram: 211
Rayner, Sgt Raymond: 274
Reed, Henry: 22
Rees, Bob: 274, 282
Reschke, Ofw Willi: 279, 280
Richardson, Lt Cdr Ralph: 54
Rickard, Flt Lt Cecil: 9, 10, 44-47, 137-142
Robb, Wilhelm: 70, 71
Robbins, C J: 253
Robertson, Flg Off Arthur: 36
Robinson, Sgt: 97, 99
Rodrigues, SKC Alfred: 208
Rökker, Hptmn Heinz: 50, 92, 114-116, 207, 208, 223-234, 246, 271, 276, 280, 281
Rommel, Feldmarschall Erwin: 197, 207, 246
Rook, Sqn Ldr Anthony: 184
Rooks, Sgt A: 104
Rose, Wg Cdr Jack: 63-65, 76, 77, 213, 268, 269
Rosholt, Capt Norm: 20, 57, 111, 112, 131, 132, 283
Ross, Jack: 182
Routley, Cdr Jack: 13, 14, 54, 55, 196-199, 217-219, 284
Rudel, Oberst Hans: 289
Ryabzev, Mikhail: 179
Safonov, Sqn Commander Boris: 183, 186
Schmidt, Oblt: 230, 231
Schnaufer, Major Heinz-Wolfgang: 92, 220, 227, 280
Schomberg, Sgt Jack: 33
Schulz, Hptmn Albert: 115
Scully, Sgt P J: 33
Seiler, Hptmn Reinhard: 154
Selyutin, Senior Lt Arkadiy: 174
Semenov, Grigoriy: 52
Seydel, Flt Lt Gabriel: 68
Seymour, William Keen: 59
Shakhaev, Viktor: 156
Sheen, Earl: 114
Skelton, Sqn Ldr Bill: 289
Smith, Flt Lt Philip: 24
Smith, Flt Lt Rod: 193, 278
Smith, Plt Off Jerry: 193
Spooner, Sqn Ldr Tony: 133

Spoden, Hptmn Peter: 16-18, 81, 226-229, 280, 281
Stalin, Joseph: 18, 19
Stapleton, Sqn Ldr Gerald: 143
Steele, AVM C R: 271
Steinhoff, Oberst Johannes: 289
Stewart, Col Everett: 87
Stewart, Sgt: 222
Stirling, Major David: 203
Stock, Sgt E P: 104
Stracey-Smyth, Wg Cdr John: 240
Streib, Hptmn Werner: 93
Strolin, Sgt A C: 104
Tayler, WO Norman: 253
Taylor, Flt Sgt David: 96
Taylor, Plt Off E M: 104
Taylor, Sqn Ldr Jimmy: 260
Thomas, Sgt 'Taffy': 46
Thomsett, Flg Off Alan: 118-120
Thwaite, Sgt J F: 104
Tikhomirov, Lt Col Vladimir: 18, 162-175
Timms, Dan: 146, 147
Timoshenko, Marshal Semyon: 51
Torrans, WO John: 126, 272, 273, 275
Trautloft, Oberst Hannes: 162, 167
Tritton, Flt Lt D C: 41
Tuck, Wg Cdr Robert Stanford: 77
Turnbull, Sgt Tommy: 204, 205
Turner, Flt Lt Doug: 117, 118, 142, 143
Valyaev, Senior Lt Alexei: 53, 151, 152, 281
Vass, Sgt Gus: 33
Viney, Flg Off Reg: 65, 66, 254
Vlasov, General Andrei: 177
Wade, Sgt Jack: 237, 264, 265
Wainwright, Sqn Ldr Michael: 66, 67, 71, 115, 117, 220, 221, 242, 243, 257, 258
Waldron, Sgt: 46
Walker, Flg Off Derek: 189
Wallis, Barnes: 118
Walsh, Sub Lt R W M: 198
Waltham, Bob: 197
Wareing, Sqn Ldr R: 126
Waughman, Flt Lt Russell: 94
Wavell, Field Marshal Lord Percival: 216, 237, 240, 241
Way, Plt Off S W A: 99
Weeks, WO Les: 101, 102, 222
Weir, Gp Capt C T: 128
Weissenfeld, Oblt Egmont: 43
Wells, Wg Cdr Oliver: 126, 127, 131

Wellum, Sqn Ldr Geoff: 28, 69, 70, 193, 194, 249
Whitaker, Flt Sgt John: 1, 205, 206
White, WO, Frank: 115
Whiter, Master Navigator Bill: 26-28
Williams, Flg Off E: 104
Williams, Flt Sgt Ron: 33
Wilson, Flt Lt Norman: 3, 24, 135-137, 284, 285
Winder, Sid: 146, 147
Wingate, Brigadier Orde: 237
Withers, Wg Cdr Harold: 241
Wittgenstein, Major Prinz Heinrich zu Sayn: 227
Woodacre, WO Sidney: 275, 276
Woods, Flt Lt 'Timber': 266
Wynn, Sqn Ldr Charles: 221
Wynne-Eyton, Wg Cdr Charles: 240
Zhanteev, Ibrahim: 247
Zhukov, Misha: 247
Zvyagin, Senior Lt Ivan: 19, 52, 155

MILITARY ORGANISATIONS & OPERATIONS
Battle of Britain: 2, 8, 10, 16, 29, 69-78, 88, 89, 91, 116, 143, 182, 196, 249, 254
British Army
6th Airborne Division: 274
8th Army: 206
Air Landing Brigades: 274
Glider Pilot Regiment: 274
Oxfordshire and Buckinghamshire Light Infantry: 274
Parachute Brigades: 274
Royal Army Service Corps: 274
Special Air Service: 203, 270
British Commonwealth Air Training Plan: 54
British Expeditionary Force: 62, 65
Burma Volunteer Air Force: 216
Channel Dash: 99
Chindits: 214, 237
D-Day: 9, 43, 47, 86, 135, 143, 240, 268-271, 274, 275
Dominion Air Training Scheme: 10, 11
Empire Air Training Scheme: 11, 45
Finnish campaign: 52, 168
France, fall of: 62-68
Free French: 265
German Air Force – Luftwaffe
2 Staffel Jagdgruppe West: 162, 163

C-Schule 17: 17
Fahnenjunkerkompanie LKS III: 50
Flieger Ausbilungs Regiment: 14
Fluganwaerterkompanie: 14
Jagdfliegerschule: 50
JG7: 16, 277
JG52; 16, 54
JG54: 15, 154, 162, 163, 165, 171
JG77: 65
JG301: 279
JG302: 279
J/LG2: 63
JV44: 277
NJG1: 122, 280
NJG2: 43, 50, 223
NJG3: 280
NJG5: 16, 280
NJG6: 16, 280, 281
RLM: 229
German Navy – Kriegsmarine
   Bismarck: 12, 140
   Gneisenau: 99
   Prinz Eugen: 99
   Scharnhorst: 99, 140
   Tirpitz: 117, 118, 184
Great Escape, The: 110, 251
Highball weapon: 117, 118
Home Guard / LDV: 6, 73
Italian Air Force – Regia Aeronautica
   2 Fighter Training Squadron: 50
   2 Stormo: 19, 192
   6th Breda Flight School: 48, 49
   6 Stormo 2 Gruppo: 190
   102 Stormo 10 Gruppo: 61
   150 Squadriglia: 192
   152 Squadriglia: 192, 200
   358 Squadrigila: 192
Kamikaze: 218, 219
Long March, The: 131
Middle August, Battle of: 194
Operation Barbarossa: 149
Operation Big Ben: 120
Operation Dynamo: 66
Operation Fuller: 99
Operation Herkules: 194
Operation Gisela: 122, 229, 230
Operation Manna: 282
Operation Market Garden: 274
Operation Sea Lion: 69, 78
Operation Servant: 117
Operation Stoat: 245
Operation Varsity: 273
Prisoner of War camps
   Dulag Luft: 125, 147

Stalag VIIA: 127
Stalag XI-B: 130
Stalag XIIIC: 127
Stalag XX-A: 130
Stalag Luft I: 125, 131
Stalag Luft III: 127, 130
Stalag Luft VI: 130
Royal Air Force
Squadrons
1: 81
3: 63, 65
4: 64
7: 126, 254
13: 11, 206, 207
16: 29, 259, 260
17: 11, 181, 208, 255
18: 26
19: 10, 59, 61, 62, 67
24: 240
30: 189
32: 2, 59, 63
35: 6
37: 5
38: 2
40: 109, 251
42: 32, 212
44: 5, 44, 94, 287
45: 204
47: 42
49: 6, 7, 92-94, 96, 99
52: 204
53: 9, 137, 138
54: 218
55: 205
59: 243
64: 66, 220
65: 28
67: 81
70: 5, 203
74: 218
77: 130
81: 184
83: 5, 94, 101, 102, 222
85: 221, 289
88: 44, 271
92: 28, 77
99: 73, 94, 108, 215, 249-251
101: 94
102: 6, 9, 42, 107
103: 110, 126
105: 100
106: 92, 93
109: 43
113: 213
126: 193
134: 185

135: 211
136: 209
138: 245
140: 84, 258
150: 33
151: 72, 221
158: 4, 6, 37, 95
159: 6, 94
172: 9, 137-138
179: 9, 140
184: 268
192: 118, 120
194: 213
196: 120, 222, 273
199: 280
203: 26
205: 6, 135
207: 290
209: 3, 136
211: 205
214: 108
216: 5, 38, 201, 237, 241, 242, 245
223: 120, 121
224: 30, 240
232: 213, 243
233: 30
235: 142
237: 11, 200
242: 77
247: 143
253: 82
257: 2, 77
266: 10, 60, 67
267: 5, 239, 240, 245
269: 134
271: 2, 65, 254, 274
296: 42
299: 273
349: 68
350: 68
356: 215
358: 5, 214
408: 40, 104, 233
412: 193
433: 233
457: 2, 78, 79, 256
460: 40, 103, 272
467: 101
485: 218
486: 280
487: 270
502: 137
504: 80
543: 29
550: 33, 34, 105-107

INDEX

575: 282
582: 126
601: 187, 218
602: 2, 79, 80
603: 143
604: 221
605: 83
611: 218
616: 80, 275, 276
617: 117
618: 117
644: 42

OTHER UNITS
ACRC: 5, 8, 43, 47
1 ADU: 257
1 ITW: 4
1 LFS: 34
2 Air Armament School: 258
2 Group Support Unit: 27
2 Radio School: 35
2nd Tactical Air Force: 271
3 Ferry Unit: 264
3 Group: 203
3 ITW: 5
4 B&GS: 35
4 (Coastal) OTU: 134
4 EFTS: 47
4 ERFTS: 23
4 Glider Training School: 257
4 Group: 95
4 ITW: 12
4 Radio School: 38
4 Signals School: 36
4 SofTT: 40, 41
5 Group: 100
5 FTS: 68
5 RFU: 28
5 SofTT: 41
6 Group Battle School: 38, 41
6 Coastal Command OTU: 46, 137
7 ITW: 5
7 (O)AFU: 36
7 SFTS: 287
8 B&GS: 35
9 Air Observers' School: 43
9 (P)AFU: 55
10 Group: 80, 271
10 OTU: 137
10 Radio School: 134
11 (P)AFU: 287
12 FTS: 30
12 Group: 78
12 Radio School: 39
12 SofTT: 288
13 Air Gunnery School: 39

13 ITW: 5, 6
13 OTU: 44
14 OTU: 93
16 OTU: 35, 96
17 EFTS: 29
17 OTU: 287
17 (P)AFU: 31
19 ITW: 8
19 MU: 253, 254
21 OTU: 33, 36, 37, 40
21 SFTS: 26, 32
22 SFTS: 26
24 BG&NS: 47
24 EFTS: 261
24 OTU: 29
25 EFTS: 47
26 EFTS: 26
27 EFTS: 26
30 OTU: 40
31 B&GS: 45
31 GRS: 24
32 OTU: 27
33 ANS: 45
33 EFTS: 24
33 SFTS: 24
35 EFTS: 27
38 Group: 285
40 Staging Post: 242
44 Group: 253
45 Atlantic Transport Group: 242, 264, 265
46 Group: 273, 274
52 OTU: 257
55 OTU: 31, 256, 257
56 OTU: 255
57 OTU: 33, 259
58 OTU: 68
61 OTU: 256, 259
70 OTU: 28
71 OTU: 30, 32
75 OTU: 47
80 Group: 119
81 OTU: 28, 104
100 Group: 117-122
105 (Transport) OTU: 142, 237
109 MU: 241
142 Wing: 218
151 Wing: 181, 184
216 Group: 240
216 Group Communications Flight: 242
221 Group Communications Flight: 215
229 Group: 288
317 MU: 241
1332 HCU: 243

1654 HCU: 104
1658 HCU: 42
1659 HCU: 38
1664 HCU: 41
1665 HCU: 42
1667 HCU: 34, 103
1668 HCU: 40
AHQ (Bengal): 216, 237
AHQ India Communications Flt: 241
Bengal Command : 237
Bomber Command: 23, 29, 33, 89, 91-111, 118, 120, 122, 125, 134, 237, 238, 249, 253, 272, 280, 286
Bomber Command Instructors' School: 287
BPD: 30
Central Flying School: 255
Central Gunnery School: 218
CFS Handling Flight: 251
Coastal Command: 31, 41, 134-143, 265
Desert Air Force Training Flight: 283
Empire Flying Training School: 255
Ferry Command: 264
Fighter Command: 29
Franco-Belgian Air Training School: 68
Frontal Aviation: 169
    Military Aviation School: 18
    Molotov Naval Aviation Technical School: 52
    Normandie-Niemen: 156
HQ (Bengal) Communications Unit: 216
Meteor Training Flight: 275
Overseas Aircraft Despatch Unit: 253
Overseas Aircraft Preparation Unit: 253
Pathfinder Force: 94, 102, 126
Photographic Reconnaissance Unit: 258, 259
Royal Navy
    Fleet Air Arm Squadrons
    713: 13, 55
    755: 54
    758: 54, 284
    769: 56
    785: 55, 56
    786: 55, 56
    805: 13, 146, 196-198
    815: 146, 147
    820: 14, 219

822: 14, 148
825: 146
826: 202
885: 13, 217
887: 219

OTHER UNITS & SHIPS
British Pacific Fleet: 218, 219
HMS *Argus*: 54, 80, 181, 185
HMS Daedalus: 146
HMS *Eagle*: 193
HMS *Furious*: 193
HMS *Hussar*: 184
HMS *Illustrious*: 146
HMS *Indefatigable*: 13, 14, 219
HMS *Jackdaw*: 55
HMS *Kenya*: 184
HMS *Khedive*: 56
HMS Peewit, Deck Landing Training School: 55
HMS *Rajah*: 13, 55
HMS *Rodney*: 12
HMS *Ruler*: 13, 217
HMS St. Vincent: 13
HMS *Urley*: 55
Naval Air Fighter School: 218
South East Asia Command: 134
South African Air Force
25 Squadron: 115
Soviet Military Air Forces – VVS
2 GuIAP: 18, 51, 176
4 GuIAP: 173
12 IAP KBF: 18
32 GuIAP: 165
38th Regiment: 171
43 IAP: 19
65 GuIAP: 161
103 GuIAP: 18, 250
121 IAP: 163
176 GuIAP: 152
180 GuIAP: 53, 151
187 IAP: 161
434 IAP: 165
482 IAP: 177
566 Ground Attack Aviation Regiment: 155
653 IAP: 161
937 IAP: 177
Spanish Civil War: 19, 60, 61, 89
Special Installation Flight: 221
Transport Command: 108, 264, 265
Thousand Bomber Raid: 93, 94, 99
Tiger Force: 284

United States Army Air Force
4th FG: 87
6th Fighter Wing: 85
8th Air Force: 85, 111
8th Fighter Command HQ: 89
12th Air Force: 200
91st BG: 112, 113
324th BS: 112, 113
328th FS: 21, 87
352nd FG: 21, 86, 87, 269
355th FG: 87
452nd BG: 21
United States Navy
USS *Missouri*: 284
Upkeep weapon: 117
West Africa Communications Squadron: 242

MISCELLANEOUS
Air France: 65
Air Ministry: 10, 27, 77, 99, 251
Air Transport Auxiliary: 8, 9, 78, 261-264
2 Ferry Pool: 262
5 (Training) Ferry Pool: 261
6 Ferry Pool: 262
Armstrong Whitworth Aircraft: 4
Arnold Scheme: 12, 24, 30, 31
Belgian Resistance: 126
Civil Air Guard; 14
Fairfield Aviation Company: 103, 266, 267
French Resistance: 245
Gestapo: 109, 110, 127, 286
Gloster Aircraft Company: 28
Lancashire Aero Club: 3
Merchant ships
Britannic: 12
Catapult Aircraft Merchantmen: 143
Empire Baffin: 184
New Amsterdam: 55
Otranto: 11
Pedestal convoy: 194
Queen Elizabeth: 24, 27, 211
Queen Mary: 24, 266
Telecommunications Research Establishment: 137
VE-Day: 43, 242, 282, 283
VJ-Day: 135, 268, 284, 285